THE FIRST BIRTH
A Family Turning Point

Doris R. Entwisle
Susan G. Doering

The Johns Hopkins University Press
Baltimore and London

The Johns Hopkins University Press, Baltimore, Maryland 21218
The Johns Hopkins Press Ltd., London

Library of Congress Cataloging in Publication Data

Entwisle, Doris R
  The first birth, a family turning point.

  Bibliography: pp. 309–26
  Includes index.
  1. Children, First-born—United States—Case studies.
2. Parents—United States—Attitudes. 3. Parenting—
United States—Case studies. I. Doering, Susan G.,
joint author. II. Title. [DNLM: 1. Birth order.
2. Family. 3. Parent-child relations. WS105.5.F2
E61f]
HQ777.2.E57   306.8′7   80-22741
ISBN 0-8018-2408-7

To Hank, B. J., and Babs
and
Stefanie, Andrea, Karl, and Larry

CONTENTS

LIST OF TABLES

LIST OF FIGURES

PREFACE

It hardly needs to be said that social relations during pregnancy and childbirth have profound effects on marital life, on family relationships, on men's and women's careers, and undoubtedly on the children themselves. The scientific literature, however, has been curiously silent on these matters. In fact, when we began this research in 1972, there were no research reports that followed a group of emergent families, starting before the birth of their first child, in order to investigate the first perinatal period in the family's life cycle. Nevertheless, over the present decade there has been a growing acceptance of the life-span framework in studies of human development and an increasing interest in the relationship between social change and life patterns—two perspectives that this research employed from its inception.[1]

As social scientists, we feel it is important to inquire into the sociological and psychological aspects of a family's first birth, particularly how pregnancy and previous life experiences may affect couples' reactions to childbirth and the period of early parenthood, because this is the period in life when a couple changes into a "family." Two major premises have been that events or states of mind during pregnancy should affect birth and that couples' experiences in both pregnancy and childbirth should affect subsequent family life. Another major premise has been that the transition into parenthood may be especially sensitive to general social conditions, so that the remarkable social changes that have taken place over the past decade are likely to have affected the nature of the transition to parenthood during that period.

Our book covers many topics and its scope is hard to define. Since so little is known about families at the time point when the first child arrives, just to describe what happens to a small group of families over this period in their lives is informative. Generally we have tried to provide as broad a picture and to describe as many facets of the couples' experiences as possible. We did this in the belief that, in a largely uncharted area, only by attending to such complexity were we likely to address the key questions of a "sociology of childbirth." We also took this tack because we believe that it is impossible to study phenomena in this domain by examining variables in isolation.

[1]Rutter, writing late in 1979, says that "new" issues likely to influence future theorizing and policy formation include, among others, the process by which parent-child relationships develop and the nature of ecological influences on family functioning.

Lest the reader be misled, however, we wanted—as social scientists—to move whenever possible beyond description and to use theoretical notions derived from sociology and its sister disciplines to explain what was transpiring. In particular, we wanted to bring to bear some of the modeling techniques that sociologists had found fruitful in understanding other sociological phenomena.

In the research we studied 120 wives and 60 of their husbands. Half were middle class, half lower class. We have available from each of these people all the information that could be verbalized in ten to twelve hours of intensive interviewing. We can relate what an individual said at one time with what he or she said at another time, or can relate what one member of a couple said to what the other member said. This makes possible an exceedingly rich and informative analysis. Furthermore, by following the same people over a nine-month time span, we can speak to some questions of a causal sort—for example, whether the father's presence in delivery seems to affect his relationship with his wife or with his infant. The work is exploratory, and therefore of necessity often descriptive, but we have tried at every step to be as analytic as the data permit.

The book has two main aims: (1) to describe and chronicle the family life-cycle of a particular group of couples over the perinatal period and (2) to analyze the available information (so that social scientists will be enlightened) on a number of concerns linked to this period in life.

We have received help from many sources, most important, of course, the couples who were willing to share some of their most intimate thoughts and feelings at this turning point in their lives.

Our colleagues at Johns Hopkins have given advice and counsel—Karl Alexander, Andrew Cherlin, James Fennessey, Robert Gordon, Leslie Hayduk, Robert Hogan, Edward McDill, Richard Rubin, and Ross Stolzenberg. Those who helped us gather data or process it are Linda Bell, Muriel Berkeley, Michael DePriest, John Glascock, Jon James, Harold Nussenfeld, Vicki Pollard, John Ralph, Marijke Resnick, and Deborah Salkov.

Special thanks are due Daniel Quinlan, who undertook the Herculean task of constructing data files and who carried out many analyses. Le-yun Chang also assisted with analyses and file construction, and more recently Thomas Reilly has collaborated in data analysis. Manuscripts were prepared by Caprice Obinger, Lynette Cunningham, Linda Olson, Shelley Rojas, Nancy Scheeler, and Gloria Zepp. Linda Olson served as a research assistant during the entire period of this research from 1973 forward, and her contribution has been substantial in every phase. She and Merrill Cherlin aided in the final editing of the manuscript.

This research has been supported by NIMH Grants MH25172 and MH12525. Supplementary analyses were supported by NICHD Grant HD13103-01. Also, a Guggenheim fellowship to Doris Entwisle during 1976–77 made it possible to prepare a first draft of the manuscript.

THE FIRST BIRTH

1 | BIRTH IN AMERICAN SOCIETY

INTRODUCTION

Hardly a week goes by without several articles appearing in leading news-papers and magazines on sex or sexual behavior. There is talk of abortion, of homosexual unions, of the perils of the pill, of how women's rights are tied to issues like abortion or birth control. In the face of all this "news" about sex that is not connected with reproduction, it is easy to forget that most adults still become parents and that every single child has two parents. Here, as in other industrialized societies, parenthood continues to be almost universal, and most women and men are still strongly socialized to the norms of heterosexual marriage and parenthood.

There is also much "news" about the family; its imminent demise has been highly exaggerated. There have, of course, been some striking changes in family structure over the last decade. There are now many one-parent families; couples are having fewer children; many persons in their twenties are remaining unmarried; a fair number of couples are voluntarily childless; and many mothers of preschool children work. A principal reason for these changes, which have political as well as ideological roots, is the high degree of conception control, including abortion backup, now possible.

What may not be so obvious is that the structural and demographic changes in the family are paired with changes of another sort—in the *quality* of family life. Attitudes and behaviors of young couples starting families today reflect this. For example, choosing to have fewer children probably means that a family attaches a social premium to producing and nurturing each child. Scarce commodities are always valued more highly, and as the status of children through history testifies, this is no less true if the commodity is a child.

Parents now embarking on parenthood want to savor the experience. Young people going through a pregnancy and a first birth realize that this pregnancy may be a one-and-only experience for them. One consequence of the decline in marriage rates for adults in their twenties is that many of those who do

1

marry and decide to bear a child take on their childbearing task with considerable enthusiasm and forethought. Both men and women today seem to view
their parental roles rather differently than parents did a decade ago. Many
couples want to experience every part of parenthood together, starting with
the changes of pregnancy and continuing on to nurturing the neonate. Change
in family attitudes and behaviors seems particularly noticeable in the case of
fathers.

The quality of family life is also changing because both men and women
have broadened their conceptions of sex roles. Just about all young women
now work from before marriage up to the time their first child is born. Many
return to work soon after. With wives working, young men often share in
household tasks. Also, what were formerly exclusively female tasks—
childbearing and the care of the very young infants—are tasks many husbands
now wish to share and actually do share. Many men wish to be present at and
to assist in the delivery of their children. A number of parents see little incon-
gruity between a masculine role and the nurturant kind of parent a new baby
needs, even though their own childhoods gave them little exposure to models
exemplifying this. The mounting number of divorced fathers seeking custody
of their own children is testimony to this expanded conception of the masculine role.

Expectations for sharing childbirth and child care have changed greatly in
the past two decades. In 1960 men almost never entertained the thought of
witnessing the births of their own children. The few who did wish to be
present were frequently barred from the delivery suite even when they themselves were physicians. Social scientists ignored fathers, and there was a
general lack of interest in them (Nash 1976). There are actually no data on
what prospective and new fathers thought about themselves prior to 1965, but
socialization for the father role was quite different from what it is today.

One manifestation of the desire of today's young couples to share in the
birth of their children is the current popularity of childbirth preparation
classes. Difficult as it is to estimate attendance at such classes on a nationwide
basis, the widespread appeal of the classes is nonetheless apparent (Watson
1977). Most urban and suburban areas now have classes available—probably
70 percent of the population could attend such classes if they wished. The
popularity of such classes increased greatly in the 1970s. In a survey of 269
mothers conducted during the late sixties (Doering and Entwisle 1975), it was
hard to find couples who were enrolled in childbirth education classes, but for
the research reported in this book (1973-76), it was hard to find pregnant
couples who were not enrolled in some sort of childbirth preparation class,
even though half the couples came from blue-collar backgrounds.

Childbirth preparation classes encourage couples to approach birth as a
joint experience. Fathers are expected to help their wives in labor and to
assist, when possible, in delivery. Class attendance may be one cause of what
seems to be a resurgence of breast-feeding. The more basic cause, however, is

probably the same as the reason for class attendance—young couples want to experience parenthood to the fullest. Many of the women in this study who did not attend classes planned to breast-feed. With fewer children expected and fewer actually being born, young parents seem disposed to treasure the experience of parenthood and to plan for it carefully, and the desire to experience all facets of parenting was as characteristic of the young men in this study as it was of the young women. Today's expanded sex-role attitudes, in fact, allow new fathers to share more comfortably in the care of young infants than was true in the past.

THE PLACE OF BIRTH IN FAMILY FORMATION

A couple's first pregnancy, followed by the birth of the child and the ensuing early months of the infant's life, actually constitute a critical period in the evolution of a family. Even now, despite the mushrooming of childbirth-preparation classes, there is little formal socialization of parents for their new roles. If a couple manages to cope well with the arrival of their first child, one would expect the threesome to be off to a successful beginning as a family, as reflected in the role integration of both parents. The man must integrate the father role with roles he has previously held, his husband role, his work role, and others. The woman must also integrate the mother role into a role set she possesses, including that of wife, daughter, and possibly employee. A successful beginning to parenthood may also be reflected in an increase in both parents' sense of well-being, an improvement in the couple's marital relationship, and most important, in the enhancement of the developing relationship between parents and child.

If, on the other hand, a couple copes poorly with pregnancy, childbirth, and the early weeks of parenting, problems may ensue, and problems at one stage can create others at the next stage. During pregnancy, for example, if the *couple* does not take steps to prepare realistically for the birth, the birth event may be traumatic for one or both spouses and may actually drive them apart. The husband may feel he has been deserted. Or if the young woman becomes overanxious, she may not be able to help herself during delivery and may require obstetrical assistance (drugs, forceps). She will then take longer to recover. Later, because of the difficult delivery, she may be so frightened at the thought of becoming pregnant again that she avoids sexual relations with her husband. This kind of behavior could erode the marital relationship and perhaps spill over and lead to physical or emotional problems for the infant. Situations like these could get the new family off to a bad start.

It is easy to underestimate the stress incurred by the arrival of the first child. Although not all social scientists are willing to label the period as one of crisis (Lamb 1978) and the view that early parenthood is a strain on marriage is not always supported (Fawcett 1978; Hobbs 1965, 1968; Hobbs and Cole 1976; Hoffman and Manis 1978*b*), childbirth and the early weeks of an infant's life

call for a couple to make drastic readjustments. New behavior patterns are called for as soon as the birth occurs. Furthermore, social supports for first-time parents are weak, partly because the traditional supports of the extended family—the maiden aunt or the live-in grandmother—have been replaced by institutional, depersonalized supports in present-day society. The hospital obstetrical unit, rather than the home, is usually the scene of the birth, for example, so when it occurs, parents are screened off from friends and relatives and are cared for by medical personnel, who can be detached and distant. A few days after the birth, the couple is left completely on its own. Confused new parents trying to soothe a distressed infant have few places to turn. Young people's prior experience gives them little competence in their tasks as parents of a new baby, yet the whole tone of the family's future and the welfare of its members may be influenced by the way the couple handles the birth crisis and the events of the ensuing few weeks.

Surprisingly, despite sociologists' extensive research on the family as a social unit, and despite a widely held opinion that the arrival of children has a negative impact upon marriage (Rollins and Galligan 1978), little attention has been paid to the normal family at the time when its first child arrives—the exact moment when the couple becomes a "family." And what little attention has been paid has mainly centered on the mother. Fathers have been neglected for the most part.

Many sociologists have commented upon birth as a life-cycle event, noting that parenting is a role for which our society offers little preparation and that there is no period of apprenticeship analogous to the courtship preceding a marriage (Hill and Aldous 1969; Hobbs 1968; Lopata 1971; Rossi 1968). But there is not much research on families at this critical point in their history—aside from a few early studies with mixed findings (Dyer 1963; Hobbs 1965, 1968; LeMasters 1957) and some recent surveys looking at the general effects of children on a marriage (Campbell, Converse, and Rodgers 1976; Hoffman and Manis 1978a). The lack of sociological research on emergent families is all the more curious when one considers that society as a whole tacitly recognizes the challenge posed by pregnancy and childbirth. Just the fact that there are specialized personnel and institutions concerned with pregnancy and birth is proof that society recognizes the need for support at the time of birth.

A number of medically oriented researchers suspect that stress would have negative effects on pregnancy and its outcome (Gorsuch and Key, 1974; Nuckolls, Cassel, and Kaplan 1972; Syme and Berkman 1976). In this context, social class can be seen as one source of stress: the lower the level of a mother's socioeconomic resources, the higher stress may be during pregnancy and arrival of a first child. Having to resign her job, for example, may put more of a strain on the budget of a lower-class mother than on that of a middle-class mother, because often lower-class income (hourly pay) is less regular. A middle-class husband who stays home for a few days with a cold

does not have less pay at week's end. In addition, the more stereotyped sex-role standards of lower-class couples as compared to middle-class couples could cause lower-class women to tolerate the bodily changes of pregnancy less well than their middle-class counterparts. On the other hand, the lower-class mother may have a number of advantages. Resources other than financial ones are not necessarily correlated with high social status, the best example being the more extensive support of kin in lower-class and disadvantaged groups. Indeed, Furstenberg (1976) found that father absence was apparently much less critical than might have been expected for the adjustment of low-income black adolescent mothers, because the adolescent's family of origin provided the necessary social support. Findings are similar for other solo black mothers of low income (Takai, forthcoming). In addition, a lower-class mother is not necessarily expected to plan a lifetime work career, so the interruption in work caused by arrival of an infant may not be as psychologically stressful as for a career-oriented middle-class mother. Nonetheless, whether or not social class affects the stress a family feels at the time a first child arrives, and how great a source of stress it may be, is not well understood.

RESEARCH AIMS

To provide more information about what actually happens to modern couples during the critical period of family formation, this research focused on 120 couples experiencing the birth of a first child. They were questioned starting in the sixth month of the pregnancy and were then followed up until their infants were six months old. Both mother *and* father were interviewed before and after the birth.

By following these emergent families, the research aimed to provide descriptive information of several kinds. One kind pertains to these families as social units. Most previous studies of birth concentrate exclusively on the mother. Here, both mother and father, as well as their interactions with the child, are described. Another kind of information concerns the degree of stress these couples faced as a result of their experiencing childbirth in the seventies, a time during which there has been much social change affecting young families.

Because it includes a narrative description of couples at one life stage, this research is in some ways like an anthropological study. It is a case history that inquires into the life experiences and outlooks of a set of people with common problems. The narrative history asks, among other things: What do husband and wife worry about during pregnancy? How do couples find out about modern customs of labor and delivery? How do they go about seeking the kind of childbirth care they prefer? What are their views on child care before they

have a child? How do these views change when a child arrives? To whom do the young parents look for advice? How do they feel about their own parents? What are their reactions to the early days of infant care? In the sense that this study is descriptive, it is particularistic. It is based on a small sample of volunteer couples who live in Maryland, so the description that emerges here may not apply to couples in general. Yet the problems that beset these couples are probably not peculiar to any one section of the country. When checked against more representative samples (Yankelovich, 1974), the circumstances and outlook of the couples in this panel who resided in central Maryland at the time their first children were born (1973–76) were similar in most ways to those of other young adults of similar socioeconomic status in the United States at that time.

In other ways, this research is analytic—exploring associations or possible causal links between variables. On this account it resembles many psychological and sociological studies. To examine intersections among variables, it is not as essential as it is for descriptive work to have a representative sample of people, although it is desirable for the sample to span a considerable range of persons. The sample of couples surveyed in this research was therefore chosen to ensure a wide distribution on how well the couples were prepared beforehand for the birth—we suspected that prenatal preparation would affect how the couples coped with the crisis of childbirth. Couples from different social-class and religious groups were also systematically selected (half were middle class, half blue collar, and approximately one-third belonged to each major religious group). Following a set of carefully chosen couples for a period of time is a helpful strategy in analyzing potential cause-effect relationships, particularly for topics as complex and intimate as those involved in family relationships. Only lengthy and detailed questioning would yield the kind of information we deemed essential. This kind of research should shed considerable light on events or states of mind that may be causally related. For example, it should be possible to draw some conclusions about the events, attitudes, or activities during pregnancy that may influence couples' birth experience and early parenting.

This book, then, follows the unfolding of life-cycle events affecting 120 young Maryland couples. The sample of couples, the design of the survey, and its methodology are described in chapter 2, with the more technical details given in Appendix A. Chapter 3 deals with the pregnancy, and succeeding chapters deal with the birth and early parenting. At each step, the aim is to describe the couples at that particular point in their lives and then, using sociological or psychological theory when possible, to seek out particular relationships that may account for what is transpiring. A careful analysis of the life histories of this set of first-time parents should elucidate some of the basic questions about early family formation that perplex social scientists.

The remainder of the present chapter will present a brief overview of prior research on pregnancy, childbirth, and the period of early parenting.

PRIOR RESEARCH

The Perinatal Period and Stress

Childbirth, as Macfarlane (1977:2) says, is an "emotional and immeasurably complex aspect of existence that means a great deal to the individuals involved, both at the time itself and later." The family's first pregnancy is a turning point. It is an *exciting* time. Besides posing a challenge to both husband and wife as individuals, pregnancy constitutes a major hurdle for the family, because it leads to an upheaval in family relationships. And although each person might deal with the pregnancy and birth in a way satisfactory to him or her as an individual, some modes of individual coping may threaten the family as a unit. If a new mother relies heavily on *her* mother's help, for example, she may safeguard her own well-being, but at the same time she may prevent her husband from learning how to handle the new baby. A balance must be struck—individuals must cope, but the family must learn how to function as a unit.

In our society a child's arrival forces a couple to take that final step into their adult roles. The birth crisis forces the reorganization of the family as a social system—"roles have to be reassigned, status positions shifted, values reoriented, and needs met through new channels" (LeMasters, 1957:352). If, as Nye (1976) says, family roles encompass the essential activities of family life—and the more competently each spouse enacts these roles, the more satisfactory family life becomes—clearly the first pregnancy can pose a threat to the quality of family life, or even to the family's existence. With the advent of a third person, the couples' roles change with respect to each other and to the larger society. In addition, each spouse adds a new role to his / her repertoire, that of parent.

The early sociological literature defined the arrival of the first child as a family crisis (Hill 1951; Waller 1938), but until recently, actual research on pregnancy and childbirth has been conducted mainly along two other lines—medical and psychiatric. Because both of these disciplines emphasize the pathological, research on the sociopsychological concomitants of pregnancy, birth, and early parenting in the normal, well-balanced adult is rare. There is increasing recognition, however, that the perinatal period can be a time of crisis for even the average young woman (Gorsuch and Key 1974; Larsen 1966; Nuckolls, Cassel, and Kaplan, 1972; Syme and Berkman 1976). Nonetheless, how stress affects a woman, or what particular kinds of stress are hardest to bear, is not yet well understood, even though physical as well as mental ailments have been linked to stress (Syme and Berkman 1976).

Research on fathers is even scarcer than research on mothers, but pregnancy and childbirth are no doubt psychologically stressful for husbands as well (Arnstein 1972). The psychiatric literature mentions a few fathers who could *not* handle the stress, reporting extreme reactions such as sexual acting

out (Curtis 1955; Freeman 1951; Hartman and Nicolay 1966; Towne and Afterman 1955). But again, little is known about stress the average father faces either before or after childbirth, how that stress affects his well-being, or how his reactions to stress may affect his wife's or his child's well-being.

So far, stress has been talked about mainly in relation to the birth itself. However, in addition to the new sources of tension that childbirth creates, it probably also catalyzes or multiplies the other usual sources of tension in a family—sex, money, relationships with relatives. All these could be pushed into the foreground by the impending arrival of an infant. Women in the last trimester of pregnancy often desire sex less frequently than their husbands do, or not at all (Solberg, Butler, and Wagner 1973). Also, increased financial worry could be predicted because of an interruption or an end to the wife's paycheck, possibly coinciding with some hospital and doctor bills. Such changes could increase marital tension, for it is well known that economic resources are linked to marital stability (Cutright 1971; Furstenberg 1976; Scanzoni 1970). The stresses of childbirth, then, are often coupled with several other kinds of stressful family events: the pregnant woman resigns her job or takes a leave of absence to have the child; the couple moves because the apartment that was well suited to the needs of a couple is too small for a family with children; the husband perhaps changes from student to breadwinner, or takes on a second job to make ends meet.

There are two major thrusts to the problems of new parenthood. First, pregnancy challenges the mother and father as individuals. Second, pregnancy also challenges ''the family''—it tests the bonds between husband and wife, it exposes the husband as well as the wife to high levels of stress, and—by producing a third individual who must be socially (as well as physically) integrated into an already existing group—it tests the viability of the family as a social organization. A three-person group, whatever its nature, is inherently less stable than a two-person group (Simmel 1950; Stryker 1964). (In fact, most other kinds of three-person groups eventually disintegrate into a two-person group and a social isolate.) The couple must expand to include a newcomer who, besides being an intruder, is completely helpless. It seems likely that whatever coping style the couple develops over this period probably does much to set the style the family will employ in meeting other kinds of challenges in the future, especially those posed by the arrival of succeeding children.

THE MOTHER

The crisis character of the first pregnancy in a female's life has long been recognized (Benedek, 1970b; Bibring et al. 1961; Haas 1952; Larsen 1966; Menninger 1943). Shainess (1963:146), in fact, referred to this period as a ''crucible tempering the self'' and recognized the possibility that the tempering process may go wrong, resulting in damage to the self, and by implica-

tion, to the self's relationship with others. Chertok (1969) speaks of pregnancy as a progressively developing crisis with the labor and delivery as its peak, both because of the traditional final results of the confinement (separation of mother and child) and its isolation in time as an *event*.

The literature on stress theory offers some guidance on how mothers may cope with a first pregnancy and birth. Janis (1958:7-8) used the crisis of major surgery to formulate his theory of normal stress behavior. It involves three phases: the "threat phase," occurring when the individual became aware of the impending crisis; the "danger impact phase," when the actual crisis (surgery) occurred; and the "post-impact victimization phase" (convalescence). He interviewed patients both before and after surgery and found three clearcut groups emerging, each of which displayed distinct methods of facing stress before it occurred and distinct reaction patterns during and after the crisis. The groups were distinguished during the threat phase by their anticipatory fear. One large group, the "low anticipatory fear" group, claimed to be unperturbed about the surgery and sought no information about what would happen. Essentially, they denied the coming crisis. When it occurred, they found it an unpleasant surprise and reacted with outrage, belligerence, and a need to blame others for their discomfort in the period of convalescence. They were seen as very difficult patients by the hospital staff. A second large group, those who felt moderate anticipatory fear, admitted some anxiety about what was to happen and sought information. They did what Janis (p. 353) calls the necessary "work of worrying" (after Freud's "work of mourning"). They went through surgery well and were considered model, cooperative patients by staff. These two groups were the predominant ones in Janis's population.

A very small third group had high anticipatory fear, with many symptoms of emotional disturbance. They had a panic reaction, as compared to mere worrying. At times they sought information, but then ignored it. Their post-impact behavior as patients was equally changeable, ranging from being cooperative to the point of childlike dependence to creating occasional disruptive incidents of total noncooperation. They demanded endless reassurance and attention from medical personnel.

Janis's theory has considerable relevance for the childbirth experience, for pregnancy can be seen as the threat phase, labor and delivery as the impact phase, and the recovery period as the postimpact phase (Lapidus 1968; Levy and McGee 1975). Futhermore, the theory can be applied to the husband as well as to the wife.

What evidence is there on the validity of Janis's formulation in relation to childbirth? Research on how new parents handle the stress of a premature birth point to several findings like those of Janis (Caplan 1960; Kaplan and Mason 1960). Parents of premature infants who managed the crisis in a healthy way constantly sought information, planned for the future (the infant's homecoming), admitted their feelings (negative as well as positive), and

accepted reassurance and help. By contrast, the couples whose responses to this crisis were unhealthy did not seek information. They practiced denial, both of the current crisis and of the future homecoming. They denied needs for help and were hostile and suspicious toward those who offered it.

In some earlier research, we sought to apply Janis's model directly to women undergoing childbirth. In a cross-sectional study of 269 women who gave birth to full-term infants between 1965 and 1969 (which in many ways served as a pilot work for the present investigation), it turned out that mothers who had sought knowledge beforehand required less medication during labor and delivery (Doering and Entwisle 1975). Their degree of preparation for childbirth during pregnancy was linked to the amount of medication they required during delivery, and even minimal preparation was better than none. Most important, the prepared women experienced significantly more positive feelings for their new infants at first meeting. These initially positive reactions to their babies were associated with better early mothering: prepared mothers were more likely to care for their own babies in a rooming-in arrangement and were more likely to breast-feed and to continue breast-feeding longer. Although the one-shot nature of the study and its narrow focus place clear limits on its conclusions, a realistic anticipation and some actual training during pregnancy appeared to help these women cope with the birth crisis.

This prior research on childbirth, then, as well as research with parents of premature children, is consistent with Janis's observations concerning surgical patients: ability to cope well with stress is correlated with previous information-seeking. Optimistic denial of approaching threat is dysfunctional; the "work of worrying" is a healthy reaction.

Most other prior research on mothers' degree of preparation and the childbirth experience attends to *physical* events surrounding delivery, not to emotional or social events. The negative effect of fears and anxieties during pregnancy, for instance, upon the course of labor and delivery has been consistently documented (Davids and DeVault 1962; Grimm 1961; Kartchner 1950; McDonald and Christakos 1963; Winokur and Werboff 1956). Also, the efficacy of various programs of preparation for childbirth has been thoroughly researched, with most studies reporting physical or medical advantages, i.e., shorter labor, fewer complications, lowered rate of surgical intervention, and decreased need for drugs (Hughey, McElin, and Young 1978; Laird and Hogan 1956; Miller, Flannery, and Bell 1952; Pearse, Easley, and Podger 1955; Thoms and Wyatt 1951; Zax, Sameroff, and Farnum 1975). (Preparation programs commonly include information about what will occur in labor, specific techniques for dealing with it, airing of attitudes and emotions, and provision for help during the actual labor period.) Other research (Chertok 1969; Huttel et al. 1972; Tanzer 1968; Yahia and Ulin 1965) has begun to emphasize psychological benefits to the mother, ranging from increased self-esteem to reports of a peak experience as defined by Maslow (1954).

In all the studies that have been mentioned so far, however, data were procured at only one point in time, and it was difficult or impossible to make causal inferences. Also, early studies all stopped short of investigating what happened subsequent to delivery—what effects preparation of the mother had on the newborn infant or on her well-being or her husband's in the days following delivery. Except in Doering and Entwisle (1975) and in some other studies just now appearing (Eichler et al. 1977; Feldman and Rogoff 1977; Grossman 1978; Norr et al. 1977; Peterson, Mehl, and Leiderman 1979), there is no information about events after delivery.

Social conditions, of course, are changing in ways that make questions about behavior after delivery especially pressing. For example, many mothers of young children now wish to return to the job market as quickly as possible because two paychecks are needed to keep the family solvent. At the same time, many new mothers are eager to breast-feed. These conflicting demands must be carefully assessed if they are to be reconciled. Other conflicts are a consequence of the fact that attitudes toward motherhood have not kept pace with changes in attitudes toward women in other roles. For example, in present-day society there is still widespread suspicion of women who delegate child care.

THE FATHER

Much less is known about how the birth of a first child affects the father. Our previous study (Doering and Entwisle 1975) did not include fathers. The psychiatric literature (Benedek 1970a; Jones 1942; Towne and Afterman 1955) recognizes that the impact of pregnancy and the birth of a first child can be a serious crisis in a man's life and can affect the marital relationship, but little firm research is at hand. In one study (Trethowan and Conlon 1965) expectant fathers, compared to a nonexpectant control group, experienced more toothache, nausea, and loss of appetite, with symptoms at their worst in the third month of pregnancy. Symptoms cleared up just before or just after delivery. This kind of study is rare. Firsthand accounts by new fathers in the lay literature suggest, as one would expect, that active preparation and participation during labor and delivery strongly affect the father's earliest reactions to his newborn, as well as his feelings toward his wife (Bing 1970; Eldridge 1970; Roberts 1969), but these topics are just beginning to be studied scientifically. As Richman and Goldthorp (1978) point out, most existing knowledge about fatherhood concerns men who are atypical in some respect, men for whom fatherhood precipitated mental illness or who were in prison or in military service.

In reports that concentrate on the wife's emotions, there are a few passing references to fathers. For example, the fears and anxieties of a group of husbands who, with their wives, attended an encounter-type group throughout the pregnancy are discussed (Colman and Colman 1971). Until recently, the

only empirical data available on how expectant fathers coped with the crisis of birth were found in wives' reports of their husbands' behavior (Henneborn and Cogan 1975; Tanzer 1968) or in the lay literature; since the present research began, however (early 1973), some empirical studies of the expectant and the postpartum father have begun to appear (Coley and James 1976; Cronewett and Newmark 1974; Eichler et al. 1977; Fein 1974; Feldman and Rogoff 1977; Grossman 1978; Russell 1974; Wapner 1975; Wente and Crockenberg 1976). These studies call attention for the first time to how birth affects the father himself and how it affects his relationship with his wife.

The birth crisis must be stressful for the male, even though the crisis character of a first pregnancy and childbirth was not recognized as clearly or as soon for men as for women. The Janis model most likely applies to fathers as well as mothers. True, the father is spared the bodily changes of pregnancy, but the fact that some men experience morning sickness or other symptoms mimicking their wives' ailments suggests that stress on first-time fathers may be severe. At the very least, there could be indirect stress because the wife calls upon the husband to help with her own stress.

Men must respond to the pregnancies of their wives and to the birth of their first child in terms of their own self-image and role behaviors. Birth must also affect a man's relationship with his wife, if only because both he and she assume additional roles at the birth of an infant. Furthermore, in taking on the parent role, fathers do not abdicate any other major role, so the new role calls for integration and readjustment. Adding roles creates the possibility of role strain or incompatibility. The role of father, for example, may not be entirely compatible with the role of successful breadwinner. Babies cry at night, new mothers get overtired, relatives may overstay their welcome, and the new father must therefore attend to tasks at home that interfere with his work responsibilities. Conversely, the baby may be a source of such pleasant distraction that the husband's attention strays from his work—he calls home to check on the baby and literally spends hours every day playing with the infant. In the sociological literature much has been said about role strain for employed women, but little is known about role strain for new fathers.

It was pointed out above that pregnancy confronts women with new demands and responsibilities which climax at the birth of the child, and that for the new mother, successful coping with the stress of pregnancy and childbirth can be a "crucible tempering the self" (Shainess 1963). It seems reasonable to state similar hypotheses about the father, even though the demands upon him are more psychological than physical. In particular, the birth of a child places financial burdens upon the family. Despite the egalitarian work ethic many modern couples espouse, these burdens still fall more heavily on the male. Many young mothers now choose to work, but the presumption persists that the fathers can assume full support—and will, if need be. If both members of a couple have been employed, a significant reduction in spending must occur when the wife leaves the labor force, either temporarily or permanently.

Such sources of worry could be particularly acute for the fathers included in this research, which happened to take place over a time (1973–76) when the Consumer Price Index rose 20–25 percent.

Fathers face other demands too. Childbirth poses the risk of having a sick mate. Many women experience morning sickness in the first trimester. An increasingly large number of women give birth by Cesarean delivery, and this requires an extended period of convalescence. A significant proportion of women experience some kind of depression after the birth. Wives may turn to husbands for extra support in coping with all these health problems.

Other sources of worry to fathers are babies born long after the due date or those born prematurely. Some couples have the misfortune to bear an infant who is deformed or ill. And although it may seem trivial compared to issues like the health of the infant, a fair number of fathers must reconcile themselves to the arrival of a child whose sex is the opposite from what they had hoped for.

Another kind of stress, which might be classed as social, comes about because the father must sacrifice privacy. Relatives or other helpers invade the household. The father may find it awkward to deal on an intimate basis with some of these persons—say with his mother or mother-in-law. If he works at home or deals with clients or customers at home, he may have to readjust his work schedule. The new mother could undoubtedly experience these same kinds of stress, but since she is the center of attention, it may be easier for her to handle such problems. She can more easily tell helpers to leave or to leave her alone, for example.

In addition, the father may suffer some loss of his wife's attention, for she is necessarily engrossed in caring for the infant. She can no longer be a carefree companion, ready to go out on the spur of the moment or glad to entertain his friends at short notice. Having occupied first place in his wife's attention, a husband may resent second place. As discussed above, two-person groups are generally more stable than three-person groups—partly, no doubt, because each person can bask in the undivided attention of the other.

Some new demands (mentioned above in passing) are placed upon fathers as a consequence of an outlook peculiar to this decade. Society has begun a profound reconsideration of the proper roles for men and women, and this has led to a disintegration of earlier sex-role stereotypes. Many young adults see less-stereotyped sex roles as highly desirable: if women can be engineers, men can be house-husbands. Even for more traditional couples, such ideas cause the birth of a child to place more explicit and more varied burdens upon a man than was formerly the case. A generation ago a father was not expected to take a very active role in infant care. Now, however, fathers are seen as major caretakers of infants, especially by mothers. Today's fathers are expected to care for the infant while the mother goes shopping or visiting, and in addition, they often are expected to take the baby to the pediatrician or to stay home with the baby while the mother works.

The weight of the new burdens is increased by the ambiguity that the new, more flexible roles create. Role strain, in fact, must be very likely. Is the young father expected to take an active part during labor and delivery even if it conflicts with a critical work assignment? Should he take time off from work when his wife comes home from the hospital even if his pay is docked? Should he allow himself to be tied down while his wife is earning money? Should he stay home from work if the baby is sick?

Because today's sex-role expectations are novel, men's earlier socialization for the father role is out-of-date. Young men of today seem to know little more about pregnancy and birth than their fathers did—perhaps even less because of the decline in agrarian life-styles and because their childhood was spent in an isolated nuclear family, where there is little chance to obtain firsthand experience in caring for infants and young children. Young men in American society are brought up to attend to achievement and mastery, to deny affect, to neglect expressive roles, and above all, to avoid being "sissies." Even playing with girls is suspect. How can such men find it easy to express their affection for a helpless infant? How can they readily take up diaper changing, meal fixing, and house cleaning when they, like most of society, classify such tasks as menial? How can they reconcile the television stereotype of the slim, carefree modern female presented for their admiration all through their youth with the vision of the parturient or lactating mother?

Further, mothers, more than fathers, derive the satisfactions of active achievement from childbirth. Most cultures place motherhood at the apex of female achievement (Blake 1972; Flapan 1969; Hoffman and Wyatt 1960). In present-day American society, even high-achieving women are rated on family as well as on professional activities: women's proper task still includes raising children. Becoming a father is socially important—i.e., as proof of sexual prowess, the continuation of the bloodline, and the existence of an heir—but the acting out of the nurturant part of the father role as the infant matures yields few socially important gratifications for men. We have "gold-star mothers," not "gold-star fathers"; we hear about "motherhood and apple pie," not fatherhood. The fact that most mothers are still awarded custody of minor children in divorce actions is evidence of the secondary role assigned to fathers. Society rather generally views the infant as the "mother's property"—if the infant is healthy and well cared for the mother is congratulated; if the infant is dirty or malnourished, the mother is held to be at fault. The deemphasis of the father's role in relation to the infant is, then, only one of the possible psychological stresses experienced by the first-time father. It is unclear whether or not the birth of a child is usually a negative marital factor for the father, but research on the subject is past due.

There are almost no data on how the status of fatherhood affects the marital relationship, despite the growing literature on how men respond to becoming fathers (Bernstein and Cyr 1957; Fein 1974; Greenberg and Morris 1974; Parke, O'Leary, and West 1972; Pedersen and Robson 1969). Survey data

confirm that fathers are somewhat less interested in parenthood than mothers (Hoffman and Hoffman 1973; Lowenthal, Thurnber, and Chiriboga 1974; Maas and Kuypers 1974). Except for evidence to be provided in this study and a preliminary report by Feldman and Rogoff (1977), literature on how father's attitudes may affect mother's parenting is scarce.

The father's response to his first child, besides being important for his psychological well-being and for the integration of his own role set, may be a dominant factor in his wife's role behavior. Cohen (1966) had not planned to include husbands in her study of expectant mothers, but was forced to do so when she discovered that husbands had a crucial effect on their wives' functioning during pregnancy. (See also Gladieux 1978.) Husbands are also thought to be exceedingly important in determining women's work roles; for example, husbands are strong determinants of whether a wife works (Blood and Wolfe 1960; Duncan, Schuman, and Duncan 1974), and one study indicates that legitimation and support by a valued male is essential for women in pursuing a career and maintaining a nontraditional family life (Tangri 1969). Everything points to reciprocal influence between mates, with one helped or hindered by the other. Role integration, although not researched until lately, is a critical aspect of adjustment to parenthood for which the spouses' influence on one another could have important consequences for family functioning.

Finally, although what is written above emphasizes the difficulties and role strain of fatherhood more than its gratifications and rewards, Chilman and Elbaum (1976) report that 23 percent of the fathers of older children found child rearing was much more satisfying than other jobs they might have, and about one-fifth of the fathers particularly enjoyed preschool youngsters. In the same survey, more fathers than mothers thought that parenthood had strengthened their marriage. Such findings suggest that there are ways for fathers to cope with the advent of children that will strengthen them as individuals and will strengthen their marriage ties as well.

THE COUPLE

In the 1976 Chilman and Elbaum survey, few men and women saw children as playing an important part in marital adjustment, but this finding does not necessarily deny that arrival of a first child may threaten marital harmony or may set the style for how other kinds of stressful events will be handled. For one thing, respondents in that survey were years past the actual event (the birth), and they were not being asked specifically about their reaction to the birth of children. When couples are asked specifically about that period, most report that they experienced a fair amount of stress and had difficulty adjusting (Dyer 1963; LeMasters 1957; Meyerowitz and Feldman 1966). There are also reports that children are a threat to conjugal solidarity because time and energy spent in child care is often at the spouse's expense (Pohlman 1969). The healthier a couple's marriage, however, the less difficulty they appear to

experience in adjusting (Dyer 1963; Hobbs 1968). Yet the level of marital satisfaction for couples with (first) infants is reported to be significantly lower than for a control group of couples married for the same period but without a child (Feldman in Hobbs 1965). There is also reported to be a significant overall decrease in marital satisfaction for both husbands and wives at the birth of a first child (Feldman and Rogoff 1977; Ryder 1973). Hoffman and Manis's (1978b) conclusion, based on a national sample of parents, is that the marital relationship changes rather than deteriorates, however. Those in the early stages of parenting reported great satisfactions from children, even though they had severe complaints. The effect of the birth experience per se on the marital relationship, however, has thus far only been hinted at (Bing 1970; Tanzer 1968).

The birth event could affect couples in different ways because of variability in the experience itself. Some couples have extensive financial resources, uncomplicated births, and infants who are easy to handle. Other couples face an operative delivery, become parents prematurely, or have the misfortune to bear a malformed infant. Outside of the work of Gordon and Gordon (1960), however, little prior research focuses upon identifying the variables causing stress around the time of birth. In particular, little attention has been paid to what could be done to assure a more satisfying experience.

There have been marked changes in the roles of marriage partners since World War II. The postwar baby boom led, perhaps out of necessity, to a social climate of family "togetherness." With shortened hospital stays, brought about by the postwar shortage of obstetrical beds, husbands in the fifties had more responsibilities thrust upon them even before the time when today's questions about sex-role stereotypes became so pressing. Long before society's notions of sex roles began to broaden, there was a decline in the family's economic (production) function. Industrialization and urbanization caused the family to give up a life-style in which women and children helped to provide food, clothing, and other necessities of life, and so the family now seems to fulfill mainly psychological functions (Parsons 1955). Men and women began to look at their marriages primarily as a means for personal fulfillment and satisfaction. Specific expectations today for extensive husband participation in pregnancy and delivery are greater than in the fifties and sixties. Men are encouraged to remain with their wives during labor and delivery, and most wives now expect it. But husbands' preparation for what will happen over the perinatal period is limited. They certainly are not as well prepared as they could be, if only because they have had few role models available. Another problem for couples could be that, despite giving lip service to broadened sex roles, young mothers may subconsciously discourage, rather than encourage, their husbands from taking an active part in caring for the newborn; by monopolizing the infant, they can increase their relative power within the family. Such behavior could lead to conflict for the male. Modern husbands are urged to participate in home chores and infant care, and

they could be in a dilemma if these ideals are consciously or unconsciously opposed by their wives. In fact, several researchers note that *women* more than men oppose changes in the traditional division of labor in the family (e.g., Pleck 1981).

Social conditions today do not allow fathers more time with infants than they had in the last generation. Fathers can seldom get paternity leave, as all new fathers do in Sweden. Most men's jobs have rigid hours. Few young men have spent much time around young babies. In childhood an active father role was not anticipated—boys a decade ago did not spend time "playing father," nor, in most cases, did they spend much time with their own fathers. While it has always been assumed that most young males will become fathers, the father role is one that men were expected to know mainly by instinct, and they have had few role models to follow for the nurturant role behaviors now expected of them (Fein 1974).

These days it is fashionable for both husband and wife to subscribe to complete equality, but when the first child arrives, it may be exceedingly difficult for the couple to maintain this ideal. For one thing, only the mother can give birth and produce milk. For another, not many husbands can take an infant along to their workplaces. Men's work schedules are usually rigid, and if the baby cries through the night, it is often the wife who deals with the crying and then tries to catch up on her sleep in the daytime. These problems are not easy to resolve, and they threaten the popular egalitarian ethic.

Parent-Child Relationship

Research into the effect of prenatal experiences and the birth itself on the parent-child relationship has been scarce until recently. Early parenting is, for the most part, a period shrouded in mystery. Folklore has it that people raise children the way they themselves were raised, and there seems to be more than a kernel of truth in this hypothesis. Child abusers, for example, are often those who have themselves suffered abuse when children (Hunter et al., n.d.). It is hard perhaps to see how a mother or father could copy behavior of their own parents toward them at the time of their infancy. If they were loved as babies, however, even if they have no current recollection of it, they are probably more likely to be able to display love themselves and to seek emotionally warm relationships.

There are a few scattered reports on how events before or during the birth of one's child affect later adjustment to motherhood. Davids, Holden, and Gray (1963) demonstrated an association between anxiety during pregnancy and mother-child adjustment eight months postpartum, but skipped the intervening crisis of confinement and early mother-child interaction. Moss and co-workers also did not attend to the birth event, but noted relations between measures of maternal warmth obtained during pregnancy and the quality of early mother-infant interaction (Moss 1967; Moss, Robson, and Pedersen

1969; Robson, Pedersen, and Moss 1969). Very recently a preliminary report by Eichler et al. (1977) points to relationships between the mother's emotional state during pregnancy and both marital satisfaction and the infant's health. Tanzer (1968) reported a correlation between preparation during pregnancy and a positive childbirth experience, but nothing about mother-child relationships afterward. Other research (Newton 1952, 1955) suggests a link between a positive birth experience and a close relationship to the infant immediately after birth, as measured by desire to breast-feed, to have rooming-in, and the like. Our previous cross-sectional study of mothers in the sixties (Doering and Entwisle 1975) found that breast-feeding was continued longer by prepared women. In that research, women who were better prepared for the birth received less medication during labor and delivery. Thus, preparation could lead to positive outcomes at several subsequent points, both because of direct effects, and because of domino effects—good things are likely to trigger further good things. A mother with a good delivery experience could be more disposed, because of this alone, to persist in her efforts to breast-feed. Also, if she requires less medication because she is well prepared, she may find herself in better physical shape after delivery and so have both the psychic and physical stamina to endure a few setbacks when she tries to learn how to breast-feed. Recent preliminary reports (Eichler et al. 1977; Grossman 1978) are consistent with this hypothesis.

Despite social scientists' general lack of attention to pregnancy and birth, there has been an enormous amount of psychological research lately on infant attachment, particularly with regard to the mother (see Ainsworth 1969, 1973; Ainsworth, Bell, and Stayton 1974). Until recently, such research had focused on behavior of children at least six months old, because methodologies for use with younger children were not available. Observational techniques have now improved to such an extent, however, that even attachment of the youngest infants is being studied, and the amount of research on very early attachment behavior of neonates is becoming substantial (Barnett et al. 1970; Brazelton, 1961; DeChateau 1976; Fanaroff, Kennell, and Klaus 1972; Greenberg, Rosenberg, and Lind 1973; Klaus and Kennell 1976b; Klopfer, 1971). There is, of course, no lower limit for the age at which infant attachment may occur. For all we know, human infants may experience the analogue of early imprinting in animals. Klaus and Kennell (1976b) believe there is a "maternal sensitive period" within the first few hours after birth when close contact between mother and infant leads to long-lasting, positive consequences of several kinds.

Some theorists believe that attachment can develop only after there has been enough cognitive development so the infant can distinguish one person from another (e.g., Lamb 1977), but other research suggests that attachment begins as soon as the baby is born, or even during pregnancy (Klaus and Kennell 1976a). Attachment, however, like every other aspect of child socialization, is a two-way process. The behavior of infants has occupied re-

searchers' attention more than the behavior of parents, but parents' attachment behavior is important as well. The parents have no need to wait until the infant is several months old before their own attachment behavior can begin.

Lately, attachment research has concerned itself with the father as well as the mother (Cronewett and Newmark 1974; Fein 1974; Golluber 1976; Greenberg and Morris 1974; Lamb 1976, 1977; Peterson, Mehl, and Leiderman 1977; Wente and Crockenberg 1976). It is suspected that the father, like the mother, may have highly significant attachment experience when the infant is still very young.

With the exception of Parke and O'Leary (1975), very little research has been done on behavior of *both* parents in relation to infant attachment, and there is a dearth of research on other aspects of very early parenting as well. The present research is novel because it investigates some of the parents' behavior before, during, and shortly after the infant's arrival, and reports in particular about their interaction with the young infant.

Though little has yet been published on how couples' coping with pregnancy is related to parent-child bonding or to other important events early in a child's life, there is no reason to believe such linkages are absent. Until fairly recently, however, when electronic data processing allowed quick analysis of large amounts of complex data, elaborate hypotheses concerning family formation could not be readily tested.

THEORETICAL CONTEXT

The theoretical context for this research can best be described as eclectic. Some theories of limited scope can be brought to bear rather powerfully on particular aspects of the research. For example, Janis's stress theory (1958) is useful in interpreting how parents react to the crisis of childbirth. Klaus and Kennell's theory (1976b) about early contact and the quality of mother-infant attachment can be tested rather specifically. Kohn's theory (1969) linking class values to parenting helps explain social-class differences in the nature of early parenting behavior. But other theoretical notions are less well crystallized and so mainly provide a frame of reference or a set of concepts to serve as a backdrop for the analysis. In particular, the various theories of the family that emphasize roles, life-cycle notions, and social exchange provide useful concepts but at present are too loosely formulated to serve as strictly testable propositions.

The life-cycle approach to human development calls attention to the life cycle of the family as well as that of individuals. Any given period in the life cycle is the staging area for the next, and passage from one period in the cycle to the next is often accompanied by stress. However, there is little in the theory that is explicit enough to be applied directly to our data. For example, there are no specific predictions about conditions that will mitigate stress or

aggrandize it, and very little in the way of predictions about social rites de passage.

Role theory also provides a loose set of theoretical notions that helped guide our thinking (see Nye 1976; also Pleck 1981) but that, again, is useful mainly in supplying concepts rather than in specifying testable relationships. The parent role is imposed suddenly, and both husband and wife must quickly integrate that role with the others they already fill. Having acknowledged that *role* is a key concept, one has little guidance on how to proceed further. There are no particular clues to clarify the reciprocal roles of husband and wife in pregnancy or how couples perceive each other in the role of expectant parent. At this point in history, furthermore, assumption of the parent role is both more ambiguous and more problematic than in the past—ambiguous because in the wake of the feminist movement there is much blurring of sex roles and problematic because when women combine work and parent roles they create role strain for themselves *and* their husbands. There is further uncertainty because of the current acknowledged transitoriness of family roles. A parent will always be a parent, but wives and husbands in increasing numbers find themselves without partners. Awareness of the possibility of becoming a solo parent may make new mothers hesitate to leave the labor force or make new fathers reluctant to encourage their wives to do so.

Social-exchange theory provides a different, but again limited, kind of insight. According to these theories, individuals choose modes of interaction or coping styles that they hope will maximize benefits to themselves. Thus, a wife may wish to become pregnant because she perceives that as a mother the social rewards accruing to her over a child's lifetime will outweigh the shorter-term financial and emotional costs of caring for a young baby. Or she may choose motherhood mainly because she believes her husband wants children and she has no other option if she wants to maintain a stable long-term marriage. Likewise, a husband may opt for fatherhood despite its acknowledged financial burdens because he perceives the social rewards as larger than the dollar costs.

The possible relevance of exchange theories to family formation could be more clear-cut now than in previous decades because of conception control. Whereas a large percentage of conceptions could formerly be classed only as accidents, unplanned pregnancies are less common now. In this research sample, only four women said their pregnancies were completely unplanned. It is reasonable therefore, to think of couples actually weighing the costs and benefits of becoming parents. Another reason that exchange theory may now be more readily applied is that many modern couples are committed to expanded sex roles. Both the number of roles and the possibilities for their enactment are increased. Thus, there is more opportunity to bargain, or to play one option off against another. Many more women with young children now work than was true a generation ago, and the possibility of full-time work late into pregnancy has become so common it is almost taken for granted.

Men, too, have more role choices, partly as a consequence of broadened sex roles and the egalitarian ethic now characterizing so many marriages. Most young men share in what were formerly seen as women's tasks— housekeeping, food preparation, and even remaining at home to care for an infant while the mother works.

The life-cycle concept, role theory, and social-exchange theory all provide considerable perspective on the unfolding of life-cycle events for young couples, but social-science theory is just not well-enough articulated to provide a consistent set of testable propositions in this research area. In fact, a pressing need exists for factual information that could inform theory-builders; one purpose of the descriptive part of this research is to fill part of that gap.

A further word is needed about the multidisciplinary perspective adopted in this research. Pregnancy and birth have medical aspects that cannot be ignored. The physical changes that occur as pregnancy progresses, or the decrease in physical well-being following a surgical delivery, must affect the psychological outlook of couples as well as their social relationships. Throughout the book, emphasis is placed mainly on the psychological or the sociological concomitants of pregnancy, childbirth, and early parenting, with a view toward understanding change in individuals and in families during this important phase of the life cycle. But it is clear that the psychological and the sociological aspects cannot be separated, and that both depend on biological or medical imperatives. The book therefore moves back and forth between the two social-science perspectives while trying simultaneously to take account of the "health" context. Partly for this reason, both the units of analysis (individuals or dyads) and the emphasis in the book vary from place to place. At some times the approach is wholly descriptive. At other times the approach is rather severely analytic. This places a burden on the reader, but there seems to be no sensible alternative. It is hoped that the book will widen and enrich discussion of early family formation by presenting more data, and more incisive data, about persons in this stage of the life cycle than has heretofore been available.

SUMMARY

This book presents a detailed longitudinal study of 120 women and 60 of their husbands around the time that their first child is born. The data cover that critical period when a family changes from a dyad to a triad.

Because there is a dearth of information available on families during this period, one aim of the research is to provide rich descriptive data. Little is known about how emergent families function, and the pace of social change has lately quickened to such an extent that a careful description of this point in the lives of families should yield considerable insight into how young couples have organized their lives in the seventies. The sample is not necessarily

representative, however, so the descriptive data may not hold for other couples in the country at large. In that way, this research is like an anthropological field study.

A second aim of this research is to provide an analysis of the life experiences of the panel of couples at the time their first child arrives. In this sense, the research is like other analytic social science studies that focus on the intersection or the overlap among variables. Such associations are usually rather robust in terms of sampling fluctuation, so the analysis may offer insight into the dynamics of family functioning despite the purposive nature of the sample. The analytic portion of this research tries to link the quality of the parents' childbirth experience and early parenting to prior life experiences of the couple, especially during pregnancy. It also inquires into the specific effects of the birth experience on the new mother, the new father, their perceptions of one another, and the ongoing husband-wife relationship. Two key concepts throughout the analysis are preparation during pregnancy and the social-class identification of the women.

The analysis, we hope, will point up critical factors that help or hinder young couples in coping with the arrival of a first child.

2 | THE PARENTS-TO-BE

In prefacing this chapter we note the obvious: childbearing is a central task of women in all societies. Furthermore, all societies allocate the care of young children to women, even when, as in the Israeli kibbutz or the urban middle-class commune (Kanter, Jaffe, and Weisberg 1975), parents are not the primary caretakers of their own children. But perhaps *because* birth is such a common occurrence, variables affecting women's desire to give birth and their satisfaction from doing so have received little scientific attention. Often the key to understanding a society lies in what it ignores rather than in what it attends to. And as Miller (1973) says, social scientists, including Freud, have concluded that since most married women become pregnant and somehow cope with pregnancy and birth, normal pregnancy is instinctive, explicable in terms of the intrinsic attributes of human nature. Anthropologists apparently also have held this view, judging by the scarcity and brevity of ethnographic accounts of normal births. A less benevolent view is that the lack of attention to birth may stem from the fact that pregnancy and birth are experiences specific to women, a relatively low-status group whom researchers and policymakers do not find it rewarding to work with (Stewart and Erickson 1976).

The expectation that all adults will someday become parents is so taken for granted that it is rarely mentioned. There are norms against childlessness. Although there has been some erosion of these norms among persons currently of childbearing age, it would be a mistake to underrate their strength. The recent lowered fertility of women in their twenties is largely a consequence of postponement of childbearing, either because the woman wishes to establish herself in the labor market or because the couple wishes to test the long-term viability of their marriage. Most childless couples plan to have children eventually, for a recent national sample found that only 7 percent of childless couples did not ever want to have children (Hoffman and Manis 1978*a*). Apparently underlying predispositions in favor of parenthood, which must have started earlier in life, are not easily cast aside.

Despite recent changes in society's views of female participation in the

labor market, woman's role and identity in the United States are still defined primarily in terms of marriage and motherhood (see Busfield 1974). The contrasting identities ascribed to the two sexes can be seen in the set of connotations called up by *spinsterhood* and *bachelorhood*—the former is a somewhat pejorative term, assuming that the woman remains single involuntarily. Almost two decades after the beginnings of the women's liberation movement, there is still a strong bias for American mothers of young children to stay at home unless financial stringencies require outside work (see Yankelovich's survey of parents, 1977, and a survey of teenagers by Herzog, Bachman, and Johnston, 1979). Young mothers themselves, however, are not very happy with the institution of motherhood as it exists in America today (Bernard 1975). Most do not see the role as one capable of fulfilling a woman's whole life. Women are perplexed, however, about how they can combine a mother role with other roles, and when not to do so.

In the remainder of this chapter the particular sample of expectant parents will be described in terms of demographics, attitudes, and opinions. Further details on the sample are given in Appendix A. As we have already noted, these couples are not a representative sample of young adults in the United States today, but their views of themselves do appear to reflect trends seen in the larger society and do provide a background for understanding their reactions to becoming first-time parents.

WHO THE WOMEN ARE

Except in one instance,[1] none of the 120 pregnant women from the Maryland area who participated in this research had had a child before. (Of husbands previously married, nine were already fathers and therefore were not interviewed.) Three of these women were not married, but lived with the prospective fathers of their children in stable relationships. (Two couples remained unmarried throughout the study. One couple was married when their child was about three months old.) For the sake of simplicity, all men in the study are referred to as "husbands," all women are referred to as "wives," and all couples are referred to as "married pairs." No distinctions are made in the analyses regarding a couple's marital status or whether this was the husband's first marriage, except that the men who had children from a previous marriage were excluded from interviews.

All couples were white; half of the wives were of blue-collar origin and half of middle-class origin. All the middle-class couples lived in dwellings by themselves. About 15 percent of the blue-collar couples shared their dwellings with relatives, usually the wife's parents. The women in the sample are about

[1]One respondent had given up a baby for adoption at age sixteen; she had not taken care of that child and had never seen it except for a glimpse through glass after it was born. Several women (11 percent) had had abortions prior to the present pregnancy.

equally divided among the three major religions: thirty-eight Protestants, forty Catholics, thirty-eight Jews, and four who professed either other religions or no religion. The Protestant women were half middle-class, half blue-collar. There were more lower-class Catholic women (thirty vs. ten) and more middle-class Jewish women (twenty-nine vs. nine). Twenty-seven percent of the middle-class women and over half the lower-class women reported attending religious services regularly or often. These figures agree rather well with Yankelovich's survey (1974:90) reporting that 23 percent of college women and 42 percent of noncollege women see religion as a "very important personal value."

The women's average age at the time of the first interview (end of sixth month or beginning of seventh month of pregnancy) was 24.7 years. Thus, they were a little older at the time their first children were born than the average delivery age for women in the United States generally (22.4 years: U.S. Bureau of the Census 1975b). The average age of middle-class women was 25.5, and of blue-collar women 23.9. The range in age among the women was about fourteen years—two women in the sample were 18, and at the other extreme, three women were 31 and one was 32.

The women's median age at marriage was 21.8, and on the average, husbands were slightly more than two years older than their wives. Seventeen of the respondents (14 percent) came from homes broken by divorce or the death of a parent. For the ten respondents whose parents had been divorced, the father was the missing parent in all cases. In the seven where death had broken the family, the respondent's father had died in three cases, mother in three cases, and both in one case.

WOMEN'S PLANS FOR WORK

Exactly half of the respondents either planned to continue working almost to the moment of delivery (fifty-one women) or else did not plan to stop work at all (nine women). Of the remainder, almost all had worked for some portion of their pregnancy (fifty-one women). Only nine women had not worked at any time after conception. Thus when the research started, 92.5 percent of the women were working or had recently worked, a high rate no matter what group they are compared with. In March 1974, for example, 82 percent of single women aged 25 to 29 were in the labor force (U.S. Dept. of Labor 1975). The percentage of mothers of preschool children who were employed in 1970 was 36.9 percent. Probably the percentage of working women in our sample exceeds even the percentage of employed single women in the 1974 study because there are no women in this sample who fall at the lowest educational levels.

The usual relation was found between expected fertility and labor-force participation. Women who expected to have larger numbers of children tended to be those who dropped out of the labor force before or relatively early

TABLE 2.1. Mean rankings by wives and husbands for sources of satisfaction
(1 = most important; 8 = least important)

	Wives' actual ratings			Husbands' estimates of wives' ratings		Husbands' actual ratings		Wives' estimates of husbands' ratings
	W-1[a]	W-2[b]	W-3[c]	H-1[d]	H-2[e]	H-1[d]	H-2[e]	W-2[b]
Baby	2.6	2.2	1.8	2.0	1.8	2.5	1.8	2.3
Friends	6.1	6.0	6.0	5.9	6.1	6.4	6.3	6.5
Home	5.3	5.4	5.2	5.1	4.8	5.5	5.7	5.7
Other relatives	6.2	6.1	6.3	6.5	6.3	7.2	7.3	6.7
Parents	4.5	4.4	4.5	4.5	4.7	5.0	5.0	4.9
Self	2.7	2.8	3.0	3.0	3.0	2.9	2.9	2.9
Spouse	1.3	1.6	1.7	1.7	1.8	1.4	1.4	1.5
Work	7.1	7.2	7.6	7.3	7.4	5.2	5.2	5.5

[a] Wife's interview when six to seven months pregnant.
[b] Wife's interview when nine months pregnant.
[c] Wife's interview two to three weeks after the birth.
[d] Husband's interview during ninth month of pregnancy.
[e] Husband's interview four to eight weeks after the birth.

in pregnancy ($r = .18$, $p < .05$). There was no relation between time of stopping work and the occurrence of either first or second trimester symptoms.

There is no difference according to social class in the work intentions of women for either the immediate or the remote future, although seven of the nine women who did not plan to stop work at all were middle class. Different motives were given for continuing work by the women in each group, however. Middle-class women spoke of the self-fulfillment: "For my own personal enjoyment—my satisfaction," and "I very much enjoyed teaching ... loved working with kids and it's something I'd want to go back to." Lower-class women cited financial pressures: "Mainly money," and "The extra money would be nice." There thus seem to be different motivating factors for middle-class than for working-class women's work plans, a finding consistent with Yankelovich's survey (1974:40) of women college students, who saw their way clear to combining marriage with a fulfilling career, while those not in college saw work as a way to make ends meet rather than as a fulfilling career. As an analysis of sources of satisfaction given in table 2.1 will show, all women in this sample, irrespective of class, rated work as the lowest source of satisfaction in their lives at this time, and husbands of both classes also rated work as very low in their wives' values.

WOMEN'S PLANNING OF MARRIAGE AND PREGNANCY

One would expect life plans to be related to the planning of pregnancy itself, and there are strong indicators of pregnancy planning in this group of women. Over 54 percent of the women in this sample reported that they did

not become pregnant until at least two years after marriage, and almost one-fifth of them were married from four to six years before they became pregnant. In addition, seventy-five women (almost two-thirds) reported that the pregnancy was completely planned, and forty-one (34 percent) reported it was somewhat planned. Only four women in the sample had totally unplanned pregnancies. (Miller [1973:77] found 68 percent total planners, 23 percent "sort-of planners," and 9 percent unplanned pregnancies in a sample of forty-seven women.) In this study, respondents were put in the "totally planned" category if they had specifically stopped using (or had never used) contraceptives in order to conceive. "Sort-of-planners," adopting Miller's definition (1973:77), were "irregular and uncommitted contraceptive users." These women knew about birth control but slipped up once, occasionally "forgot," or "didn't get around to" doing whatever was necessary. In discussing the question, many of the "sort-of-planners" said flatly that they had wanted to become pregnant; others wondered whether that had been the case. None was seriously upset over the conception. In the 1970s, most women who really did not want to become pregnant either managed to avoid it or resorted to abortion when contraception failed and thus would not appear in this sample. From this standpoint, finding only four women who report completely unplanned pregnancies is not surprising.

The four unplanned cases were explained as follows. One was an IUD failure. Another couple was using withdrawal, but the husband did not withdraw in time on one occasion. A third couple, with a very young, naive wife, were on their honeymoon, and the new husband was "taking care of everything." She said that she was unaware that he did not use a condom once and could not imagine what was causing her physical symptoms a month later. The fourth case involved teenagers who were using condoms, but did not on one occasion.

The desire to postpone pregnancy reflects life-style changes and young adults' concerns about women's roles and about the population explosion. The availability of reliable contraception with abortion as a backup enabled them to postpone pregnancy. Thirteen women reported having had a previous abortion—seven middle class and six lower class. The couples in the sample expect to have fewer children than either husband or wife would prefer if they could have as many children as they really wanted. The sentiments of couples in the sample reflect those seen in the country as a whole. Yankelovich (1974:124), for example, reports that over one-quarter of both college and noncollege youth favor government limits on the number of children a family can have.

The expected class differences show up in the relationship between time of conception and marriage. Seven (12 percent) lower-class women,[2] but only one middle-class woman, acknowledged that pregnancy occurred prior to

---

[2]Of the seven lower-class women who became pregnant before marriage, only three stated that pregnancy was completely unplanned, which suggests that premarital pregnancy may not have been particularly stressful for those who "planned" it.

marriage. In addition, all but about 13 percent of lower-class women had
produced a child by their fourth wedding anniversary, but over 23 percent of
the middle-class women were married more than four years prior to bearing a
child. The ability and the desire to postpone pregnancy may be class related,
but in this sample the effects of religion and class cannot be separated completely. Fifty percent of the lower-class women are Catholic, compared to 17
percent of the middle-class women. Also the middle-class sample has a high
percentage (48 percent) of Jewish women.

Similar life planning is indicated by the length of courtship. This was
measured by asking: "How long were you going together as a steady
couple?" Only 39 percent of the wives reported a courtship of one year or
less. Of the sixty husbands interviewed, 45 percent of the lower-class and 50
percent of the middle-class husbands reported courtships of one year or less.
There is some disagreement between husbands' and wives' reports on length
of their courtship, and there is no way to tell whether spouses' different
reports on courtship are due to wives seeing courtship (steady dating) as
beginning sooner than husbands, or merely to the fact that the sixty husbands
who were interviewed happened to have shorter courtships than the husbands
not interviewed. The former appears more likely, because wives whose husbands agreed to be interviewed reported only slightly longer courtships than
wives of husbands not interviewed. Averages of both groups were well over
one year, almost two years in fact.

The extensive period of courtship and the average two-year delay in conceiving suggest a great degree of life planning—with respect both to marriage
itself and to starting a family. Recent literature offers no data on length of
courtship, perhaps because the term *courtship* is so hard to define. Formal
engagements are much less common now than a decade or two ago and, in any
case, would probably not be very reliable barometers of actual length of
courtship. At present, many couples live together before marriage; 21 percent
in the present sample fell into this category. This could be considered "courtship" behavior, but again, the term eludes precise specification.

WOMEN'S DESIRE FOR CHILDREN

Women in this sample would ideally like to have more than three children
(an average of 3.32), but they actually planned to have two or possibly three
(an average of 2.28), including those they might adopt. Eleven women (9
percent) planned for this to be their only child. Obviously, no women in this
sample expected to remain childless. National probability samples of fertility
plans reveal that 9 percent of white women age fourteen to thirty-nine planned
to have only one child (U.S. Bureau of the Census 1975b) and 58 percent of
married women age eighteen to twenty-four expected to have two children
(U.S. Bureau of the Census 1976). The desire of women in this sample to
have two or three children is in sharp contrast to Yankelovich's finding
(1974:90) that having children is an important personal value for only 31

percent of college women. The desire for what is, by today's standards, a relatively large number of children underscores again the fact that the sample of women in this panel may be representative of pregnant women but not of all women age twenty to thirty in the United States.

The fact that the women plan to have fewer children than they might like undoubtedly reflects a mix of motives, including concern about world over-population. But a primary motive spontaneously expressed by them is the recognition that children are expensive, coupled with the belief that one should not have more children than one can afford. In this the sample reflects findings noted by Rainwater (1965) in families in Chicago, Cincinnati, and Oklahoma City and by Hoffman and Manis (1978b) in a recent national survey. We did not ask about sex preference for children other than the one about to be born, but it seems likely that sex composition of the family interacts with desired family size—a couple with two girls is more likely to try for a third child than a couple with two boys or with children of both sexes. Hoffman and Manis found that most couples preferred a mixture of boys and girls, but when forced to make a choice by sex, the majority chose boys.

As would be expected, there is a strong correlation ($0.65 \ p < .01$) between the number of children wanted and the number of children the women planned to have, but the variance associated with the number wanted consistently exceeds the variance associated with the number planned. That is, some people would like a very large family (a dozen children), but none plans a large family.

WOMEN'S SEX-ROLE ATTITUDES

The strong elements of planning just mentioned might be taken as symbolic of women's liberation, except that the women in this sample are rather tra-ditional in their sex-role attitudes. Forty-three percent of them feel, for exam-ple, that men "have it better in life," but more of them (49 percent) feel that women have it better. (Eight percent were unable to decide.) There are no social-class differences in these opinions. Fifty-three percent of them feel that women's work—housekeeping and raising children—is more interesting than most men's work, but there is a significant interaction with class, for 64 percent of women who think men's work is more important are middle class. These findings are in line with Yankelovich's report (1974:41) that 63 percent of college women and 42 percent of noncollege women felt (in 1973) that women were discriminated against.

The women in this sample supported traditional views of marriage—close to 59 percent disapproved of couples living together before marriage; surpris-ingly, this view is held irrespective of social class level. Only 18 percent of middle-class and 23 percent of working-class women would fully approve of living together before marriage. Those who disapproved said things such as: "Living together is just dumb; I can't see anything in it. If you really love somebody, you want to get married, you don't want to live with them first. I just couldn't do it; it doesn't appeal to me." As mentioned, however, there

were three couples in this group who were unmarried at the time of the birth, and 21 percent of the group had lived together before marriage. Their views came out in remarks like those below:

> It just seemed the right thing to do at the time, the natural thing. He just slept over one night and never left [laughs].

> Well, at first, we just kind of fell into it, actually. I just ended up staying there most nights, so . . . I gave up my apartment and moved my things in. I loved to be with him all the time, and we both had busy schedules. If I didn't see him at *night,* I didn't *see* him.

Peterman, Ridley, and Anderson (1974) report that 33 percent of a college-student sample had lived together at some point during college, and a recent census report estimates that out of a total 43 million couples living together, 1.1 million couples are unmarried (U.S. Bureau of the Census 1978). But having children out of wedlock is something else. Yankelovich (1974:161, 67) reports that 65 percent of housewives without a college background and 40 percent of college youth disapprove of having children without a formal marriage. The same pattern is seen in this sample—much more willingness to live together until pregnancy occurs. However, by selecting young women who are experiencing their first pregnancy one would expect the sample to be biased in the direction of social conservatism. Young adults who postpone marriage for longer times, who forego childbearing entirely, or who have "deviant" life-styles are not represented in this sample.

WOMEN'S SOURCES OF SATISFACTION

An even stronger indicator of the traditional outlook of this particular sample of women is the order in which they rank significant sources of satisfaction in their lives. The women were asked to rank in order of impor-tance in their lives eight items: baby, friends, home, husband, other relatives, parents, self, and work (see table 2.1). When these sources of satisfaction were ranked from 1 (most important) to 8 (least important), on the average, "husband" (1.3) was ranked far ahead of either "baby" (2.6) or "self" (2.7) at the time of the first interview (sixth month of pregnancy). "Self" and "baby" were virtually tied. "Home" (5.3) rated far above "work" (7.1). Indeed, "work" was decidedly at the bottom—rather surprising considering that half of these women intended to continue work up to delivery and one-third planned to resume outside employment by the time the baby was six months old.

Table 2.1 also provides husbands' estimates, at both the nine-month inter-view and the interview right after the birth, of how they believe their wives would rank the various sources of satisfaction. Both the agreements and the disagreements are provocative. At the nine-month interview, husbands be-lieve they themselves are ranked a little lower by their wives than their wives

actually ranked them in either interview before the birth (1.7 vs. 1.3 and 1.6). Husbands also believe their wives ranked the anticipated baby rather more highly than was the case (2.0 vs. 2.6 and 2.2). There is close correspondence between how other sources of satisfaction are actually ranked by wives and what their husbands estimate these rankings to be before the birth.

Both before and after the birth the husband's estimates of his wife's rankings are close to her estimates, but his guesses agree a little better with her later rankings than with her earlier ones. This suggests that the baby's arrival is probably not perceived by the husbands as altering his wife's regard for him, whereas from the wife's point of view there is a modest downward shift in importance attached to her husband, while the relative position of the baby goes up. Others have also noted that baby and home increase in salience after childbirth (Meyerowitz and Feldman, 1966).

These changes and displacements are not hard to understand. Most women today are unprepared for the strong and unremitting demands imposed by a newborn baby—relatively few in this sample had much prior experience caring for very young babies. Also, there are strong emotions associated with nursing and caring for a helpless infant. Women who breast-feed, in particular, may experience biological forces that bind them to the infant. The mother role may be one for which there is increasingly less prior rehearsal of any kind as girls' upbringing comes more and more to resemble boys'—with sports and competitive games favored as play over such traditional activities as tending dolls in toy cribs and baby carriages.

Even though, as Bane (1976) notes, nuclear families have always been the rule and families now are not much smaller than they were a century or two ago, in times gone by there were more real-life opportunities for women to practice the mother role. For one thing, kin lived closer together and helped one another through crises such as childbirth and the chores of caring for young children. (Klatsky's [n.d.] data suggest that at present this pattern may persist more in lower white-collar groups than in blue-collar groups.) For another thing, infant and maternal mortality rates have changed in the past few generations. Even at the turn of this century many children did not survive the early years of childhood. With such mortality patterns those females who did survive to bear their own children would, in most cases, have been provided opportunities to care for other young children, tending the many babies who did not survive as well as those who did. Many more young children suffered maternal bereavement and were mothered by older sisters. The society was largely agrarian, with adult females active in gardening, milking, making clothing, and the like; care of other siblings, when necessary, was therefore likely to fall to young girls.

The very high and approximately equal scores assigned by wives to husbands and by husbands to wives in all interviews underscores Parsons's observation (1955) that the American family serves primarily as a psychological bulwark. Home, friends, relatives, and especially work are far down on the

scale compared to mate. Although some of these couples could be regarded as
still being in a honeymoon phase of the marriage relationship, it should be
remembered that on the average, pregnancy was postponed until these couples
had been married two years.

The very strong attachment between mates early in a marriage may, in fact,
be one of the weak points in the American social system. Such strong commitment is virtually impossible to maintain over time. As Brown (1965:84)
has remarked, "Being in love is a . . . precarious combination of sentiments
of value and intimacy," and Etzioni (1977) points out that probably the most
widely held but destructive social myth is the quest for the *perfect* relationship. "The incessant search for 'more' is a direct descendent of American
optimism and romanticism which looks for a marriage which will be harmoni-
ous and loving, full of communication, understanding, mutual respect, joy
and fulfillment through children. When all this is found out to be as close to
the reality of most families as Marcus Welby is to your M.D., a million
Americans a year take to the exits" (p. 8). The couples in this study generally
reported themselves to be in the "perfect relationship" but at several points,
as will be seen, the relationships appeared to be more perfect on the surface
than they were in actuality.

At the time of the first interview, these couples had no children, and so
most were buffered from financial pressures by having two paychecks. They
were also relatively shielded from other interpersonal responsibilities, and no
doubt husbands' needs could be given a high priority by wives and wives'
needs could be given a high priority by husbands. Thus, a very high rating for
the spouse as a source of gratification does not lead to conflict with other
demands. Put another way, prior to the birth of a child, husbands and wives
monopolize the domestic scene and both have relatively few home responsibilities. Later, when the husband must adjust to the infant's presence
and / or his wife's return to outside employment, he may experience a relative
deprivation of attention, and there was a small drop in wives' ranking of
husbands as sources of gratification after birth as compared with before. As
might be expected, the baby increases in importance for both parents after
birth as compared with before.

As mentioned above, there is *no* difference in the present sample by social
class in women's commitment to work. On the average, all the women—
regardless of class—ranked work as the lowest source of satisfaction. In the
Mason, Czajka, and Arber (1976) study, there was no class difference in
commitment to equal job status among women respondents, but there was
stronger desire to work for personal fulfillment among better-educated
women, a tendency also observed in this sample. Also, Yankelovich
(1974:41) notes that 64 percent of college women compared to 47 percent of
noncollege women endorse the statement "Women's place is in the home is
nonsense." The present sample—married at age twenty-two and pregnant, on
the average, two years later—thus seems in many ways at the conservative

end of the "new morality" spectrum. On the other hand, college women—who have perhaps not yet experienced sex discrimination in job opportunities and the strong societal pressures for women to assume subservient roles—may hold unrealistic views about the actual job opportunities for women with bachelor's degrees, especially now that there is no longer a teacher shortage. Despite progress in job equality for women, it is still the case that many women with bachelor's degrees take secretarial jobs, while male graduates start as a stockbroker apprentices or sales trainees in heavy industry. Jobs that hold potential for high *future* earnings still seem much more accessible to males who hold bachelor's degrees than to females who do.

In the present sample the women's average job prestige is lower than their husbands'—about five points on the Siegel (1971) index—whether couples are middle class *or* lower class. These men tended to select as mates women who are below them in job prestige, and who will not be serious competitors in terms of jobs; no doubt this tendency is widespread. The women in this sample do not have high career aspirations, one indication being that only fifteen had done any graduate work. Nevertheless 91 percent believed that most women want the kind of husband who is willing for a wife to work outside the home if she wishes, and 65 percent believed that a woman's personality suffers if she is involved only in keeping house and raising children (see Appendix B, opinion items 12 and 15).[3]

The order in which women rank sources of satisfaction in their lives is similar between classes, with two exceptions. First, working-class women rank their expected baby somewhat higher than middle-class women do; in particular, they rank their expected baby above themselves, while middle-class women rank themselves a little higher than their baby. Second, and rather surprisingly, middle-class women rank their friends lower than working-class women do, and their parents noticeably higher. Since the sociological literature generally stresses the small social distance between blue-collar women and their kin (Bott 1957), the reversal of these relationships by class in the present data deserves notice.

WOMEN'S SEX-ROLE IDEOLOGY

The women in this panel see themselves in terms of typical American myths and roles. As they begin their mother role—conception, pregnancy, and birth—their life-style follows recently evolved societal patterns. Their pregnancies are planned, they delay birth of a first child for a considerable period after marriage, and so on. But at the same time these women seem destined to face some problems, because while one-third of them intended to return to work within six months following childbirth, they nevertheless rated work far below other sources of gratification. The women acknowledged little emo-

---

[3]All opinion items with response percentages are given in Appendix B.

tional investment in a job, and their husbands saw work as of low importance to their wives. Given this set of commitments, it is hard to see how the women can avoid frustration and conflict in the future. If they return to outside work, their husbands' needs will necessarily be displaced to some extent by the unavoidable demands of babies and jobs. This adds up to planning a course of action, i.e., returning to work, that both spouses see as not particularly gratifying.

The prevalence of feminist ideas has not led to widespread structural changes in society so far. For example, maternity leaves are usually without pay. Paternity leaves are virtually unheard-of. Day-care centers rarely take children under two years of age. Few firms allow flexible or staggered working hours for husband and wife, or make other arrangements so it is easy for both parents to work. Such institutional arrangements would make it much easier for women to accord a central place in their lives to their own development, especially to their own vocations. Changes in employment conditions would reduce the conflict these women seem bound to encounter when they try to combine working outside the home with child care.

Division of Household Work

To evaluate division of labor within the household, we devised a scale patterned after one used earlier by Blood and Wolfe (1960), but we included only household tasks commonly considered women's work. Items such as "repairs around the house" or "paying the bills" were omitted. Scores could range from 0 (all household tasks done by husband) to 18 (all household work by wife). If a husband "usually" or "always" shopped for the groceries, did the laundry, vacuumed, washed the dinner dishes, got breakfast on weekends, and straightened up when company was coming, his score on "division of labor" would be the lowest possible.

Husbands and wives were asked at separate interviews about division of labor within the household. The tasks scored were: (a) Who does the grocery shopping? (b) Who gets breakfast on weekends? (c) Who takes care of the laundry? (d) Who washes the dinner dishes? (e) Who straightens up when company is coming? (f) Who does the vacuuming? Zero was assigned for each item which husbands "always" or "usually" did; one was assigned if husband or wife was "equally likely" to do the task; two was assigned if the wife "usually" did the task; three was assigned if the wife "always" did the task.

Husbands' scores (in the ninth month) averaged 10.2 (SD = 3.36) and wives' scores (in the sixth month) averaged 10.7 (SD = 3.65). An "average" score implies a pattern such as the following: the husband always does the grocery shopping and gets breakfast on weekends; he washes dinner dishes as often as his wife and occasionally does the vacuuming. In the aggregate, then, there is close agreement between husbands and wives in reporting on

division of labor within the household, and there is *considerable* sharing of tasks by husbands. A rather surprising amount of household work was performed by husbands in this sample, and there was no social-class difference—lower-class husbands carried out just as many household chores as middle-class husbands. This is an unexpected finding, of course, because lower-class men generally hold more traditional views of sex role. Most research suggests that there is more egalitarianism in middle-class marriages, but such findings are closely linked to the age of the couple. Here, of course, all couples are young.

Because the husbands were interviewed very near the end of pregnancy, they might have been helping more around the house than usual. As a matter of fact, in another question, 57 percent of the husbands did report that they had been helping more than usual, and only one reported less than usual. But the wives' reports at six months suggest that considerable sharing was the rule even before the woman's physical condition might require it. Thus, despite the fact that couples might be expected to shift toward an increasingly traditional division of labor as pregnancy progressed and as women withdrew from the work force, the available data do not suggest such a trend in this sample.

WOMEN'S EXPECTATIONS FOR CHILD CARE

The women in this sample had unrealistic expectations in *many* areas. When questioned shortly before childbirth about how long they expected to breast-feed or bottle-feed their infants, almost all women expected their infants to be completely weaned by the first birthday. Yet most of these women must have observed youngsters two years or older toddling about feeding themselves from bottles. They also expressed confidence in their ability to care for a newborn unaided, although considerably more than half of them had *no* previous experience in baby care whatsoever. Over half of them expected their infants to sleep through the night before the age of eight weeks.

While optimism in young people is the rule, more realistic assessments of current problems and more down-to-earth expectations about their coming infants probably would have been helpful for these young pregnant women. Childbirth will challenge them in a way that none has yet been challenged, and on several fronts at once—their own physical stamina will be tested, their ability to maintain a viable relationship with their mate over a stressful interval will be tested, and they, who have been used to personal freedom and mobility, will soon find themselves virtually immobilized and isolated with infants who make demands that are hard to interpret. Most will also experience financial pressures greater than any experienced heretofore, for baby-sitting fees or the cost of a year's supply of formula will be added to a budget already strained by the (at least temporary) loss of one of the family wage earners. Perhaps the least-expected sources of stress, and therefore the hardest

to handle, will be the unremitting nature of infant care and the unpredictability of infant demands. Even a baby with the sunniest disposition can suddenly become ill, and most infants take months to learn to sleep through the night.

WOMEN'S PERSONALITY MEASURES

In this research, a limited appraisal was made of a few personality traits for both men and women, the traits being those thought to be important for coping behavior in connection with pregnancy, childbirth, and parenting. Fortunately, differences according to personality measures or pregnancy symptoms were negligible across social-class groups.

"Femininity" is clearly one such variable. Scales to measure "masculinity-femininity" are few in number and not well grounded in theory (Constantinople 1973). Most scales measure what might be called "social femininity," the extent to which a female accepts the stereotypically feminine social role: concern with physical attractiveness, with being passive and helpless in male-female interactions, with behaving in expressive rather than instrumental fashion, and with domestic affairs. For the present research, the Femininity (Fe) Scale taken from Gough's California Psychological Inventory (Gough 1952) seemed the most valid of the existing scales for measuring "social femininity" because of both its careful construction and its prior use in other field studies. Accordingly, a subset of items measuring masculinity-femininity was taken from this scale. Because Gough's items were designed and validated before 1952 and women's liberation has raised the consciousness of the general population to the point where many of its items are now invalid, some items were deleted, and only part of the scale was used.

Considerable prior work by Doering (1975) and other researchers indicates that femininity is at least a two-factor characteristic, one factor being "social femininity" (as described above), the other being "biological femininity"— how a woman feels about her body and its functions: menstruation, sexuality, pregnancy, childbirth, and lactation. Further, it appears that these two dimensions of femininity are *negatively* correlated with each other (Doering 1975; Loevinger 1962; Newton 1955). For this research it seemed particularly important to have a good measure of biological femininity, so using Loevinger's extensive work, Doering developed a scale of "biological femininity" on a subsample ($N = 70$) of the women in the panel. (For a full report, see Doering 1975.) Scores on this scale were eventually obtained for all women in the panel.

Anxiety is another variable that would seem pertinent in this research. Do women who are pregnant become more anxious as pregnancy progresses, and do pregnant women have specific childbirth-related anxieties that are different in type or quantity from anxieties of nonpregnant women? As pointed out in chapter 1, a certain amount of anxiety is probably healthy, and indeed the

work of worrying can lead women to take specific steps to prepare themselves for the childbirth event. In fact, from the viewpoint of the Janis model (1958), women who refuse to worry and who therefore deny the coming crisis of childbirth may be at severe risk in both medical and psychological terms.

Testing the notion of the work of worrying requires a way to separate general anxiety from pregnancy-specific anxiety. Obviously, chronic anxiety is not what Janis had in mind. Such anxiety would be expected to have a deleterious rather than a beneficial effect. Therefore, some items from the Taylor Manifest Anxiety Scale (Taylor 1953) were used to measure generalized anxiety, and the worries and anxieties specific to pregnancy and childbirth were then measured separately (see chapter 3, especially table 3.1). If the correlation between the two kinds of anxiety is low, one would take this as evidence that the two forms of anxiety are relatively independent and would then try to explain coping ability in terms of only the pregnancy and birth worries. On the other hand, if the correlation is sizeable, the conclusion would be that worriers worry irrespective of particular life events and that a life event does not so much accentuate worry as focus it. (In addition, of course, Janis's work of worrying may include activities or behaviors: taking childbirth classes, preparation of a nursery, and so on. It is much broader concept than a single worry score.)

For this sample of women at the time of the first interview, the correlation between Taylor anxiety scores and total worry scores related to pregnancy and childbirth was rather large (0.41, $p < .01$). There is thus a relationship between anxiety in general and pregnancy- and birth-focused anxiety; women who have fewer anxieties associated with pregnancy have fewer anxieties of other kinds as well.

Answers to the single question: "How much do you worry about childbirth?" (scored from $1 =$ constantly, to $5 =$ never) provided some additional information about relative worrying. The total pregnancy-worries score and answers to this single question were related ($r = .47$, $p < .01$), but there was little relation between this question and the Taylor score ($r = .16$, $p < .05$).

A third variable—locus of control, or efficacy—has enjoyed enormous popularity in sociological research in the last decade, especially following its inclusion in the report of Coleman et al. (1966). Despite its potential attractiveness for use in the present research—if a woman felt in control of herself and her life, one would think this would predict coping ability—locus of control was not a variable that correlated with other variables in this study either for women or for men. For this reason it will not be discussed further.

All in all, psychological measures that were tailored specifically to this research—pregnancy worries, rating scales for spouses, and the like—led to interesting findings, while the parts of traditional psychological tests that could be used in this study were generally disappointing.

WHO THE MEN ARE

As noted in Appendix A, of the 120 husbands, 57 were interviewed both before and after the birth. Four were interviewed at the first interview only, and one of these interviews was lost. Of the 59 husbands not interviewed, 33 refused. Of the remainder, 9 were fathers already; 14 were missed for various other reasons, including the fact that their wives experienced an early delivery; and 3 were unable to take part for valid job-connected reasons. Husbands who were interviewed turned out to be somewhat younger and to have slightly less prestigious jobs than those not interviewed, and they were also more interested in the pregnancy. But for most variables of interest in this research, the interviewed and noninterviewed husbands seem comparable (see table A.4). The biggest difference between the two groups appears to be that the wives of those husbands who were interviewed were more likely to plan to breast-feed their infants, and they then went on to carry out those plans. (A statistically significant difference in preparation level is small in magnitude—0.45 on a 7-point scale.)

Of the 60 husbands interviewed, 27 were Protestant, 22 were Catholic, 10 were Jewish. One was not raised in any of these three religions. About one-third of these husbands (21) reported themselves as religious, while the remainder (39) indicated that they attended religious services "seldom" or "never." Catholics were most likely to attend religious services. *All* the Jewish men who were interviewed reported that they seldom went to religious services.

There is considerable agreement between the religious backgrounds of husbands and wives (58 percent matched) and an even higher degree of correspondence between the religiosity of husbands and wives ($r = .77, p < .01$).

The average man in this study is close to 27 years old and a little more than 2 years older than his wife. One of the largest differences between husbands who were interviewed and those who were not is in average age—husbands not interviewed were almost 1.5 years older. The range in husbands' ages, as would be expected, was greater than the range for wives—two husbands were 17 (the youngest wife was 18), and one husband was 40. The average age of middle-class husbands was 27.8; that of blue-collar husbands, 25.1. Of the 60 husbands interviewed, 51 had been raised in families with both parents present. When a parent was missing, it was the father in all but one case.

MEN'S PLANNING OF MARRIAGE AND PREGNANCY

Of husbands responding, 45 percent of the lower-class group, and 50 percent of middle-class reported courtships of one year or less. As mentioned above, they reported shorter courtships than their wives, for reasons that are not entirely clear. Sixty-two percent of the husbands said the pregnancy was "entirely planned" and another 31 percent fell into the "sort-of-planned"

group. For four fathers (7 percent) this pregnancy was "completely un-planned." (Four women in 120—3 percent—acknowledged the pregnancy to be a complete surprise. In every case these were *not* wives of men who acknowledged completely unplanned pregnancies.)

MEN'S DESIRE FOR CHILDREN

The men who responded wanted to have three to four children. ("How many children would you *really* like to have, if you could have as many as you wanted?") Their average, 3.28, was essentially identical to the average number wanted by their wives. Almost twice as many men as women (19 percent vs. 10 percent) would like very large families (five or more children) if they could have as many children as they wanted.

The men interviewed planned to actually have two or three children, how-ever, with most (59 percent) planning two. The men's plans agree very well on the average with the plans of the women. Plans for number of children also agree rather well on a couple-by-couple basis ($r = .65$, $p < .01$). There are no cases in which the husband wants several children and the wife wants only one.

MEN'S SEX-ROLE ATTITUDES

Sixty percent of the husbands believe men "have it better in life." Thirty percent of the men see women as having it "definitely better."

Forty-five percent of the husbands disapproved of couples living together before marriage (compared to 59 percent of wives), and as was true for wives, the percentage of husbands disapproving did not differ by social class. In comparing these figures with husbands' reasons for marriage, one concludes that more men than women favored living together as a substitute for mar-riage, but wives' views prevailed. This interpretation is strengthened by the lack of agreement, case by case, between husbands and wives on this topic. The couple-by-couple agreement between husbands' and wives' views on cohabitation is practically zero.

MEN'S SOURCES OF SATISFACTION

Husbands, like wives,[4] rated their mates highest among the eight sources of satisfaction (see table 2.1). In the ninth month the men rated themselves at 2.9, not quite as high as women rated themselves (2.8). Husbands rated their coming baby a little lower than their wives did (2.5 compared to 2.2) and did not rate the baby quite as high as their wives thought they did (2.3). Husbands rated their parents somewhat lower than their wives rated *their* parents (5.0 vs. 4.4), but husbands still rated their parents higher than work (5.2).

[4]Comparisons are made with wife's nine-month interview, the closest one in time to the husband's prepartum interview.

Perhaps husbands who agreed to participate might rate work lower than other husbands, because if work is taken very seriously it might have conflicted with agreeing to participate in this research. However, as table 2.1 shows, all wives believe that work rated 5.5 for their husbands. It therefore seems likely that the husbands who did respond rated work in a way comparable to other husbands.

Analysis of differences by class shows that, for most ratings, such differences are negligible. On the average, husbands of both classes rate themselves, their wives, their babies, and, most surprisingly, their work almost the same. The largest difference shows up in ratings of home (5.1 vs. 6.0)—almost a full point—with middle class lower.

Middle-class husbands are somewhat more accurate in their perception than lower-class husbands, for wives of both classes rate their husbands about where middle-class men estimate that rating to be. Lower-class men see their wives rating them as very close in importance to the baby, whereas the women actually rate their husbands a full point ahead of the baby. Men of both groups believe their wives rate the baby higher than the wives' actual rating, however, with the error more pronounced for middle-class men (2.8 vs. 2.1).

The relatively low rating assigned to work by men in this sample agrees with other surveys,[5] and, rather surprisingly, the average rating given work by lower-class respondents was similar to that given by middle-class respondents (5.1 vs. 5.2). (This contradicts Kanter's [1976:61] finding.) Middle-class respondents were more variable in their ratings than lower-class respondents, however—some rated work relatively much higher, others much lower. The figures suggest, nonetheless, that the more educated men with more prestigious jobs do not (early in their careers at least) value work more highly than lower-class men do in comparison to other sources of satisfaction. These findings, incidentally, are consistent with Hoge's (1976) data for University of Michigan and Dartmouth men in 1974—over 50 percent in both groups expected to get their greatest satisfaction in life from family relationships rather than from careers, and 25 percent or less expected the opposite. The 1974 data on college men, when compared with data from earlier historical periods, reveal that a higher percentage of men expected to get their greatest satisfaction from family relationships in 1952 than in 1974. One implication is that present-day sex-role ideology has not strengthened men's overall family commitment so much as it has defined the channels by which that commitment will express itself. Fathers in the early fifties were not in the delivery room, but they were committed to the notion of large families and family togetherness, perhaps more than men are now. Men of today take an active role in childbirth but see the quality of their own lives as a separate important life goal.

[5]Although work is important in that a large majority would continue even if they did not need the money, a happy marriage is more important as a determinant of the quality of life in the survey by Campbell, Converse, and Rodgers (1976).

Men's Personality Measures

The same personality measures used with wives were used with the husbands who agreed to participate. As would be expected, their Gough femininity scores are lower than their wives', but husbands' and wives' scores overlap to a considerable extent, a common finding with masculinity-femininity scales (Constantinople 1973; Maccoby 1966). On the Taylor Manifest Anxiety Scale men scored lower (less anxious) than women.

A contrast is provided by the total worry score, which enumerated different kinds of worries about pregnancy and childbirth. In the ninth month the husbands' average total worry score was significantly higher than the wives'. Thus, although husbands are less anxious in general as judged by the Taylor scale, which has many items related to physical well-being, they acknowledged more childbirth-related worries than their wives.

As was true for wives, husbands' pregnancy-related anxieties tend somewhat to follow a pattern. Husbands who report many worries about childbirth are also those who report worrying about childbirth more often ($r = .31$, $p = .01$), and husbands who reported worrying more than usual also had more specific worries about childbirth ($r = .27$, $p = .02$). The correlation between the Taylor scale and amount of worrying about childbirth is rather large and negative ($r = -.37$, $p < .01$). There thus appears to be a work-of-worrying phenomenon for husbands. They are more worried about specific childbirth events than their wives, the increase in their worries is sharper, and those who worry most are those who are least anxious about other things.

MEN'S AND WOMEN'S ROLE BEHAVIORS

Sex Roles

Because of the renaissance of feminism in the past two decades and because of more general questions about sex-role stereotypes, people in late adolescence and early adulthood today are looking at their roles in life much more critically than was true a generation ago. And their views of sex-role stereotypes are affecting their behavior. The proportion of persons refraining from marriage in the twenty to twenty-four age group has increased noticeably in recent years. In 1975 60 percent of men and 40 percent of women in that age group were unmarried, compared to 53 percent and 28 percent respectively in 1960 (Carroll and Morrison 1976). Yet since in the present sample all but three couples are married, these respondents are probably more conventional in their attitudes concerning sex roles than many other persons their age. The opinion data collected in this survey bear on these issues. There are curious reversals in Appendix B, e.g., only 16 percent of women think men are more interested in sex than women, in line with feminist thought on this topic, but 52 percent see women's work at home as more interesting than

outside work, a departure from standard feminist thought (opinion items 19 and 13).

In the country as a whole, young adults have been more susceptible than older persons to the new sex-role ideology—shifts in ideas about sexual equality are more pronounced in persons below the age of twenty-five. The percentage of college freshmen who feel married women should devote themselves to home and family, for example, dropped from 67 percent to 36 percent for men and from 44 percent to 18 percent for women between 1967 and 1975. In 1975, 92 percent of all freshmen favored job equality for women (Carroll and Morrison 1976).

Most formal research on effects of sex-role ideology has dealt with females' having jobs outside the home, the ability of women to attain high-level jobs, or the effect on childbearing of holding a job. Relatively little attention has been paid to sex-role behavior as it affects family life. What research there is suggests that household tasks are still segregated by sex (Duncan, Schuman, and Duncan 1974), but that husbands of working wives help somewhat more (Doering 1975; Hoffman 1963; Holmstrom 1973). In this panel there was less segregation of household tasks than previously reported, but the timing of the questions (in the ninth month of pregnancy and immediately after birth) may cause these findings to be exceptional.

Feminists have consistently voiced notions about equal division of labor within the house, but this kind of egalitarianism may be the rarest of all. Most researchers agree that equal status in "public" work is more the rule than equal status in "private" work. In Mason, Czajka, and Arber (1976), for example, the traditional sex-role division of labor within families continued to receive more support from women than from men. Unequal division of labor within the household, particularly after a baby arrives, is a complicated phenomenon, no doubt related to feelings about sharing the infant and to how great the need for household help is. In this sample, there appears to be considerable sharing of household tasks just before birth, and many husbands helped their wives in the first week after birth, but help dropped off quickly in the second week. Deutscher (1970) confirms the finding of increased husband help around birth and adopts a psychological explanation—the use of household work by husbands as an outlet for their anxieties about being abandoned by their wives upon the arrival of an infant. In this sample, sharing appears to be more a consequence of altered sex-role standards, because it begins long before the birth. Today's young men and women do not see men's cooking or cleaning as a threat to masculinity.

Feminist thinking has also led many women to question the desirability of a passive role during childbirth (Rothman 1976). In this sample a large proportion of women sought some kind of preparation or training, and it was hard to find couples with no preparation. Their seeking preparation implies that women are now looking for a more active role in birth. A recent national poll of both first-time mothers and women who have had children before revealed that 74 percent had attended some sort of preparation class (Waterfall and

Morris 1976), and a study of who attends classes (Watson 1977) showed that classes tend to attract the better-educated expectant parent with higher job status.

Many women now wish to take a more active maternal role, beginning in pregnancy. They want to participate actively in the birth process rather than to be passively delivered by a (usually) male obstetrician. Feminists, as well as other researchers, have pointed to the links existing between female sexuality, menstruation, pregnancy, birth, and breast-feeding (Doering 1975; Goschen-Gottstein 1966; Masters and Johnson 1966; Newton 1955, 1973; Rossi 1973). Furthermore, many women—not just active feminists—now believe that an uncomplicated birth should be primarily under the mother's and father's control rather than being controlled by medical professionals, and that *both* parents should be active rather than passive (Arms 1975; Elkins 1976; Haire 1972).

WOMEN'S WORK ROLE

In terms of work plans, the persons in this sample seem fairly typical compared to other young men and women recently researched. For example, the couples accept the idea that mothers of young children can work. About one-third of this sample of women planned not to stop work at all or to resume outside work before their infant was six months old, and 65 percent planned to be working by the time their children are six.

At a time roughly equivalent to the time when this sample was drawn, 45 percent of all women sixteen years and over were in the labor force, compared to 33 percent in 1950 (U.S. Department of Labor 1975). Furthermore, according to the 1970 United States Census, over one-third of women with at least one child under six were employed full-time (compared with only 14 percent in 1950). In 1975 the number of employed women had increased to the point that 39 percent of the mothers of preschool children were in the work force and 55 percent of mothers with children six to seventeen were in the work force (Kaplan and Anderson 1976). The upward trend is likely to continue. Furthermore, the figures cited are probably underestimates, because mothers with part-time jobs and those who have stopped searching actively are not tabulated in census statistics. Both numbers, especially part-time workers, must be substantial for young mothers. Our sample, therefore, has proportionately more women who plan to be in the labor force at various points in their child-rearing years than would be predicted from current census data, but data for women in this sample may be more accurate because all kinds of employment are tabulated.

MEN'S FAMILY ROLES

Other trends that may be powerful, although not well documented in terms of previous research, are those indicating that women now look for a more active role in lovemaking and expect their husbands to participate more ac-

tively in infant care. Eighty-four percent of the females in this sample think women are just as interested in sex as men (Appendix B, opinion item 19). Even more think that husbands should be in the labor room and should be willing to baby sit (opinion items 33 and 11).

Even though many men are trying to measure up, the husband's upbringing may not have prepared him very well for such expectations. Thus, 84 percent of the women in this sample wanted the husband to be present during labor and delivery (73 percent of those not wishing husbands to be present were lower-class women), yet many of the husbands were ill-prepared for such an active role. For example, over 25 percent of the husbands refused to take part in this research, which required only two interviews. If a husband is to take an active role in the labor room, to interact with nurses and other caretakers in the labor and delivery rooms, and to become heavily involved emotionally in his wife's birth experience, it is somewhat anomalous that he would refuse to discuss with a male interviewer what his views on pregnancy and childbirth are. In other words, if a man is not interested in discussing events related to his wife's pregnancy and birth experience, probably he would also be less interested in meeting her demands for participation in the birth event. Some data support this conjecture. Husbands unwilling to be interviewed were seen by their wives as significantly less interested in the pregnancy than husbands who were willing, and they also showed more negative feelings during the actual delivery of the baby than willing husbands (see table A.4).

The sex-role ideas learned early in life by men who are now young adults have probably not prepared them very well either in practical or in emotional terms for the husband and father roles that their wives and much of society now expect them to play (Fein 1974; Harlow 1975). Pleck (1981) notes that the basic American value centering upon the importance of the family and the well-being of children has now been extended to include men, but deep-lying sex-role ideology of *both* sexes conflicts with men's active family participation. Only a minority of persons believe men should do more family work, and women reject this belief as much as or more than men. The sample of couples in the panel expressed views congruent with Pleck's conclusions—both husbands and wives expected to have relatively few children (an average of just over two), and many wives planned to return to work. The division of labor within their households before the arrival of the first child was fairly liberal. The new sex-role ideology, however, is reflected more in a rearrangement of wives' commitments than as a change in husbands' commitments. Although 93 percent of the husbands in the present study said that they had had *some* experience with newborns, only 21 percent felt that they knew "a lot" or "all" about infant care (compared with 30 percent of wives). Perhaps there is a barrier or end point in accepting changes in family and sex roles coinciding with the arrival of the infant. Before marriage, cohabitation is looked upon with considerable favor, and early in marriage, wives' working and careful family planning are seen as desirable. But once an infant is on the

scene, it may be that both parents slip back into the traditional sex roles because there are no real alternatives.

FATHERS AND PARENTING

Prior to 1970 fathers were almost entirely neglected in research involving infants. In fact, their role with the infant was downgraded. For example, Bowlby (1951, 1959) saw the father as of importance mainly to the mother. Lately, however, considerable research on infant attachment is aimed at fathers, either primarily (e.g., Ban and Lewis 1974; Greenberg and Morris 1974; Lamb 1976, 1977; Parke and O'Leary 1975) or secondarily (e.g., Pedersen and Robson 1969; Rebelsky and Hanks 1971). Apparently Pedersen and Robson's report is the first study of fathers and infants.

As part of a full description of the perinatal period, one major aim of this research was to cast light on the father's role before, during, and after the birth event. A number of other reports appeared soon after the present research began (1972-73) (Cronewett and Newmark 1974; Fein 1974; Greenberg and Morris 1974; Wapner 1975; Wente and Crockenberg 1976). Apparently only three studies, however—the present one, Eichler et al. (1977), and Peterson, Mehl, and Leiderman (1979)—try to link events during pregnancy to later fathering behavior. A father's feeling and attitudes toward his child, are bound to be shaped by the prior events of pregnancy and delivery—as are a mother's. Also, the father's relationship to his spouse would be expected to influence his relationship with his baby. A newborn child is talked about, is planned for, and must be dealt with from the moment of birth by the father as well as by the mother, even if the father deals with it by ignoring it and absenting himself from home as much as possible. The father as well as the mother must cope with stress during pregnancy and childbirth, and he will probably cope better if he has some prior preparation.

It is a curious fact that fathers in the United States, especially during the past half century, have been almost completely shut out from the birth event and the period of early infancy. Even in the sixties, fathers wishing to witness their children's birth were steadfastly barred from most delivery rooms (Goetsch 1966; Schaefer 1965; Stender 1965; Stewart 1963). Yet in other cultures the custom of the couvade—the husband taking to his bed and being cared for when his wife is confined—suggests the deep psychological meaning of birth for men. This custom was still being practiced in the Basque regions of France at the end of the nineteenth century (Chertok 1959:215). Furthermore, in many primitive cultures fathers hold and caress infants and show considerable interest in babies (see Greenberg and Morris 1974).

Until recently, new fathers in our culture have been forced to play stereotyped, sterile roles. The devaluation of the father role at the time of birth is manifest in many subtle ways. Television situation comedies portray fathers as totally inept in dealing with their offspring. The father's role at birth has

been especially ridiculed—the father being caricatured as driving his wife to the hospital with his hands trembling at the wheel, and then breathing a sigh of relief as he drops his wife, along with his responsibilities, at the door. In novels and plays fathers are shown ready to panic with the first labor pain and eager to be relieved by females of the care of their newborns. Expectant fathers are painted as psychological weaklings who wear themselves out pacing the hospital waiting room, only to faint when told of the birth. Until recently, hospitals have excluded fathers almost completely from meaningful roles at the time of birth. Because of a real lack of interest in fathers, even by social scientists, we have no data on what fathers themselves really thought about their role in childbirth prior to about 1965 (see Nash 1976).

In the United States a largely urban society forces a complete separation of work and parent roles for many adults. It is the rule for fathers or mothers to work far away from home. A 1972 survey (Hill 1974) found that only 16 percent of workers interviewed lived less than two miles from work. For men the job often requires absence from home for over twelve hours a day, and some must also work evenings or weekends because they travel or entertain customers. Some fathers work odd hours or even double shifts and must sleep when the rest of the family is awake. This enforced father-absence has led many fathers to perceive little or no role for themselves in connection with their infant children. Furthermore, because of the stereotyped male role in American society—success in the job combined with machismo—men have tended to dissociate themselves from tasks considered feminine, like childbearing.

As the child grows, many men continue to perceive only stereotyped roles for themselves, and interact (mainly with their sons) in ritualized encounters involving roughhouse and baseball. The presumption seems to be that a child should not make demands upon the father, but rather should be an amusing toy. (The parallel to men's views of women as sex objects is obvious.) In fact, both because of culturally prescribed empty family roles for men and because of the fact that fathers desert the family more often than mothers (15 percent of the men and 12 percent of the women in this study were raised in father-absent homes), young fathers are apt to have no adequate role models at all. Their own fathers were either not present or fulfilled stereotyped (i.e., distant) roles as they were growing up. New fathers in Fein's (1974) study, however, hoped to be closer to their children than their fathers had been to them.

Some wives may reinforce father-infant separation by regarding an infant as "their property." An infant sometimes is conceived mainly to provide an occupation for the wife. Wives who actively foster social distance between fathers and their children may do so to compensate themselves for achievement that they are denied outside the home. Whatever the case, both social structure and psychodynamics probably often work together to push fathers away from the young child, and unequal division of labor within the house-

hold may be part of the same picture. By controlling resources, including the baby, within the household, the wife may try to maximize her power within the husband-wife team.

It is easy to gloss over how odd modern perceptions and role scripts are for fathers—and, in fact, how closely they are bound to present-day American society.[6] History gives some perspective on these matters. For example, Roman children were placed upon the earth as soon as they were born, and were then seized by *the father* and raised up (Belmont 1976). The father's part in the ritual signified his recognition of the child as his offspring. The raising up was a ritual permeated with religious meanings. A similar ritual, kneeling, was part of an ancient Germanic-Scandinavian tradition in which the father accepted the newborn child as his by placing it on his knees (Onians 1954). Such rituals involving the father are not limited to European historical cultures. An apparently accurate description of the naming of children in West Africa in the eighteenth century (Haley 1976) recounts that the father alone decided on the name of a newborn child and then conferred it by whispering it in the infant's ear when the child was about a week old. The custom is said to persist to the present day in West African groups. The couvade, prevalent among primitive societies, has also been mentioned above. The meaningful—and long overdue—integration of the father into events surrounding birth is a step forward, but actually this integration can be seen as a return to customs that prevail today in more primitive groups or that prevailed more than a thousand years ago within European cultures.

As mentioned, fathers have not only been discouraged from being in the delivery room but have been forbidden. Fortunately, the "mystique surrounding parturition created by the medical profession" (Nash 1976:80) is now being broken down. Childbirth is becoming an experience in which wives *and* husbands see themselves as the main actors, with medical personnel as assistants. This trend has accelerated tremendously over the period of this research project. In this sample, 66 percent of fathers were present at delivery, and another 7 percent wanted to be there but were not permitted. Even though attendance at preparation classes is obviously likely to lead husbands to be present in the delivery room, 73 percent of fathers actually being present or wishing to be present is still an impressive statistic. With changes in attitudes toward sex roles in the seventies, particularly those aspects concerned with legitimizing men's nurturant and expressive roles, the social climate is becoming much less hostile toward fathers who participate actively in the birth event and the period of early infancy. Perhaps before long the father will remain in the hospital with the mother, or the prevalence of births at home will rise even

[6]Although maternity leaves are being sought militantly now by feminist organizations in the United States, paternity leaves are not. In Sweden, husbands whose wives have given birth are allowed up to seven months of leave at 95 percent of salary to stay at home helping with housework and the care of the baby (Pifer 1976).

more than it already has. In this sample 30 percent of the 115 women choosing hospital deliveries said they were mildly or strongly in favor of home deliveries. Five had a planned home delivery with medical attendants.

Sex ideology aside, the mere fact that many more women, particularly more mothers of young children, are in the labor force now than a generation ago has implications for men in their home roles. With wives at work, household tasks must be dealt with at night or on weekends. Conflicting pressures may build up upon women as a consequence of role strain between work and home roles, and some of this pressure is probably displaced on husbands. (See Pleck, 1981.) None of the couples in this panel was a "two-career" family, in which both wife and husband had high-prestige occupations, however. Also, persons most committed to nontraditional sex-role ideologies are the least likely to be found in a sample of young expectant couples, so those in this panel may experience less role strain than other young adults. On the other hand, almost all wives were working prior to birth and many planned to return in the near future. So, in addition to assuming a parent role, these couples must adjust to a part-time or full-time work role for the mother along with motherhood. In most cases, the nature of the father's work role may also change, at least for a time, in that he will be the only breadwinner.

3 | THE COURSE OF PREGNANCY

Throughout history the conviction has been held that the child is affected by events before birth, whether events are caused by "magic, the gods, . . . the planets," by the infant's own actions, or by external circumstances surrounding the mother. A thousand years ago the Chinese ran prenatal clinics "to ensure tranquility in the mother, and through her, in the baby" (Macfarlane 1977:5 ff). Nonetheless, precise scientific evidence on how psychological and sociological circumstances of pregnancy affect the child after birth is a rarity. A few early studies link prenatal maternal anxiety to severe food intolerance (Sontag 1941) or to vomiting in the infant (Turner 1956), and Abramson, Singh, and Mbambo (1969) observed that severe stress during pregnancy was associated with a low level of motor development at birth. An ongoing study (Eichler et al. 1977) in Boston reports: "Most significantly, we found a very strong relationship between the mother's emotional state measured early in pregnancy and the infant's irritability at three days postpartum. . . . We found that the more positively both parents had rated their marriage [during the first three months of pregnancy] the better the infant looked physiologically [at two months of age]." The findings that do exist are impressive, but on the whole research linking pregnancy to events after birth is scarce.

Research is also scarce on the *couple* during pregnancy. Soule (1974) reported that differences in attitudes between husbands and wives were few —mainly that husbands were less ambivalent about pregnancy than were their wives—and Gladieux (1978) reported that women's expected satisfaction with motherhood depended on husband and wife having consonant and traditionally oriented attitudes. But other writers point to husbands' envy of pregnancy (Horney 1926; Liebenberg 1973) that, if present, could have a negative impact on the marital relationship. LaRossa (1976) argues that a first pregnancy will create marital strain if the work role is the primary role for one or both partners. Whatever the case, there are many unanswered questions about how pregnancy affects the couple as a social unit, or how pregnancy impacts on birth and other later events.

As part of the present study, both husbands and wives were interviewed

during pregnancy, in the hope that events during that period would shed light on the birth event and on family functioning after birth. In two interviews before the birth, information was collected on the women's perceptions of their own health during pregnancy, their attitudes concerning pregnancy and the physical changes that go with it, their feelings and beliefs about the upcoming birth, their reactions to their physicians or midwives, their perceptions of their husbands over this period, their expectations concerning the baby's sex, how they planned to feed and care for the baby, whether they would return to work and how soon, and so on. Husbands, in a single interview in the ninth month of their wives' pregnancies, were asked many questions about their wives' symptoms and health, their own feelings during this period, their expectations concerning the birth event, and their expectations concerning the baby. It is, therefore, possible to see for this panel how some events before birth—including those involving the father—may affect the birth event, the infant, or the functioning of the family after birth.

During pregnancy *both* husband and wife are preparing themselves for the impending birth. The importance of pregnancy as a preparation period is clear from research that links psychological stress at this time and negative attitudes about pregnancy to prematurity, repeated spontaneous abortion, the woman's excessive vomiting, delivery-room difficulties, and above all, the physical status of the newborn baby (see Heinstein 1967 for citations). However, data linking women's and men's psychological status during pregnancy to their family relationships after birth are almost nonexistent. For example, there is little information on how the mother's attachment to the infant and her relationship with her husband after birth depend on happenings prior to birth. So far as we can determine, the "Collaborative Perinatal Study" (Niswander and Gordon 1972)—despite its stated aims (p. 3) that "social and economic conditions" affecting pregnancy were to be a target of study—did not treat such topics either in the 540-page volume itself or in any subsequent reports. The exceptions are some small studies (Davids and DeVault 1962, Davids, De-Vault, and Talmadge 1961, Davids, Holden, and Gray 1963, Davids and Rosengren 1962), that do follow a few patients from the collaborative study on into the period after birth.

One barrier to understanding the birth process is that each specialty is devoted to a narrow set of problems. Obstetricians, pediatricians, psychiatrists, and other medical workers each attend to separate aspects of the birth. For example, the pediatrician supervises the baby but shies away from problems in breast-feeding. Another barrier is that records are kept only on individual patients. The birth event is most often viewed from the perspective of the mother *or* the child rather than as a joint occurrence. Women are usually seen isolated from their social contexts, not as persons closely tied to others in social networks. The present study tries to take a comprehensive view by studying members of the family within their family contexts and by cataloguing psychological and social aspects of the family's life both before and after

birth. For example, the husband's ideas and opinions about breast-feeding expressed during pregnancy are studied in relation to the success and duration of breast-feeding, or the mother's being breast-fed as an infant is studied in relation to her own success in breast-feeding.

One purpose in taking this broad view is to discover, if possible, the importance of some factors previously overlooked. The quality of a woman's marriage, although hard to measure, may bear directly on how well the pregnancy is tolerated and on how the birth event is handled. The woman's views of herself in terms of sex role, and how her husband views her in that role, could also have a direct bearing on her health during pregnancy. In fact, as women become increasingly involved with clinicians over the course of pregnancy, they may be treated in ways that encourage dysfunctional behaviors. A survey of practicing psychiatrists revealed that their professional judgments of good mental health in women were almost identical to stereotypes of "proper" feminine behavior (Broverman et al. 1970), but male traits—"proper" male behavior—were considered more mentally healthy and socially desirable than female traits. Thus, a double standard of mental health apparently exists for men and women. A "typical woman," as seen by some clinicians, displays traits that are less mentally healthy than traits ordinarily displayed by "typical men." (See also Scully and Bart 1973). By interacting during pregnancy with a clinician who holds such views, a woman's reaction to pregnancy and to herself could be altered in a dysfunctional direction. In any case, there is little information available to describe the social climate in which the pregnant woman exists. But social supports, or their lack, are probably of particular importance for her.

This chapter describes the physical symptoms of pregnancy as husbands and wives in this panel perceived them. They include the anxieties and worries about pregnancy and birth expressed by husbands and wives, the couples' sources of information about childbirth, and both parents' expectations concerning birth and early care of the infant. This chapter also covers the couples' sexual behavior during pregnancy, a topic that is not treated extensively elsewhere in either the medical or the social science literature. Clearly, pregnancy would be expected to influence sexual behavior, and through it the quality of the marriage relationship.

INCIDENCE OF SYMPTOMS

The women in the panel described themselves as having fairly easy pregnancies. In fact, when asked what problems or difficulties they found associated with pregnancy, the majority of women mentioned no more than three problems. Most of the problems mentioned were relatively mild, such as not being able to do as much as usual, being uncomfortable, lack of energy, clumsiness and awkwardness, or "not fitting into any of my clothes." Eigh-

teen symptoms were inquired about. These included backache, bleeding, constipation, depression, diarrhea, dizziness, heartburn, insomnia, irritability, lack of interest in sex, loss of appetite, nausea, painful intercourse, shortness of breath, swollen ankles, tiredness, vomiting, and weakness. Wives were asked about symptoms of the first six months in the first interview and about symptoms of the last three months in the second interview. (Husbands were asked about their wives' symptoms in the interview held with them about a month before the birth.) A total symptom score for each three-month period was constructed as follows: any symptom that was mentioned as occurring "often" was scored 3, while a symptom experienced "occasionally" was scored 1. These scores were then added up for all symptoms, so the possible range for the total symptom score is from 0 to 54. In the first three months of pregnancy the average score for wives was 13.3; middle three months, 11.4; last three months, 13.0. Scores derived from husbands' reports, for the last three months only, averaged 15.9.

As expected, reports of nausea and vomiting decreased after the first three months. The *total* number of symptoms per person also declined after the first three months. Nevertheless, the incidence of six symptoms increased (backache, heartburn, insomnia, painful intercourse, shortness of breath, and swollen ankles). Symptoms that might be classified as most subjective (irritability, lack of interest in sex, tiredness, and the like) were those that became less common as pregnancy progressed.

Almost half of this sample of women experienced nausea or vomiting *often* in the first three months, and such findings agree with the results of other studies (Poffenberger, Poffenberger, and Landis 1952; Robertson 1946). Furthermore, nausea and vomiting seemed to serve as "triggers" and were significantly associated with the other symptoms that declined over pregnancy. Nausea, for example, was significantly related to depression, dizziness, insomnia, irritability, lack of interest in sex, loss of appetite, tiredness, and weakness, but was *not* related to symptoms like heartburn or painful intercourse—the symptoms that increased over pregnancy. Further confirmation of the trigger role of nausea can be seen from the strong relationship between nausea and the total number of symptoms in the first three months ($r = .69$, $p < .01$) and the much smaller relationship between nausea and the total number of symptoms in the middle three months ($r = .19$). It seems likely, therefore, that nausea and vomiting accentuate other early symptoms that are largely subjective. Since nausea occurs mainly in the first three months, the other, "triggered" (subjective) symptoms occur primarily then also.

There is a definite link between menstrual discomfort and discomfort during pregnancy, as evidenced by correlations between menstrual-symptom scores and pregnancy-symptom scores, which are significant for every trimester (.42, .36, .35). Menstrual-symptom scores and pregnancy-symptom scores

for every trimester are significantly associated with both the Taylor anxiety score and the total worry score (correlations in the low .30s), but not with the Gough femininity score. The implication is that women who experience reproductive-system symptoms when not pregnant are those more likely to experience discomforts associated with the pregnant state, and that anxiety may mediate both kinds of symptoms. Such reasoning is consistent with reports of Wenner and Cohen (1968) and Rosen (1955) correlating stress with vomiting. But the actual causal direction of the influence of anxiety is problematic—symptoms could cause anxiety, but anxiety could also make symptoms worse. Menstrual and pregnancy symptoms could also be associated because some women cast themselves in the "sick role," which is a role society at least partly approves for both the menstruating and the pregnant woman if she wishes to adopt it.

In an effort to clarify relationships between role strain and symptomatology, Doering (1975) carried out an extensive analysis for seventy women in this panel to see how women's notions about their own sexuality and proper sex role related to their reactions to pregnancy and birth. Women were classified as "biologically feminine" (those who were comfortable about their own feminine bodily functions and who were not passive or dependent in outlook) or "socially feminine" (those who held stereotyped views, e.g., that women should let their husband's sex drive set the pace for their sexual activities, should be passive, should devote themselves exclusively to homemaking). Socially feminine women also regarded the physical aspects of femininity such as menstruating and breast-feeding as either embarrassing or unpleasant. It turned out that (as reported also by Newton 1955), women who were more socially feminine experienced more menstrual and early pregnancy symptoms, and their symptoms became more noticeable as pregnancy went on. High biological femininity was very mildly associated with trouble-free menses and pregnancy ($r = .13, .16$ respectively).

Women in this sample felt some discomfort with advanced pregnancy, for the number of symptoms increased in the last three months. The most noticeable increases were in tiredness, lack of interest in sex (closely related to tiredness), and heartburn. Still, the most frequent symptom—tiredness—was reported by only 41 percent of the women in the sample, and except for heartburn (36 percent) no other symptom affected more than 26 percent of the sample often.

These women looked upon themselves as being healthy. Only 23 percent saw themselves during pregnancy as being less healthy than usual. Considering the large number of symptoms inquired about and the fact that some symptoms are almost bound to appear in any pregnancy (or for that matter at any other time in life), one can say only that these women had very positive views of their own health.

Twenty-five percent of the husbands saw their pregnant wives as being less

healthy than usual. There was some agreement between husbands and wives on the state of the wife's health ($r = .36$, $p < .01$), but agreement was far from perfect.

Earlier it was noted that a large fraction of the women in the sample planned to work until late in pregnancy or planned not to stop work at all, and that there was no relation between the time of stopping work and whether a woman experienced nausea in the first three months. Staying at work is, of course, another indicator of the highly satisfactory health of the women in this sample. Again, however, the causal direction is equivocal—women could have continued to work because they were healthy, or working may promote health in that physical activity, getting out of the house, focusing attention on things other than the self and the pregnancy, and continuing familiar life patterns are beneficial for health.

Almost all of these women did not believe that being pregnant is equivalent to being ill, and as mentioned, the vast majority of the women at the time of the second interview reported that they felt as healthy as usual, or healthier. Also, there is likely an interplay between the women's positive attitudes about their health and their body images. At the end of the sixth month, only 19 percent felt that women are clumsy or unattractive when pregnant, and even by the ninth month only 24 percent felt that way. Of those who do feel pregnant women are clumsy and unattractive, more are middle class than lower class (64 percent vs. 36 percent). Almost all the women (95 percent) felt that after the birth a woman could get her figure back if she really tried.

Symptoms reported by wives for the last three months were compared with the symptoms the husband perceived at approximately the same time. The men tended to see some symptoms more often than their wives (lack of interest in sex, constipation, weakness, insomnia, swollen ankles, backache). Wives' admission of being tired near the end of pregnancy was the one symptom that they reported much more often than did husbands.

There was considerable agreement within couples on the total symptom score at the time of the nine-month interview ($r = .51$, $p < .01$). There was particularly good agreement on sex-related symptoms (pain during sex and lack of interest in sex). Thus pregnancy-related physical difficulties of the wife were viewed similarly by both members of the pair, suggesting that there is good communication between husbands and wives on these matters. This agreement may be overrated, however, because data exist for both members of a couple only when the husband was willing to be interviewed—these husbands may be more sensitive to their wives' symptoms than husbands who refused to be interviewed.

Not surprisingly, there was a negative relationship between spare-time activities with the husband and the total number of pregnancy symptoms ($r = -.21$, $p < .01$). This suggests, rather reasonably, that a wife's anxiety and/or physical debility is a negative influence on the couple's time spent together. The husband may choose to spend his time elsewhere when the wife

is not a relaxing and pleasant companion. Again, however, the argument can proceed in the opposite direction: if a husband is not around much and does not join his wife in recreation, this may lead her to pay more attention to her symptoms and anxieties.

INCIDENCE OF WIVES' WORRIES

Information on specific types of worries and anxieties related to pregnancy and childbirth is given in table 3.1. Although the number of pregnancy- and birth-related worries could have increased as pregnancy went on, it did not. Three substantial sources of worry noted in the sixth month of pregnancy— weight gain, losing the baby, lack of interest in sex—became less important by the ninth month.

The lessening in these three areas of worry is offset by a number of small increases in worries specifically tied to the childbirth event—worry about not being sure when labor begins, going to the hospital too early, etc. Other workers have found increased worry near the end of pregnancy (Colman and Colman 1971; Davids, De Vault, and Talmadge 1961; Erickson 1967; Newton 1963), but in this sample of women the overall level of worrying did not increase significantly from the sixth to the ninth month. In fact, when asked just prior to the birth about whether they tended at that time to worry less than usual, the same, or more than usual, about two-thirds of the women replied that they worried the same as usual or less than usual. There is a strong relationship between the total number of *different* worries and the women's reports about how much they worried—as would be expected ($r = .56$, $p < .01$).

Higher preparation levels are associated with less worry ($r = .25$ or .16, depending on the interview). Whether or not the pregnancy was planned was not related to worry or to anxiety. Also, there appears to be no relation between social class and worry level. This lack of a relationship between class and level of worrying would not necessarily be expected because the lower-class women were less well-off financially and had somewhat more stereotyped views of their own sex roles.

The most common worry women reported was about weight gain, even though research suggests that effort to hold weight gain to a minimal amount (15–20 pounds) may actually be harmful to the developing baby (Brewer 1966; Committee on Maternal Nutrition 1970). Twenty-nine percent of the women were told to hold weight gain to twenty pounds or less. Of the remainder, 26 percent were told twenty-one to twenty-five pounds; 11 percent, twenty-six to thirty pounds; 7 percent, thirty or more pounds, and 28 percent had not yet been told anything about weight gain when they were asked this question in the sixth month. Many of the respondents said that they were going by what they had read or by what friends had told them about

TABLE 3.1. Pregnancy- and childbirth-related worries (percentages)

Worries	Wife—6th month		Wife—9th month[a]		Husband—9th month	
	Worry a lot	Worry a little	Worry a lot	Worry a little	Worry a lot	Worry a little
Pregnancy-related						
Aches and pains	7	46	3	54	57	35
Disagreement with Dr.	3	13	4	25	2	20
Husband unfaithful	0	13	0	8	0[b]	38[b]
Lack sex interest	10	33	3	35	9	39
Lose baby	23	41	7	41	16	52
Sex hurt baby	5	27	4	28	7	40
Weight gain	43	42	32	43	n.a.	n.a.
Childbirth-related						
Baby born dead	12	41	7	38	11	39
Baby deformed	23	61	17	56	20	63
Being torn or cut	3	38	5	30	5	40
Complications	7	54	7	56	13	70
Do good job in labor	15	53	14	54	n.a.	n.a.
Hospital too early	2	13	4	22	0	13
Hospital too late	4	20	3	25	5	50
Left alone in labor	9	25	6	29	n.a.	n.a.
Lose control in labor	8	52	13	44	n.a.	n.a.
Mix up babies	0	4	0	3	0	13
Not enough drugs	0	14	4	13	2	21
Not know when in labor	8	37	10	49	4	46
Pain during labor	13	53	16	53	20	63
Scream during labor	1	25	3	25	7	25
Too many drugs	11	35	7	35	9	41
Postpartum						
Care of baby	27	55	27	53	27	48
Financial responsibility	n.a.	n.a.	18	48	34	46

n.a. = not asked.

[a] Six women who delivered early not included.

[b] Worded differently for husbands: "Are you worried about the temptation to be unfaithful?"

weight gain—usually a twenty-pound limit. Actually, if respondents' statements are taken at face value, holding down weight often seemed to them to be the major goal of the monthly visit to the obstetrician.

By the first week of the ninth month, 19 percent of the respondents had gained twenty pounds or less, but the average gain was twenty-seven pounds. When asked if the doctor had said anything about their weight gain, women reported few compliments (even if their gain was twenty pounds or less) and much of what they called "scolding" or "yelling at me." Doctors' comments

ranged from mild ("Now don't gain anymore") to insulting ("How does a dietitian gain two pounds in two weeks?"). The latter respondent, who had conscientiously kept her gain to twenty-four pounds, retorted, "How does a doctor get sick?" but admitted to being very upset by her obstetrician's remarks. Often scare tactics were used also. A teenager, who had gained twenty-three pounds, reported, "He yells at me every visit. He says I eat too much. I just get so depressed. He says my delivery is going to be harder because of my weight gain." Certainly sudden weight gain can signal serious problems, but the weight is a symptom, not a cause. Only one respondent was told by her physician of the importance of the type of food ingested (especially protein) rather than of calorie counts.

The other most prominent worries of these pregnant women concerned labor, about pain or losing control, and the baby, about how to care for it after it was born and whether its health would be good.

INCIDENCE OF HUSBANDS' WORRIES

The pregnancy and childbirth-related worries reported by husbands are also given in table 3.1. On the whole, the men were more anxious than their wives, and they reported being far more worried about their wives' aches and pains than their wives were. More of them also acknowledged fear about the temptation to be unfaithful than their wives were aware of.

As was true for wives, husbands who were anxious about things in general tended to be those who reported more worries related to pregnancy and childbirth ($r = .37$, $p < .01$). Concerning the worries related directly to childbirth, husbands were anxious about getting to the hospital in time (perhaps because that is considered to be their responsibility), and they admitted to a few more fears than their wives about the baby being born dead or deformed. They voiced considerable anxiety about the financial responsibility of raising a child—a logical concern given society's expectations, and a concern other researchers have also noted (Benson 1967; Lynn 1974).

On the average both husbands and wives admitted worrying a little more than usual during pregnancy, but (as already noted) wives worried less than husbands. Both admitted some worries about childbirth; one might expect that the wife would be more worried than the husband because she is the one who will give birth, but this was not true. The woman's average score on worrying about childbirth (with constant worry coded 1 and lesser degrees of worry coded 2, 3, 4, and 5) was 2.50, compared to men's average of 2.19. Although both spouses were concerned about the baby, the subjects of greatest worry differed for husbands and wives. Weight gain was a greater source of worry to the wives, whereas husbands worried more than their wives did about finances, getting to the hospital on time, and losing the baby. It appears that

the lower average score for wives can mostly be accounted for by the husbands' greater concerns about their wives' discomfort and about getting to the hospital on time.

For both husbands ($r = .18$) and wives ($r = .25$), preparation was associated with lower total worry scores in the ninth month, but the tendency is not strong. The interpretation is problematic: people who are preparing themselves well may worry less as a consequence, but worriers may be persons who do not take realistic steps to prepare. In other words, they may worry, but do not act.

PHYSICAL FITNESS

In the nine-month interview a number of questions were asked about the kind of exercise women got during the two-week period immediately preceding the interview. Generally speaking, except for ordinary household tasks, these women obtained exercise during the ninth month *only* by climbing stairs, walking, and by engaging in "pregnancy exercises" (e.g., leg lifts, tailor sitting). Ninety-two percent reported climbing stairs regularly, 28 percent took long walks regularly, and 34 percent did pregnancy exercises regularly. Almost none jogged, swam, rode bikes, or engaged in sports. In other words, toward the end of pregnancy, unless a woman was enrolled in childbirth-preparation classes, she engaged in almost no exercise. The amount of exercise women engaged in was not related to whether the woman saw herself as worrying more or less than usual, but those with the highest worry scores got the least exercise ($r = .23$, $p < .01$). The relation between final preparation level and total worry score does not explain this. That is, when preparation level is held constant, there was still a relationship between worry scores and exercise (a partial correlation of .24), so the relation noted earlier between higher preparation levels and lower worry scores does not account for the relation between lack of exercise and worry.

ATTITUDE TOWARD PREGNANCY

WIVES

In both the sixth and ninth months, women were asked probing questions about what they found to be nice in being pregnant. Their replies were coded into five categories as follows: $0 = $ *nothing* nice; $1 = $ selfish things (i.e., extra attention, get to stop work, buy new wardrobe, etc.); $2 = $ joint effort (i.e., "brought my husband and me closer"); $3 = $ some enjoyment of the pregnant state; and $4 = $ enthusiasm for being pregnant (i.e., love to feel baby move, enjoy bodily changes, "glowing," etc.). On the average, women

scored on the negative side at both the sixth-month (1.96) and the ninth-month (1.86) interview. Views generally resembled the reaction of one woman who said: "Well, I was constantly on diets before I was pregnant. . . . I don't like being pregnant." Enjoyment of pregnancy, a less common feeling, was expressed as follows: "I really like the feeling of something living inside you. It's just an incredible feeling, to think there's another life in you. It makes you think more seriously about things, about life." At the ninth month 52 percent of the women (compared to 47 percent in the sixth month) were negative about being pregnant.

The average number of pregnancy-related problems mentioned by the women in the ninth month was 3.29, a few more problems than seen by the men (2.63). There is a relation between the number of problems the wife sees as being associated with pregnancy and the state of her health as estimated by both her husband ($r = .30$, $p < .01$) and herself ($r = .31$, $p < .01$).

The women's generally negative attitude toward being in the pregnant state could be interpreted as an indication of the negative attitudes society has about female bodily functions. In other words, the women could be responding to negative evaluations of them made by others. (The relationship between "typical" feminine characteristics and common ideas of mental health was noted above.) On the other hand, such attitudes could have their genesis within the women themselves. There is no correlation between the number of problems experienced in pregnancy and enjoyment of the pregnant state, but the modest correlation between the respondents' biological femininity score and their attitudes toward pregnancy ($r = .22$, $p < .01$) suggests that women's sex-role ideology is somehow involved. The relative importance of others vs. the self in generating these attitudes cannot be evaluated completely.

Since quickening occurs between the fourth and fifth months, every woman in the sample had experienced fetal movements by the time of the first interview. Sixteen percent registered clearly negative feelings toward fetal movements, with remarks such as "it's a pain in the neck," "really annoying," and "it hurts, and I wish it'd stop": "I . . . I'm shocked! I just didn't believe it would move that much; I really didn't. . . . It's very uncomfortable." Thirty percent were neutral or ambivalent. However the majority, 55 percent, were positive: "Oh, I love it! It's my favorite part of being pregnant. It feels like it's gonna come out dancing. It's a wonderful feeling that there's life inside."

There is a relation between the women's attitude toward fetal movements and their enjoyment of pregnancy ($r = .22$, $p < .01$), and also between their own and their husband's attitudes toward fetal movements ($r = .24$, $p < .01$). Although 46 percent of the women were not enthusiastic about fetal movements, over 79 percent of the husbands were reported to enjoy feeling the baby move—attitude toward fetal movements may depend on whose abdomen is being kicked.

HUSBANDS

There was only one man among the sixty husbands interviewed before the birth who said he was "not very interested" in his wife's pregnancy, and none reported no interest whatsoever. About 77 percent of the husbands reported themselves as "very interested" in the pregnancy. Also, there was a correlation between husband's degree of interest and how positive his attitude toward the pregnancy was. The association between the wife's report of her husband's reaction to news of the pregnancy (rated from "very negative" to "enthusiastic" on a six-point scale) and his initial interest in pregnancy reveals that if the wife perceived a negative reaction when the husband first heard the news, he tended not to be very interested in the pregnancy in the ninth month, according to his own report ($r = .27$, $p < .05$).

Husbands were asked about the problems of pregnancy. The average number of problems mentioned was 2.63. Husbands mentioned their wives' tiredness first (just as wives had). Another common problem was her being irritable "all the time." Husbands frequently mentioned two other problems that were rarely alluded to by the female respondents: sex (or lack of it) and money. As one man put it: "Our sex life has certainly slowed down—no, it's come to a screeching halt." Financial worries, suddenly realized after the wife quit her job, were also commonly mentioned.

When men were asked: "What's nice about the pregnancy?" their replies ranged from negative through seeing the pregnancy as bringing the couple closer together. For example,

[laughs] . . . uh . . . the nicest thing. . . . Huh! I can't think of anything.

[Anything you enjoy about her being pregnant?] There's not much enjoyable. . . . uhh—I can't think of *anything*.

She's starting to look more motherly, I guess. Other than that, it really hasn't been that nice.

She won't be pregnant much longer. [laughs] . . . She's had a very rough pregnancy, so it's hard to find anything nice about it. I think the best thing, the neatest thing, is when you can feel the baby move.

I think she looks good. I think she looks pretty. She looks happy. [Else?] It's brought us, like, it's brought us together. Not that we were apart before it. . . . It brought us a certain feeling between us—that's good. And it's brought out a quality in her that I'd never seen before.

The fact that she's carrying something that is both of us, and in a short while we'll be able to see the product of our love.

Planning of pregnancy was *not* related to the wife's attitude toward being pregnant but was strongly related to the husband's first reaction to pregnancy as reported by the wife ($r = .45$, $p < .01$). ("How did your husband react to the news that you were pregnant?"—coded from 1 = very negative, to 6 = enthusiastic.) In view of their interest, it is paradoxical that 28 percent of the

husbands interviewed saw nothing nice about the pregnant state and only 23 percent were actually positive about their wife's pregnant state.

LEVEL OF PREPARATION FOR CHILDBIRTH

Couples in the 1970s were far more interested than couples formerly were in knowing what will happen to them during labor and delivery and were even more interested in having some control and choice over this experience. In the sixth month, very few of the women (7 percent) thought that they wanted to be asleep when their babies were born, and by the ninth month, only 1 percent felt that way. (Physicians were reported as telling women that it is not safe for the infant for the mother to be unconscious, thus persuading them to stay awake.) In the sixth month, 57 percent wished to be awake and feeling everything at the moment of birth, while 37 percent wanted to be awake but numb. By the ninth month, of the 114 women reporting, 54 percent still hoped to be awake and feeling everything, and 45 percent wanted to be awake but numb. Some women who wished to be awake and feeling everything were not Lamaze-trained, evidence of how the changing social customs surrounding birth are spreading to persons in all segments of society.

The women who were more biologically feminine—those who were less likely to subscribe to stereotyped views of feminine behavior—were also more likely to wish for little or no medication during delivery. Typical views were:

> I don't see how I could help if I were drugged. And I want—to experience it—I think it's going to be a very beautiful feeling. . . .

> It's something you should feel everything. . . . And you can help with the childbirth; you're not a victim.

Women who were less biologically feminine saw themselves in passive-bystander roles and said things such as: "I'd rather just be asleep and get it all over with. . . . Just wake me up when it's over with and show me the baby and that'll be fine. I couldn't see without my glasses anyway."

The women's "preparation level" was evaluated by combining information from several questions they answered in all three interviews. This variable measured the final level of preparation the women achieved by the time birth occurred, and it included the women's knowledge about labor and delivery received from magazines, books, movies, and medical training, as well as from the different types of classes available. The final preparation level[1]

---

[1] Medical training *only* was rated below training courses aimed specifically at expectant parents because medical training teaches the medical attendant how to help and care for the laboring patient; it does not teach her *at all* how to be the laboring patient, i.e., how to cope with contractions in her own body. Of four R.N.'s in the sample, three took Lamaze training and the other read childbirth manuals and qualified at level 3. Also, there were two L.P.N.'s, one of whom took Lamaze and the other a hospital course, and two medical technicians, both Lamaze trained. There was one "nurse's aide" who worked at a state mental hospital and who had no medical training whatsoever for childbirth. She was scored "1".

ranged from 1 to 7, with meanings assigned as shown in table 3.2. The sample of women in the panel was selected to provide as much variation in preparation as possible; 44 percent of the women had Lamaze training, 26 percent had hospital-class preparation, and 29 percent had little or no preparation.

By design, the average level of preparation for middle-class women in this sample is about the same as for lower-class women (see "The Sample," Appendix A). The average preparation levels look somewhat different by religious affiliation (for Catholic women, 4.25; for Protestant women, 4.92;

TABLE 3.2. Final preparation level (percentages)

Final preparation level[a]	Degree of preparation	Wives (N = 120)	Husbands (N = 57)
1	Nothing	8	21
2	Pregnancy manuals[b] or medical training only[c]	17	9
3	Childbirth manuals[d]	4	0
4	Hospital-based classes or department-store classes[e]	13	12
5	Level 4 plus childbirth manuals	13	11
6	Lamaze[f] training	16	28
7	Level 6 plus childbirth manuals and / or childbirth movie	28	19

[a] Information was obtained from all three women's interviews in order to ascertain preparation level. If two-thirds or less of the classes in a series were attended, the value of "final preparation level" was reduced by one unit.

[b] Pregnancy manuals are books that describe pregnancy and postpartum events in detail, but indicate that labor and delivery are something that doctors and nurses do *for* the woman. (Eastman and Russell 1970; Fielding 1971; Hall 1972; Mitchell and Klein 1969; Seidman and Albert 1956; Spotnitz and Freeman 1974.)

[c] Medical training *only* has been placed in this category because, prior to 1970, students in most nursing schools learned only the physiology and possible pathologies of labor, and how to care for the patient in labor (in the sense of giving perineal shaves, enemas, and medication). How it felt to *be* the laboring woman, let alone how she could help herself, was not commonly a part of the curriculum at that time. We noted that even those women whose medical training had included learning about preparation for childbirth all chose to take classes, thus placing themselves in one of the higher categories.

[d] Childbirth manuals are books that emphasize labor and delivery as something the mother must learn how to do, with the help and support of mate, doctors, and nurses. These books describe in detail how to cope with labor and how to give birth. (Bing 1967; Bradley 1974; Chabon 1966; Dick-Read 1959; Karmel 1959; Kitzinger 1972; Vellay 1960.)

[e] Hospital-based classes take an approach half-way between pregnancy manuals and childbirth manuals. They tend to concentrate on socializing the pregnant woman to be a good patient in their particular obstetrical department. She learns about labor and delivery, but only as they are performed in that hospital; options are not usually discussed, and choices are discouraged. Department-store classes prepare a woman for labor and delivery even less thoroughly than hospital classes do. One investigator (S.D.) attended full series of all but one of the classes placed in level 4, in order to ascertain how thoroughly they were preparing couples for labor and delivery. One series of classes did not permit visitors; in that case a pregnant and knowledgeable nurse friend attended and reported back.

[f] All Lamaze classes were taught by certified instructors of the Childbirth Education Association of Baltimore. One investigator (S.D.) attended several different trainers' classes and found the quality of instruction to be uniformly high.

and for Jewish women, 5.11), but the difference in proportions of trained women across religious groups is not statistically significant.

When asked how much they practiced for labor—in the sense of rehearsing the relaxation, breathing, and pushing learned in preparation classes—forty-eight women reported they did not practice because they did not have anything to practice or had not heard of "practicing." Four others had learned, but did not practice. Of the sixty-eight who did practice, the average amount of practice was about three times per week.

Not surprisingly, the amount of practice by husbands and wives is closely related ($r = .79$, $p < .01$), but wives tended to practice more than their husbands. There is a close link between the amount of practice couples engaged in and the final level of preparation for childbirth ($r = .40$, $p < .01$). Lamaze classes stress the importance of daily practice. Hospital classes take a more relaxed approach toward practicing.

There was no relation between when women stopped working and final preparation level. Classes are commonly taught in the evening so that husbands can attend, and this timing therefore does not interfere with women's jobs either.

Preparation level is of importance in this research in two respects: (1) as an outcome—that is, as a possible consequence of age, education, or other variables; (2) as a predictor—that is, as a possible cause of successful coping with the birth event and later parenting demands. Put simply, one purpose of this research was to determine what persuades women to prepare themselves in advance for the birth event. A second question was how that preparation affected their ability to cope successfully with childbirth and parenting. It was possible to obtain much more information on the latter question.

A basic thesis for this research and for other research that preceded it is that successful coping will be predicted by preparation for childbirth. The prediction is that the more prepared the woman, the more favorable the outcome. The well-prepared women should manifest a superior state of psychological well-being both during and after birth, and their family relationships should also be superior to those of poorly prepared women. We based these hypotheses on an earlier cross-sectional study of 269 women (Doering and Entwisle 1975), which suggested that those who were better prepared had a more positive attitude toward the baby, were more likely to breast-feed, and actually breast-fed longer. Preparation level was thus correlated with the quality of mother-infant relationships after birth in that study.

As noted in chapter 1, one theoretical context for explaining the benefits of preparation in this research is adapted from Janis's theory (1958) about how individuals cope with stress. Another relevant theoretical context is the notion that transition between life-cycle stages is made easier by anticipatory socialization. An extensive literature documents the medical benefits of preparation (shorter labors, less medication, and the like), and evidence in addition to the authors' previous work confirms some psychological and social benefits of

preparation (Eichler et al. 1977; Henneborn and Cogan 1975; Norr et al. 1977). In general, however, research linking events in pregnancy to later adjustment is rare.

Preparation for childbirth now enjoys tremendous general popularity. However, Lamaze preparation is characteristic of better-educated women and of women residing near major population centers (Watson 1977). Perhaps the most remarkable testimony to the popularity of childbirth training was the difficulty encountered in this research (from 1973 to 1976) in locating women who were *not* prepared. It was only by diligent searching that any relatively unprepared women (preparation categories 1, 2, and 3) could be located. This experience contrasts with experience in the latter part of the sixties, when the unprepared woman was the norm and the prepared woman was the one who had to be sought out (Doering and Entwisle 1975).

PRECURSORS OF PREPARATION LEVEL

In this sample, there was no relation between a planned pregnancy and preparation level. The relation between preparation for childbirth and husband's interest in pregnancy, as reported by him, is also nil.

There is a small relation between wife's interest in sex and preparation level ($r = .18$, $p < .05$) and between the wife's report of husband's sex drive and preparation level ($r = .21$, $p < .05$). Those reporting stronger interest in sex planned to continue sex the longest during pregnancy. Overall, the pattern of relationships with sexuality suggests that openness on the part of both partners is associated with higher preparation levels. Probably those who are the most sexually active and uninhibited are also less anxious in general, not just about sexuality. These more-open attitudes lead to a desire to participate in childbirth, and for that purpose, to a seeking of knowledge about the birth process. Biological femininity scores and final preparation level are also closely related ($r = .44$, $p < .01$). Here again, however, the direction of the relationship is equivocal. Higher levels of preparation could lead to more openness, rather than vice versa. Findings that link sexual adjustment and low anxiety to preparation, and thereby to better coping, are in line with a recent report by Grossman (1978), who noted that low anxiety and better sexual adjustment were the most important variables associated with a good early adjustment of new fathers.

A SOCIOPSYCHOLOGICAL MODEL

The data from the panel contains some useful information on the intersection of preparation with other variables, but for several reasons these data are not ideal for determining the factors that may induce women to prepare themselves for childbirth. For one thing, many women in the panel had read books and had decided whether or not to take classes by the time they joined the study. For another, preparation level, social class, and religion were intentionally balanced in the sample, so distributions of women according to

these variables are arbitrary. Since information on factors inducing couples to prepare for childbirth is generally scarce, however, the data from the panel will nevertheless be explored from this standpoint.

Three main lines of exploration were pursued. First, a number of reports suggest an association between preparation level and education (Mann, Woodward, and Joseph 1961; Watson 1977; Yankauer 1958), and this was checked. Second, by using respondents' answers to several questions on woman's role, it was possible to investigate whether an active vs. a passive outlook (a woman's wish to take an active part in birth and early parenting) was associated with higher levels of preparation. Third, although the hypothesis has not actually been tested, previous research suggests that closeness of the husband-wife relationship might predict a decision to prepare for childbirth (Cohen 1966; Deutscher 1970). In this panel whether wife's spare-time activities were shared with the husband was *not* related to preparation level. For a different measure of closeness—a measure of couple communication—the hypothesis was confirmed, however. Couples were asked what they were most likely to quarrel or disagree about, and the disagreements were probed in detail. Answers were then rated for how severe the conflicts were and how the couple handled them (i.e., by severe quarrels and conflicts or by communication and compromise). Couples who communicated well and quarreled little are significantly more likely to prepare for childbirth ($r = .30$, $p < .01$).

Putting these findings together leads to an explanation accounting for wife's preparation that has both psychological and sociological components. Quality of the couple's communication (QCOMM), the woman's desire for an active role (ACTRL), and the wife's education (WEDUC)[2] are all taken as determinants of the wife's preparation level (WPREP) in a multiple regression model. Of these, the woman's desire to take an active role is by far the most influential factor affecting wives' preparation, with a standardized coefficient of .482 (table 3.3). In fact, even if the quality of communication and wife's educational level are ignored, preparation is still predicted well by only the woman's preference for an active role ($r = .518$).

Apparently the women who are more highly educated, whose communication with husbands is good, and who wish to take an active role in childbirth are those who ended up at higher preparation levels in this sample. It is not entirely clear from this analysis, though, whether the wife's personality characteristics or her preconceived ideas about motherhood lead her to seek more preparation, or whether for some couples a certain mutual compatibility of ideas and attitudes leads to more preparation. The most promising linkage to explore in future research is that between biological femininity and preparation.

It would be desirable to know more about what or who persuades women to prepare. In this sample Protestant women were more likely to follow through

---

[2]Full information on how these variables were measured is given in Appendix C.

TABLE 3.3. Predicting women's preparation level

	Dependent variable Preparation level (WPREP)	
	Metric coefficients	Standardized coefficients
Independent variables		
Wife's educational level (WEDUC)	.240	.226*
Quality of communication in marriage (QCOMM)	.287	.171*
Woman's desire for active role (ACTRL)	.878	.482*
Variance accounted for	35.7%	
Constant term	3.830	

	Correlation coefficients (listwise present) N = 120				
	WEDUC	QCOMM	ACTRL	Mean	SD
WEDUC				14.13	1.99
QCOMM	.124			3.23	1.25
ACTRL	.078	.109		4.86	1.13
WPREP	.284	.251	.518	4.80	2.06

*Coefficient 2.0 or more times its standard error.

on their plans than others, and Catholics seemed to involve the husband more in the decision to prepare than other religious groups. Other research suggests that middle-class and more highly educated women are more likely to attend classes (Mann, Woodward, and Joseph 1961; Watson 1977; Yankauer 1958), and data for the panel are consistent with these findings. At present, however, there is an increasing fad among pregnant women to take classes, and almost all pregnant women attend classes of some kind. It may therefore be important to determine what induces women to select one kind of preparation from among the many kinds available. Also, in predicting preparation of women more generally, educational level is very likely far more important than the present data suggest, because in this sample the restricted range on wives' educational level probably attenuates the strength of the relationship. There are no seriously disadvantaged women or women without male partners in the panel, nor are there any women with education beyond a master's degree.

SOURCES OF CHILDBIRTH INFORMATION

WIVES

Women in this sample wanted to find out about childbirth. To the question "How much do you want to know about childbirth?" over two-thirds of the women (68 percent) responded that they "wanted to know everything."

Another 24 percent wanted to know "most things." Only one woman admitted wishing to "know nothing." However, because this is a volunteer sample, persons who are "information seekers" are probably overrepresented. Many respondents requested copies of the results of the study each time they were interviewed.

Women's pursuit of knowledge about childbirth turned out to be mainly through channels outside the doctor's office, however. Although 80 percent of the women admitted wondering about childbirth "sometimes" or "often" at the time of the first interview, over half (55 percent) reported asking their physicians two questions or less per visit. Middle-class women were just as inhibited about seeking information from their physicians as lower-class women were, for exactly 55 percent in both social-class groups asked two questions or less per visit. Also, the number of persons wanting to know little or nothing about childbirth is less than 10 percent of each group and does not appear to be class related.

In the sixth month of pregnancy, 93 percent of the women reported that they felt it was important that the obstetrician describe what labor and delivery were like, but in the ninth month, 73 percent reported that their doctors had not so far described childbirth at all. Ninety-four percent of the sample felt that the physician should explain what drugs he / she planned to use during labor and delivery; in the ninth month, however, only 40 percent of the women had received any information from their obstetricians about what medications would be used, and of those who were informed, most had brought up the issue themselves. Since their obstetricians did not supply information, women turned to other sources to find out about the coming event. This thirst for information was probably a major reason why women agreed to participate in this research.

Apparently the women's need for information was met at least partially by magazines and books. At the time of the first interview, about half of the women (51 percent) acknowledged obtaining information about childbirth from magazines, especially ones like *Baby Talk,* a free magazine aimed at pregnant women. Books served as an additional source of information . Over 75 percent of the women had read at least one specialized book on the topic of pregnancy and childbirth by the time of the first interview, and 44 percent of the women had read two or more such books by then. Two-thirds of the women reported asking friends and relatives for information on what childbirth would be like. Many others received information from friends and relatives even when they had not requested it.

Middle-class and lower-class women used magazines equally as sources of knowledge. More middle-class than lower-class women, however, read specialized books on the topic of childbirth—92 percent had read at least one book, compared to 60 percent of lower-class women. This class difference is also seen in a tally of how many women read two or more books—57 percent vs. 30 percent. Active seeking of formal information differed by class in this sample.

The wish for information, and the active pursuit of it, was also signified by the fact that 87 percent of the women definitely planned to attend some kind of preparation classes at the time of the first interview (71 percent of all the women carried out such plans), and more than half of the women (53 percent) planned to attend Lamaze classes (44 percent actually did). In such classes, of course, people not only ask questions themselves, but hear the answers to questions posed by their classmates. On the other hand, what is learned in classes is not usually tested, and it is possible for a woman to attend classes and to remain surprisingly ignorant about important events. (One well-educated woman who had attended hospital classes, for instance, was astounded and angry at being asked to push as the baby was passing down the birth canal. She was so upset that she refused to do so. She had thought that the doctor reached up and pulled the baby out with forceps.)

By the nine-month interview, 84 percent of the women had either taken a tour of the hospital or planned to take one soon, and over 76 percent of the women had seen at least one movie on childbirth. Only 4 percent said both that they had not seen such a movie and that they would not want to. Eleven women in the sample had actually seen a human birth (9 in the process of medical work of one sort or another, and 2 while attending friends' home births), and close to half (48 percent) reported they would like to see a birth if given the opportunity. On the other hand, almost as many women (46 percent) were sure that they would *not* want to see a woman giving birth because they felt it would be too bloody, gory, or embarrassing.

Many women (47 percent) reported that *no* information about childbirth had been given to them by their mothers. Another 19 percent at first said they had received no information from their mothers, but probing revealed that they actually had. Mothers, clearly, are not major sources of childbirth information for women in this sample. The major sources are formal—classes and / or reading materials.

HUSBANDS

Exactly half of the husbands interviewed had male friends, already fathers, who had told them something about labor and delivery. A minority (20 percent or less) acknowledged receiving such information from women friends or from male relatives. Comparatively few of the husbands in this panel obtained childbirth information from magazines or pamphlets (20 percent and 37 percent, respectively). (At the time of the first interview, a majority of wives reported obtaining such information from magazines.) Close to half the men acknowledged reading specialized books on childbirth (compared to 75 percent of wives at first interview).

A surprisingly large percentage of the husbands (19 percent) had witnessed an actual human birth. This reflects the number of physicians and various medical technicians and assistants in the sample, though one man had inadvertently

observed a birth while in Viet Nam. Eighty-two percent of them had seen at least one movie on the topic of childbirth. (Of wives, 10 percent had seen an actual birth and over 76 percent had seen a childbirth movie.) The data on husbands' sources of information and the extent of information possessed by husbands make one suspect that willingness to participate in this research and prior knowledge of birth are strongly related. There are no data on the sixty husbands not interviewed, and therefore there is no way to settle the issue. It would seem unwise, however, to believe that the husbands who agreed to be interviewed are exactly like those not interviewed in terms of knowledge about birth.

EXPECTATIONS ABOUT LABOR AND DELIVERY

WIVES

The women in this sample expressed an overwhelming desire to have a companion present during labor and delivery. Only one woman did not want one. Furthermore, given a choice of companions (doctor, nurse, relative including mother or sister, childbirth trainer or midwife), almost all women (94 percent) preferred their husband. The few women who did not want their husbands present said things such as:

> Well, he'd get sick. I can't see making him stand something like that. I really think he'd throw up! [Laughs]

> No *way* is he coming in there. You're not at your *best* you know—I've seen that delivery table, and there's no way my husband's going to see me in that position. Oh, my! It . . . it would embarrass me too much.

Much more commonly, however, women expressed strong wishes for their husbands to share the birth experience with them.

> It's an experience that he should be there for, to see his child being born. I think it brings us all closer. He was a part of making the child. . . . I think he should be part of bringing the child into the world. It's as important to *him* as to *me*.

> I want him there, so he can see the baby coming out, and because he'll be helping me the whole time. I don't know if I could do it without him. It's to share . . . share it . . . we want to be together when it comes.

The women's expectations about what their doctors would do during labor spanned a wide range. The average expectation was that the physician would be present in the room about one third of the time, but 6 percent of the women expected the obstetrician to be present 5 percent or less of the time they were in labor, and at the other extreme, 8 percent expected him or her to be there continuously.

When asked how they expected their doctors to help them during labor, the

women's most common response was "just by being there." Asked what they thought their doctors would *do* that might help, most responded with a variation on the theme of giving encouragement: "For support!"; "Keep telling me I'm doing a good job!"; "Reassure me that everything's all right"; "To tell me everything's going well"; "He'll give me confidence and tell me I'm doing good." An equally common reply to this question cast the physician in the role of information giver: "He'll tell me how far along I am"; "To check me and say how much dilated"; "Explain what's going on"; "Tell me when I can push." A less common response indicated expectations for help if complications arose, "He'll deliver the baby," and, least important, "Give me medication, if I need it."

Women expected a nurse to be present a little less than 50 percent of the time. The respondents were less likely to be certain of what nurses might do to help them during labor. With nurses, the most common expectation was for physical comfort measures: "Get you pillows"; "Hold my hand or rub my back"; "I hear they bring you crushed ice, cool washcloths." The women were also aware of medical measures the nurses would be taking, such as shaving the pubic hair and giving an enema, checking vital signs, tidying the bed periodically, and checking progress in labor and the baby's heartbeat.

All the women but one were aware that they could do things to help *themselves* during labor. Whether or not they had attended classes, most respondents were aware that it was best to try to relax during labor. Those who had not gone to classes hoped that nurses would teach them the proper breathing. Many spoke of trying to maintain a positive (cool, calm) mental attitude and not to panic. A minority were aware of the importance of position, massage and pressure, and concentration in helping oneself.

The women's knowledge of what would transpire during labor and delivery was often incorrect, and erred in the optimistic direction. For instance, when asked in the nine-month interview how long the average woman having her first child can expect to be in the first stage of labor (cervix opening up), 47 percent gave the correct answer (12–16 hours), but 43 percent of the women thought it would take 11 hours or less, and only 9 percent expected it to be 17 hours or longer. However, their expectations about duration of the second stage of labor (the time it takes the baby to pass down the birth canal) for a first-time mother showed error in the opposite direction; they thought it would be longer than is usually the case. Only 37 percent were correct (1 to 1½ hours).

The respondents were asked how much pain they thought a woman having a normal, uncomplicated labor would feel during the first stage and then during the second stage if the usual drugs were given. They were asked to imagine the same situation if *no* drugs at all were given. Their expectations are tallied in table 3.4. Regarding the first stage of labor, only one woman in the entire sample expected terrible pain when the usual drugs were given, and no one thought that there would be *no* pain at all. The large majority (61 percent)

TABLE 3.4. Degree of pain anticipated by wives and husbands

	Degree (percentages) of pain					Average degree anticipated
	1 None	2 Slight	3 Moderate	4 Bad	5 Terrible	
	Wives' expectations					
With usual drugs						
First stage	0	20	61	18	1	3.0
Second stage	39	37	20	4	0	1.9
With no drugs						
First stage	0	10	50	38	3	3.3
Second stage	8	21	23	29	19	3.3
	Husbands' expectations					
With usual drugs						
First stage	3	20	47	25	5	3.1
Second stage	15	35	33	15	2	2.5
With no drugs						
First stage	0	18	38	37	7	3.3
Second stage	3	10	35	32	20	3.6

expected moderate pain. The remainder were equally divided, some expecting bad pain (18 percent), the rest "occasional, slight" pain (20 percent). The women expected that, given the usual drugs, the second stage of labor (pushing) would be much easier than the first stage. In fact, 39 percent expected no pain at all during that stage, and 37 percent expected only occasional, slight pain.

When queried as to what might be in store without drugs, there is naturally some shift toward anticipating more pain in both stages of labor, but the shift is more pronounced for the second stage, as table 3.4 shows.

The women were also asked what they thought would be *the* most painful period in the whole process of labor and delivery if no drugs were administered. Forty-one percent were aware that this point usually occurs when the cervical opening is dilated 7–10 cm. Eighteen percent thought it was sometime when the baby was in the birth canal, and 34 percent expected it to be the birth itself, i.e., as the head was actually emerging. The remainder thought it might be early in labor, during the episiotomy, during delivery of the afterbirth, or when being sewn up. Since pain is subjective, the amount of pain women experience and when it peaks vary, and events triggering it vary somewhat even from one birth to another in the same woman.

Given the high average level of preparation in this sample of women, distortions and gaps in their knowledge about delivery are surprisingly numerous.

HUSBANDS

Eighty-two percent of the husbands who were interviewed expected to remain with their wives during the *entire* labor (94 percent of wives wanted husbands there), and 72 percent of the husbands expected to be *next* to their wives when delivery occurred (78 percent of wives had this expectation). A small minority of husbands (8 percent) and of wives (7 percent) expected the husband to remain in the waiting room. In the aggregate, there was good agreement between husbands' and wives' expectations for where the husband would be during labor, but wives expected more participation by husbands, especially during labor, than husbands foresaw.

Thirty-seven percent of the husbands were correct in their estimates of how long labor is in the first stage for a woman having her first child. Only 15 percent expected it to last seventeen hours or more, and 48 percent thought it might be shorter than twelve hours. Forty-five percent of men were correct in estimating the length of the second stage.

Husband's expectations about the amount of pain women experience during labor and delivery are summarized in table 3.4. The figures seem to follow the same patterns as those seen for wives.

PLANS FOR INFANT CARE

Feeding has a central position in the mother-infant relationship. Breast-feeding is thought to produce close physiological and psychological ties (see Newton 1955, Winters 1973). Even for the bottle-fed infant, however, it is still most often the mother who ministers to the child's needs and who responds to the baby's need for food.

For many years the rate of breast-feeding in the United States was dropping. A national survey of hospitals in 1946 showed that at the time of discharge from the maternity ward, 65 percent of babies were wholly or partially breast-fed (Bain 1948). By 1956, only 37 percent were on the breast at the time of discharge (Meyer 1958), and during the sixties, the percentage had dropped to 27 percent (Meyer 1968). However, there may be a swing back toward breast-feeding (see *Consumer Reports* 1977; Hirschman and Hendershot 1979; Sauls 1979; Waterfall and Morris 1976), and the present sample illustrates this. This resurgence of interest in breast-feeding coincides with the mounting evidence favoring it on medical and psychological grounds (see Jelliffe and Jelliffe 1978; Klaus and Kennell 1976*b*), but we suspect that social reasons are more persuasive for women in this sample.

FEEDING INTENTIONS AT FIRST INTERVIEW

About 68 percent of the women at the time of the first interview stated an intention to breast-feed their infant: 28 percent "probably," 40 percent "definitely." (In Waterfall and Morris's survey [1976], 72 percent planned to

nurse or were nursing.) Of those planning to bottle-feed (32 percent), most were definite in their intention to do so. It thus appears that the decision to breast-feed is a harder one to make, because more tentative replies were given to questions on breast-feeding. The actual decision on feeding shows no relation to social class, probably because of the special composition of this sample, but generally more middle-class than lower-class women choose breast-feeding (Hirschman and Hendershot 1979; Hirschman and Sweet 1974; Sauls 1979). As will be discussed later, however, the reasons women in the present sample choose breast-feeding or bottle-feeding seem to differ by class. Feeding choice was related to biological femininity; the more biologically feminine women in this sample were more likely to plan to breast-feed ($r = .36$, $p < .01$).

There is little doubt that, if the mother is able, breast-feeding has health advantages for both mother and child (see Gerrard 1974; Harfouche 1970; Jelliffe and Jelliffe 1978). Colic and other digestive disturbances are supposedly less frequent in breast-fed infants. Various kinds of immunities to infectious disease are known to be transmitted to the infant through its mother's milk. The full advantage of breast-feeding may still be underestimated, however. It has been shown recently, for example, that specific resistance to organisms in the mother's own birth canal are present in human milk (Klaus and Kennell 1976b:75). The mother also benefits: the return of the mother's uterus to its prepregnancy condition is stimulated by the nursing infant (Committee on Nutrition 1976; *Consumer Reports* 1977; I.P.A. Seminar 1975). This is not the place to make a case for breast-feeding, except to point out that in addition to the medical advantages cited above and many others as well, there are thought to be extremely important psychological advantages for mother and for infant. (Klaus and Kennell 1976b; Sosa et al. 1976; Winters 1973; and references cited therein.) If the mother breast-feeds she must be physically close to the infant for much of a newborn's waking time. Further, breast-feeding is pleasant and rewarding to the mother, whereas holding a bottle provides less gratification. Also the same person— the mother—must be involved. If bottles are used, infants may be fed without being held close to the mother, and a variety of persons can feed—husbands, relatives, neighbors, etc. It is also tempting to prop the bottle and turn attention to other things. With feeding carried out by one person who is physically close several times a day, strong attachments between mother and child develop more easily. Mother-child attachment may be linked to later child adjustment *and* maternal adjustment (Klaus and Kennell, 1976b). The attachment process from the mother's side is not well understood, but it is suspected to be biologically based or programmed, just as infant attachment may be. That is, the mother may form strong emotional bonds with her infant as a consequence of either hormonal influences or built-in human tendencies. If this is so, unsatisfied maternal attachment needs could have negative consequences for the mother.

An important question for this research was: What factors during pregnancy

shape women's decisions on baby feeding? As would be expected, prospective breast-feeders tended to be women with more preparation, but the relationship between preparation and intentions to breast-feed was smaller than expected ($r = .33$, $p < .01$), perhaps because of the strong trends toward breast-feeding in the population as a whole. Feeding intentions are extremely important, however, because those with strong intentions tended to be the successful breast-feeders.

REASONS FOR BREAST-FEEDING

Women in this sample cited closeness to the baby as an important reason for breast-feeding, and this reason was given equally often by both middle-class and lower-class women. Of those choosing to breast-feed, over 75 percent mentioned closeness, whereas only 16 percent of those choosing to bottle-feed mentioned closeness. The potential breast-feeders talked about closeness in various terms:

> It's an emotional experience for the mother and the baby. It's . . . it's closeness, and warmth.

> It's the more natural way to feed, in which the baby can relate to you better. You physically *feel* it when you feed the child, you're not so detached.

Bottle-feeding mothers most often mention "convenience," which, when probed, translates to "not being tied down to the baby" or "someone else can feed it." They said:

> You're not tied down. You can go anywhere you please and do what you want. My husband can feed the baby a bottle at 2:00 A.M. and 6:00 A.M.

> I'd feel like a *cow* if I breast fed. . . . I can leave the baby with my mother for a week if I want to.

Breast-feeders cited advantages to the baby as well as to the mother, and there was no difference by social class. Of those citing advantages to the baby as the reason for their choice, 92 percent planned breast-feeding, while only 20 percent of those planning bottle-feeding mentioned advantages to the baby.

The women in this sample obtained information about feeding from several sources. Only 5 percent of the women had no friends who had discussed infant feeding with them. Various kinds of written materials also served as sources of information about infant feeding. Pamphlets were read the most frequently (77 percent), and baby-care books next most frequently (69 percent).

The difference in infant feeding practices between this generation and the last is pointed up by the percentage of women in this sample who reported that they themselves were bottle-fed as infants—69 percent.

Despite much previous research pointing to social-class differences in attitudes toward breast-feeding in the last generation (see Jackson, Wilkin, and Auerbach 1956; Bronfenbrenner 1958; Salber, Stitt, and Babbott 1958), rea-

sons for breast-feeding differed in only one respect across social-class groups in the present sample. Exactly 57 percent in both groups mentioned closeness as a reason for breast-feeding and about the same proportion of women in each group mentioned advantages to the baby in breast-feeding (63 percent and 70 percent). There was, however, a sharp difference on a third question, in that 65 percent of lower-class women admitted inhibitions about breast-feeding with other people around, compared to 45 percent of middle-class women. A greater number of inhibitions is acknowledged by lower-class women whether or not the woman herself intended to breast-feed. Of those lower-class women who did *not* plan to breast-feed, all but one acknowledged inhibitions; whereas among middle-class women, a lesser percentage (60 percent) of those not planning to breast-feed acknowledged inhibitions. Among those planning to breast-feed, a class difference in expressed inhibitions is also evident (39 percent for middle class vs. 52 percent for lower class). The more stereotyped feminine sex-role ideas held by lower-class women probably account for their greater feeding inhibitions.

FEEDING INTENTIONS AT SECOND INTERVIEW

By the time of the second interview all but 3 percent of the women had decided whether to bottle- or breast-feed, and they felt that whatever mode they had chosen was "important" or "extremely important" to them. There was thus a crystallization of feeding intentions prior to the baby's birth. The firming up of intentions by the end of pregnancy is not surprising, because drugs to inhibit milk production must be given soon after birth if the mother does not plan to breast-feed. She therefore must make up her mind before she delivers.

There is an association between a woman's choice of feeding mode and whether or not she herself was breast-fed as an infant. Disregarding those who were undecided about feeding mode, those who were not sure whether they themselves were bottle- or breast-fed, and the six women who missed the nine-month interview because of an early delivery, the choice between breast- and bottle-feeding differed significantly according to whether or not the woman herself was breast-fed as an infant ($\chi^2 = 7.21$, $p < .01$). Of those who were themselves breast-fed (thirty women), ninety percent planned to breast-feed their infants, while only 61 percent of those who were bottle-fed planned to breast-feed. If this pattern continues into the future, bottle-feeding might be rare two generations from now.

In the single interview fathers had before the birth, they were asked about their wives' feeding intentions. Of sixty fathers, forty-eight (80 percent) indicated that breast-feeding was planned, twelve indicated bottle-feeding. Thus, a higher percentage of husbands reported breast-feeding intentions than wives. In those couples where responses of both members about feeding intentions can be compared, there were four cases of disagreement. In three,

the husband reported "breast-feeding" and the wife reported "definitely bottle-feeding," and in one case the husband reported breast-feeding and the wife reported "probably bottle-feed."

To sum up: a large majority of both mothers and fathers (but particularly fathers) anticipated breast-feeding. Whether or not the woman was herself breast-fed was strongly associated with her own feeding intentions. In analyses below of actual feeding behavior, husbands' and wives' intentions about feeding will be discussed further.

OTHER IDEAS ABOUT INFANT CARE

Twenty percent of the husbands acknowledged "a lot" of experience with newborns, 7 percent "none," and the remainder something in between. They saw their wives as much more experienced than they were—70 percent thought that their wives knew "all" or "a lot" about infant care. Only one man did not think his wife knew much about it. Actually, 57 percent of the women admitted they had *no* experience at caring for a child under six weeks of age. About 30 percent had had "full-charge" experience with a newborn. Of those with experience, twenty-three were lower-class, thirteen middle-class.

A husband's experience with newborns was significantly related to his interest in the pregnancy ($r = .21$, $p = .05$) and also to when his wife plans to return to work ($r = .27$, $p < .05$)—if he knows a lot about newborns she plans to return to work later. Also, there is some indication that if the husband is knowledgeable, the wife plans to breast-feed longer ($r = .19$, $p = .07$). These observations suggest that prior life experience of some husbands has prepared them in a very real sense for childbirth.

During the second interview the women were asked a number of questions about how rigid or flexible they planned to be in caring for the infant. Of these questions, one—whether the mother intended to follow a rigid feeding schedule, a moderately structured schedule, or a completely infant-determined feeding schedule—turned out to be the most important among several "rigidity-flexibility" items. Twenty-three percent of the women intended a rigid schedule, 32 percent intended a modified schedule, and 45 percent intended to feed by infant needs.

A minority of women (38 percent) planned to have the infant sleep in the same room with them. Fifty-two percent expected the infant to be sleeping through the night *before* the age of two months. Regrettably, husbands were not queried on their expectations for sleeping. Thirty-five percent of women expected to wean the baby before six months, 22 percent between six and nine months, and the remainder planned later weaning. (Many of those who breast-feed may plan to wean from the breast to the bottle, but unfortunately, they were not asked when they thought weaning from the bottle would then occur.) The women's expectations seem rather optimistic.

One of the few striking differences in women's opinions by social class concerned whether women already loved their babies during pregnancy or whether women learn to love their babies after they are born (Appendix B, opinion item 48). A majority of the women in the sample (64 percent) believed women already loved their babies before birth. Of those who disagreed, however, 72 percent were middle-class.

SEXUALITY

The Kinsey reports (1948, 1953) led to recognition by scientists and by the public at large that the range of human sexual behavior is broader than was previously thought. For instance, they found that a large fraction of the male population engages in homosexual behavior at one time or another. That report led to a change in outlook involving frank and open discussion of previously taboo topics, and so paved the way for other, more careful analytic studies like Masters and Johnson's. Publicity given these and similar studies made it acceptable in the present research to inquire about sexuality during pregnancy or after the birth, for respondents saw such inquiries as scientifically legitimate.

An outstanding feature of the women's liberation movement is its emphasis upon sexual activity and sexual pleasure for women, and the prevailing views women now hold about men reflect this. In the Yankelovich survey (1974), for example, the third most important quality women look for in a man (after being a good provider and having strong views about right and wrong), is concern with a woman's sexual satisfaction—78 percent of noncollege and 80 percent of college women express this view. Eighty-four percent of the women in this panel (and 93 percent of the men) believed that women are just as interested in sex as men (Appendix B, opinion item 19).

But feminist concerns aside, sexual activity is important as an indicant of marital closeness and / or satisfaction. If the arrival of an infant not only causes interruption in lovemaking activity but decreases its frequency after the birth, there is a possible threat to overall marital satisfaction. Also, if the birth is such a traumatic event that a woman becomes fearful of another pregnancy, she may avoid sex, which may lead to serious marital problems. This is less likely now than formerly—both because of more dependable contraception and because of the wide availability of abortion—but the possibility certainly exists.

Over the period of a pregnancy and the first few months thereafter, sexual activity often stops for at least a while. Although few solid data are available on sexual activity during pregnancy, such activity usually does not stop completely. Previous data on sexual activity during pregnancy were for the most part obtained by asking people to recollect what they had done in the past— sometimes even several years previously—and the accuracy of memories

about something as emotion-laden as sexual behavior has been questioned. The present research covers sexuality as an ongoing activity, and for this reason it may be more accurate than some previous reports.

Masters and Johnson (1966), the only other workers who asked pregnant respondents about ongoing sexual activity and interest, questioned 111 pregnant women (43 having a first child and 68 women who had had at least one child before) in each third of pregnancy and again after birth. These workers observed loss of interest and concomitant reduction of activity in the first three months, a resurgence of interest and activity in the middle three months, and an even greater loss of interest and reduction of activity in the last three months. Colman and Colman (1971), who agree with Masters and Johnson on the patterning of sexual activity during pregnancy, based their observations on an encounter-type group of pregnant couples followed over time. Landis, Poffenberger, and Poffenberger (1950) and Solberg, Butler, and Wagner (1973) disagree, but since their respondents were interviewed after the birth and asked to recall prepregnancy as well as pregnancy behavior, the reliability of their data is questionable.

The present panel of respondents was asked several questions in each interview pertaining to opinions on sexual matters and sexual practices. Data were secured concerning sexual practices before and after birth. In this survey, there was a decrease in the wife's sexual desire rather early during pregnancy, for 53 percent of the wives reported in the six-month interview that they were less interested in sex than they had been prior to pregnancy. Perhaps more surprising, 29 percent of the wives reported that their husbands "want less sex now" (sixth month). Thirty-six percent of the women felt that their interest in sex was the same as prepregnancy, and 63 percent reported that their husbands' sex drive was the same. As for the remainder, 11 percent of the wives and 7 percent of the husbands wanted more sex in the sixth month of pregnancy than they had previously. Overall, there is some drop in sex drive for both partners, more noticeably the wife.

In the six-month interview, women were also asked to compare their sex drive with their husband's "at the present time." For almost half the couples (46 percent) the husband wanted sexual intercourse more often than the wife; in 7 percent this situation was reversed. When wives were queried about sex drive in their husbands and in themselves, they saw more correspondence ($r = .48, p < .01$) between spouses' sex drive than did husbands asked the same question ($r = .28, p < .01$).

At the first interview (sixth or seventh month of pregnancy), 117 women reported having sexual intercourse a little more often than twice a week on the average. (Three women refused to answer this question.) This figure includes 14 respondents (12 percent) who had not had intercourse at all in the previous two-week period, so if only those couples who were sexually active are counted, the average is about 2.5 times per week. There was a good deal of

variation around this figure, however. Besides the 12 percent noted above who had not had intercourse, another 10 percent reported only one instance in the preceding two-week period. On the other hand, 19 percent of the women reported sexual activity about every other day, and an additional 12 percent even more frequently than that. These findings on frequency of intercourse at this stage of pregnancy are similar to the data of Solberg, Butler, and Wagner (1973) (2.33 per week), although as noted earlier, their data on the patterning of activity over pregnancy do not agree with either Masters and Johnson's findings or the present study.

Respondents in the panel were asked to recall the frequency of intercourse prepregnancy in order to compare rates during pregnancy with those before. Although prepregnancy frequencies may be somewhat unreliable because of errors in recall, the figures may be more accurate than those reported in previous studies (except Masters and Johnson) because the women in this sample had to remember back only six or seven months, and no traumatic intervening event (childbirth) had yet occurred. Prepregnancy, the wives reported intercourse on an average of 3.5 times per week. None recalled having no intercourse in any two-week period, but 3 percent estimated an average of only once per two weeks. Twenty-five percent thought that they had had intercourse approximately every other day, and 34 percent reported more frequent sexual activity than every other day. (Solberg, Butler, and Wagner's prepregnancy frequency [1973] is lower [3.11 per week], but their sample included women who had had several children.)

Respondents were not asked to estimate frequency of intercourse for the first three months of pregnancy, so it is not possible to address directly the question of whether sexual activity diminished in the first three months and then increased in the middle three months, as Masters and Johnson found in their sample, or whether desire declined steadily over the entire nine months, as other work suggests. However, women's lack of sexual desire was inquired about because the women were asked in both interviews to recall whether they had felt less interest in sex "often," "occasionally," or "never" during the first three months of pregnancy and then were asked the same question for the present. Answers are shown below:

	Often	Occasionally	Never
1st trimester	21%	34%	45%
2nd trimester	15%	38%	47%
3rd trimester	26%	40%	33%

The trend in the first six months is in the direction of Masters and Johnson's findings. The trend in the last three months is larger and in the direction reported in all research on sexuality during pregnancy.

WHEN SEXUAL ACTIVITIES STOP

At the time of the first interview the women were asked when they thought they would have to stop sexual activity. Twenty-three percent responded that they did not plan to stop and 26 percent planned to continue up to, or partway through, the ninth month. At the other extreme, 11 percent had already stopped or thought they would very soon. In the second interview (early ninth month) women were again asked about stopping or continuing, and results are shown in table 3.5. Then more women were continuing (33 percent) than had planned to earlier. Another 22 percent had continued into the ninth month before stopping. Only 4 percent recalled actually having stopped in the sixth month or before, although in the six-month interview 11 percent reported that they had stopped by then or would stop soon.

Solberg, Butler, and Wagner (1973) report similar findings. Over 48 percent of their sample reported abstaining from coitus sometime in the ninth month, leaving about 52 percent who evidently did not. In the present sample, when the 10 percent who had not stopped by the time of the nine-month interview but who had planned to are added to the 33 percent who planned to continue, there are 43 percent who "might continue" (or an abstention rate of 57 percent).

Time of stopping was related to when respondents began to find intercourse uncomfortable or painful. At the nine-month interview, 24 percent of the women reported pain. Since this figure includes only those who were still continuing in the ninth month, however, the symptom could be more widespread. Only very small numbers (1 percent to 5 percent) had reported this symptom during the first six months of pregnancy.

For women who said they had stopped intercourse by the nine-month interview, a further question was asked about their physicians' recommendation concerning sexual activity. Among this group, 39 percent of the women reported their physicians had not mentioned anything at all about the matter.

TABLE 3.5. When couples stopped sexual activity
(9th-month interview; percentages)

	Wives[a] (N = 113)	Husbands (N = 60)
Before 3rd trimester	4	9
During 7th month	10	7
During 8th month	32	40
During 9th month (or planning to)	22	25
Not stopping	33	20
Average	Late in eighth month	Mid-eighth month

[a] One respondent refused to answer, and six respondents did not have a nine-month interview because they delivered early.

Another 22 percent of the women reported their physicians said that they did *not* have to stop intercourse. All but 3 percent of the remainder (39 percent) reported that physicians recommended stopping in the eighth or ninth month. This is certainly a change from Masters and Johnson's (1966) findings—78 percent of their respondents expecting a first baby were told that they had to stop in the ninth month or earlier.

There is a strong relationship between the women's attitude toward intercourse in the ninth month and when it was discontinued ($r = .80, p < .01$). Also, and not surprisingly, reports of pain or discomfort (including awkwardness) are related to a negative attitude (correlations range from .23 to .33, depending on the exact question asked).

The women's attitudes toward sexual activity in the ninth month were coded from a long-answer question dealing with whether the couple was still ''able'' to have intercourse, why or why not, and how they felt about stopping or continuing. Thus, one woman could have stopped because her doctor said she had to, or because her husband had lost interest even though she still had a positive attitude herself; another woman, who was continuing, could be rated as negative because she obviously was not enjoying it and longed to be able to stop. Twenty-three percent of the women felt *very* negative (all of these had already stopped). An additional 33 percent were mildly negative (two-thirds of these women had stopped). Forty percent were mildly positive (7 percent of these women had stopped regretfully; the rest were continuing). Four percent were still really enjoying sexual activity.

Considering the negative recommendations made by most obstetricians and pregnancy manuals until very recently, the rate of sexual activity during pregnancy observed in this sample is noteworthy. It is no doubt attributable to the research of Masters and Johnson—which questioned whether increased infection rates, damage to the fetus, or premature birth were caused by sexual activity—and to the swift dissemination to both the medical profession and lay persons of their findings to the contrary.

The point at which intercourse stops is of interest in itself, but it may be more important for the marital relationship whether the decision is mutual. If the husband wishes to continue but the wife refuses, or if the wife would welcome more sexual activity than the husband (both these situations were reported spontaneously by many individuals in the sample), tensions and resentments could build up that might affect the future of the marital relationship.

The data point to many reasons for continuing or discontinuing sexual activity during pregnancy. Definite but small relationships emerged between when the wife reported the couple would stop sex and the incidence of symptoms during pregnancy (r-value below .30). Also, women who worried about childbirth reported they planned to stop sooner ($r = .20$). More direct causes for stopping have already been mentioned in the earlier part of this chapter. One would expect, first, that pain and / or discomfort would predict when

sexual relations would be discontinued; second, that a positive or negative attitude toward sexual activity, however derived, would affect sex behavior; and third, that recommendation by the obstetrician might be a factor.

In *every* instance, a woman's reported negative attitude toward sexual activity late in pregnancy was significantly related to the timing of sexual abstinence. Discomfort during sex could lead to a negative attitude, but did not always do so. Pain or discomfort in themselves, apart from attitude, had very little bearing on when couples discontinued sexual activity. If the woman's physician expressed an opinion, this apparently contributed to stopping sexual activity but had little effect on women's attitudes.

HUSBANDS' REPORTS ON THEIR SEXUALITY

Husbands were asked to report whether their own and their spouses' sex drive was more, the same, or less than prepregnancy. There is a significant but small tendency for husbands to see the same level of sex drive in themselves and their spouses ($r = .28$, $p < .05$). That is, if they reported their own sex drive had increased, they tended to report that their wife's sex drive had also increased. There is only a small relation between the frequency of intercourse as reported by the husband in the ninth month and his level of sex drive ($r = .24$, $p = .03$). The overall validity of both spouse's answers to sex-related questions is borne out by the good agreement between husbands' and wives' answers to questions on sex drive ($r = .56$, $p < .01$).

Husbands reported at the ninth month an average frequency of intercourse in the preceding two-week period of about once per week. However, twenty-seven of them (45 percent) reported that there had been no sexual intercourse in the past two weeks, so the average frequency for those sexually active was close to twice a week. This is very similar to what wives reported at the same point in time. When asked to recall frequency prepregnancy, the men estimated an average of a little over three times a week. This is not much less than what wives recalled, even though the husbands had to think back a full nine months by the time they were asked this question.

Over three-fifths of the husbands reported in the nine-month interview that their sex drive equalled or exceeded their sex drive before the pregnancy. Women in their nine-month interview were not asked about their husbands' sex drive, but at the time of the first interview (sixth month), 29 percent reported that their husbands wanted less sex than before pregnancy. There is also agreement in couples' perception of wife's sex drive. At the six-month interview, 53 percent of the wives reported they wanted less sex than prior to pregnancy. Forty-five percent of the husbands (in the ninth month) reported that wives wanted less sex than formerly. Altogether, reports of husbands and wives with respect to sexual desires and frequency agree rather well.

To a question on relative sex drive, 40 percent of husbands reported wanting more sex than their wives. Another 20 percent reported that their wives wanted sex more often than they themselves did. (Wives at the six-month

interview reported that 46 percent of husbands wanted more sex than they did, but only 7 percent of wives acknowledged a greater sex drive than their husband's.) This divergence in findings may be an artifact of the particular set of sixty husbands who agreed to be interviewed—those more willing being those more open in acknowledging their own and their wives' sexual preferences.

Again, by comparing responses for specific pairs of spouses, some additional observations are possible. Only three men perceived their own sex drive as having risen, but seven perceived their wives' drive as being greater than formerly. There are two cases, in fact, where the husband reported his drive had decreased but his wife's drive had increased. *All* seven women whose husbands reported an increase in wife's sex drive are women who planned to breast-feed. Of the twelve women who planned to bottle-feed and whose husbands consented to be interviewed, the majority (seven) were reported by their husbands to have less sex drive than prepregnancy. This may be a further indication of differences between biologically and socially feminine women.

There is strong agreement between husbands' and wives' reports of sexual frequency prior to pregnancy—both report close to every other day. Reports of plans for stopping sex (those who had not stopped were asked when they planned to stop) were less similar between husbands and wives—33 percent of wives and 20 percent of husbands reported they would continue indefinitely or would stop only when labor began.

As might be expected, those husbands reporting the highest rates of sexual activity in the ninth month were those planning to stop very late in pregnancy or not at all ($r = .48$, $p < .01$). There is a significant but smaller relation between husbands' reports about frequency of sexual activity in the ninth month and frequency reported prior to pregnancy ($r = .30$, $p < .01$).

When asked about resuming sexual activity, all sixty husbands planned to resume by the time the baby was two months old, and 37 percent planned to resume before the wife had her six-week checkup. Wives all expected to resume sexual activity when the baby was six weeks old, the typical time when the obstetrician schedules the mother's first physical checkup after birth. Physicians frequently counsel patients not to resume sexual activity until after this checkup.

Of the sixty husbands interviewed, almost one-third (31.7 percent)[3] said they had felt tempted to be unfaithful to their wives during this pregnancy, but only one admitted to having been unfaithful. This kind of question was not asked of wives, although they were asked about whether they ever worried about their husband's being unfaithful. Only 8 percent even occasionally felt worried about unfaithfulness, and most laughed and said "Never" with great conviction.

[3]This was a different question from the "worry" question reported in table 3.1.

THE COURSE OF PREGNANCY IN PERSPECTIVE

The key findings: This sample of women enjoyed good health during pregnancy and rejected the sick role. Those who had the most symptoms were also those who were the most anxious, although whether symptoms led to anxiety or the reverse is unclear. Wives worried relatively little, and their worst worries centered on weight gain. Given the high proportion of planned pregnancies and the commitment of these women to modern ideas about sex roles, it is surprising that so many were decidedly negative about being in the pregnant state. This negativism, furthermore, does not seem to stem from actual problems related to pregnancy. It could be a hangover from views of women's bodily functions that prevailed earlier in the century, or perhaps it is just a consequence of the fact that pregnancy interferes with normal routines. Being awakened by a fetal movement in the night, for example, is a nuisance. There is a contrast between women's views of their public and private sex roles, because most of these women were committed to work during pregnancy (public role), but often found the state of being pregnant less than enjoyable (private role). They seemed to accept a more modern sex role for their social life, but many were influenced by a more traditional sex role in their feelings about their biological functions. In an extensive study of part of this sample, a negative relation was found between the biological and social aspects of femininity (Doering 1975).

Although most couples planned their pregnancies, those who did not completely plan them seemed to adjust rapidly to the fact. Husbands seemed especially resilient on this score. (This may be a consequence of the ease and availability of abortion now; persons who were *really* negative may have terminated the pregnancy and thus have automatically been excluded from this sample.)

Preparation level was related to wife's educational level, to the quality of the couple's communication, and to the woman's desire for an active role in childbirth and child care, but to little else. Exploration of the data suggests that what induces women to seek preparation may not be the same from one religious group to another, but patterns could not be clearly traced out in this sample.

There were many matters relating to pregnancy and childbirth upon which couples in this sample were poorly informed or were misinformed, and many of their ideas about childbirth and parenting were overly optimistic. The expectant partners had exaggerated ideas about one another's capabilities with newborns, and they underestimated the probable duration of labor.

Data on sexual activity for this set of expectant couples agree remarkably well with reports of others. The reader should note, however, that in the present research sexuality can be studied in a sample of persons who have volunteered for a research project directed mainly at *other* topics. For this reason the reports on activity may be particularly valid, because the respon-

dents are not self-selected on willingness to volunteer sex-related information. In many surveys of sexual activity, the respondents who participate are suspect because of their willingness, or even eagerness, to give information on taboo items. Such eagerness is often interpreted to mean that respondents could be unusual people in terms of sex behavior.

4 | THE BIRTH EVENT AND THE EARLY POSTPARTUM PERIOD

This chapter describes couples' experiences during the birth event and the early postpartum period. Emphasis is placed on how preparation during pregnancy may have affected the couples' reactions in childbirth and events of the early postpartum period.

As would be expected, there was more stress at birth for some couples than for others. Of the 120 women in the sample, 20 (16.7 percent) experienced a Cesarean delivery, only one of which was definitely planned in advance. For the twenty couples whose child was delivered surgically and the fourteen couples who experienced a variety of other serious complications at birth, stress associated with the birth event was naturally greater and the experience qualitatively different than for couples whose child was born without serious problems. Other kinds of stress also occurred, such as a baby being born rather long after the due date or a lack of help at home after birth. These differences in stress will be taken into account whenever possible in considering the couples' reactions to childbirth and their early parenting.

There are many more surgical deliveries now than formerly (Patterson, Mulliniks, and Schreier, 1967). However, the full explanation for the skyrocketing rate of surgical delivery in the 1970s is not entirely clear. It apparently is *not* a consequence of population shifts. Although more teenagers, especially those who belong to minority groups, and more women in their thirties are now giving birth to a first child than was true in the 1960s, and such women are at greater risk of surgical delivery, Gibbons (1976) in a careful regression analysis was unable to link race, age, or any of a number of other demographic variables to recent changes in rates of Cesarean delivery for women having a first child in Baltimore. Whatever the causes, however, a surgical delivery now often accompanies the transition to parenthood, and it is one form of stress requiring careful consideration in the panel of couples taking part in this study.

The severity of complications at birth was almost exactly equivalent for the two social-class groups. The division in terms of Cesarean delivery was

86

exactly even—ten women in each group experienced a surgical delivery. Other complications (artificial rupturing of membranes, artificial stimulation of labor, or any of a number of other problems, including fetal distress) were very similar for the two class groups, especially complications that could be classed as serious.

The number of problems mentioned ("When you look back over your whole labor and delivery, what was the most upsetting thing about it?... What else?... What else?") was a little larger for lower-class mothers, but not significantly so—an average of 2.35 problems vs. 2.05 problems for middle-class women. (See table 4.1) (The averages may distort

TABLE 4.1. Comparison of mothers' birth experience by social class

	Middle class			Lower class			
	N	Mean	SD	N	Mean	SD	t-value[a]
Woman's birth experience[b] (BESCL)	58	17.98	5.46	59	18.56	6.14	0.54
Sum up whole childbirth experience 4 = neutral 5 = slightly positive	60	4.75	1.87	60	4.45	2.02	0.84
Level of awareness at birth 3 = gas or sedation, no conduction 4 = conduction only, mind clear	60	3.70	1.99	60	4.08	2.09	1.03
Worst pain, first stage of labor 3 = moderate 4 = bad	57	3.50	0.97	60	3.50	0.93	0.00
Worst pain, second stage of labor 2 = slight 3 = moderate	49	2.65	1.47	50	3.04	1.60	1.25
Delivery time vs. due date 4 = within one week of due date	60	4.03	1.36	60	4.08	1.27	0.21
Number of childbirth problems mentioned (What was most upsetting about labor and delivery?... What else?... What else?)	59	2.05	1.25	60	2.35	1.35	1.25
Length of postpartum depression 4 = 3 to 6 hrs. 5 = 6 to 12 hrs.	44	4.36	2.43	48	4.46	2.55	0.18
Seriousness of postpartum depression 1 = momentary or mild 2 = medium	60	1.60	1.06	60	1.70	0.85	0.57

[a] Two-tailed.
[b] This scale is the sum of scores on five items measuring the quality of a woman's birth experience. Higher scores indicate more positive birth experience. See Appendix C for full explanation.

the picture a little, for sixteen lower-class women mentioned four or more problems and only five middle-class women mentioned that many.) There were no significant differences between classes on level of awareness at birth, the rating of pain in either the first or second stages of labor, whether or not the infant arrived early or late, and in either the length or the seriousness of postpartum depression. Furthermore, there was no difference by class in how much babies were reported to cry or in how rested the mother felt when questioned in the interview three weeks after birth—almost equal percentages (78 percent and 77 percent) were "more tired than normal."

All these facts lead to the conclusion that, insofar as information is available, the physical stress of delivery and the early postpartum period as experienced by these mothers was equivalent by class.

THE BABY'S SEX

Of the 120 women in the study, 63 gave birth to boys and 57 gave birth to girls, including one pair of twin girls. (Two stillbirths occurred before the ninth month, and these women were not included in the final sample of 120 couples.)

Even though approximately half of the mothers produced a baby whose sex was opposite to their earlier-expressed preference, the vast majority were neutral or mildly pleased about the baby's sex when questioned after the birth. Only 12 percent of the women expressed disappointment about the baby's sex, and as many mothers of sons were disappointed as mothers of daughters. Twenty-nine percent of the mothers said they "didn't care" about the sex of their baby. The remainder (59 percent) were pleased or overjoyed about the baby's sex. Nevertheless fifteen mothers of sons, compared to five mothers of daughters, were "overjoyed," indicating a slight bias of mothers in favor of boys.

The fathers, however, had keener feelings about the sex of their infants. The men's preference for boy babies was strong in the nine-month interview. At that time, 71 percent of the men wanted a boy, 13 percent wanted a girl, and 16 percent did not care. (Father preference for boys agrees with Liebenberg's [1973] finding.) Surprisingly, of the eight men who expressed preference for a daughter, seven were lower class.

Of fathers expressing disappointment in their baby's sex, all but one were fathers of girls. Only one father of a boy was disappointed, compared to eight fathers of girls. By contrast six fathers of boys were "overjoyed," while only one father of a girl was "overjoyed." However, the majority of fathers, like mothers, was either neutral or pleased. All in all, both parents were somewhat more enthusiastic about having a boy, but men were actually disappointed with a girl, while women were not.

THE BIRTH EVENT

TIME OF BIRTH

Seventeen percent of the infants were born between midnight and 6 A.M., 22 percent between 6 A.M. and noon, 35 percent between noon and 6 P.M., and 27 percent between 6 P.M. and midnight. Previous research shows that, when minimal interference in the labor process occurs, babies are born fairly randomly around the clock. For example, Eastman and Russell (1970) report the respective percentages for quarters of the day as 28 percent, 26 percent, 22 percent, and 24 percent[1]; while Guttmacher (1950) found 28 percent, 27 percent, 23 percent and 23 percent.[2]

Thirteen percent of women in this sample had labor induced from the beginning, and another 20 percent were given stimulants for a labor already in progress.[3] Obviously, induction could cause data on time of birth to be distorted.

The babies ranged in size from two pounds and ten ounces (2½ months premature) to nine pounds and eight ounces, the average being 6.85 pounds.

Most babies (78 percent) arrived within two weeks in either direction of the calculated due date. Seven babies were born more than three weeks before the estimated date of confinement, and six of the seven mothers missed the nine-month interview because of these early arrivals. An additional five babies arrived two to three weeks ahead of the due date. Eight babies arrived two to three weeks past the due date, and six others were more than three weeks overdue.

There was a weak association between whether or not the baby was overdue and the seriousness of the mother's postpartum depression ($r = .18$, $p < .05$). There was also a weak relation between the baby's arriving on time and whether the woman saw the baby as contributing to marital happiness ($r = .18$, $p < .05$, for women delivered vaginally). When asked to "sum up the whole birth experience," the fourteen women whose babies were two or more weeks late expressed significantly less positive views than other mothers (an average of 4.36, compared to an average of 4.63, for all other mothers on a 7-point scale where 4.00 is neutral and 7.00 is highly positive). The twelve women whose babies arrived two or more weeks early summed up delivery very positively, rating it at 5.00.

[1]Eastman and Russell quote DeLee's report on 1,000 confinements at Chicago Lying-In Hospital, no dates given, probably pre-1950.

[2]Guttmacher reports on Myers's analysis of 134,335 births occurring between 1913 and 1935 in Nuremberg, Germany.

[3]It is estimated that at least 10 percent of all births in the United States are induced with oxytocin (Corea, 1977:98). Rindfuss and Ladinsky (1976) suggest that induction may often be undertaken for the convenience of the obstetrician. Recently the FDA has made new labeling requirements for oxytocic drugs, barring them for elective induction of labor and placing strong controls with warnings on their use in labor under other circumstances.

90   THE FIRST BIRTH

When asked how they felt about their babies when they first saw them, however, those mothers who had waited longer rated the experience slightly more positively (3.79 vs. 3.38 on a 6-point scale where 3.00 is neutral). Cognitive dissonance theorists would interpret these findings as showing that the value placed on the baby is related to the difficulty encountered in producing it—people tend to value things more highly when they have to work hard for them.

Whether a baby was born early or late could be considered a chance event, yet it apparently had some effect on the mother's reaction to the birth event *and* to the infant.

CONDUCT OF LABOR AND DELIVERY

Women reported experiencing a variety of obstetrical procedures in addition to the use of labor-stimulating drugs. Twenty-eight percent had their membranes ruptured early in labor, and another 18 percent were subjected to this procedure later. For those women who were asked about fetal monitoring,[4] 47 percent reported having been monitored, and 53 percent said that they were not. Except for women who experienced a Cesarean delivery (and so were not candidates for episiotomy), all but 6 percent had episiotomies. Use of forceps was common—64 percent of the women who were delivered vaginally were sure forceps were used, and another 4 percent thought so. Only 32 percent pushed out their own babies.

Since a few women were not certain exactly what procedures were carried out, data on forceps, induction, and the like are not definitive and will not be analyzed in detail. Nevertheless these interview data do indicate that various kinds of obstetrical procedures are common even for women delivered vaginally.

The medications used during labor and delivery are listed in table 4.2. These data are based entirely on patient reports and must be evaluated with this in mind. However, even when respondents were not clear on drug names, uses, or dosage, enough information was usually elicited to determine whether or not drugs were used, and an educated guess about type and dosage could often be made. *Only 7 percent of the women reported being given no drugs at all.* Most women received two or three types of drugs (e.g., Demerol and a sedative in mid-labor and then an epidural at 6 cm., renewed hourly.)

The data in the present study are not analyzed to point up possible drug effects on infants, because patients' reports on drugs could not be checked against hospital records. The reader should be aware, however, that even small amounts of *local* anesthesia lead to changes in infants, and drug risks to neonates are extensively documented (Borgstedt and Rosen 1968; Bowes et

[4]Fetal monitoring was still fairly unusual when this study was begun (September 1973), but use of monitors increased rapidly over the time that the research covers. Since the question was not asked early in the study, only 63 percent of the women reported on fetal monitoring.

TABLE 4.2. Drugs given to women during labor and delivery (patients' reports)

Type of drug[a] or form of anesthesia	Percent[b]
Sleeping pills (barbiturates)	4
Sedatives and / or tranquilizers	50
Demerol	58
Paracervical block	4
Epidural or caudal	23
Spinal	8
Saddle block (low spinal)	39
Whiffs of gas	4
General anesthesia[c]	8
Pudendal block	18
Local infiltration	6
No drugs	7

[a] Scopolamine is not listed, because the women were unaware of receiving it. This does not mean that the drug was not used.

[b] Respondents were classified as receiving a drug if they received any of the drug, whether the dose was large or small and whether they received one dose or many.

[c] Although only 8 percent of the women were unconscious at birth due to general anesthesia, many others were unconscious at various times during labor or delivery because they were given a combination dose (a sedative or tranquilizer plus Demerol) strong enough to put them to sleep.

al. 1970; Brackbill et al. 1974; Brazelton 1961, 1970; Cohen and Olson 1970; James 1960; Kron, Stein, and Goddard 1966; Rosefsky and Petersiel 1968; Scanlon et al. 1974; Shnider and Way 1968; Sinclair et al. 1965; Standley et al. 1974). Also, although use of barbiturates has supposedly been abandoned because of the well-documented depressing action of this drug on neonatal respiration (see, e.g., Macfarlane 1977:383), at least 4 percent of the women in this sample apparently received barbiturates. (The FDA still has no requirements that obstetrical drugs be proved safe for the fetus, although more warnings are being considered.)

Table 4.3 sums up women's preferences concerning medication and their actual experience at the birth. Since experience for women delivered vaginally and women delivered surgically is so different, the table has separate parts for each group.

Fifty of the hundred mothers who were delivered vaginally wanted to be "awake and feeling everything" at the moment of the birth. Only 54 percent of them achieved this experience. Another forty-three of these mothers wanted to be "awake but numb" at that moment; 48 percent of them were actually awake and numb. Altogether, twenty-nine women undergoing vaginal

TABLE 4.3. Awareness desired and level of awareness achieved at birth

	Desired awareness					
	Asleep		Awake but numb		Awake and feeling everything	
Awareness level[a]	N	%	N	%	N	%
Women delivered vaginally *(N = 100)*						
1 = unconscious (asleep)	0	0	2	5	0	0
2, 3 = confused and numb	4	57	20	47	5	10
4 = awake but numb	2	29	16	37	15	30
5 = whiffs of gas	0	0	1	2	3	6
6, 7, 8 = awake and feeling everything	1	14	4	9	27	54
Women with surgical delivery *(N = 20)*						
1 = unconscious (asleep)	1	50	7	64	2	29
2, 3 = confused and numb	0	0	3	27	3	42
4 = awake but numb	1	50	1	9	2	29

[a] The method by which the woman's level of awareness (AWARE) at the moment of the birth was coded is described in Appendix C.

delivery were "confused and numb," something no one wanted. The extensive use of drugs for these Maryland women (93 percent of those with vaginal deliveries were given some kind of medication) should be compared with rates of 5 percent in Holland and 12 percent in Sweden (Macfarlane 1977:40).

The average length of labor for women in this sample was within the range usually cited: 12 to 16 hours for the first stage, and 1.0 to 1.5 hours for the second stage. In this sample, however, the average length of labor and the variability in length of labor were significantly different for women admitted to the hospital in the daytime (8:00 A.M. to 7:59 P.M.) and for those admitted during the night (8:00 P.M. to 7:59 A.M.). This is an observation that, to the authors' knowledge, has not previously been reported. Those admitted in the night hours had significantly longer labors (18.18 hours vs. 13.78 hours), and the length of labor was significantly more variable for them also. There might be less variation in length of labor for day-admitted patients, however, because patients admitted for elective induction are always scheduled for the daylight hours. Also, labor stimulants are given to day-admitted patients more often (perhaps because they are supervised more closely).

There was a negative but not significant relation between total length of labor and women's view of their childbirth experience for women who were delivered vaginally. Although other workers have observed longer labor times for women with higher anxiety scores (Davids and DeVault 1962), there was

no relation in this sample between a woman's anxiety score and the length of her labor. The frequent use of labor stimulants in the present sample could certainly mask such a relationship, however, and the many differences between this study and others prevent a straightforward comparison across studies of the relation between anxiety and length of labor.

Forty-one of the women were never left alone during labor or delivery. At the other extreme, twenty-two (18 percent) were left alone for periods ranging from one and one-half hours to eight hours or more. On the average, women were left alone about fifty minutes, but of course this average is markedly affected by the few women who were left alone for long periods. The doctor was present in the room 28 percent of the time on the average. All doctors were in the hospital after the patient was admitted, except for five unable to get there before the baby arrived. Fifty percent of the women had a nurse with them in the same room at least half the time.

PAIN

Twenty-nine percent of the sample reported that childbirth was much more painful than they had expected it to be, but 22 percent found it much less painful than expected. On the average, birth was a little more painful than the women had expected.

The women were asked to describe the *worst* pain they felt at any point in the first stage of labor and then at any point in the second stage. Thus pain described as "terrible" could have lasted for only one or two contractions, and in many cases it did. Four percent reported no pain at all in the first stage of labor, whereas 9 percent felt terrible pain or agony at some point during this time. Almost half (49 percent) said that, at the worst, they felt "bad" pain in the first stage. Overall, first-stage pain at its worst averaged midway between "moderate" and "bad." Thirty percent found the second stage painless, while 19 percent said that, at the worst point, they felt pain to the point of defining it as agony. But relatively fewer (20 percent) reported "bad" pain in the second stage as compared with the first. The average report was between "slight" and "moderate."

Another assessment of pain was derived by asking women what point in the whole experience was the *most painful* of all. Answers to this question suggest that transition—the time when the cervix is approaching full dilation (7-10 cm.)—is *the* most painful time (38 percent reported this), while the actual birth of the head is least likely to be the acme of pain (8 percent). Four percent of the women reported no pain at any time. Another 12 percent found that—rather than anything to do with the birth process per se—the insertion of intravenous needles, fundal pressure, and other ancillary procedures were the most painful. These women's reports do not agree with some obstetrical texts—with Greenhill and Friedman (1974:197), for example—who report the greatest anguish when the head emerges.

One might anticipate that woman who received conduction anesthesia (epidurals, caudals, spinals including saddle blocks) would report the least pain, and that women who had only local anesthesia or no drugs would suffer the greatest pain. Actually the relation is complex, but those who were more fully conscious reported less pain in the second stage. (See table 4.4.) In the group of twenty-nine women who were both sedated and given conduction anesthesia, 62 percent reported bad or terrible pain, and 35 percent reported no pain or slight pain. Thirty-three women received conduction anesthesia only (minds clear), and 45 percent of them felt bad or terrible pain, while 42 percent were relatively painfree. Of the thirty-two women who were awake and feeling everything, only 19 percent (six women) suffered bad or terrible pain, while 56 percent reported no pain or slight pain. There is thus a relationship for the women in this sample between the worst pain experienced in the second stage and the amount of medication given—those who received the least medication reported the least pain.

The issue is not a simple one, however, because those reporting the greatest pain may have been given more medication in an effort to counteract the pain, and / or the timing of the medication may have been poor. Another approach to this complex question is to look at the relation between amount of medication and women's experiences, adjusting for differences in pain. *Controlling for pain,* the correlation is large between negative experiences and amount of medication (partial correlation of .411 for physical feelings and .595 for emotions). This analysis casts doubt on the effectiveness of anesthetics for the women in this sample.

TABLE 4.4. Interaction of drugs with pain in second stage

	Awareness at birth[a,b]					
	2, 3 Semi-conscious		4 Awake but numb		6, 7, 8 Awake and feeling everything	
Pain in second stage	N	%	N	%	N	%
1 = none	8	28	13	39	9	28
2 = slight	2	7	1	3	9	28
3 = moderate	1	3	4	12	8	25
4 = bad	10	34	9	27	1	3
5 = terrible (agony)	8	28	6	18	5	16
Average pain	3.28		2.82		2.50	

NOTE: Data are for vaginal deliveries only.
[a] The method by which the woman's level of awareness (AWARE) at the moment of birth was coded is described in Appendix C.
[b] Two cases were unconscious (category 1). One reported "terrible pain" before she went to sleep, the other "no pain." Four women received "whiffs of gas" (category 5). Of these, three reported "slight pain" and one "moderate pain."

What about expectation of pain beforehand in relation to pain experienced? Rather surprisingly, and contrary to some previous reports (Kapp, Hornstein, and Graham, 1963; Kelly 1962; Newton 1970; Robertson 1946; Zuckerman et al. 1963), when women's reports of pain are tallied against their expectations for first stage and (separately) for second stage pain ascertained before the birth, there is no relationship between the pain they expected and the pain they experienced. Levy and McGee (1975) report a similar finding. There is a relationship between women's total worry scores and their reports of pain in the second stage ($r = .31$, $p < .01$), however, so the women who are more anxious (have more worries) do find the delivery more painful. There was no correlation between worry scores and the duration of either stage of labor.

Husbands' worry scores did not turn out to be associated with women's reported pain. Women might be affected by their spouses' frame of mind; those with husbands who were anxious might "catch" his anxiety. Actually, Grossman (1978) observed that husbands' anxiety scores were good predictors of wives' experiences—the more anxious the husband, the poorer the wife's experience. In fact, this was the main way the husbands' outlook seemed to affect wives in that study. In the present research, however, wives' "total number of worries" was the only link between anxiety and pain, although a diligent search was made to uncover relationships between worry or anxiety and pain.

The findings concerning pain and level of awareness can perhaps be best explained in terms of the strong relationship between level of preparation prior to birth and consciousness at birth. In reading table 4.4, it is important to note that the women who were "awake and feeling everything" were not all equally well-prepared. Of the six women who felt "bad" or "terrible" pain in the second stage, only one had had Lamaze training (i.e., had learned how to push properly[5]), and her baby was born in an unusual position. *All* women who were fully conscious, and who reported "no" or "slight" pain in second stage, were Lamaze-trained. (Klopfer, Cogan, and Henneborn [1975] reported that in highly prepared women use of medication was not associated with pain relief in the second stage.) There were significant, although modest, relationships between preparation and less pain in both the first stage ($r = .22$) and the second stage ($r = .29$).

The birth experience altered some women's opinions about pain in labor. Before birth, 50 percent of the women thought that "nature did not intend childbirth to be a painful experience" (Appendix B, opinion item 38), but after experiencing birth themselves, only 42 percent held that opinion. In the ninth month, 94 percent of the women said that "labor pains are not as bad as some women say they are" (opinion item 32), but afterward fewer (74 percent) held that opinion.

[5]Women who had learned to push correctly and to simultaneously relax the muscles around the birth canal reported that the moment of birth feels good, not painful. Some women even liken the sensation to that of a tremendous orgasm (Kitzinger 1972; Masters and Johnson 1966; Newton 1973). Women who tighten those muscles, while pushing hard, report excruciating pain.

WIVES' FEELINGS ABOUT THE BIRTH

The women were all asked, "How did you feel?" at the moment of birth or during their first conscious moment thereafter. If a woman answered by describing her physical feelings, she was subsequently asked about emotions, and vice versa. Emotionally, 30 percent felt negative. Examples of very negative feelings are the following responses: "Very disappointed, just not *caring;* as if I had been dying," and "Pain—the pain just blocked everything; I was so scared." Mildly positive women said things like: "Relieved and happy" or "kind of excited and kind of unbelieving, you know," without any enthusiasm showing. Women who were scored as "ecstatic" or as having a "peak experience"—of whom there were 14 percent—gave such responses as:

Oh—ah! Glorious! Fantastically excited! We were crying, my husband and I were crying and laughing and yelling, "It's a girl!" and I was kissing him and yelling—the feeling is—I don't think I've ever been happier. It's—you're so proud, you're so excited, you're—it's impossible to—put the emotion into words—none of the words I'm saying come anywhere near—the overwhelming emotion of it—

I kept yelling to my husband: "Get the camera! Get the camera!" [How did you feel?] Really ecstatic. I felt really great. I was just so happy. I was ready to get up and call everybody. It was really great. I was just sitting there all smiles.

As for physical feelings right at the moment of birth, almost half (47 percent) of the women said they felt "somewhat bad" or "awful." Examples of responses rated "awful" are as follows: "Lousy. I was throwing up and had double vision. I was looking at my husband and he was a big blur." Answers such as "So totally exhausted—just tired" and "Empty and relieved; weak and dizzy; oh, I was shaking like crazy" were rated "somewhat bad." Neutral was exactly that: "Nothing; I felt nothing," "Nothing hurt," etc. and 18 percent were in this category. Answers such as "fine" and "okay" and "I wasn't tired at all" were rated as "good," and 32 percent of the women felt "good" or even "wonderful," with responses such as: "I felt great; I felt like I could run around the block" and "I felt—fantastic, you know? Like I could get up and run the 100-yard dash."

There appears to be an association between how the women felt, both emotionally and physically, at the moment of birth and the amount of medication they had been given. Table 4.5 suggests that the more medication a woman had received, the worse she felt both emotionally and physically. Since the use of drugs is often justified on the basis of improving women's birth experience, the data of Table 4.5 and the data on pain in labor discussed in the preceding section suggest that this assumption should be seriously reexamined. Later, an explicit model will be developed to explain how a woman's level of awareness may contribute to her birth experience (see table 4.10).

TABLE 4.5. Association between drugs and feelings at delivery

	Awareness level at birth[a,b]							
	1 Unconscious		2, 3 Semi-conscious		4 Awake but numb		6, 7, 8 Awake and feeling everything	
	N	%	N	%	N	%	N	%
Emotions at delivery								
1 = very negative	3	25	1	3	0	0	0	0
2 = negative	5	42	17	49	7	19	3	9
3 = neutral	1	8	3	9	1	3	2	6
4 = mild positive	3	25	12	34	16	43	3	9
5 = solid positive	0	0	2	6	11	30	9	28
6 = peak experience	0	0	0	0	2	5	15	47
Felt physically at delivery								
1 = awful	2	17	2	6	0	0	1	3
2 = bad	9	75	18	51	16	42	8	25
3 = nothing	1	8	10	29	8	22	2	6
4 = okay, good	0	0	5	14	12	33	13	41
5 = great	0	0	0	0	1	3	8	25

[a] The method by which the woman's level of awareness (AWARE) at the moment of birth was coded is described in Appendix C.
[b] Only four cases were in category 5, "Whiffs of gas," and they rated as follows: for "emotions at delivery," one was rated 4 and three were 5; for "felt physically at delivery," one felt "2," two felt "4," and one felt "5."

As would be expected, when asked to sum up the whole birth experience, women who experienced a surgical delivery were much more negative in their average rating: 2.60 (on a scale from 1, "very negative," to 7, "very positive," with 4 "neutral"). By contrast, women who were delivered vaginally rated the whole childbirth experience at 5.00—slightly positive.

HUSBANDS' PARTICIPATION FROM THE WIVES' VIEWPOINT

It is now becoming more and more common for husbands to stay with their wives during labor and delivery, and the present sample reflects this. Eighty-four percent of the husbands were present during labor and almost all (80 percent out of the 84 percent) were reported by their wives to have helped in some way. Sixty-six percent of husbands were present in delivery. It is not as easy for husbands to help in delivery, because if the wife has been given conduction anesthesia, the physician tends to deliver the baby, usually with forceps. Nevertheless, fathers helped "just by being there," and 8 percent managed "to help a lot" during delivery. One father delivered his own baby, and needless to say, he and his wife both perceived him as extremely helpful.

Table 4.6 shows how wives felt about having their partners present. The women who had their husbands with them during labor were positive about it in 96 percent of the cases. Of the women whose husbands were not with them, close to half felt negative about his absence.

Findings are identical for husbands' presence in the delivery room. When the husband did not attend the delivery, 45 percent of the women had negative feelings about his absence. One said: "I can't even describe the disappointment. It was just devastating that the doctor wouldn't let him. I just couldn't understand why he wasn't there. We really worked on this and planned for it and looked forward to it, and suddenly, without warning . . . it was pretty hard to take." This mother plans to change obstetricians next time, because it is so important to her to have her husband present.

TABLE 4.6. How couples felt about husband's presence in labor room and in delivery room

	In labor room: if husband		In delivery room: if husband	
	absent	present	absent	present
Wife feels				
1 = very negative	17%	0%	18%	0%
2 = negative	31	1	27	0
3 = didn't care	10	3	22	5
4 = mild positive	31	29	27	26
5 = solid positive	10	40	7	42
6 = extreme positive	0	27	0	26
Average	2.86	4.89	2.78	4.89
Husband feels (by wife's report)				
1 = very negative	29%	7%	14%	0%
2 = negative	39	15	42	4
3 = didn't care	25	24	14	5
4 = mild positive	4	18	23	25
5 = solid positive	4	22	7	31
6 = extreme positive	0	15	0	35
Average	2.14	3.79	2.67	4.87
Husband feels (own report)				
1 = very negative	27%	0%	44%	0%
2 = negative	55	7	44	0
3 = didn't care	0	7	0	5
4 = mild positive	18	44	11	26
5 = solid positive	0	31	0	51
6 = extreme positive	0	11	0	18
Average	2.09	4.13	1.78	4.82

Another woman, who had chosen a hospital where husbands are not allowed because she thought it would not be important, said: "I was—really sorry. It was just fascinating, and I know he would have been as fascinated as I was. I really regretted his not being there. I almost hated to tell him later on about how thrilled I was, because he didn't get to see it."

Of the women whose husbands were not present, 34 percent felt positive about his absence; most were women who underwent a Cesarean delivery. One said, for example: "I felt fine about it. I wouldn't have wanted him to watch when I was being operated on. That's not something he has the stomach for."

Others didn't want the husband present because they felt inhibited about it: "I was glad he wasn't there. He wanted to be there but—[Why were you glad?] Well, it's kind of unattractive. You lose your last shred of dignity."

Ninety-four percent of the women whose husbands were present felt positive about having their husbands at their side (including three women with a Cesarean delivery) while *none* felt negative about his presence. The following description of one mother's feelings is representative of the positive viewpoint: "I really wanted him there. It would have been a shame for him to go through the whole labor and not see the final thing. And it'd be hard to try describe it to him. There are experiences you just like to be together for. I think it's very important—the birth of our baby. It was a good feeling." Another woman, who had a home birth, said: "I was thrilled. I was very proud of myself. He told me he had never seen such a neat delivery—closer to nature than he had ever seen in hospitals, with women all doped up and babies pulled out with forceps." (Husband is a physician.)

Fathers of both social classes actually participated to an equal extent in labor and delivery. Nevertheless, a difference bordering significance ($\chi^2 = 3.44$, $p \cong .07$) appeared in women's general opinions on this matter—over twice as many lower-class women as middle-class women (sixteen vs. seven) believed "most men would not want to see the birth of their own baby."

PREPARATION IN RELATION TO FEELINGS ABOUT BIRTH

Women's preparation level was related to their feelings about having their partners join them in labor and delivery. Women at the highest levels of preparation (6 and 7) on the average "wanted very much" for their husbands to be present in labor and delivery, and they differed significantly from women at intermediate levels of preparation (4 and 5) in the strength of their desires to have their husbands present in delivery (see table 4.7.) There is also a significant difference between how women summed up the whole birth experience according to level of preparation when those at the highest levels are compared to those at intermediate levels.

Explicit models will be developed later, in an effort to understand how preparation affects both men's and women's birth experience.

TABLE 4.7. Comparison of parents' birth experience by preparation level

	Levels 1 to 3			Levels 4 or 5			Levels 6 or 7			t-value[a]	t-value[b]
	N	Mean	SD	N	Mean	SD	N	Mean	SD		
For mothers											
Wanted husband to be present during labor 1 = want very much 2 = in favor of	35	1.31	0.47	32	1.28	0.52	53	1.13	0.34	0.27	1.59
Wanted husband present during delivery 1 = want very much 2 = in favor of	35	1.69	0.58	32	1.50	0.62	53	1.15	0.36	1.26	3.28**
Sum up whole childbirth experience 3 = slightly negative 4 = neutral 5 = slightly positive	35	3.77	1.86	32	4.19	1.84	53	5.40	1.78	0.92	3.00**
For fathers											
Importance of sharing labor 1 = extremely important 2 = important	13	1.75	0.93	15	1.13	0.35	27	1.22	0.42	2.47*	0.69

Importance of sharing delivery 1 = extremely important 2 = important 3 = didn't matter	8	2.25	1.49	15	1.27	0.59	27	1.22	0.42	2.28*	0.28
Sum up whole childbirth experience 2 = negative 3 = neutral 4 = slightly positive 5 = solid positive	14	2.86	1.41	16	4.50	1.41	26	4.31	1.44	3.18**	−0.42
Quality of emotion at moment of birth 3 = neutral, nothing 4 = mild positive 5 = very positive	14	3.79	1.25	16	4.81	1.11	27	4.22	1.22	2.38*	1.59
Reasons for enjoyment of childbirth 1 = drugs given 2 = that it "wasn't bad" 3 = help and support of medical personnel 4 = husband being able to help and support wife	14	1.57	1.70	15	3.13	1.55	27	3.81	2.11	2.59*	1.09

*$P(t) < .05$, two-tailed.
**$P(t) < .01$, two-tailed.
[a] t-tests run between levels 1 to 3 and levels 4 or 5.
[b] t-tests run between levels 4 or 5 and levels 6 or 7.

MOTHER'S FIRST REACTION TO THE BABY

Eighty-five percent of the women saw their babies at once—that is, they saw the baby as it was born or immediately thereafter. Another 8 percent saw their babies while they were still in the delivery room. Asked, "What did the baby look like?" for that very first glimpse, the mothers responded as follows: 13 percent, very negative; 20 percent, negative; 14 percent, neutral; 24 percent, mild positive; 24 percent, solid positive; and 5 percent, enthusiastic. Women who experienced a Cesarean delivery rated their baby's appearance in just about the same way as the rest of the women (3.50 and 3.41, respectively, where 3.00 is neutral).

Some examples of very negative first reactions are: "It just looked all gooey. I looked at him and looked away." "He looked—terrible, you know? Red and *scrawny*—" or "She looked—awful. All that gunk hanging off her—bloody." Neutral responses are variations on: "It looked like a baby. What else can you say?" Positive women found much to say, including: "A nice round head and his ears were close to his head," or "She was pretty from the minute she was born. Really good coloring, and her forceps marks weren't too bad...." Examples of enthusiastic reactions are:

> He looked so wonderful. He came flying out and B. put him on my belly and his little forehead wrinkled up and he was matted with vernix and squinched up and very nice. Very wet. He was yelping [laughs], making himself known.

> She was *beautiful*. I didn't know a newborn could be that beautiful—she was soft, and calm—and content and happy. She had just been born, and it's *hard* getting born, but—she—she *impressed* me.

When asked about their *feelings* toward the baby when they first saw it, rather than what the baby looked like, many fewer women were negative— only 8 percent admitted they did not like the baby at first, and another 22 percent said they were neutral.

Women's reported feelings toward the baby not being in complete agreement with their comments on the baby's appearance is consistent with findings in an earlier cross-sectional study of 269 mothers (Doering and Entwisle 1975). Then, a high percentage of women also expressed negative views when asked a question about the baby's appearance, to which the socially approved answer was not obvious. Few women will openly state negative feelings toward their infants. In answering a semiprojective question such as "What did the baby look like?" however, a great deal of negativism surfaced both in this study and in the earlier study. Other workers (Grey et al., n.d.; Robson and Moss 1970) have videotapes of mothers showing "distinct distaste and disgust as the baby was presented to them," so observation of maternal negativism is not peculiar to the present study.

General negativism is also revealed by answers to another question—how the new mother felt about holding and touching her baby right away. Twenty-eight percent of the women in this study said that it did not matter to

them whether or not they held the baby soon after it was born, and 34 percent actually said that they did not want to. Only 25 percent *did* hold the baby immediately or while still in the delivery room. Another 28 percent were permitted to hold the baby for the first time in recovery.

In terms of mothers' reaction to the baby, social-class differences are inconsequential. Except for lower-class women being more enthusiastic about their baby's sex (57 percent of them had boys), the mothers' reactions by class are much the same in terms of, for example, how they felt about the baby on first seeing it, how they felt about not being able to hold the baby, whether they breast-fed, and whether they fed on schedule or demand.

Often considerable time elapsed between the birth and the time when parents were permitted to hold their babies (table 4.8). Only 53 percent of the mothers held their babies during the first hour of life. Twenty-nine percent of the mothers were separated from their newborns for more than twelve hours.

Only 26 percent of the breast-feeders fed their child in the first hour after birth, while 6 percent waited two days or more. *All* those who fed their babies for the first time more than forty-eight hours after birth were women who had had Cesarean deliveries. Other aspects of mother-infant interaction also differed greatly depending on whether or not the woman experienced a surgical delivery.

Many persons feel that the first few contacts between mother and infant are critical to the success of breast-feeding. They believe that if the infant does not require supplemental feeding and / or the mother can begin feeding promptly so that breast problems are minimized, breast-feeding is usually more successful than if there is a struggle between bottle and breast beginning in the hospital. Also, since this research was begun, it has been asserted that close and immediate contact between mother and child right after birth may be crucial for optimal attachment to occur between mothers and babies (Klaus and Kennell 1976*b*; Sosa et al. 1976). Sosa et al. found more infection, shorter breast-feeding, and other negative consequences following separations of twelve hours or longer following birth, and other reports hint that later child abuse is correlated with prolonged separation of parents and newborns (Hunter et al., n.d.). There is even some suggestion that long-term cognitive

TABLE 4.8. When parents held babies for first time

Time elapsed until parents first held baby	Mothers		Fathers	
	N	%	N	%
More than 2 days later	5	4	10	18
25–48 hours later	10	8	3	5
13–24 hours later	20	17	7	12
7–12 hours later	15	12	0	0
1–6 hours later	7	6	1	2
Not in delivery room, but in recovery room or hall	33	28	7	12
In delivery room	30	25	29	51

development may be influenced by the amount of contact between mother and child right after birth (Ringler et al. 1978). Others (Greenberg and Morris 1974:526) have pointed to a parallel phenomenon for fathers— "engrossment"—hypothesized to be an innate potential of fathers to become intensely involved with their infants, "by the first three days and often earlier." Some possible consequences of parents' lack of early contact with the infant will be explored in chapter 7.

HUSBANDS' FEELINGS ABOUT THE BIRTH

Of the fifty-seven husbands interviewed after the birth, only one was outside the hospital when his baby was born. Thirteen percent remained in the waiting room, 27 percent were with their wives for part of the labor, and 58 percent were with their wives through the entire labor. Sixty-eight percent of the men who agreed to be interviewed were in the delivery room with their wives (as compared to 66 percent of the whole sample).

As would be expected, most husbands who were inside the labor room were positive about being there, and those outside were negative about being absent (see table 4.6). The small difference in father's participation in the birth event according to social class is not significant.[6] Nine middle-class and ten lower-class fathers were not present for any part of labor, with two and three, respectively, being absent by choice. Eighteen middle-class and twenty-three lower-class fathers were not present in delivery, with two and six, respectively, absent by choice.

Of the fifty-seven husbands queried directly, seven were fathers of Cesarean-delivered infants. Like their wives, they were decidedly negative in their summing up of the whole childbirth experience (2.00 on a scale like that for wives in table 4.1), whereas other fathers who responded were, on the average, slightly positive.

Sharing the delivery was evidently more important to men than being in the labor room. When they were not in the delivery room, 88 percent of the husbands felt negative about it. One said: "I felt anxious. Very anxious. Boy, it's taking a long time. And disappointed, like I'd let her down. Because I heard her—a nurse came out, and I heard my wife saying, "I want my husband!" and I thought: Oh, God what's happening? I felt like—possibly—I hadn't done my job. I don't know why he [the doctor] made me leave." Another husband, who had known all along that he would not be permitted in the delivery room, was equally unhappy: "Distressed. I called and asked the priest on duty to come up. I needed a little moral encouragement. It kinda hit me—kinda hard—I just sat there and tried to pull myself together."

[6]It is likely that in the population at large there is a difference favoring presence of middle-class fathers in labor and delivery, however, because more middle-class couples take preparation classes. By forcing equivalence of social-class groups in terms of preparation in this sample, the equivalence of father participation is likely to be forced also.

The husbands who were present at the deliveries of their infants were overwhelmingly enthusiastic. Ninety-five percent were positive, 5 percent neutral, and *none* negative. (Three husbands were present for Cesarean deliveries.) The neutral husbands were physicians, who said that they had seen too many births to become excited about this birth.

One of the fathers who was present described his feelings as follows: "I felt tremendous. It was just an experience I'd never—had before, and it's a good experience. I felt like I was part of it too. I was feeling *great,* tremendous." Several fathers were unexpectedly invited into the delivery room, although they had not attended classes and had not expected to be part of the birth. One such father stated: "I felt honored. Privileged. I felt pleasure—excitement—gratitude—curiosity. I had no idea why he invited me in. I guess it's somewhat of a compliment. And it was a very personal and very sharing thing. For me, it was extremely important. I wasn't afraid of blood or being shocked—it was an emotional thing. Indescribable."

Besides being asked how they felt about being or not being with their wives in the delivery room, all male respondents were also asked: "How did you feel?" for the moment of birth if they were present at the birth, or for the moment when they were told that the baby was born. Interviewers probed for both emotions and physical feelings, as in the wives' question, but only men's emotions could be coded. The average score for all interviewed fathers was 4.28, somewhat higher than the wives' average (3.80). The new fathers' feelings were probably more positive than those of the new mothers because the men did not have to contend with negative physical sensations and / or with the emotion-dulling effects of drugs.

Whether the new father was present at the birth of his baby affected his feelings about the birth event. Husbands (32 percent) who were in the waiting room averaged 3.61 (or neutral) in their emotions at the news of the birth, while husbands (68 percent) who were present as their babies were born averaged 4.59 (positive) in their emotions. Furthermore, 23 percent of those present, but none of those absent, reported an "ecstatic, peak experience."

Examples of the fathers' negative reactions are the following: "Disappointment that it was a girl—but relief that everyone was okay" and "Well, I was really a nervous wreck. All I could think was: what the hell happened? I was sure something had happened." Mildly positive responses went along the following lines: "I was really—uh, happy" and "I wasn't surprised . . . by very much, and—it was, uh, in a way—fascinating." Examples of an ecstatic or peak experience are:

I was elated. I was filled up. There was no—to me there was no room for words. I was crying. Just looking and crying. I was just dumbfounded, really. Everybody's saying, "Wow!" and "Far out!" and I just—didn't say anything.

As *joyful* as I've ever been in my life. That is—the *greatest* experience of anything I've ever done. It was just—a very happy time—a feeling I've *never* had before.

The man who delivered his own baby put it this way: "It was just—sort of—far out. There it is. Happy. I was as happy as I could be—a real rush—I'd go anywhere to see a baby born. I wouldn't have missed it for the world. I put the baby up on B.'s belly, and then just moved out of the way and let the midwife take over. I just sat there—looking at the baby and at B. . . . It's—there are no words." No husband felt that he had too much knowledge about labor or delivery, and 31 percent of the fathers who responded wished they had known more about what to expect. (The mothers felt better informed.)

As was true for women, there was also a relation for men between preparation level and the strength of desire for the husband to share in labor and delivery. The largest differences occurred for fathers between those at levels 4 and 5 (intermediate) and those at the lowest levels, whereas for women differences occurred between levels 6 and 7 and lower levels (table 4.7). Apparently any kind of preparation class was sufficient to kindle these fathers' desires to be present.

As mentioned, there was no difference by social class in whether or not husbands were present during labor and delivery, and men of the two social classes expressed equivalent sentiments for being present at delivery. A statistically borderline difference by class exists in men's opinions about whether "Most new fathers would like to hold and touch their babies right away" or "Most new fathers are just as happy to view their babies in the nursery" (Appendix B, opinion item 7). More middle-class men (23 vs. 16) agreed that fathers would like to touch their babies; lower-class fathers expressed somewhat happier feelings on the average about the baby's sex;[7] and middle-class fathers seemed to enjoy fatherhood somewhat more. On all other measures, differences between fathers according to class are small and inconsequential.

FATHER'S FIRST REACTION TO THE BABY

Fathers were asked when they first saw their babies—68 percent saw the baby as it was delivered; 20 percent saw it first in recovery or on its way to the nursery; 12 percent did not see the baby until hours (or days) later. Asked "What did the baby look like?" at this first view, the fathers' responses were tallied as follows: 7 percent, very negative; 19 percent, negative; 11 percent, neutral; 26 percent, mild positive; 25 percent, solid positive; 12 percent, enthusiastic.

The men expressed more extreme views on their infants' appearance than did their wives, and often in more colorful language. Examples of very negative descriptions are:

[7]Although in the sample as a whole there were a few more boys born to lower-class than to middle-class couples, the sex ratio for interviewed fathers was equal (fifteen boys and fifteen girls for middle-class fathers, thirteen boys and fourteen girls for lower-class fathers).

> All beat to hell. I was stunned—It's very *shocking*. It had a big blob of blood on its head and a bruise—two bruises on each side of its face—and milky-looking and yucky—It threw me. It really did.

> I'll tell you what he looked like. He looked like he'd been run over by a Mack truck—that's what!

Many came right out and said "ugly," a word that the wives almost completely avoided.

When the fathers were enthusiastic, they were equally articulate about their feelings:

> Well, she was beautiful. She was absolutely gorgeous. I mean—a lot of them look like rats, you know. I'm not the greatest fan of little babies. But *she* was an absolutely gorgeous child. There's no doubt about it. I mean, even the nurses said so.

> They tell you to expect the worst—and—I was surprised. He wasn't five minutes old and—um—he was just beautiful. *In my eyes*—he was really pretty. He had a white color, not reddish or anything.

The fathers appeared more enthusiastic than the mothers, but the most enthusiastic fathers in the sample were probably the same ones who agreed to take part in this research. Also, many of the women were sedated when they first met their babies, which would dull their enthusiasm considerably.

Fathers were asked when they were first allowed to hold their infants (table 4.8). Surprisingly, a larger percentage of fathers than of mothers (51 percent vs. 25 percent) held babies while still in the delivery room. Probably, if the father is there, the physician lets him hold the baby unless there is some reason against it. The father, of course, is not lying down with an intravenous tube inserted in one arm and perhaps a blood pressure cuff on the other. Many mothers expressed resentment about being unable to hold their babies because their arms were restrained.

When asked to rate the whole childbirth experience, men were slightly positive on the average. (Wives were between neutral and slightly positive on the average.) Actually, 30 percent of the men were negative to very negative, but the most negative opinions came from fathers who had not been present. Of the 21 percent of husbands who found nothing enjoyable about childbirth and expressed profound relief that it was over, most had been in the waiting room.

The fathers' statements of what was *most* enjoyable about labor and delivery included being able to help their wives (16 percent) or actually witnessing the birth (14 percent). When asked what was the nicest thing about the days while mother and child were in the hospital, only 23 percent of the men spontaneously mentioned the baby as being the nicest thing. Fifty-three percent failed to mention the baby at all in discussing the hospital stay. This may reflect the fact that many hospitals still do not let the father hold or touch his

baby. When asked a similar question concerning the nicest thing about the first few days at home, 37 percent of the men mentioned the baby as the "nicest thing" or that they "enjoyed the baby." To a query put when their baby was four to eight weeks old—"Why is your marriage happy?"—close to half (44 percent) cited the baby as a primary or secondary reason.

These answers suggest that the men assumed the father role gradually, by no means universally at the moment of birth. Fatherhood likely requires interaction with the baby, and fathers were often separated from their infants for the first days of the baby's life. As mentioned in chapter 1, little in the past experience of these men has prepared them for an active role at the time their first child is born. Now that many hospitals are allowing fathers an active part in the labor and delivery, perhaps sharing of the birth experience should be further extended so that more parents can share the early days *after* birth. When a woman has rooming-in, of course, the new father can care for his baby as often as he wishes, but fathers whose wives choose nursery care should also be given opportunities to hold the baby. Fortunately, this privilege appears to be becoming more common.

PERCEPTIONS OF THE BIRTH EVENT

Both husbands and wives were asked to sum up the childbirth experience from their own point of view. For couples where both responded, views compared very well ($r = .64$, $p < .01$). There is also a significant relationship between preparation level and how both men and women summed up their birth experience ($r = .39, .48$, respectively). (See also table 4.7.)

There are also data on what husbands did during labor and delivery, and how wives perceived their husbands' feelings and actions. The data already reviewed show that husbands who were with their wives during labor were positive about it (see table 4.6). Wives estimated their husbands' feelings during labor for those who were present as mildly positive (3.79) and for those who were absent as negative (2.14). For husbands who were interviewed, agreement between their feelings about delivery and their wives' perception of their feelings is very close.

Husbands were more enthusiastic about delivery than labor, perhaps for two reasons: only the most enthusiastic husbands elected to be present during delivery, and delivery is relatively fast and exciting—the culmination of all previous events, including labor. Husbands saw themselves as being helpful during labor (4.34, where 3 = "just being there," 4 = "being there and some specific helps," and 5 = "engaging in several helpful activities"), but wives on the average saw husbands as less helpful (3.43). Likewise, husbands saw themselves as more active during delivery than their wives perceived them to be, but there is not as much difference in husbands' and wives' recollections of delivery. In general husbands' and wives' recollections of events during delivery are in better agreement than their recollections of events during labor.

EARLY DAYS AFTER THE BIRTH

Husbands spent considerable time visiting their wives in the hospital—on the average, between three and four hours a day. Twenty-one percent spent an average of six hours a day. (The five home deliveries in the sample were coded as "over six hours.")

For women with vaginal deliveries, the less medication a woman had at the birth, the better she felt when she first tried to walk. There are probably at least three reasons for this, the first being simply drug hangover. The second is that complications of all kinds lead to increased use of medication—more complicated deliveries lead to more medication, and such complications may have other consequences as well. The third reason is that when large amounts of medication are used at birth, the mother's pushing ability is impaired or eliminated, making forceps almost a necessity, so women with higher levels of medication at birth are more likely to suffer the discomfort of forceps abrasions and larger episiotomies. By contrast, the six women who did not have episiotomies all reported feeling "good" or "wonderful," and three of the six were up and taking a shower within one hour of the birth.

The women's apparent good health during pregnancy and their positive estimates of their own health continued through the days right after birth. There are large differences, however, in the rates of recovery according to whether or not the woman experienced a Cesarean delivery (see table 4.9). For example, the women who were delivered vaginally had their first meal about seven hours after birth, and 36 percent of them said they were "starving" at that time. The first meal for women who had a surgical delivery was delayed an average of twenty-four hours after delivery.

The costs of a Cesarean delivery are considerably more with respect to all symptoms asked about. These women were hospitalized longer, required more drugs in the hospital, and in general were sicker. Vaginally delivered women returned home on the average in less then three days, whereas the others spent close to a week in the hospital. Surgery also negatively affected the mother's perception of the quality of her birth experience.

INFLUENCE OF PREPARATION ON THE WOMAN'S BIRTH EXPERIENCE

A connection between women's preparation and a positive birth experience has been observed repeatedly. In an early Soviet study of 500 women, failure to control pain either fully or temporarily occurred in 47 percent of women given drugs, compared to 33 percent of women who had undergone psychoprophylaxis (Chertok 1959). Put another way, preparation produced a higher percentage of relief than was afforded by drugs. In Bergström-Walen's study (1963) of 250 Swedish women and Tanzer's smaller but carefully controlled study (1967) of 36 American women, those who had trained for childbirth

110

TABLE 4.9. Recovery while still in hospital for women experiencing Cesarean delivery compared to all others

	Vaginal delivery			Cesarean delivery			
	N	Mean	SD	N	Mean	SD	t-value
First meal after birth 1 = more than 48 hrs. later 2 = 24 to 48 hrs. later 4 = 6 to 12 hrs. later 5 = 1 to 6 hrs. later	99	4.72	0.73	20	1.90	1.02	14.66**
Appetite at first meal 2 = fairly hungry 3 = not very hungry	99	2.10	1.04	20	2.35	1.14	0.96
Slept in hospital 2 = fairly well 3 = poorly	100	2.05	0.89	20	2.10	0.85	0.23
Sleeping pills taken 0 = never 1 = one night only	100	0.61	0.92	20	1.15	0.88	2.41*
Pain killers in hospital 2 = 2 or 3 doses 3 = 4 or 5 doses	100	2.20	1.67	20	3.40	0.94	3.11**
Other drugs taken in hospital (excluding vitamins, iron, laxatives) 2 = 2 or 3 doses 3 = 4 or 5 doses	100	2.52	1.70	20	3.00	1.62	1.16
When got up and walked after birth 1 = more than 24 hrs. 2 = 18 to 24 hrs. 4 = 8 to 12 hrs. 5 = 4 to 8 hrs.	100	4.30	1.50	20	1.90	0.72	6.98**
When first urinated 2 = 18 to 24 hrs. 3 = 12 to 18 hrs. 4 = 8 to 12 hrs. 5 = 4 to 8 hrs.	100	4.82	1.86	20	2.05	1.19	6.41**
When first bowel movement 3 = 4th day 4 = 3rd day 5 = 2nd day	99	4.33	1.32	20	3.00	1.41	4.06**
Laxative required 1 = once 2 = more than once	100	1.26	1.05	20	1.45	1.19	0.72
When returned home 3 = 3 days 2 = 4 days 1 = 5 to 7 days	100	3.60	1.27	20	0.90	0.64	9.24**
How felt about going home 1 = glad to leave hospital 2 = didn't matter	95	1.18	0.52	20	1.30	0.73	0.87

*P(t) < .05, two-tailed.
**P(t) < .01, two-tailed.

reported a far more positive birth experience. Other studies of German (Huttel et al. 1972), Canadian (Enkin et al. 1972), and French (Chertok 1969) women are consistent with these conclusions. In a careful review of the large literature now extant on this topic, Charles et al. (1978) concluded that preparation has positive effects net of background factors. In other words, although women with a more favored socioeconomic background are more likely to receive preparation, socioeconomic background alone cannot explain the positive effects.

A persistent problem in evaluating effects of preparation has been whether personality characteristics or motivation is chiefly responsible for benefits conferred by preparation, rather than the preparation per se. Women who seek preparation could be different in many respects from women who do not seek preparation, and such differences—present before preparation—could explain why prepared women weather the birth event better. However, if women seek preparation but—because the instruction they receive is of varying quality— are actually prepared to varying degrees, then an assessment of effects of varying levels of preparation can be made with "motivation to prepare," held constant. This strategy of analysis, begun in an earlier study (Doering and Entwisle 1975), was continued in the present study. Women at preparation levels 4 and 5 had obviously sought preparation, but their preparation was not as complete as that of women at levels 6 and 7. Data in tables 4.7 and 7.2 reveal that in many ways women with the highest levels of preparation (6 and 7) were better off than women who attended classes but whose preparation was not as thorough (levels 4 and 5). For example, the most highly prepared mothers summed up their childbirth experience in significantly more positive terms than mothers with an intermediate level of preparation.

Partly because of personality or motivation, it would be expected that inter- mediate levels of preparation would be better than little or no preparation, and the data bear this out. For example, women with hospital classes were more positive in their opinions about their babies' appearance than women who did not attend classes of any kind (table 7.2).

It is sometimes thought that physicians resort to a surgical delivery when women are poor at coping with labor. If this were true, one would expect a negative relation between occurrence of surgical delivery and degree of prepa- ration. The present survey does not support this association; the proportions of surgically delivered women are *not* significantly different by preparation levels, although the size of our sample is very small for a test of this kind. Lack of an association between preparation level and operative delivery was also observed by Halstead and Frederickson (1978), but Hughey, McElin, and Young (1978) in a sample of 1000 women found a large and significant association. The reasons for these divergent findings are not clear, although the varying nature of the samples and the small size of our sample could easily be the cause.

In the present study, if women experienced a surgical delivery, preparation

was unrelated to how they rated their childbirth experience, and preparation conferred no emotional benefits. For women who delivered vaginally, however, there was a strong zero-order correlation between preparation and how the women rated their childbirth experience (see table 4.10), and high preparation was associated with more positive views of the experience no matter what the length of labor.

A MODEL TO EXPLAIN EFFECTS OF PREPARATION FOR WOMEN

Although a positive association between preparation for childbirth and the nature of women's birth experience is frequently reported, the exact mechanisms by which preparation achieves its salutary effects are not clear. In research on surgical patients who had knowledge about their operations in advance, Janis (1958) concluded that psychological preparation was a major defense against stress. Individuals forewarned by their physicians of likely unpleasant aspects of surgery were much less disturbed than other individuals whose physicians minimized unpleasant aspects or told them nothing. Janis (1958:353) postulated that the "unpleasant task of mental rehearsal" is apt to be shirked unless patients are given "approximate preparatory communications before being exposed to potentially traumatizing stimuli." From a psychoanalytic perspective, the "work of worrying" is a healthy phenomenon. It mobilizes the individual's psychological resources in a way that allows effective coping with stress.

Janis (1958:384) also noted the importance of the physician informing the patient of "overt actions he can execute" to minimize aches and pains. Although Janis emphasized the "active control" notion less than the "work of worrying" notion and did not attempt in his analysis of surgical-patient data to disentangle the two as precursors of more positive responses to surgery, in his discussion he explicitly distinguishes between control and worrying.

The application of Janis's theory to childbirth is relatively straightforward. Preparation classes teach women what to expect during labor and delivery and forewarn them of unpleasant events that may occur. Classes encourage women to air their concerns ahead of time, and they teach pregnant women and their partners many techniques that will help during childbirth. Furthermore, for childbirth, information about active control and benefits to be derived from self-help appear to greatly exceed those that are possible for a person facing a surgical operation. A surgical patient can help himself or herself to a limited extent in the postoperative period, but a parturient woman can take direct action to help herself during labor and delivery as well as in the recovery period.

In addition, the more intensive kinds of preparation classes strongly encourage active husband participation in labor and delivery. Such social support, of course, is rarely feasible for patients undergoing surgery, and consequently

Janis does not consider it. Women in childbirth thus have potentially greater opportunities and means for coping with stress than surgical patients—a greater freedom to act themselves and wider social support.

Recent reports are consistent with these arguments. Henneborn and Cogan (1975) found that in a group of forty women who had attended preparation classes with their husbands, those whose husbands elected to remain through delivery reported less pain and required less medication than those whose husbands chose to remain only through labor. And recently, Norr et al. (1977) offered evidence that both preparation in pregnancy and husband presence were positively associated with the quality of women's birth experience, although husband's presence seemingly had no direct effect on pain perception.

Our earlier cross-sectional study revealed not only that the quality of a woman's birth experience was associated with the extent of her preparation for childbirth but also that the effect of preparation on birth experience was not altogether direct (Doering and Entwisle 1975). A considerable portion of preparation's positive effect seemed to be mediated indirectly through women's awareness, or level of consciousness, during delivery (related to the amount and type of medication received). The conclusion from that study was that preparation operates through two mechanisms to enhance the birth experience: the first mechanism operates by way of providing the requisite psychological support (the direct effect), while the other mechanism entails an increase in physical and mental awareness, allowing the woman to be more actively in control.

Drawing upon Janis's stress theory and the previously discussed empirical studies of birth experience, we formulated a recursive model to explain the quality of the woman's birth experience. In the model both woman's preparation and husband's participation are taken as exogenous. Woman's preparation level is strongly associated with husband's participation in the birth event, since the more intensive kinds of preparation classes strongly encourage prospective fathers to attend classes with their wives and to be present during labor and delivery. During these classes men as well as women are taught skills that aid in coping with labor and delivery. It seems doubtful, however, that the woman's preparation is the only cause of husband participation, since the wife's preparation by no means guarantees the husband's participation. Indeed, for some couples, it may be the husband's desire to take an active role in the birth event that motivates them to enroll in a preparation class rather than preparation leading to participation. Hence, a plausible argument can be made for assuming reciprocal causation between wife's preparation level and husband participation, and so the variables are treated as jointly exogenous in the model.

Direct paths link both wife's preparation and husband's participation to pain. Earlier work, already alluded to, documents the possible influence of women's preparation on pain. In addition, one would suspect that the father,

by encouraging and comforting the mother, would reduce her anxiety (closely related to pain), and that in any case pain would be more bearable with him present to work with her in controlling contractions. Several studies agree that husbands can serve as an effective analgesic (Anderson and Standley 1976; Henneborn and Cogan 1975; Tanzer 1967).

Both pain and the two variables prior to it are expected to act directly upon level of awareness at the moment of birth—with less pain, less medication is required. Also, a husband might persuade his wife, or might support her own decision, to use less medication either because of danger to the fetus or because of prior commitments to avoid medication as much as possible—thereby yielding a direct path from husband participation to level of awareness at birth. Finally, our earlier work points to a direct effect of the woman's preparation level upon her level of awareness, probably attributable to techniques women learn in preparation classes to reduce or control pain so that they are less likely to require medication.

The quality of a woman's birth experience, the last variable in the chain, is assumed to be directly affected by all the prior variables for the following reasons. First, in addition to methods of coping with pain and avoiding medication, preparation covers many topics related to factual knowledge about what will happen. These and other effects of preparation are represented by the direct link between preparation and birth experience. Second, husband participation has the potential of enhancing birth experience directly—apart from any influence it has on pain or level of awareness—in that the simple sharing of the experience could make the birth experience more gratifying to the woman, everything else held equal. Next, the level of pain would obviously be expected to have a dampening effect on the quality of the woman's birth experience. And last, there is evidence from our prior study that links level of awareness to the quality of the woman's birth experience. Moreover, a woman assuming an active role by maintaining a high level of awareness would be expected, on the basis of Janis's thinking, to derive more pleasure from the birth experience, and in line with feminist thinking, women who actively give birth may find childbirth more gratifying than women who are passively delivered.

This rationale yields a fully recursive model with woman's preparation and husband's participation jointly exogenous, and with pain, level of awareness, and woman's birth experience as successive endogenous variables.

Measurement of Variables in the Woman's Model

Because women undergoing Cesarean delivery have birth experiences markedly different from the experiences of women delivered vaginally, women in this sample who were delivered by surgery (twenty cases) are excluded from the analyses that follow. A brief description of how each variable in the model was measured will now be given, with more complete information provided in Appendix C.

Women's preparation level (WPREP), already discussed in chapter 3, combines all sources of women's knowledge about what to expect in labor and delivery and how to implement this knowledge.

Husband's participation (HPART) is based on a six-item scale measuring husband's participation in labor and delivery in both behavioral and emotional terms. Due to the fact that only about one-half of the husbands in this sample were interviewed, this variable was constructed using information gathered from wives. A careful investigation of the overlap between husbands' and wives' replies to questions about husbands' participation, as well as a comparison of alternative parameter estimates in the model using information obtained directly from husbands vs. estimates based on information about husbands supplied by wives, suggests that any differences are inconsequential. Accordingly, the variable measuring husbands' participation was constructed from data supplied by wives, leading to a case base of 96, the set for which complete information was available on all other variables.

The measure of pain (PAIN1) is extracted from a question soliciting a description of the worst pain women experienced in the first stage of labor. Women were asked to rate the *most severe pain they experienced*—whether it lasted for only a contraction or two or went on for a considerable period.

Level of awareness (AWARE) is a subjective measure, derived from careful evaluations of women's replies to several long-answer questions about medication they received and their level of awareness during the actual delivery. It should be emphasized that *awareness* refers to both mental and physical consciousness. Thus, a woman who had been given a saddle block was scored in the middle of the scale because, although her mind was clear, she had lost consciousness of physical sensations in the "saddle area."

The quality of a woman's birth experience (BESCL), represented by a score on a five-item scale, covers how the woman felt both physically and emotionally immediately after the birth, how she felt 30–45 minutes later in recovery, and what she thought right after the birth about having another baby.

ESTIMATING THE WOMAN'S MODEL

The coefficients estimated for the recursive model suggest a number of interesting linkages among variables (table 4.10). Although the respondents do not form a probability sample, coefficients exceeding 1.5 times their standard errors are tagged for the reader's convenience.

As found in the earlier cross-sectional study (Doering and Entwisle 1975), preparation acts to increase the likelihood of a woman manifesting a higher level of awareness at the time of delivery, indicated by the significant standardized regression coefficient (.451). For the present sample, however, the effects of preparation on the woman's birth experience tend to be *largely* mediated by level of awareness. The direct effects of preparation on birth experience are small relative to other variables, as indicated by the size of the standardized coefficient (−.055) and its sign. The indirect effects, on the

TABLE 4.10. Model for explaining the woman's birth experience (Cesarean deliveries not included)

	Dependent variables					
	Worst pain in first stage (PAIN1)		Level of awareness (AWARE)		Woman's birth experience (BESCL)	
	Metric coefficients	Standardized coefficients	Metric coefficients	Standardized coefficients	Metric coefficients	Standardized coefficients
Independent variables						
Preparation level (WPREP)	−.090	−.197	.429	.451*	−.144	−.055
Husband's participation (HPART)	−.005	−.041	.062	.226*	.193	.254*
Worst pain in first stage of labor (PAIN1)			−.309	−.148†	−1.035	−.178*
Woman's level of awareness (AWARE)					1.446	.522*
Variance accounted for	5.0%		43.7%		52.0%	
Constant term	4.026		1.969		13.196	

Correlation coefficients (listwise present)
N = 96

	WPREP	HPART	PAIN1	AWARE	Mean	SD
WPREP					4.76	2.07
HPART	.590				22.38	7.20
PAIN1	−.222	−.157			3.48	0.94
AWARE	.617	.516	−.283		4.32	1.97
BESCL	.457	.519	−.354	.670	19.47	5.46

†Coefficient 1.5 to 1.99 times its standard error.
*Coefficient 2.0 or more times its standard error.

116

other hand, are fairly large. Multiplying the coefficients linking preparation to awareness and awareness to birth experience yields 0.235, a figure suggesting that the indirect effects of preparation on birth experience are substantially larger than the direct effects. Preparation acts to raise awareness at the time of delivery, and awareness in turn operates to increase the quality of the birth experience.

Husband's participation contributes both directly and indirectly to the woman's birth experience. The standardized coefficient linking husband's participation to level of awareness, .226, tends to indicate that husband's participation enables a woman to manage with less medication. A sizeable coefficient, .254, linking husband participation directly to birth experience, also exists. The direct effect of husband's participation on the woman's birth experience surpasses its indirect effects through level of awareness (.226 × .522 = .118), although the indirect effect is substantial enough to consider seriously.

As would be expected, the effects of pain on birth enjoyment are negative (−.178). Pain directly reduces the quality of the woman's birth experience, and more pain seemingly reduces level of awareness (more medication is required)—although the coefficient here fails to exceed twice its standard error (−.148). (This finding agrees with the relation noted in table 4.5 between amount of medication and how women felt, net of pain.) Neither preparation nor husband's participation are observed to have much effect on the worst pain a woman reports, and only about 5 percent of the variance in pain is explained by these two factors.

The importance of level of awareness in predicting the woman's birth experience is clearly revealed in this analysis. The standardized coefficient of 0.522 connecting awareness to the woman's birth experience is more than twice the absolute size of any other direct effect. Thus, the maintenance of a high level of awareness seems to increase the likelihood of a woman experiencing an enjoyable birth. Furthermore, it appears that remaining in control (receiving less medication) is much more important to a woman's birth experience than simply experiencing less pain.

It appears, then, that the major impact of preparation on the woman's birth experience is by way of increasing level of awareness. In this analysis, awareness is the most critical determinant of the quality of a woman's birth experience. Husband's participation seems to exert both a direct effect and an indirect effect (through awareness) on birth experience, the former effect probably one of social support at the time of delivery. Neither preparation nor husband's participation exert any substantial effects on pain, and pain is weakly and negatively related to a woman's birth experience. Finally, it is noteworthy that when estimated by ordinary least squares assuming perfect measurement, this model accounts for over half of the variance in a woman's birth experience and that when estimated by full-information maximum-

likelihood methods with measurement error also taken into account, it explains 78 percent of the variance in birth experience. (Conclusions about overall structural patterns are the same for both methods of estimation, and parameters are consistent in size.) This suggests that the model is specified rather completely, even though variables related to the birth attendant are not included.

DISCUSSION OF THE WOMAN'S MODEL

Janis's theory (1958) provides a powerful means for explaining the benefits of preparation, and other researchers have also noted that counseling before surgery confers significant benefits (see Andrew 1970; Egbert et al. 1964). *Preparation* as defined for the present collection of women included reading books, attending movies, and other forms of self-preparation, as well as previous medical training or enrolling in formal classes. This preparation is presumed to stimulate the work of worrying, since it causes women to air their concerns and to ask questions about what is likely to happen. But such preparation also teaches women how to help themselves in labor and delivery.

The model suggests that preparation is effective *mainly* because it leads women to retain active control in labor and delivery. In Janis's data, "control" and "worrying" were confounded. Here they can be separated to some extent by examining the direct and indirect effects of preparation on the woman's birth experience, and it appears that "control" is the more important in accounting for the quality of the women's birth experience.

The model also elucidates how social supports, mainly husband's presence, may help. Husband's participation probably is beneficial from three standpoints: (1) his very presence is comforting, and the couple together appreciate the birth experience more fully than would be possible alone (a direct effect); (2) most husbands who participate have attended some preparation classes, and this teaches them how to assist their wives in retaining control, especially late in labor when fatigue and confusion could complicate matters (an indirect effect); and (3) the husband's presence may lead to better relationships between the woman and the hospital staff, because he can lessen his wife's demands on the staff and also because his presence enables his wife to retain control (both direct and indirect).

The careful and comprehensive study by Norr et al. (1977), based on a single postpartum interview with women delivered at the Michael Reese Hospital in Chicago, also offers evidence that husband's presence in delivery positively affects the quality of a woman's birth experience. Their findings agree with ours, in that husband's presence has no significant effect on pain but has a significant impact on a woman's enjoyment. However, contrary to our observation that preparation has no significant effect on pain, they found a significant partial regression coefficient between preparation and pain. Their

analysis, though, does not separately conceptualize level of awareness. The specificiation in this study of paths from preparation to pain, from pain to level of awareness, and from preparation to level of awareness is a more complete structural analysis of how these three variables are related to a woman's birth experience. Our analysis indicates that there is a large indirect path from preparation through level of awareness to birth experience, implying that preparation aids in coping with pain and remaining in control, and that coping and remaining in control substantially enhance the birth experience. This path is much larger than the other two indirect paths linking preparation to pain. Hence, our results suggest that pain is a relatively independent factor and that the benefits that accrue to those women who are prepared are those of more successfully coping with pain and of remaining in active control in delivery. Despite these divergent findings, both our model and that of Norr et al. are able to account for over half the variance in least squares estimates of women's birth experience, and both agree in finding social support (husband's presence) to be of critical importance.

The relative sizes of parameters for the present set of cases are somewhat different from those based on a simpler model estimated earlier (Doering and Entwisle 1975; see also table 5.4). In particular, the earlier study uncovered relatively greater direct effects of preparation on "attitude toward childbirth" (roughly similar to "woman's birth experience" in the present study), but the structural connections revealed by the two studies are broadly similar.

When social-class groups are studied separately, the model structure appears similar. For both middle-class and lower-class women, preparation exerts its effects through awareness. Detailed models by class are not given here, but similar structures can be clearly seen in table 7.4, where preparation, awareness, and woman's birth experience are included as part of a more extensive model.

The structural model advanced to explain the quality of a woman's birth experience suggests that for this panel of women, the mechanisms explaining the relation between preparation and the quality of the woman's birth experience is awareness at delivery rather than the reduction of pain per se. The model also suggests that stress can be diminished by a patient's direct action and that overt action may overshadow work of worrying as a protection against stress. "Overt action" was a factor mentioned by Janis, but it was of less applicability in the surgical patients he studied than it appears to be for women giving birth. The model provides more evidence that husband's participation contributes considerably to a woman's birth enjoyment, and it points to social support as an additional defense against stress. (See Doering, Entwisle, and Quinlan 1980 for further discussion of the model.)

As noted earlier, in this sample preparation had no detectable influence on whether or not delivery complications occurred. Furthermore, if complications did occur, preparation did not appear to mitigate their negative effects.

The reasons why preparation does not improve resistance to complications are not clear, but one reason may be that preparation raises women's hopes about the satisfaction they will feel at birth—the prepared women has her sights trained on a positive, gratifying, even thrilling event. If instead she goes through a negative experience such as a surgical operation, her disappointment may be even more acute because her high expectations fail to come true. But a more direct reason why preparation is ineffective for women with complications may be that preparation classes prepare women for a normal birth. Although most classes presently do not do so, they could cover information that would prove useful if a surgical delivery were necessary (how the operation would be performed and for what reasons, what to expect in the postoperative period, how to breast-feed despite the operation, and so on), information along the lines of that which Janis (1958) and others (Andrew 1970; Egbert et al. 1964) have found useful in preparing surgical patients. Perhaps if women were forewarned that the possibility of a surgical delivery always exists and were then informed of the negative aspects of such a delivery, they would be led to do the work of worrying recommended by Janis. Since the rate of surgical deliveries is already high and seems to be increasing (Klassen 1975), the preparation curriculum probably should expand to include topics related to these problems, and in some places it already has.

INFLUENCE OF PREPARATION ON THE MAN'S BIRTH EXPERIENCE

Since society has paid little attention to the man's role in birth and until lately has even excluded him from the birth event, it is not surprising that previous research on men and the birth crisis deals exclusively with how husbands affect wives' birth experience. There are, to our knowledge, no reports dealing directly with the quality of a man's birth experience, although the birth of a first child can be considered a crisis for men as well as for women. If Janis's thinking is correct, previous preparation could strengthen men's ability to cope with the stress of the birth crisis. By attending classes or by reading, men could acquire information about the progress of labor and delivery that would make witnessing these events less threatening. Men can also learn techniques that enable their wives and themselves to remain in control during the birth. The application of Janis's theory involving preparation as a defense against stress is applicable in an even more straightforward way to the man's birth experience than to the woman's, because a man's reactions are emotional (not physical) and neither pain nor medication come directly into the picture for him. Most important, of course, is that classes encourage men to be present for the birth event.[8]

[8]Of those whose wives did not attend preparation classes, 28 percent were present for delivery, compared to 77 percent of those whose wives attended.

Since 95 percent of those present during the birth were positive in their reactions—including those who did not attend classes—attendance turned out to be gratifying experience for men. In addition, if hypotheses about parents' early contact with newborns are correct, the father's presence in delivery could be important for father-infant attachment.

As was true for mothers, many of the benefits associated with preparation for men involve reactions to the birth event—men enjoyed the birth event considerably more if they had some preparation.

A MODEL TO EXPLAIN EFFECTS OF PREPARATION FOR MEN

This line of thinking leads to the formulation of a recursive model to explain the quality of the man's birth experience that is reminiscent of the model constructed for women. Both a man's preparation during pregnancy (WPREP) and his participation in labor and delivery (HPART) are taken as exogenous variables in this model for the same reasons as in the woman's model. Since both preparation and the degree of husband's activity during birth were earlier shown to contribute to the woman's birth experience, they play the same role here, and both are assumed to contribute directly to the quality of the woman's birth experience (BESCL), the first endogenous variable in this model. The man's birth experience (MBESCL) is assumed to be directly affected by the level of prepartum preparation, in accordance with Janis's theory that the work of worrying provides defense against stress. Also, being able to take an active part is assumed to directly affect the quality of a man's birth experience in a positive way because (again according to Janis's theory) taking part contributes to feelings of control. It seems likely that Janis's "active measures" notion could apply to husbands as well as to wives. Finally, it is assumed that the quality of a wife's birth experience directly affects the quality of her husband's birth experience. If a woman has a particularly difficult delivery, for example, or reacts to birth with very negative emotions, it seems likely that she will dampen her husband's enjoyment. On the other hand, a man with little enthusiasm beforehand may find birth thrilling or satisfying if his wife does.

Preparation, husband participation,[9] and the quality of a woman's birth experience were fully discussed already. Measuring the quality of the man's birth experience was accomplished by summing three scores related to the husband's emotions at the precise moment of birth and his perceptions of his labor and delivery experience. The scale is described in Appendix C.

ESTIMATING THE MAN'S MODEL

Altogether, the quality of a man's birth experience is rather well accounted for by the structural model (table 4.11), with over 61 percent of the variance

---

[9]For simplicity's sake, the same measure of husband participation is used again here as was used in the wives' model. An alternative measure based only upon husbands' own estimates of help in labor and delivery performed similarly in this model.

TABLE 4.11. Model for explaining the man's birth experience

	Dependent variables			
	Woman's birth experience (BESCL)		Man's birth experience (MBESCL)	
	Metric coefficients	Standardized coefficients	Metric coefficients	Standardized coefficients
Independent variables				
Preparation level (WPREP)[a]	.349	.124	.135	.070
Husband's participation (HPART)	.417	.543*	.214	.408*
Woman's birth experience (BESCL)			.292	.427*
Variance accounted for	37.1%		61.1%	
Constant term	0.721		0.698	

	Correlation coefficients (listwise present) $N = 54$				
	WPREP	HPART	BESCL	Mean	SD
WPREP				5.02	2.00
HPART	.448			21.98	7.34
BESCL	.367	.599		18.13	5.63
MBESCL	.410	.695	.698	11.37	3.85

*Coefficient 2.0 or more times its standard error.
[a] The correlation between women's and men's preparation level was 0.95, estimated to be equal to the reliability of the measure.

explained. Lack of a direct effect of preparation on the woman's experience replicates what was seen in the previous model. Lack of a direct effect of preparation on the quality of a man's experience would not necessarily be expected, however, because for men the psychological component of preparation could be the *chief* one. As was true for women, however, a man's preparation acts mainly in an indirect way to shape the quality of his experience.[10]

Also consistent with the earlier model for women, the extent to which the husband took an active part in delivery strongly affected the quality of the woman's experience. Here, his active participation directly affected the man's experience as well (standardized coefficient of .408). Taking an active role in delivery definitely seems to indirectly improve the quality of a man's birth experience also. (The indirect path through wife's birth experience is .543 × .427 = .232.)

[10] Further evidence that the psychological component is small is that there is no correlation between men's worries about childbirth (measured in pregnancy) and the quality of their birth experience.

The direct path from the quality of the woman's experience to the man's experience is large (.427). A woman who has a positive birth experience contributes to her husband's birth enjoyment.

All in all, preparation again has a minimal direct role, suggesting that the work of worrying is less important than active control. On the other hand, preparation induces men to participate and / or contributes to the quality of women's birth experience through awareness so it leads indirectly to a more positive birth experience for fathers as well as for mothers.

Little previous research addresses the possible importance of a positive birth experience for fathers, but the man's birth experience could have impact on both father-infant attachment and marital cohesion. The transition to the parent role that the father experiences may be even more critical than that experienced by the mother, in the sense that the biological imperatives that link men to children are presumably weaker than those affecting women.

THE BIRTH EVENT IN PERSPECTIVE

In the past decade social customs surrounding the birth of a child have changed greatly. In this sample almost all the women, and a very large percentage of the men, wished to have the husband participate actively in the birth event. The degree of husbands' activity in labor and delivery suggests that the young men in this sample have expanded roles compared to what was true of fathers in earlier decades. In a study of middle-class couples in the sixties for example, none of the fathers was present for delivery, and when told of the birth, several fathers fainted—presumably in the waiting room (Shereshefsky and Yarrow 1973:109). In the present sample fathers' active involvement in the birth event is particularly impressive because close to one-third of the couples were not enrolled in preparation classes, and yet even among these, ten men were in delivery with their wives. Some of the least prepared couples must have adopted attitudes or viewpoints on modern customs associated with childbirth from the press or other informal sources.

Another way in which this sample reflects the zeitgeist of the seventies is that almost all the couples were having a child by choice, and couples had the means available to discontinue pregnancy if they wished. The fact that 11 percent of these women had previous abortions testifies to the actual freedom they exercised in conception control. By contrast, in a middle-class sample interviewed in the sixties, 27 percent acknowledged unplanned pregnancies (Shereshefsky and Yarrow 1973), and in a nationally representative sample, the rate of unwanted pregnancies was estimated to be much higher (less than half of the youngsters whose mothers were included in the survey were planned in the sense that the mother "wanted to become pregnant at that time," Foundation for Child Development 1977).[11]

[11]Other estimates are that one in every twelve marital births was unwanted by parents in 1976 compared to one in five a decade earlier (Russo 1979).

Nevertheless, these couples probably resemble couples having children in earlier decades in other ways. For example, 71 percent of the men wanted a son as a first child, and the majority of mothers preferred that hospital personnel care for the new baby.

Altogether, the number of obstetrical complications, in particular surgical deliveries, turned out to be larger in this sample than was anticipated, especially because the women were so healthy in pregnancy. However, comparisons of this sample with other recent reports suggest that it is not atypical in terms of the rate of surgical delivery (Gibbons 1976; Jones 1976; Klassen 1975).

The psychological and sociological effects of delivery complications have not, to our knowledge, been described previously. Surgical delivery in this sample led to a longer and much less pleasant hospital stay for the mother. Also, because these mothers see and hold their babies later after delivery than other mothers, early mother-infant bonding may be impeded.

The amount of medication women in this sample received seems substantial in view of experience in other countries, particularly since 57 percent of these women said in the six-month interview that they were ready to do without it. The evidence assembled here makes recent statements by a prominent British physician especially thought-provoking:

> It would be difficult to deny the enormous benefits . . . which medical advances have brought about . . . [but this] has meant more and more interference in the processes of birth. . . . To a certain extent we seem to have reached a point of diminishing return: increasing interference provides less and less in terms of improved outcome. [Macfarlane, 1977:1]

> If I have any one strong belief after reviewing the research and my own experiences, it is that childbirth is, in the main, a normal physiological process that might be enhanced if women felt, and were encouraged to feel, competent at it and confident in themselves and their bodies. [Ibid., p. 125]

Preparation, although unrelated to the incidence of surgical delivery or to other complications, appeared to enhance both men's and women's birth experience indirectly, and there are only minimal differences by class in its effects. For women there were large indirect effects by way of level of awareness and / or husband participation, and for men large effects by way of the woman's experience. The woman who remains aware allows the couple to stay in control, and this active role is apparently the key to the quality of the woman's and of the man's birth experience. Furthermore, for both spouses, sharing the experience appears to be extremely important and enhances the quality of the birth experience for both.

Few social-class differences appear in any of the topics examined in this chapter, and those that do appear should not be weighed very heavily, because *many* differences were examined. Also two other facts about social class deserve emphasis. First, the forced equivalence of social-class groups with

respect to preparation level may distort the picture, because it is likely that just those aspects of class that might produce different reactions to the birth event are minimized by equating on preparation. Second, the range in social class in this study is small. None of the women in this sample was disadvantaged, all had considerable education, most women in this sample were married, most definitely planned the baby, and all were in good health. For these reasons although the present study sheds some light on class differences, it is not ideal for exploring possible relations between stress associated with social class and events of the perinatal period.

5 | THE FIRST FEW WEEKS AFTER BIRTH

A major purpose of this research was to investigate how a couple's style of coping with a first pregnancy and birth affects their relationship with their newborn child early in the baby's life. As mentioned in chapter 1, there is little prior research that examines the family continuously over the period when it changes from a two-person to a three-person group, during that critical period of adjustment in the first few weeks of an infant's life. Also, much family research deals with the pathological or problem family, for example, with parents who are child abusers or alcoholics. Such research, although valuable for policymaking and needed for remedial work, is probably misleading as a source of information about development of normal parent-child relationships.

Along different lines, attachment between mother and child is a topic that has heavily engaged the attention of social scientists in the past two decades, leaders being Bowlby (1969) in England and Ainsworth (1969, 1973) in the United States. But there is a dearth of information about father attachment, or about how parents interact jointly with babies, especially in the earliest weeks. Furthermore, although Ainsworth, Bell, and Stayton (1971) have directly observed mother-child interaction during the first year of life and a number of other workers have made more limited cross-sectional studies (e.g., Beckwith 1972; Bell 1970), longitudinal data pertaining to early family behavior are scarce. Few studies are sensitive to social-class differences. The present research has its own limitations, but it does inquire into very early parenting behaviors of a sample of new parents carefully selected in terms of social-class membership.

In this chapter, the first few weeks after birth will be described, especially in terms of the couple's individual and joint parenting activities. Also we will try to analyze the relations between events or attitudes the parents held prior to birth and their later behavior as new parents. For example, length of breast-feeding will be studied in relation to feeding intentions before birth and general attitudes toward infant feeding determined prior to birth.

A word is needed about the organization of this chapter. First, the early

days of life with a new baby will be described: adjustment to homecoming, the mother's postpartum depression and possible longer-term response to complicated delivery, feeding modes and schedules, and caretaking behavior—especially in response to baby's crying. Later in the chapter, analyses will explore the precursors and possible determinants of breast-feeding and parents' reactions to the baby in relation to its sex. (Chapter 7 will cover further analytic work on parenting behavior and its precursors.)

RETURNING HOME

The women in this sample typically stayed in the hospital two to three days, except that those delivered surgically remained hospitalized close to a week. The large majority of women did not have rooming-in, and so, on their return home, most mothers were fully confronted with their new parental respon-sibilities for the first time. However, for most women the transition was smoothed by full- or part-time help at home.

Only two women reported no help from either husband or anyone else in the first week home. During the first week 21 percent of husbands took vacation time, while another 8 percent gave much help, although they did not take time off. Seventeen percent of the women had either ''baby nurses'' or other strangers to help. The rest had either a friend or a relative part-time (15 percent) or full-time (38 percent), with most of such help provided by the woman's mother.

In the second week 5 percent of the women still had a baby nurse, 18 percent had a friend or relative full-time, and 11 percent had a friend or relative part-time. Ten percent of husbands took two or more weeks off to help their wives. During the second week 25 percent of the women were completely on their own, and another 30 percent had some help from their husbands, but their husbands were not taking time off.

Most wives reported a great deal of help from their husbands during the first week at home. In addition to husbands who were their wives' sole source of help, another 32 percent were reported to give ''a lot more help than usual.'' In 26 percent of the couples, however, wives reported no extra help from their husbands even during the first week.

Help from husbands dropped off quickly in the second week, with 65 percent of husbands giving only ''a little more help'' or ''no more help'' than usual. Other researchers note that husbands help less with housework after arrival of a first child than they did before (Hoffman and Manis 1978b) and that fathers with more children do less than those with fewer children (Robin-son 1977). Fourteen percent of the husbands in this study had not changed any diapers by the time the baby was two to three weeks old.

About 33 percent of the women reported that things did not go well the first week at home. A higher percentage (38 percent) of women reported things did

not go well the second week (when more of the women were on their own), but only 23 percent of the women wished they had more help in the second week. Things "going well" or "not going well" almost always translated into how the baby was behaving. Mothers for whom things were not going well expressed themselves as follows:

> It was crazy. He ate so *erratically* and *frequently*—and then he'd go a couple hours and I'd get engorged. If he eats frequently, that's a problem, and if he goes four hours, that's a problem. And my nipples were sore and *that* was a problem.

> Oh, she was making me so tired. Because she'd be up all night, fussing. You're so tired with no sleep. Everytime she'd start to cry, I'd go: [groans] "Please!" It just got on my nerves. But then I'd go in and look at her and she was *so* sweet—she can't help crying, you know.

Because young middle-class couples may be more likely to live at a distance from kin and also because their income may be more dependable than that of lower-class couples (salary rather than hourly pay), the patterns of household help in the first two weeks at home were analyzed separately by class. All but two women, as mentioned, had some kind of help in the first week at home, and the percentage of full-time help did not differ by class. In fact, the only difference by class appears to be that the lower-class husband was more likely to take time off from work to help full-time at home (28 percent vs. 14 percent) and the middle-class couple was more likely to hire a full-time baby nurse (22 percent vs. 3 percent). Although the total percentage of each class with full-time help in the first week is about the same, the sources are somewhat different. By the second week, most of the baby nurses had been dismissed, half of the grandmothers had departed, and only 7 percent of the lower-class fathers were still at home, so both the amount and sources of help were practically identical for the two classes after the first week. As already noted in relation to other factors, the picture according to social class is also remarkably homogeneous in regard to household help during the first two weeks at home.

Perhaps as a consequence of the large amount of help given by the women's mothers, it turned out that women judged their own mothers more favorably after birth than they had before. Using semantic differential rating scales that provided twenty pairs of descriptive adjectives (see Appendix A, table A.3), the women rated a number of persons, including their own mothers, before and after the birth. Their views of their own mothers improved significantly after the birth, as compared with before. On sixteen out of twenty scales, a significant majority of women's views of their mothers were *more* positive after their baby was born.

It is not surprising that women are more favorably disposed toward those who help them through a crisis. (The next chapter reveals that the wives' views of their husbands are also related to the amount of support provided

during the perinatal period.) It is also likely that new parents revise their memories of their own childhoods and become closer to their own parents as a consequence of assuming the burdens of parenthood themselves. From a psychoanalytic viewpoint, women who perceive their mothers positively may find it easier to value themselves as mothers, and the change in their views of their mothers may have begun early in pregnancy. Arbeit (1975), in fact, reported that women undergoing a first pregnancy became more empathic toward their own mothers as pregnancy progressed. The *total* improvement registered in women's views of their mothers over the whole period of pregnancy and birth could be greater than the improvement measured in our sample, because measures were taken over a short time span (late in the sixth month of pregnancy and again two to three weeks after the birth.)

PREVIOUS KNOWLEDGE OF BABY CARE

By the time of the interview after the birth, 68 percent of the women were fairly confident, and another 23 percent were very confident of their ability to care for a newborn. Women who "felt like a mother" a little sooner were those who reported that they enjoyed motherhood and baby care the most ($r = .20$, $r = .28$; $p < .05$). There is some overlap between husbands' and wives' previous experience in infant care for the sixty couples where both husband and wife were interviewed ($r = .35$, $p < .01$), but the wife's confidence in her ability to care for her infant was not associated with either her own or her husband's previous baby-care experience.

Although knowing how to care for a baby might make childbirth less threatening, all in all it seems that child-care knowledge does not substantially affect women's perceptions of labor and delivery or their postpartum depression. Wives' perceptions of labor and delivery were essentially unrelated to any measure of previous baby-care experience,[1] and the seriousness of a woman's depression after birth appears to be unrelated to the wife's or husband's previous experience with newborns or knowledge of baby care. In particular, the seriousness of depression was not related to the husband's prior experience with newborns, the husband's knowledge of baby care, or the wife's confidence in her ability to care for a newborn. Although previous baby-care experience appears to have little bearing on how women in this sample weather the birth crisis, nevertheless in future work this hypothesis should be rechecked, because the range of baby-care experience in the present sample is very restricted.

---

[1] Husband's experience with newborns was related to the wife's evaluation of her entire delivery experience ($r = .28$, $p < .05$), but this single exception should probably be disregarded. Also, a later analysis in table 7.4 shows a *borderline* direct effect, and very small negative indirect effects for middle-class women only, of previous baby-care experience on women's birth experience (the zero-order correlation is .206).

WHEN THE WOMAN FEELS LIKE A MOTHER

At the time of the six-month phone interview, all the women were asked when in the previous six months they had started to "really feel like a mother." (See Appendix C for details on scoring.) Nobody replied "not yet," but 9 percent said that it had not happened until the baby was five or six months old. Nineteen percent felt that way either while pregnant or immediately at birth. The average was at about six weeks. The women were asked what they felt the turning point was, what exactly made them feel like a mother. Those who felt like a mother right away or within a few days mentioned touch, closeness, cuddliness, and especially breast-feeding. Those who felt like a mother after a week or more emphasized the responsibility: "She was dependent on me," "I was doing everything for him," "She got very sick, and we had to take her to the hospital." Those who did not have the feeling till after the first month felt that it was triggered by the baby responding to them: "He seemed to notice me," "She started smiling," or "She recognized me." Several mothers felt that it happened when they were out in public with the baby, as if they had to be labeled "mother" by others before they could feel it in themselves. Those who did not feel like a mother till several months had passed referred to more negative reasons for feeling that way: "I began to *really* feel tied down," "He was more demanding; I couldn't ignore him," "He was sick, and I realized how much I cared about him," or "He wasn't sleeping as much."

These data differ sharply from Macfarlane's (1977:116), who asked ninety-seven English women a different question ("when they first felt love for their infants"). He reports that 41 percent replied "during pregnancy," 24 percent "during birth," and over 27 percent "before the end of the first week." For only 8 percent was more than one week required.

The bottle-feeding women who were employed full-time were very late in feeling like mothers (three to five months) and *all* said that it happened when they were on vacation and taking care of the baby themselves, i.e., when they had total responsibility. Of the breast-feeding mothers who worked full-time, three felt like mothers in the early days, before they returned to work, for reasons of closeness and warmth, or reasons of responsibility. Only one (the one who returned to work at 2 ½ weeks) did not feel like a mother till five months, when it was summer vacation and she was caring for her son full-time and still breast-feeding.

A comparison of bottle-feeding and breast-feeding mothers reveals that they differ on the dimension of "feeling like a mother" ($\chi^2_1 = 7.63, p < .01$). Whereas 43 percent of those who ever tried breast-feeding already felt attached and close to the baby by one week, only 17 percent of the bottle-feeders did. It would be a mistake, however, to see this as a simple cause-and-effect relation, because those who decide to breast-feed may be more ready to assume the role of mother. For example, there is a small but signifi-

cant correlation between women's confidence in their ability to care for a newborn and when they reported feeling like a mother ($r = .23$, $p < .01$). The relation between feeding and maternal responsiveness is analyzed in more detail in chapter 7.

DEPRESSION

One common occurrence after birth, especially in the first week or two at home, is that many women become depressed. Actually emotional lability and slight depression are thought to affect most women after childbirth—80 percent is a figure commonly cited (Breen 1975:44; see also Yalom 1968). Causes for the blues after childbirth are not clear, although physicians and laymen alike frequently attribute depression in new mothers to hormonal imbalance.

Only 19 percent of the women in this sample reported *no* episodes of depression by the time of the postpartum interview. Of those who did experience the blues, 17 percent had them during their hospital stay (the traditional "third day blues"), and the remainder after they returned home. The reasons for depression in the hospital were several, but something wrong with the baby was the main reason (born deformed, premature, jaundiced, aspiration pneumonia, and so on). Other reasons included painful stitches or hemorrhoids, not being able to see the baby enough, having a sleepy baby who would not suck, or mother-in-law problems.

Those who experienced a depression after returning home, the vast majority, cited many reasons: baby fussing or crying too much, feeding problems, the responsibility, physical problems (especially exhaustion), friends or relatives "getting on my nerves," husbands not being understanding enough. But an interesting fact emerged when these reasons were checked further: almost without exception, the depression developed within a day or two of the time when the new mother first had full responsibility for the baby. (Melges [1968] makes a similar observation.) In other words, whether the woman recognized it or not, depression occurred on the fourth or fifth day if she came home from the hospital on the third day and had little or no help, or on the tenth day if her mother had left on the ninth, or on the fifteenth day if she had had a baby nurse for two weeks. The connection occurred in so many cases (seventy-five out of the eighty-one who succumbed to the blues after they came home) that a hormonal explanation for depression can be questioned. The increased incidence of depression among women who experienced a Cesarean delivery is also contrary to a hormonal explanation.[2]

For women who reported depression, the average blue period lasted less than six hours. Thirteen percent said that it lasted half an hour or less, while

[2]A hormonal basis for depression can also be questioned on the basis of reports of "postpartum equivalent" reactions after *adoption* of a child (Breen 1975:39).

for 24 percent it went on for more than forty-eight hours. Eighteen women (15 percent) experienced a serious depression (rated by how long it lasted and how hopeless the respondent felt), and eight of these women had undergone a Cesarean delivery.

No doubt the 80 percent or 81 percent incidence figure for depression somewhat overrates how often the blues are triggered by childbirth, however, because most people experience changes in mood over short periods. If probing questions were asked of *any* group of people about mood changes over a two- to three-week period, there would probably be some reports of depression. In effect, there is no way to judge how much depression occurs in new mothers above and beyond what would be experienced by any group of young women.

Women in this sample overcame their depressions by crying, getting angry, and talking to friends or relatives; some reported that the condition cured itself. The majority of those who experienced depression saw the husband as no help in overcoming it (57 percent). Twenty-nine percent thought the husband gave a little help in getting over depression, and 14 percent attributed a great deal of help to the husband.

It also turned out that women who underwent a Cesarean delivery were more likely to have longer depressions—35 percent of the women who were delivered surgically experienced a long depression (over twenty-four hours) compared to 17 percent of those delivered vaginally. Furthermore, among women who were not delivered surgically, those who experienced more complications and whose recovery took the longest were likely to experience long depressions ($r = .48$, $p < .05$).

There was a strong relation between awareness at birth and rate of recovery ($r = .51$, $p < .01$), suggesting that aftereffects of medication could be a cause of depression. Another explanation might be that a mother's dissatisfaction with the quality of her delivery experience could lead to depression. Preparation per se had little to do with depression. Putting everything together, it seems that dissatisfaction of the mother with the quality of her birth experience is a less likely cause of depression than the physical demands of caring for a new baby, especially for women whose recovery was slow and difficult.

In fact, there are associations between the severity of depression and just about every obstetric intervention: fetal monitoring ($r = .32$), use of forceps ($r = .21$), use of fundal pressure ($r = .24$), and all complications combined ($r = .31$). (More obstetrical interventions were carried out when women were given medication.) A more extended recovery period followed all kinds of extra delivery procedures, and no doubt there is a connection between physical vigor and psychic vigor. Consistent with the foregoing, if husbands and wives summed up the delivery experience in a more negative manner, the seriousness of the woman's postpartum depression was greater ($r = .20$, $p < .05$, for husbands; $r = .28$, $p < .01$, for wives).

Two causes mentioned for depression—exhaustion and the baby's fussiness—were explicitly investigated to see if the women's feelings about the cause of depression were accurate.

Almost all women noted some fatigue. When asked how tired they felt at the moment (coded from 1 = totally exhausted to 5 = very well rested), the average woman was "somewhat tired" (3.02) at the time of the interview after the birth.

There were no relationships between how rested the woman reported feeling at the time of the interview after birth and several variables: the woman's confidence in her ability to care for a newborn, whether or not the husband was likely to pick up the baby when it cried, how the woman felt about going home from the hospital, whether the husband helped at home in the first or second weeks,[3] or when depression occurred. There is a significant, although small, relationship, however, between how tired the woman reported feeling at the postpartum interview and the seriousness of her postpartum depression ($r = .26$, $p < .01$). Fatigue and depression are associated, however, so it is hard to tell which is the cause. Depression makes people tired.

How much the baby cried (either the amount of crying reported or the woman's feelings about the crying) did not relate to depression for women with vaginal deliveries. Only fatigue and delivery complications appear to correlate with the seriousness of depression, except that women who wished they could stay in the hospital longer experienced worse depressions ($r = .24$, $p < .01$).

LATER EFFECTS OF CESAREAN DELIVERY

Immediate costs of a surgical delivery have been emphasized up to now— more symptoms in the period immediately following birth, more negative ratings of the childbirth experience, and the like. But there were also more negative effects later on. Information obtained in the interview a few weeks after birth and from the later phone check when the baby was six months old indicated that, in addition to depression, a mother's early relation to her baby and her reaction to events in the early weeks of the baby's life may also have been adversely affected by surgical delivery (table 5.1).

For example, women who underwent surgical delivery were less positive in their feelings about caring for a newborn (ambivalent actually) and less likely to mention the baby as a source of happiness in marriage. (The question was

[3]An unexpected finding was that the more the husband helped in the first week, the more serious the woman's depression. One interpretation is that those women who needed help most (especially women recovering from Cesarean delivery) were the ones whose husbands did help. Given the number of indicators we have examined, however, we think it best to disregard this isolated finding.

TABLE 5.1. Reactions of women experiencing Cesarean delivery compared to all others (Variables measured at three-weeks' postpartum interview, except as noted)

	Vaginal delivery			Surgical delivery			
	N	Mean	SD	N	Mean	SD	t-value
Sum up whole childbirth experience 2 = negative 3 = slightly negative 5 = slightly positive	100	5.00	1.72	20	2.60	1.82	5.65**
How felt about holding baby for first time 3 = neutral 4 = mild positive 5 = definitely positive	97	4.10	1.41	20	3.70	1.70	1.12
Frequency of quarrels 1 = never 2 = seldom	100	1.82	0.58	20	1.80	0.62	0.14
Amount baby cries in 24 hrs. 3 = 2.5 hrs. daily 4 = 1.5 hrs. daily	100	3.74	1.20	20	3.10	1.48	2.09*
Seriousness of depression 1 = momentary, very mild 2 = average, medium	100	1.56	0.94	20	2.10	0.97	2.34*
How feel about caring for newborn 3 = very ambivalent 4 = somewhat ambivalent 5 = mild positive	100	4.32	1.32	20	3.65	1.66	1.98*
Baby mentioned as source of happiness in marriage 2 = mentioned secondarily 3 = mentioned primarily, but in abstract terms	100	2.67	0.89	20	2.30	0.73	1.75†
When felt like a mother[a] 3 = 1 to 2 months 4 = 3 wks. to 1 month 5 = 1 to 3 wks.	99	4.62	2.41	18	3.89	1.71	1.24

†$P(t) < .10$, two-tailed.
*$P(t) < .05$, two-tailed.
**$P(t) < .01$, two-tailed.
[a] Question asked at six-month phone check.

"Would you say that you and your husband are always happy, usually happy, or never happy? What is it about circumstances right now that make you [happy / unhappy]?" Only if the baby was spontaneously mentioned as a primary source of happiness was the highest score assigned.) The babies of women who had Cesarean deliveries were also reported to cry significantly more per day.

Some differences in breast-feeding were registered between women delivered surgically and others, but these differences must be discounted. Whereas 31 percent of women delivered vaginally selected bottle-feeding from birth

on, 55 percent of surgically delivered women did so. In percentage terms, this difference appears large (24 percent), but statistically the percentage difference does not attain significance, and when asked about feeding intentions in the six-month interview, more of the mothers who were delivered by section had already determined to bottle-feed (45 percent vs. 29 percent). In this sample most women stuck with the feeding mode they had favored before the birth. However, two of the six women who changed from breast to bottle had Cesarean deliveries. (Of the two women who changed from their before-birth intention to bottle-feed to breast-feeding after birth, neither was a woman who had undergone a surgical delivery.)

The number of surgically delivered women who started to breast-feed (9) is too small to support an analysis of persistence at breast-feeding, but insofar as there is evidence, persistence appears comparable. There also appears to be no difference in rooming-in according to mode of delivery, but the number of cases is really too small to support an analysis.

FEEDING

Thirty-five percent of the women bottle-fed their infants from birth, while 65 percent began by breast-feeding (down from the 68 percent who had planned to breast-feed in the sixth month of pregnancy). The number of bottle-feeders was exactly the same in each social-class group. The reasons for changes in feeding plan were as follows: one mother was considering putting the baby up for adoption because the father had not married her, one mother had a positive TB test just before the birth, one baby was born with a cleft palate, one was born prematurely, and two women who underwent Cesarean delivery were given hormones to suppress the milk supply before they regained consciousness. With the premature baby and the two Cesareans, the mothers were told that they could not nurse, although other mothers in this sample successfully breast-fed premature babies or breast-fed after a surgical delivery. Of these women, the five who had to change from breast- to bottle-feeding unexpectedly for health reasons said that they planned to breast-feed their second babies.[4] Two women who planned to bottle-feed changed to breast-feeding at the time of the birth, so the net change from breast to bottle was four (3 percent).

Of the bottle-feeders, 61 percent planned to keep the child on the bottle ten months or more. Only 21 percent of the breast-feeders planned to keep the baby on the breast ten months or more. Most breast-feeders (62 percent) planned to wean the child from the breast by six months of age. (Unfortunately, they were not asked how long they would bottle-feed after that.)

---

[4]Also, two other women were unexpectedly rehospitalized at five and eleven days after birth and were forced to wean.

Women who were still breast-feeding at the time of the postpartum interview were asked about how they would feel if they had to stop breast-feeding sooner than planned. Twenty percent did not answer the question because they could not imagine any reason for stopping before they wanted to, and another 49 percent they would mind very much. Only 13 percent said that it would not matter. For those women who persisted over the first few weeks, then, there is a strong commitment to breast-feeding.

Most women would choose the same kind of feeding again. Twelve percent of the bottle-feeders wanted to breast-feed a second baby, while 8 percent of those who attempted breast-feeding planned to bottle-feed from the start with the next baby. Another 10 percent were not sure how they would feed next time.

Of the breast-feeders who had weaned between birth and the sixth month (forty-three), six were very disappointed and fourteen were somewhat disappointed that they had had to stop breast-feeding. For example, one mother, whose physician said she had to stop because her baby sucked "too long" (at three weeks, feedings often took an hour), was quite unhappy about the situation. "I was real upset because I didn't want to stop at all. I was real upset that day. I guess I had my heart set on breast-feeding him. It was really a blow when I couldn't." For the remainder, giving up breast-feeding was either of no consequence or a relief. One woman said:

> I stopped because all she ever wanted to do is eat. So I called the doctor and he said: "Do you want to put her on formula?" And I said, "Yes!" I wasn't that gung-ho anyway. See, it really bothered me that I couldn't go on a diet, because I had to drink all that milk. I was desperate; I couldn't fit in any of my clothes. I didn't have anything to wear. And besides, I'm not the type to breast-feed in front of people, so every time, I had to leave the room. . . . So it was just easier all the way around, for me and for her, to stop.

Thirteen women who weaned before six months reported severe problems, especially with leaking and pain from fullness. All of these women had attempted to wean abruptly (two were hospitalized suddenly; five were sick themselves or the babies were sick; and the rest took a strong dislike to breast-feeding). If women cut down gradually, substituting one feeding per day, then two, and so on, lactation gradually diminished in response to diminished stimulation. This approach is much more effective (and pleasant) than other remedies suggested, such as a drastic cutback on fluid intake and binding the breasts. The topic is not a trivial one, for some women who experience severe weaning problems are discouraged from breast-feeding another infant. This is an example of a kind of problem that develops because the pediatrician looks after the infant but not the mother, and after her six-week checkup, the obstetrician is no longer in touch with the mother.

Thirty-five women (29 percent of the total sample) breast-fed six months or longer.

There was little difference in weight at six months of age between children who were bottle-fed and those who were ever breast-fed. The infants breast-fed for any amount of time were slightly, but not significantly, heavier (17.00 lbs. vs. 16.18 lbs.). There was even less difference between those who were breast-fed more than three months and all others (16.90 vs. 16.81).

Forty-one percent of the infants for whom the information was secured were started on solids *before* the first month was over and another 16 percent before they were two months old—contrary to advice of the American Academy of Pediatrics (Committee on Nutrition 1976; IPA Seminar 1975) that solids be withheld for *at least* four months, and preferably six. All but two of the sixty-five mothers who started solids before their babies were two months old had been told to do so by their pediatricians. (The other two did it on their own.) Many hoped that the introduction of solids would help the baby go longer between feedings (33 percent) or sleep through the night (10 percent), but when asked if solids *did* help, most laughed and said no. All the babies reported on had begun solids by the six-month phone interview, though 21 percent of the mothers had waited till after the fourth month to introduce them. In most cases women reported that their babies liked solids (70 percent), but a few (9 percent) reported strong dislike. An analysis of the time relation between starting solids and stopping breast-feeding suggests that introduction of solids played a negligible role in causing women to wean from the breast. About one third of the breast-feeders who persisted six months or more started solids in the first two months, and as many of the mothers who weaned before two months started solids *after* they weaned as started before.

There was a relation between feeding intentions before birth and preparation level (see table 5.2), the more highly prepared being more likely to plan to breast-feed. A parallel relationship is seen after birth as well, for only 16 percent of the Lamaze-trained women began bottle-feeding initially. Also, preparation level is related to duration of breast-feeding. In the Lamaze-trained group, 42 percent of the women breast-fed longer than six months, compared to 6 percent and 19 percent in the other two groups. This relation between preparation and breast-feeding is consistent with earlier findings (Doering and Entwisle 1975), but the causal direction of the relationship is equivocal. Later analyses (table 5.5 and chapter 7) suggest that the causal direction may even differ according to social-class background, for there is some suggestion that lower-class women who intend to breast-feed seek out preparation classes rather than the reverse.

Because of its high educational level, this sample is not unusual in its high rate of breast-feeding (Hirschman and Hendershot 1979). In evaluating reports of breast-feeding, however, it is important to remember that frequencies in most surveys are based on those breast-feeding at the time of leaving the hospital. In the present study, the rate of breast-feeding on departure from the hospital (65 percent) dropped off rapidly—only 49 percent of the mothers were still breast-feeding when infants were one month old. Therefore it is

TABLE 5.2. Relation between preparation level and feeding

| | Preparation level | | | | | |
| | 1–3 | | 4–5 | | 6–7 | |
	N	%	N	%	N	%
Feeding plans before birth (six-month interview)						
Bottle	17	49	12	38	9	17
Breast	18	51	20	62	44	83
Actual feeding mode						
Bottle	21	60	14	44	7	16
Breast						
1 month or less	6	17	5	16	8	18
1–3 months	3	9	3	9	5	11
3–6 months	3	9	4	12	6	13
Over 6 months	2	6	6	19	27	42

probably at least as important to study why women persist in breast-feeding as why they choose to breast-feed in the first place. Persistence in breast-feeding will be discussed later in this chapter.

FEEDING SCHEDULES

At the time of the mother's postpartum interview, 26 percent of the babies were kept on a rigid feeding schedule, 48 percent were semischeduled, and 26 percent were being fed whenever they were hungry (demand or need feeding). (In the nine-month interview the comparable figures were 23 percent, 32 percent, and 45 percent, respectively.) The average baby was fed every three to four hours (seven times per day), but eighteen women reported going regularly five or more hours between feedings (only four or five feedings per day) at three weeks of age, and nine women had babies eating every two hours or less (twelve or more feedings per day).

Bottle-feeders and breast-feeders show a significant difference in choosing scheduled vs. need feeding, and also in giving a very large number of daily feedings (table 5.3). Only 2 percent of bottle-feeders were on demand schedules, and only 7 percent of long-term breast-feeders were on rigid schedules. Although there appears to be a relation between scheduling and persistence in breast-feeding (of those who stopped, 21 percent were feeding on demand as compared with 44 percent in the group who persisted), the percentage difference is not statistically significant in a sample this size, and an analysis with preparation and other prenatal variables controlled fails to

find much relation between type of schedule and breast-feeding success in the first month *or* between type of schedule and breast-feeding persistence. (Scheduling would be expected to have its greatest effect on *early* success, but type of schedule has no effect on feeding success in the first month for either middle- or lower-class women. For lower-class women there is no significant effect on persistence, and for middle-class women there is only a borderline effect of scheduling on persistence.)

Only half the women (51 percent) adhered to the feeding schedule they were planning at the time of the nine-month interview. After birth many more women shifted to scheduled feeding (34 percent) than shifted to need feeding (15 percent). The tendency to shift to more rigid scheduling was highly significant ($\chi^2_1 = 8.64$, $p < .01$).

Social customs mostly press toward scheduling—the expectations of baby nurses and other helpers, many of whom were socialized in the previous generation, are for scheduling (Bronfenbrenner 1958). Father's or mother's employment is usually geared to cycles of sleep at night. Other family preferences, such as for uninterrupted mealtimes, also encourage scheduling. In fact, it is hard to think of any social customs encouraging demand feedings. The scarce scientific evidence related to scheduling points to the importance of stimulation contingent on the infant's signals (Ainsworth and Bell 1974). In

TABLE 5.3. Feeding mode and scheduling

| | Feeding mode | | | | | |
| | Bottle | | Breast stopped[a] | | Breast continued | |
	N	%	N	%	N	%
Type of feeding schedule						
Rigid (N = 31)	21	50	6	32	4	7
Semischeduled (N = 58)	20	48	9	47	29	49
Demand (N = 31)	1	2	4	21	26	44
Feeding frequency per day						
4 to 5 times (N = 18)	8	19	3	16	7	12
6 to 7 times (N = 66)	32	76	11	58	23	39
8 to 13 times (N = 36)	2	5	5	26	29	49

[a] Those who stopped breast-feeding within the first few weeks.

other words, developmentalists generally believe that the infant's development is helped if caretakers respond or take action when the infant cries,
smiles, or gives other cues. Feeding is the major opportunity for contingent
responding to a neonate.

Despite the shift after birth toward scheduling, there is a tendency for
women's feeding intentions of another sort—how long they plan to breast- or
bottle-feed—to be stable over that period ($r = .53$, $p < .01$). Breast-feeders
carry out their intentions on duration less well than bottle-feeders, but there is
a strong relation between the commitment to breast-feeding beforehand and
duration of breast-feeding—those who were firmer in their intentions[5] breast-
fed longer ($r = .67$, $p < .01$). In the models discussed below, the role of
intentions is clarified even further.

MODELS FOR FEEDING BEHAVIOR

Feeding occupies a central position in the development of the mother-infant
relationship, and considerable evidence points to physical and psychological
benefits of breast-feeding (Jelliffe and Jelliffe 1978; Klaus and Kennell
1976b; Winters 1973). However, aside from Newton's finding (1952, 1955)
that desire to bottle-feed correlates with negative feelings about the childbirth
experience, there is very little information linking events in pregnancy
and / or childbirth with feeding behavior (Doering 1975).

The data on breast-feeding secured from women in this sample were
analyzed from several perspectives. One advantage of the present research is
that, with information procured from couples before the birth, it is possible to
draw some inferences concerning the importance of prenatal factors, including women's psychological predispositions, in determining women's feeding
behavior.[6]

To begin the analysis, we will examine data on feeding persistence obtained
in the present survey in light of data procured in an earlier survey. With that
background, we will then explore feeding behavior more extensively in the
present data in terms of wives' predispositions before birth and in terms of
how husbands appear to influence feeding.

COMPARISON WITH PREVIOUS SURVEY

In the earlier cross-sectional study, carried out between 1965 and 1969 with
data procured from mothers four to six weeks after delivery, preparation
influenced the quality of the mother's birth experience both directly and
indirectly through level of awareness at birth. (This finding agrees with evi-

---

[5]Saying they "definitely" plan to breast-feed and thinking the mode of feeding is "extremely
important."

[6]Full definition for all variables in this and subsequent models may be found in Appendix C.

dence presented in chapter 4.) There was also some indication that awareness at birth influenced the mother's reaction to her baby and that reaction to the baby affected feeding behavior. In order to study further the possible causes of feeding persistence, data from the 1965-69 study were selected that were as comparable as possible to the 1973-76 data. (The reanalysis of the 1965-69 data is based on only the 105 women who were having a first child.) Also, since 82 percent of the women in the 1965-69 sample were middle-class, only the middle-class women in the 1973-76 sample will be used in the comparison.

The same completely recursive model to explain feeding persistence, suggested by the earlier work, was estimated for both the 1965-69 and 1973-76 data. Preparation (WPREP), level of awareness at birth (AWARE), the quality of a woman's birth experience (BESCL), and the woman's initial reaction to her baby on first view (FSVIEW) are all taken as successive determinants of feeding persistence (FEED), for reasons given below.

A rationale to explain why preparation would be expected to affect level of awareness and a woman's birth experience was provided in chapter 4.

Preparation would be expected to have positive effects on a woman's first reactions to her infant, because a woman who is prepared for childbirth is anticipating her new role, and preparation classes lead women to make plans for that role. Preparation classes also call to women's attention neonates' appearances (that they will be covered with vernix, may be a little bruised or bloody, and the like), so that prepared women's expectations regarding the baby's appearance may be more in line with the baby's actual appearance.

Preparation would also be hypothesized to have direct effects on feeding behavior for several reasons, among them that preparation classes, as part of the curriculum, often cover the advantages of breast-feeding and instruct women in how to go about it. Contrary to what a mother having her first child might think, breast-feeding is not "instinctive." It takes practice, and it benefits from formal instruction and support.

The effect of level of awareness on birth experience was discussed in chapter 4.

Level of awareness would be expected to affect a woman's initial reaction to her newborn, as well; the mother who is either partially or fully sedated cannot relate well to her baby, because of either her own or the infant's grogginess. Contact may be postponed if the mother is sleepy.

Level of awareness could affect feeding behavior directly, too, because a groggy infant or a groggy mother may be easily discouraged in early feeding encounters. Sucking behavior of newborns is decreased as a consequence of some kinds of medication during delivery (Brazelton 1961). Medication could also have delayed direct effects on sucking behavior, since changes in infants have been found even when mothers had small amounts of medication such as Demerol (Richards and Bernal 1972).

In addition to affecting her initial reaction to her newborn, the quality of a

woman's birth experience could also affect later feeding behavior. A woman with a good birth experience would be expected to be more positively disposed toward her infant, not blaming it for her previous discomfort. Also, if the mother has had a good birth experience, she may be physically able to take actions that are important for establishing the mother-child relationship in the early postnatal period and may be more disposed toward interacting with her new baby. A good experience should not interfere with the physical stamina a mother needs to undertake breast-feeding. On the other hand, a woman who has undergone a difficult birth may change her mind about breast-feeding or may shield herself by allowing night feedings to be given by hospital personnel. Furthermore, a slow recovery could affect breast-feeding for a considerable period.

Finally, the initial attitude of a mother toward her newborn would be expected to affect feeding behavior, because a woman who relates positively to the baby from the start and who establishes a warm initial relationship would be predicted to be more successful in the intimate relationship that breast-feeding requires.

Before discussing differences in parameter estimates between the two surveys, a word is needed about small differences between surveys in the definitions and measures of variables. (Complete definitions of variables for the two surveys are provided in Appendix C.) Most differences are small. Preparation and level of awareness at birth are defined similarly, but preparation was scored from 1 to 9 in the earlier survey and from 1 to 7 in the later survey. Level of awareness has one more category in the later survey. The quality of a woman's birth experience was more carefully measured in the later survey (five questions in 1973–76 compared to three questions in 1965–69), but the variable was defined in much the same way for both surveys.[7]

The mean and variance of the birth-experience variable were much greater in the later survey, but the variable has the same definition and its sample distribution is approximately the same. The woman's initial reaction to her infant was coded somewhat differently: from 1 to 9, vs. from 1 to 6.

For breast-feeding there were minor differences in how categories were constituted. Fortunately for the comparison, a high percentage of women in both samples began breast-feeding (87 percent in the earlier sample and 65 percent in the later sample).

ESTIMATION OF THE MODEL

Table 5.4 gives parameter estimates for all women having a first child in the 1965–69 survey and for the middle-class women in the 1973–76 survey. The

---

[7]The reliability of the birth-experience score for the 1965–69 data could not be determined because raters provided a composite rating for all three questions rather than separate scores for each question. On the other hand, a three-item scale and a five-item scale, both derived from the 1973–76 sample, have comparable alpha reliability levels (.726 and .765, respectively). We therefore assume the measures are of approximately equal reliability.

amount of explained variance in women's feeding behavior is considerably greater in the earlier survey (41.8 percent vs. 26.1 percent).[8]

The effects of preparation on awareness look approximately the same in both surveys (.566 vs. .512). The effect of preparation on quality of women's birth experience and the effect of awareness on quality of birth experience, however, look somewhat different in the later as compared with the earlier study. Preparation has a significant direct effect on birth experience in the earlier study (.163), and although the corresponding parameter in the later study is of similar magnitude (.139), it is not twice its standard error. Awareness is a much stronger direct predictor of birth experience in the later study (.199 vs. 1.703), although significant in both. The overall structure linking preparation, awareness, and birth experience looks similar for both samples, however, and a similar amount of variance is explained (37.8 percent vs. 43.3 percent).

Awareness has significant impact on woman's attitude on first view in both models (.349 and .216, the latter borderline), with a stronger effect relative to other variables in the earlier sample. Neither preparation nor birth experience have significant direct effects on first view in either survey.

The only significant direct path to feeding behavior for the 1973–76 data emanates from preparation (.535). The path from attitude toward baby at first view to feeding is not statistically significant and is negative, and direct effects linking other prior variables to feeding are tiny. For the 1973–76 data, any influence on feeding by variables other than preparation is very small.

For the 1965–69 data, preparation has small and nonsignificant direct effects on either first view or feeding (.059 and .141, respectively). Almost all of preparation's effects are mediated through awareness, with an effect of $.566 \times .349 = .198$ on first view, an effect of $.566 \times .440 = .249$ on feeding, and a small effect ($.566 \times .349 \times .297 = .059$) via both awareness and first view on feeding.

The comparison across surveys suggests that preparation could be a determinant of feeding persistence (indirectly in 1965–69 and directly in 1973–76), although in neither case are prenatal motivational factors controlled. Awareness is a much stronger direct determinant of women's birth experience in the later study, and there are also other structural differences involving awareness.

For both sets of data any link between the quality of a woman's birth experience and later feeding behavior is very weak, although the small amount of earlier information on this topic (Newton 1952, 1955) suggested a positive relationship. Two explanations for the absence of a relationship come to mind. The first is that women's decisions on feeding mode are arrived at gradually over the latter part of pregnancy and are almost always firm by the

[8]Estimation of the model by maximum likelihood techniques with measurement error included led to a similar outcome in terms of the variance in feeding that was explained for 1965–69 and 1973–76 data (45.2 percent vs. 29.9 percent).

TABLE 5.4. Comparison of the feeding behavior models, 1965–69 vs. 1973–76

	1965–69 data, dependent variables							
	Level of awareness (AWARE)		Woman's birth experience (BESCL)		First view (FSVIEW)		Feeding persisitance (FEED)[a]	
	Metric coefficients	Standardized coefficients	Metric coefficients	Standardized coefficients	Metric coefficients	Standardized coefficients	Metric coefficients	Standardized coefficients
Independent variables								
Preparation level (WPREP)	.566	.669*	.163	.331*	.059	.071	.141	.136
Level of awareness (AWARE)			.199	.342*	.349	.352*	.440	.359*
Woman's birth experience (BESCL)					.244	.144	.105	.050
First view (FSVIEW)							.297	.240*
Variance accounted for	44.7%		37.8%		25.2%		41.8%	
Constant term	0.450		1.865		3.214		0.356	

Correlation coefficients (listwise present)
N = 105

	WPREP	AWARE	BESCL	FSVIEW	Mean	SD
WPREP					6.90	2.62
AWARE[b]	.669				4.35	2.21
BESCL	.560	.563			3.86	1.29
FSVIEW	.387	.481	.382		6.09	2.19
FEED[a]	.497	.594	.420	.484	5.46	2.71

1973–76 data (middle class), dependent variables

	Level of awareness (AWARE)		Woman's birth experience (BESCL)		First view (FSVIEW)		Feeding persistence (FEED)[a]	
	Metric coefficients	Standardized coefficients	Metric coefficients	Standardized coefficients	Metric coefficients	Standardized coefficients	Metric coefficients	Standardized coefficients
Independent variables								
Preparation level (WPREP)	.512	.518*	.139	.052	.092	.130	.535	.447*
Level of awareness (AWARE)			1.703	.629*	.216	.301†	.024	.020
Woman's birth experience (BESCL)					.028	.106	.074	.166
First view (FSVIEW)							−.204	−.121
Variance accounted for	26.9%		43.3%		21.2%		26.1%	
Constant term	1.243		11.036		1.651		0.248	

Correlation coefficients (listwise present)

$N = 58$

	WPREP	AWARE	BESCL	FSVIEW	Mean	SD
WPREP					4.78	2.04
AWARE[b]	.518				3.69	2.02
BESCL	.378	.656			17.98	5.46
FSVIEW	.326	.438	.353		3.40	1.45
FEED[a]	.481	.308	.306	.093	3.53	2.44

†Coefficient 1.5–1.99 times its standard error.
*Coefficient 2.0 or more times its standard error.
[a] Persistence in breast-feeding up to one year.
[b] Scored on a scale from 1 to 7 in 1965–69 and from 1 to 8 in 1973–76. The mean of 1965–69 is therefore approximately 1 unit higher than the mean of 1973–76.

ninth month. There is little opportunity for women to change their minds at the time of the birth event. A second explanation is that, compared to other long-lasting factors such as husband's attitude toward breast-feeding or the woman's employment outside the home, the birth event itself is transitory. Whether good or bad, it is short-lived, so that its effects on feeding persistence are overshadowed by other influences that are longer lasting. However, awareness (level of medication) does have effects in the earlier data, and of course this is one aspect of birth management, so by this route events during the birth affected feeding even when the woman's subjective reaction to the birth apparently did not.

The structural differences between the two time periods—in particular the earlier indirect effects of preparation (with awareness playing a critical role) compared to its direct effects later—may reflect changes in social customs and obstetrical management between the mid-seventies and previous decades. In particular, this model may account better for feeding duration in the earlier data, because husbands then took a less active role. In the sixties husbands were more often excluded from labor and delivery and were less likely to attend preparation classes. In the seventies husbands attended preparation classes, took an active role in labor and delivery, and most husbands who were interviewed as part of the 1973–76 survey had definite opinions on feeding. Although we do not have any data pertaining to husbands in the 1965–69 survey, we suspect that their opinions on feeding would have been much less influential than those of men in the current decade. For this reason, the model—which is based exclusively on *mothers'* experiences—may be a more reasonable representation of the causal structures influencing feeding duration during the sixties than of such structures today. The total effect of preparation on feeding persistence in the seventies probably includes effects mediated through husbands' influence, and these effects could be manifest by a direct path from preparation to feeding (like the one observed in the 1973–76 data) when there are no other variables in the model to represent husbands' influence. In the earlier decade, "wives' preparation level" probably represented a variable pertaining almost exclusively to women.

Another change in the intervening decade is the percolation of feminist ideas through all segments of society. One consequence of the notion that women should control their own bodies is that now many women wish to be active participants in childbirth, rather than to be passively delivered. This could account for the much stronger effect of awareness on the quality of women's birth experience in the 1973–76 survey.

With social class roughly equated, both surveys cast serious doubt on the conjecture that women's subjective reactions to the birth event directly influence feeding behavior. Both surveys suggest preparation has positive effects, although this model does not control on other preexisting differences that could provide alternative explanations for the link between prenatal preparation and women's feeding persistence. Those who seek preparation, for

example, may have different motivational backgrounds from those who do not. Such factors are taken into account in the next model.

A MODEL TO EXPLAIN FEEDING PERSISTENCE

A priori, a number of variables would be thought to affect a mother's decision to breast-feed and her success in continuing to do so. Social class is a prime example. There was actually no difference in either the feeding mode selected or the duration of breast-feeding by class in this study, yet because (as pointed out in chapter 3) lower-class women report a few more inhibitions about breast-feeding, the mechanisms underlying feeding behavior may differ according to class. Therefore, a model will be proposed to examine the effects of women's prenatal attitudes and intentions as well as their preparation on infant feeding, and it will be estimated separately for women of the two social classes. The model will shed light on the extent to which effects of preparation may be confounded with, or independent of, effects of other prenatal influences.

Preparation level (WPREP) would be expected to affect feeding behavior directly, for reasons given earlier.

A second variable, included mainly for control purposes, is the woman's prepartum feeding intentions (WFIN). These intentions are the outcome of prior socialization. (Although the decision to breast-feed or to bottle-feed is correlated with preparation level, the decision is not a simple consequence of preparation, because some women with no preparation breast-feed, and vice versa.) By including this variable separately, effects of predispositions and motivational patterns present ahead of time are taken into account. If women are highly motivated to breast-feed, for example, they may seek out preparation classes, and these motivational factors rather than preparation per se may account for breast-feeding success.

Another variable probably affecting feeding behavior is a set of attitudes toward breast-feeding that are also the product of a long process of earlier socialization. (See Doering [1975:69] for citations on rejection of breast-feeding.) A number of the woman's ideas—whether breast-feeding is pleasant for the mother, how long it is appropriate to breast-feed a child, whether breast-feeding is properly done only in private, whether breast-fed babies are healthier than bottle-fed, and whether or not a husband is jealous of his wife's breast-feeding—may all affect her feeding behavior. Like intentions, women's attitudes toward breast-feeding (WOPBR) are introduced into the model mainly to control on preexisting motivational factors.

Finally,[9] the amount of medication given at delivery and / or the quality of women's birth experience might influence feeding. However, effects of women's birth experience on breast-feeding persistence were shown above to be

[9]The sex of the baby, as shown below, has no discernible effects on any aspect of parenting behavior, including feeding.

negligible in the 1973–76 data for middle-class women, and awareness was important only for the 1965–69 data. To check whether these variables behaved similarly for predicting feeding persistence of the lower-class women in the 1973–76 sample, several multiple regression analyses were run. In every instance, these variables made negligible contributions to variance in feeding either directly or indirectly. The standardized path coefficients were not only below the level of statistical significance in every case but were exceedingly small. Therefore, these two variables, which are directly tied to the birth event, were omitted in the final model of women's feeding behavior.

The above notions lead to a recursive model with three exogenous variables (preparation level, the wife's prepartum feeding intentions, and the wife's attitude toward breast-feeding) and two endogenous variables. The first endogenous variable measures the woman's feeding behavior up to the time the infant was one month old (EFDBE)—including her initial choice of feeding mode—and the second endogenous variable represents the woman's persistence in breast-feeding (FEED). Determinants of short-term and of long-term feeding behavior could differ, and separation of the two endogenous variables allows any such difference to be examined, while acknowledging that early behavior is a powerful influence on later behavior.

ESTIMATION OF THE MODEL

Within each social-class group, the equation predicting feeding behavior in the first month was estimated separately by ordinary least-squares, assuming no measurement error, for breast-feeders and for all women (breast- and bottle-feeders combined). (See table 5.5.) As it turned out, this permits separation of the effects of the prenatal variables on the decision to breast-feed from the effects of those variables on breast-feeding success in the first month. For breast-feeders, the model does not account for significant variance in feeding behavior in the first month. For breast- and bottle-feeders combined, however, the model accounts for rather large proportions of variance in first-month feeding behavior for women of both social classes. The conclusion is that the choice of breast- or bottle-feeding is rather well explained by the model, but that early success at breast-feeding is not. In other words, for women who begin breast-feeding but who stop before the end of the first month, the prenatal variables are not predictive. (A supplementary analysis of possible effects of events related to feeding in the first few days after birth— how soon the women fed, how often and so on—also did not explain variance in first-month feeding behavior.)

For middle-class women, the choice between breast- and bottle-feeding is significantly linked to preparation, with intentions and attitudes controlled. For lower-class women the net effect of preparation appears negligible, although the high degree of collinearity makes parameter estimates unstable. The pattern of zero-order correlations suggests that lower-class women's intentions may lead them to seek preparation, rather than the opposite.

The parameters for predicting feeding persistence were estimated for breast-feeders only. Irrespective of class, early feeding success predicts persistence—obviously, women who stop within the first month cannot continue. In addition, for middle-class women, preparation has borderline direct effects on persistence net of intentions and attitudes, whereas for lower-class women preparation has negligible effects.

The structural patterns differ by class even though feeding behavior was the same in terms of averages for both social-class groups (3.32 vs. 3.33 and 3.65 vs. 3.87 for middle-class and for lower-class women respectively), and even though the amount of explained variance in *long*-term feeding behavior was substantial in both (62.9 percent and 49.9 percent). (Comparable figures for estimates that included measurement error are 71.1 percent and 53.3 percent, and the conclusions about effects of preparation are essentially unchanged.)

In terms of an overall picture, it is possible that intentions to breast-feed may induce lower-class women to seek out preparation classes in the first place. Having made this decision, all else is relatively inconsequential for lower-class women. Middle-class women may seek preparation for other reasons, and their decision whether or not to breast-feed appears to be responsive to preparation net of preexisting attitudes and intentions. Their persistence is independently responsive to preparation as well. This pattern suggests flexibility—a responsiveness to training and socialization.

This account of feeding behavior leaves a number of questions unanswered, especially the determinants of women's success at breast-feeding in the first month. But this analysis and the previous one suggest that for all women experience before the birth is important in affecting feeding behavior, whereas the birth experience itself is not. These analyses also suggest that for some women (middle-class), childbirth-preparation classes have positive effects on breast-feeding choice and persistence net of preexisting motivational factors. Within the two classes rather different mechanisms appear to be related to women's success at breast-feeding.

A Feeding Model Based on Couples' Responses

To shed further light on feeding behavior, a third model will now be proposed that draws upon data obtained from both husbands and wives. Because there were differences related to breast-feeding between fathers who chose to participate in this research and those who did not (see table A.4), suggestions from a model based on data from these couples could not apply to the entire sample. Also the number of cases is *very small* for an analysis of this kind, but since data on this topic are scarce, we decided to present the information available.

Husbands' behavior could easily affect wives' success in feeding. When questioned just prior to the birth, most husbands had clear intentions about feeding, in some cases not in line with their wives'. Also, it is easy to imagine differences developing in couples' attitudes about feeding after the baby is

TABLE 5.5. Model for predicting feeding behavior by social class: women only

	Dependent variables, middle class					
	Feeding, first month (EFDBE)[a]				Feeding persistence (FEED)[b]	
	All women (N = 57)		Breast-feeders (N = 39)		Breast-feeders (N = 39)	
	Metric coefficients	Standardized coefficients	Metric coefficients	Standardized coefficients	Metric coefficients	Standardized coefficients
Independent variables						
Preparation level (WPREP)	.219	.241*	.151	.251†	.217	.214†
Wife's prepartum intentions (WFIN)	.237	.369*	−.054	−.101	.170	.190†
Wife's attitude toward breast-feeding (WOPBR)	.413	.231†	.110	.071	.107	.041
Feeding, first month (EFDBE)					1.152	.687*
Variance accounted for	42.6%		7.5%		62.9%	
Constant term	−3.178		3.086		−3.884	

Correlation coefficients (listwise present) N = 57

	WPREP	WFIN	WOPBR	EFDBE	Mean	SD
WPREP					4.89	2.03
WFIN	.230				7.95	2.89
WOPBR	.292	.619			8.56	1.04
EFDBE	.393	.567	.530		3.32	1.85
FEED[b]	.464	.584	.514	.892	3.65	2.42

Correlation coefficients (listwise present) N = 39

	WPREP	WFIN	WOPBR	EFDBE	Mean	SD
WPREP					5.36	1.93
WFIN	.057				9.28	2.18
WOPBR	.135	.314			8.97	0.74
EFDBE	.254	−.065	.073		4.38	1.16
FEED	.405	.170	.179	.732	4.87	1.95

Dependent variables, lower class

Independent variables	Feeding, first month (EFDBE)[a]				Feeding persistence (FEED)[b]	
	All women N = 54		Breast-feeders N = 35		Breast-feeders N = 35	
	Metric coefficients	Standardized coefficients	Metric coefficients	Standardized coefficients	Metric coefficients	Standardized coefficients
Preparation level (WPREP)	.051	.057	.048	.101	.096	.097
Wife's prepartum intentions (WFIN)	.489	.813*	.201	.393*	.088	.081
Wife's attitude toward breast-feeding (WOPBR)	.054	.032	-.058	-.061	.278	.137
Feeding, first month (EFDBE)					1.252	.593*
Variance accounted for	75.2%		16.1%		49.9%	
Constant term	-1.486		2.786		-4.285	

Correlation coefficients (listwise present) N = 54	WPREP	WFIN	WOPBR	EFDBE	Mean	SD
WPREP					4.56	2.10
WFIN	.538				8.43	3.13
WOPBR	.498	.652			8.59	1.14
EFDBE	.511	.865	.591		3.33	1.88
FEED[b]	.522	.810	.603	.898	3.87	2.64

Correlation coefficients (listwise present) N = 35	WPREP	WFIN	WOPBR	EFDBE	Mean	SD
WPREP					5.31	1.94
WFIN	.277				10.40	1.79
WOPBR	.336	.516			9.09	0.95
EFDBE	.189	.389	.176		4.60	0.91
FEED	.278	.410	.316	.667	5.43	1.93

†Coefficient 1.5–1.99 times its standard error.
*Coefficient 2.0 or more times its standard error.
[a] When parameter estimates for this equation were derived using only data for breast-feeders, the F-value for regression was not significant.
[b] Persistence in breast-feeding up to one year.

born. If a husband is enthusiastic about breast-feeding, he might encourage his wife to persist in it. A husband's attitudes could be extremely important on a subtle level because, even though no comments are made, a woman might sense that her husband had reservations about breast-feeding or thought it "cow-like." Certainly, if a husband had negative attitudes, he could create difficulties for his breast-feeding wife, such as complaining that breast-feeding limits their recreational activities or social life. Accordingly, husbands' prepartum intentions about feeding (HSIN) were evaluated by a scale composed of three items pertaining to his desires about feeding the infant, and his opinions about breast-feeding (HOPBR) were measured by summing items evaluating his opinions on whether infants can be fed in public and the like.

TABLE 5.6. Model for predicting feeding behavior by social class: couples (breast-feeders)

| | Dependent variables, middle class | | | |
| | Feeding, first month (EFDBE) | | Feeding persistence (FEED)[a] | |
	Metric coefficients	Standardized coefficients	Metric coefficients	Standardized coefficients
Independent variables				
Preparation level (WPREP)	.335	.571*	.189	.186
Wife's prepartum intentions (WFIN)	−.167	−.267	.201	.185
Wife's attitude toward breast-feeding (WOPBR)	−.564	−.324	−.075	−.025
Husband's prepartum intentions (HSIN)	.371	.648*	.132	.132
Husband's attitude toward breast-feeding (HOPBR)	−.526	−.370†	.253	.103
Feeding, first month (EFDBE)			1.165	.673*
Variance accounted for	55.4%		78.0%	
Constant term	8.741		−4.768	

Correlation coefficients (listwise present)
$N = 19$

	WPREP	WFIN	WOPBR	HSIN	HOPBR	EFDBE	Mean	SD
WPREP							5.00	2.19
WFIN	.224						9.79	2.04
WOPBR	.551	.347					9.11	0.74
HSIN	.181	.638	.207				9.42	2.24
HOPBR	.253	.207	.171	.197			5.47	0.90
EFDBE	.356	.086	−.031	.441	−.209		4.26	1.28
FEED[a]	.503	.382	.166	.597	.070	.793	5.05	2.22

(continued)

In line with this rationale, a feeding model was estimated separately for couples of the two social classes. Both husbands' (HSIN and HOPBR) and wives' (WFIN and WOPBR) intentions and opinions about breast-feeding before the birth, as well as preparation level (WPREP), were taken into account.

ESTIMATING THE MODEL FOR COUPLES

Because so few fathers of bottle-fed babies agreed to be interviewed, the equations in table 5.6 were estimated only for fathers of breast-fed babies. Therefore, all the parameters in table 5.6, unlike those in table 5.5, pertain to

TABLE 5.6. Continued

	Dependent variables, lower class			
	Feeding, first month (EFDBE)		Feeding persistence (FEED)[a]	
	Metric coefficients	Standardized coefficients	Metric coefficients	Standardized coefficients
Independent variables				
Preparation level (WPREP)	.002	.005	.100	.112
Wife's prepartum intentions (WFIN)	.317	.555†	−.089	−.085
Wife's attitude toward breast-feeding (WOPBR)	.083	.072	−.024	−.011
Husband's prepartum intentions (HSIN)	−.039	−.073	.330	.340†
Husband's attitude toward breast-feeding (HOPBR)	.068	.048	.705	.274
Feeding, first month (EFDBE)			1.014	.556*
Variance accounted for	33.4%		59.7%	
Constant term	0.508		−5.868	

	Correlation coefficients (listwise present) $N = 20$							
	WPREP	WFIN	WOPBR	HSIN	HOPBR	EFDBE	Mean	SD
WPREP							4.85	2.16
WFIN	.450						10.30	1.84
WOPBR	.345	.530					9.00	0.92
HSIN	.288	.472	.408				9.75	1.97
HOPBR	.178	.234	−.231	−.081			5.15	0.75
EFDBE	.267	.572	.327	.216	.168		4.50	1.05
FEED[a]	.365	.502	.239	.425	.343	.653	4.90	1.92

†Coefficient 1.5–1.99 times its standard error.
*Coefficient 2.0 or more times its standard error.
[a] Persistence in breast-feeding up to one year.

breast-feeding success. It is thus not possible to see whether husbands affected the choice of feeding mode.

The most noteworthy finding is that the couples' model, unlike the wives' model, can explain middle-class women's early success in breast-feeding. The model (table 5.6) accounts for significant variance in first-month feeding behavior (EFDBE) for middle-class couples ($F_{5, 13} = 3.23$), although not for lower-class couples ($F_{5, 14} = 1.41$). The model accounts for significant variance in feeding persistence (FEED) for couples of both classes, however. For middle-class women, husbands appear to affect early success in breast-feeding, with 55.4 percent of the variance in early feeding behavior of middle-class women accounted for. Preparation level (WPREP) and the husband's prepartum intentions (HSIN) both play positive roles (standardized coefficients of .571 and .648 respectively), but the husband's attitude toward breast-feeding (HOPBR) plays a negative role ($-.370$).

The positive influence of husbands' intentions is as expected. The negative influence of husbands' attitudes is counterintuitive. Because of the small case base, very low reliability of the husband measures, and selectivity in the sample of husbands, this analysis requires much further checking.

In the couples' model, lower-class husbands' intentions have (borderline) significant direct effects on persistence (.330), and this is the only direct effect on persistence for either class group. Since both husbands' intentions and attitudes have significant direct effects on first-month feeding behavior for middle-class couples (.371 and $-.526$), however, middle-class husbands' intentions and attitudes have substantial indirect effects on persistence (.371 × 1.165 = .432 and $-.526 \times 1.165 = -.613$). The influence of middle-class husbands is large and appears early, and the influence of lower-class husbands is smaller (.330) and appears later.

COMPARISON OF FEEDING MODELS

The patterns across the wives' and couples' models for the lower-class group suggest that wives determine feeding behavior. Except for a borderline direct effect of husbands' intentions on persistence, patterns look identical. By contrast, the patterns across the wives' and couples' models are not the same for the middle-class group. Omitting husbands in the middle-class model may distort the picture. Middle-class husbands have noticeable impact on success in first-month feeding behavior, whereas their lower-class counterparts do not.

A consistent pattern in the models for couples *and* wives is the impact of preparation for middle-class couples and the lack of such impact for lower-class couples. Preparation apparently affects the decision to breast-feed and then promotes both early success and persistence of middle-class couples, net of wives' previous intentions and attitudes.

Comparisons between the analysis based on women's responses and the analysis based on couples' responses are not straightforward, however, because in terms of husbands' attitude about breast-feeding, the subset of cases for which there are data on couples is not entirely consonant with data for the entire sample.

Since the subsample of women whose husbands participated is somewhat different from the others, the strong influence of husbands on feeding behavior probably holds only for certain kinds of couples.

The structural differences by class in both models point to class as an important determinant of the *mechanisms* accounting for feeding behavior, however, even when, as here, the groups are equally well prepared, have equivalent intentions to breast-feed, and persist in breast-feeding to the same extent.

In another survey it would be especially helpful to inquire exactly when women had decided to breast-feed and whether feeding intentions were a factor in the decision to attend preparation classes.

CRYING

Women were queried about the amount of time the baby had cried in the twenty-four hours immediately preceding the interview that was held two to three weeks after the birth. The average reported was just over one and a half hours daily. There was wide variation in this figure, however, for 8 percent reported crying of more than four hours duration, and 6 percent reported thirty minutes or less. The amount of crying reported by women who were still breast-feeding is very slightly (not significantly) less than that reported by those who were bottle-feeding. Others (Bernal 1972) have noted more crying in breast-fed infants, and suggest that the usual four-hour schedule, given the caloric value of breast milk, may be too infrequent to satisfy babies' hunger. The difference in results between this study and Bernal's may be explained by the fact that about half of the breast-feeding mothers in this sample were feeding their babies every two to three hours. Of the infants who cried a great deal (more than three hours daily), almost twice as many were bottle-fed as breast-fed (24 percent vs. 13 percent), although the difference is not statistically significant in a sample this size.

Women were asked what they did when the baby cried. Only 39 percent of the mothers answered this question in a manner that could be classified as "solicitous," e.g., pick up, rock, feed, cuddle, etc. Eighteen percent let the baby cry occasionally, and 43 percent more let it cry regularly.

When asked how they felt when their baby cried, 21 percent reported negative emotions (such as "angry," "nervous," "I wish he'd *shut up*"), with no concern for the baby. Twenty-three percent reported that crying did not bother them (they felt nothing). Another large fraction (21 percent) re-

ported ambivalence: some concern, but also some negative feelings. Just over one-third (35 percent) reported mild or strong concern: ("I feel so sorry for her." "I just want to help him.").

Perhaps in modern American society there would be social pressure for mothers to feed crying infants if relatives were within earshot. In some African societies where relatives share dwellings, social customs encourage a mother's quick offers of the breast to crying infants. LeVine (1977) sees this as an example of how social customs develop to increase the likelihood of survival. Although the African mothers who practice demand feeding do not consciously recognize it, in a tropical habitat where infant diarrhea is perhaps the most serious threat to survival, frequent feeding to increase fluid intake is the most effective remedy they could employ.

Bottle-feeding and breast-feeding women differed in their reactions to their crying infants (table 5.7). Compared to breast-feeders who persisted more than one month, bottle-feeders seemed much more likely to let the baby cry regularly. Also, 59 percent of bottle-feeders reacted neutrally or negatively to the baby's crying, compared to 36 percent of all breast-feeders. Newton (Newton 1973; Newton, Peeler, and Rawlins 1968) suggests this may be because of differences in hormone levels; breast-feeding releases prolactin, which could trigger maternal behaviors. But also the breast-feeding mother possesses a winning strategy—the instant availability of food at just the right temperature and the possibility of putting something immediately in the baby's mouth, which makes crying almost impossible. The bottle-feeder must let the baby cry while she fetches and warms a bottle, and often she must let the baby cry longer while she cools down a bottle she has overheated. Wolff's

TABLE 5.7. Mother's response to crying

| | Feeding mode | | | | | |
| | Bottle | | Breast stopped[a] | | Breast continued | |
	N	%	N	%	N	%
Response to baby's crying						
Lets cry regularly, or "let cry" first response	24	57	13	68	15	25
Lets cry sometimes	4	10	1	5	16	27
Never lets cry	14	33	5	26	28	48
Feelings when baby cries						
Negative	11	26	3	16	11	19
Neutral	14	33	6	32	8	14
Ambivalent	7	17	4	21	14	24
Concern	10	24	6	32	26	44

[a] Those who stopped breast-feeding in the first few weeks.

(1969) naturalistic observations point to the unique soothing effects of feeding on babies, over and above effects attributable to holding or rocking.

In order to shed light on whether mothers' responsiveness is a consequence of personality characteristics present before the birth or a consequence of the actual act of breast-feeding (possibly a hormonal explanation), comparisons were made of three responsiveness measures for three groups of women: those who always bottle-fed, those who breast-fed, and a group of seven women who because of circumstances beyond their control were forced to abandon plans to breast-feed at the last minute or to stop breast-feeding unexpectedly in the first few days. The last group will be called "thwarted breast-feeders."

On the measure "response to baby's crying" (see table 7.2 for method of scoring) the bottle-feeders scored 2.78, the thwarted feeders, 2.57, and the breast-feeders, 3.17 (adjacent differences not significant). In terms of the mother's reported feelings when the baby cries, the respective scores are 2.40, 2.71, and 3.01, again with no adjacent difference significant. On how soon each group "felt like a mother," the respective scores are 3.75, 4.00, and 4.93, again with adjacent differences not significant. The findings are therefore not conclusive, but since continuing breast-feeders consistently exceed the other two groups, there is some suggestion that feeding itself rather than initial motivation is associated with higher levels of responsiveness. Separation of mother and baby occurred for several of the thwarted breast-feeders, however, and this could have diminished the mother's sensitivity to the infant.

Mothers' and Fathers' Reaction to Crying

There is a strong correlation between parental caretaking[10] in response to crying and the parents' reports of their sensitivity to crying[11] ($r = .62$, $p < .01$, for mothers; $r = .41$, $p < .05$, for fathers). Those who were most concerned about the baby's crying said that they were the most inclined to intervene with comfort attempts rather than to let the baby cry. Also, parents who reported having babies who cried less reported being more apt to try to comfort the child. For example, there is an inverse relation between mothers' reports of the amount of time the baby cries and mothers' comfort attempts ($r = .35$, $p < .01$). This is in line with Bell and Ainsworth's (1972) data suggesting that, contrary to what many parents believe, prompt responses to the crying infant do not spoil the child. Rather, prompt parental response apparently leads to less fussing or crying later on, a point that will be explored more thoroughly in chapter 7.

In addition, those who take action when the baby cries may be more accurate in their recollections of how often the baby does cry. That is, when

---

[10]Caretaking was measured by asking what the parent did when the baby cried, scored from 1 = "let cry" as first response to 5 = "does everything" respondent can think of.

[11]Sensitivity to crying was measured by asking how the parent felt when the baby cried, scored from 1 = negative feelings for baby to 5 = overriding concern for the baby.

158 THE FIRST BIRTH

TABLE 5.8. How mother felt when baby cried versus action she took

| | Feelings | | | | | | |
| | No concern or negative emotions | | Neutral or mixed feelings | | Real concern for baby | | Total |
Action taken	N	%	N	%	N	%	N
"Let cry" is woman's first response	5	20	7	13	0	0	12
Woman makes other responses, but lets cry occasionally or regularly	15	60	37	70	9	21	61
Woman is solicitous; letting cry not mentioned	5	20	9	17	33	79	47
Total N	25		53		42		120

asked how long the baby has cried in the past twenty-four hours, parents inclined to let the baby cry may underreport crying because they are rueful about admitting their lack of responsiveness or because they are unconsciously distorting the facts. Crying, being an aversive stimulus, may lead parents to "forget" it or "not to hear" it.

The relation between how mothers feel when the baby cries and the action they take are rather consistent (seventy-five cases lie on the major diagonal in table 5.8). When women's actions and feelings are inconsistent, women act more solicitously than they feel (24 percent are below the diagonal, compared to 13 percent above; $\chi_1^2 = 3.75$, $p = .06$). No one reports letting the baby cry while feeling great solicitude.

From before to after the birth, changes in decisions about where the baby would sleep were in a conservative direction. Eighteen percent of those who intended the baby to sleep in its own room had the baby sleeping in the mother's room at two or three weeks of age, while 33 percent of those who planned ahead of time to keep the baby in the mother's room slept separated.

HUSBANDS' REACTIONS TO THE BABY

As mentioned in chapter 4, 66 percent[12] of all the husbands saw their child in the delivery room. When questioned directly concerning how they felt about the baby on first seeing it, the fathers (unlike the mothers) expressed almost the same level of enthusiasm as would be inferred from their descrip-

[12]Slightly more (68 percent) of the husbands who participated in the research saw their babies immediately.

tion of the baby's appearance. Fathers' consistency in reported feelings toward the baby and descriptions of its appearance may reflect either that males feel less pressure to secure social approval (saying they are positive in their feelings when they actually are not) or, again, selective factors, since possibly husbands who did not participate in the research were less positive.

On the average, fathers held their babies within six hours of birth, but this average is deceptive because almost all the fathers who were present at the birth held the baby soon after its birth, whereas almost all the rest did not hold the baby until a day or more later. Fathers' feelings about holding the baby were "mildly positive" on the average.

For four fathers (all middle-class) the first week at home was "really awful" or "terrible." Most (77 percent), however, reported that things went well. Things definitely improved by the second week—no husband felt that things were "terrible" the second week at home, although the second week was harder for wives.

When questioned about their emotions during the drive home from the hospital soon after the baby was born, 55 percent reported either neutral or negative emotions, evidently a letdown after the excitement of the birth event.

I don't know—it was just starting to get to me, to hit me. After being up for so long, you're so sleepy and—everything's unreal. I was zonked out.

Emotionally and physically drained. All I could think about was getting some sleep.

But 45 percent of the new fathers described positive feelings:

Okay—all you drivers, you better watch out, because here comes a new father! Nothing can happen to me!

I felt great. I mean, I felt whipped, but quite euphoric. Exhausted, but I didn't feel like going to sleep. I called up a lot of people and watched TV—I was pretty wound up.

From wives' reports, apparently *all* husbands, not just the group who agreed to participate in the study, tended to help with the baby by holding it and by picking it up when it cried. This began in the hospital for some husbands, and for others soon after the mother and child returned home. Since there is good agreement between husbands' and wives' reports of the husbands' child-care activities for couples with both members in the study, we are inclined to credit also wives' reports concerning activities of husbands not in the study.

When asked what they did when the baby cried, 40 percent of the fathers were either somewhat solicitous or definitely solicitous (about the same percent as mothers). The remainder let the baby cry or called their wives. The responses of men were of the same type and quality as the responses of women. On the average, husbands reported that they felt "some concern" when the baby cried, and only a relatively small fraction took no direct action at all when the baby cried.

Eighty-eight percent of the women in this sample perceived their husbands as being very interested in the new baby, while 11 percent perceived husbands as somewhat interested. Only one was seen as not interested. Fathers' interest was indicated by their getting up with the baby at night—67 percent of those queried directly reported doing so occasionally, even four to eight weeks after the baby was born. On the average, the mothers reported that their husbands had held the baby one to one and a half hours on the day before their interview (when the baby was two to three weeks old). When the baby was four to eight weeks old, fathers, in their separate interviews, reported the same amount of holding.

Many of the women (65 percent) reported that husbands got up at night with the baby during their first week at home. Also, 65 percent of husbands were getting up with the baby later, at the time when the father's interview was held. These were not necessarily the same husbands, so that altogether 82 percent got up in the night at some point. There was no significant relation between women's reports of how rested they felt three weeks postpartum and whether the husband got up.

On the whole, the husbands participated very actively in the care of their new babies, especially since close to half of the women were still breast-feeding at the time of the postpartum interview. Mothers estimated that in the first two to three weeks their husbands had changed an average of 1.3 diapers per day, but the range in answers to this question was vast. Fourteen percent of husbands had not changed any diapers, while 9 percent were reported to change more than four diapers per day. By three weeks after the birth, 63 percent of the husbands had not become involved in baths at all, 19 percent had helped give a bath, and 18 percent had bathed the baby without anyone's help. When asked what else the men did with their babies, the new mothers mentioned many other activities, including passive ones such as looking at the baby, talking or boasting about it, taking pictures, calling home from work to check on the baby, and buying things for the baby. Active-interest items included playing with the baby, rocking, singing or talking to the baby ("they have conversations"), hugging, cuddling, and kissing it, and picking up the baby on his own, as well as caretaking activities.

Since most of the fathers who agreed to participate in this study were fathers of breast-fed children, it is hard to make a study of breast-feeding in relation to father's activities with the baby. Nevertheless, fathers of breast-fed children got higher ratings, although not significantly higher, on enjoyment of fatherhood in the hospital and at home and on spontaneous activity with the baby. This is an interesting point to note, because many expectant parents saw one of the possible disadvantages of breast-feeding to be that the father would then not be as involved with his new baby.

Direct comparisons are not possible, but it seems that fathers in the present study were more active with their infants than fathers studied a few years earlier. Pedersen and Robson (1969) found that fathers played with their

nine-month-old infants slightly more than one hour per day, and Rebelsky and Hanks (1971) reported that fathers spent less than one minute per day verbally interacting with infants up to three months old.

Eighteen (15 percent) of the new fathers had not yet fed their babies at the time of the mother's postpartum interview. (Seventeen of these men were fathers of breast-fed babies.) Fathers of bottle-fed babies were giving the baby a bottle on the average of once a day. Comparing breast-feeders who stopped with those who continued, it turns out that the husbands of those who stopped were also feeding an average of once a day, while on average the husbands of those who continued to breast-feed were giving a bottle only once in four days. (This was almost always a feeding of water, not formula.) Frequent bottle-feeding at this early stage could interfere with breast-feeding, because establishing a good milk supply depends on frequent stimulation. More sucking by the baby causes more milk to be produced, although many people are unaware of this fact. Women who give supplementary formula because they think they "don't have enough milk" are exacerbating their problem rather than curing it, and fathers who feed babies formula may contribute to early cessation of breast-feeding.

PARENTS' REACTIONS ACCORDING TO BABIES' SEX

Because before the birth the majority of the men preferred a male child, because after the birth some men acknowledged disappointment if the baby was female, and also because previous research pointed to differential parent reactions according to the baby's sex (Lewis 1972; Parke and Sawin 1976), it seemed possible that men with daughters might spend less time interacting with their babies than men with sons, or that the quality of the father-infant relationship might differ according to sex of the baby. Therefore, responses to questions about how the father interacted with the baby in the early weeks (extent of feeding, diapering, bathing, holding, comforting, number of play activities) were examined for differences according to the baby's sex. Also, father's reports of how they felt when they first saw the baby, how they felt when they first held it, how they felt when the baby cried, when they first felt like a father, how much they enjoyed fatherhood, and whether they mentioned the baby as contributing to marital happiness were examined. On *none* of these variables was there any significant difference according to the baby's sex.

Since sex roles and sex-role standards are likely to be more stereotyped in working-class than in middle-class families, differences in fathers' reactions to the baby were examined separately within the two social classes. For middle-class fathers there still were no differences, with one trivial exception—fathers fed girl babies for the first time before the end of the first week, as compared to feeding boys for the first time by the end of the second

week. For lower-class fathers, three minor differences emerged: fathers of *girls* more often mentioned the baby as one of the nicest things about the first few days at home, changed the first diaper sooner, and had more positive feelings at the time they first saw the baby. In sum, despite the strong preference for male children expressed by most fathers, it appears that the preference had little to do with father's treatment of the baby in the early weeks, and to the extent differences do occur, fathers favored girls rather than boys.

Mothers expressed much weaker preferences for male children (not a statistically significant difference). It therefore seemed less likely that their parenting would be affected by the baby's sex, but to check this, analyses similar to those carried out for fathers were carried out for mothers as well. For mothers there were *no* differences according to the baby's sex in replies to questions about caretaking or about their emotional responses to the baby. In particular, there was no significant difference in feeding behavior. There were two significant differences, however, in mothers' reactions to childbirth associated with the baby's sex. On further examination, these appear to be a consequence of the fact that fifteen of the twenty Cesarean births were boys. Most likely the more difficult delivery rather than the baby's sex explains the more negative average reaction to childbirth of mothers of boys.

Further study of mother's responses according to the baby's sex revealed absolutely no differences for middle-class mothers on a set of twenty-eight variables that included wives' ratings of husbands' responses to the baby as well as wives' ratings of their own responses to the baby. For lower-class mothers there was one difference—they reported that their husbands were slightly (but significantly) more likely to pick up male babies when they cried.

One further avenue was explored. If the baby's sex was extremely important for a parent in either a positive or a negative way, then there might be differences in the way babies were treated. Accordingly, an analysis was carried out to see if parents reacted differently if at the birth they said they were "overjoyed" or "disappointed" in the baby's sex. No differences appeared for fathers. For mothers, evaluation of thirty variables—including again some that were assessments of father behavior by mothers—revealed only two to be significant. (1) If a mother was disappointed in the baby's sex, she felt "neutral" on first holding the baby; she felt "mildly positive" if she was overjoyed with the baby's sex. (2) "Overjoyed" mothers were more likely than "disappointed" mothers to mention the baby as a source of happiness in marriage. Since only these two differences appeared and they are small in magnitude, the proper conclusion seems to be that baby's sex and / or the parents' emotional response to the baby's sex has very little impact on parents' responses to the child in the early weeks of life. The one small exception involves lower-class fathers' treatment of girls, and this exception is in an opposite direction to what would be predicted.

The lack of any differences in maternal or paternal caretaking based on the baby's sex is somewhat surprising, since there is much evidence that older

babies are treated and / or viewed differently according to their sex (Clarke-Stewart 1977; Kotelchuck 1975; Lewis 1972). Condry and Condry (1976) even showed that college students reacted differently to motion pictures of the same infant when the picture was labeled *boy* or *girl*. On the other hand, our finding may stem from the fact that sex-related treatment differences are absent or minimal for very young infants, an observation consistent with findings of Parke, O'Leary, and West (1972) and of Parke and O'Leary (1975). Another possibility is that the measures of parenting behavior used in this research are too gross to pick up effects. For example, Korner (1974) reviews evidence suggesting that female neonates are more sensitive to tactile stimuli, and this possibility was not checked.

SUMMARY

The early days at home are a stressful time, particularly for mothers. A large percentage of the mothers experienced some period of depression. The seriousness of the depression appeared to be more closely linked to the stress of the birth event than to the baby's or the husband's behavior.

Effects of prepartum preparation net of other variables measured during pregnancy are further documented. Preparation is substantially correlated with feeding behavior, but only for middle-class women are the two variables linked in a potentially causal fashion. Preparation seems to affect middle-class women's decisions to breast-feed and their persistence net of preexisting motivational factors. A large fraction of the women in this sample began breast-feeding, but most of those who persisted over six months were Lamaze-trained.

There is little direct evidence available on how women's initial feeding intentions are derived, except for the earlier observation that women who were breast-fed themselves as infants are very likely to breast-feed their own infants. All analyses of feeding behavior, however—including an analysis based on data for a prior decade—show the quality of a woman's birth experience has a negligible influence on feeding.

Husbands of middle-class women seem to play a role in determining early breast-feeding success, and husbands of lower-class women play some role in persistence. However, because the interviewed and noninterviewed husbands differed on a number of indicators related to feeding and because the case base is *very* small, these conclusions about husband- and class-related differences are highly tentative.

A comparison of breast-feeding based upon a previous cross-sectional survey (1965–69) and the current longitudinal survey revealed possible changes between decades. The earlier data display a number of indirect links, through awareness in delivery, between preparation and feeding, while the more recent data reveal only a direct effect of preparation, all else held constant.

Differences in the mechanisms that explain feeding behavior in the two sets of data may reflect both social changes affecting new fathers in the seventies and changes between decades in the management of the birth event.

There are no significant differences because of the baby's sex in how parents treat very young babies in either behavioral or emotional terms. In particular, analyses of feeding behavior revealed no effects linked to the baby's sex.

6 | THE COUPLE'S RELATIONSHIP

One purpose of this research was to investigate how a first pregnancy and birth, including the couple's style of coping with these stressful events, affect the couple's relationship with each other early in the baby's life. As mentioned in chapter 1, there is little prior research that focuses on the family over the period when it changes from a two-person to a three-person group, although theorists point to the instability of triadic social arrangements and there is a pervasive belief that marital satisfaction declines with the arrival of children. In this chapter the period after birth will be more fully described in terms of the couple's relationship with each other, especially with regard to changes in their beliefs and attitudes that are precipitated by assuming the parent role. The effect of becoming a parent on other roles will be another focus of interest. The ease with which the wife can combine her marital and parental roles depends in part at least on her husband's view of her in both roles. Certainly a wife's ability to reenter the labor force depends heavily on her husband's attitude toward this course of action and on both of their sex-role ideologies. As noted earlier, support of the mate is thought to be critical in a wife's combining parental and work roles.

MOTHERS' RETURN TO EMPLOYMENT

Most of the women were interviewed by telephone when their babies were six months old. (Three could not be reached.) Of these, 6 percent were employed full-time, 18 percent were back in the work force part-time, and 6 percent had tried to work but had stopped. The large majority, however, had remained at home full-time.[1]

Two of the seven women who were employed full-time when their babies were six months old worked a thirty-five to thirty-seven hour week (both were

[1] Shereshefsky and Yarrow (1973:105) found 20 percent of their sample of women back at work by the time the baby was six months old, a figure that agrees well with ours when both full- and part-time work is included.

teachers). The other five worked a forty-hour week or more. One of these five was also a teacher, two were secretaries, one was in public relations at a hospital, and one was an administrative assistant in a well-known museum.

The administrative assistant returned to work gradually, going in for one day a week when her son was three months old, increasing gradually to four days per week in his fifth month and to full-time in his sixth month. When he was younger, she often took him with her, but this became increasingly difficult. At the time of the phone check, he stayed all day with a nanny, who also cared for two other children. The other six full-time workers all returned to work abruptly rather than gradually. One went back when the baby was two and one-half weeks old, one returned at six weeks, two returned at two months, one returned at three months, and the last at four and a half months. Two hired full-time housekeepers, two used relatives as baby-sitters, and the others found women with small children who were willing to baby-sit. Previous research suggests that as more of these mothers return to work, relatives, including the husband, will provide most of the baby-sitting, particularly for blue-collar women (see Warren, 1975).

Of the twenty-one women who were employed part-time (defined as working from four to twenty-nine hours per week) ten worked ten or fewer hours per week, four worked eleven to fifteen hours and seven worked sixteen to twenty hours per week. The average work week was twelve hours. Nine of these twenty-one women either worked at home or were able to take their babies to their workplace. Most of these women were also teachers or secretaries, but a photographer, a potter, a speech therapist, a statistician, a bookkeeper, two dental hygienists, a school-bus driver, and two who baby-sat for the children of other employed mothers are also in this group. In some cases, husbands baby-sat while the part-time work went on, but relatives and friends were the usual mainstay for these women. When women were asked about work plans at the six-months-pregnant interview, 33 percent had planned either not to stop work at all or else to resume work by the time the baby was six months old. So about the same percentage had tried to return to outside employment as said they would beforehand. The large majority of those employed, however, were working part-time.

Seven women tried working, but quit before the six-month phone check. One secretary had helped out at her old job for three weeks when her baby was two months old. Her grandmother cared for the baby, and the respondent said "it worked out fine," but she had not planned to return to work, and this experience did not make her change her plans. Another secretary also worked as temporary help for only three days when her baby was two months old. She found it "too hard to manage" and did not accept any more jobs, though this type of part-time work had been her plan when she was pregnant. A medical secretary started working part-time for the extra money when her baby was three months old. She quit three weeks later because she did not like being away from her child and also felt that the baby-sitter did things "too dif-

ferently.'' Another new mother began baby-sitting thirty-two hours a week in her own home for two preschoolers when her infant was four months old. She quit before the six-month phone check because ''it was too much of a hassle.'' A cardiovascular technician tried part-time work (twenty-four hours per week) for nine days when her child was five months old. She said it was ''fine for the baby but not for me—I'll never go back to work. I thought I'd die from exhaustion!'' Two schoolteachers had also tried working and then stopped. One, who had returned to the classroom when her infant was one month, quit in June when he was three months old, as planned; she had wanted only to finish out the school year. A second teacher returned to work when her son was 2½ months old, but quit mid-year, when he was four months old. She stopped because she was too tired, baby-sitters cost too much, and her home was always in a mess.

The correlation between women's employment plans and their actual behavior (with ''not work'' coded 1, ''tried but quit'' coded 2, ''part-time'' coded 3, and ''full-time'' coded 4) is .43 ($p < .01$). There is no relation between when women plan to have a second child and when they plan to return to employment as reported in the interview after the birth, nor is there any relation between plans for a second child and whether the woman had returned within the first six months after the birth.

There are *no* significant correlations between number of children planned as reported by the wife just before and just after the birth and either earlier-reported employment plans (in the sixth month of pregnancy) or actual employment by six months after the birth. Nor are there significant correlations between work plans or work behavior and husbands' reports of number of children planned. In this sample women's employment plans appear unrelated to desired size of family. This likely is a consequence of the fact that most couples wanted small families and had arrived at this decision before the survey began. There was no difference according to social class in the timing or extent of women's return to employment.

There is a small relation between enjoyment of motherhood when first home from the hospital and women's early return to work ($r = .18$, $p < .05$), but not between work and other baby-care variables.

Women's attitudes toward outside employment and society's attitudes toward employed mothers have undergone marked changes over the past decade, and the women in this sample reflect those changes. Hoffman and Nye (1974) report that the employed mother who has adequate household arrangements is likely to fulfill the mother role as well or better than the nonemployed mother, particularly if the employed mother does not have excessive guilt about working, and Bane (1976) reports that the difference in the amount of time working and nonworking mothers spend with their children is ''surprisingly small.'' Society takes women's commitment to outside work and the employment of pregnant women and new mothers more seriously than it used to, but the majority of parents still believe mothers should

stay home unless the money they earn is essential for family support (Yan-kelovich 1977). Even teenagers believe mothers should stay home with pre-school children (Herzog, Bachman, and Johnston 1979). Most women in this sample behaved in accordance with such opinions, because they did remain at home with their infants. On the other hand, the women in this sample who returned to jobs, or planned to, did not seem to differ at all from those staying at home, either in terms of child-care variables or in their future family intentions. Furstenberg's (1976) results also point in this direction, even though his population was much poorer and younger. Returning to work may therefore be a consequence of several contingencies: absolute financial need, as for one woman whose husband was laid off; the nature of the woman's vocation— whether it is a routine job or an emotionally gratifying one; the adequacy of available child care; and the mother's ability to organize and allocate time. In the case of the mother's time organization, much obviously depends on the infant itself. A fretful, active infant, or one who has either major or minor illnesses, can greatly complicate the direct demands on the mother and can make it difficult for her to delegate responsibility. In examin-ing the case histories of the handful of women who returned to work and the others who tried and quit, the overall impression is that money per se is less important than other factors, except in extreme cases (husband's loss of job).

Although some people are of the opinion that breast-feeding is not possible for the employed mother, this is not the experience of women who have tried. As a matter of fact, they say that it is particularly satisfying to have the intimate tie of breast-feeding, which only they can do for the baby, when they are away from their babies part of the day. In this sample, women who were employed and who began breast-feeding were more likely to persist than women who stayed at home. Of those not employed, 44 percent were continu-ing to breast-feed at the time of the six-months phone check. Of those em-ployed, 53 percent were continuing to breast-feed. (Of those not employed 66 percent began breast-feeding, compared to 61 percent of those employed either full- or part-time.)

THE BIRTH EVENT IN RETROSPECT

In chapter 4 detailed analyses explored the quality of birth experience for both fathers and mothers. Preparation apparently affected the couples' experi-ences in a positive way although not directly. Another question—whether or not new parents *believe* preparation is efficacious—is also relevant, because people's beliefs could be critical in determining whether or not classes are beneficial.

Aside from any other effects preparation classes may have had, both men and women believed classes were beneficial. Of those women who had classes of any kind (85), only two said that they would not recommend classes

to pregnant friends. The same was true for husbands who had attended classes (42); all but one of them would recommend classes to other prospective fathers.

Of the 53 women who took Lamaze preparation classes, 76 percent planned to take them again for review in a second pregnancy. Twenty-four percent felt that they would not need to repeat the classes. Of the 32 women who took hospital-type classes, 56 percent said they would take classes of some kind again, but half of these women had found hospital classes wanting and so planned to sign up for Lamaze classes next time. Forty-four percent of the hospital-preparation group said they would not take future classes. When the 35 women who had taken no classes were asked if they might try such classes with a second pregnancy, 60 percent said they planned to and also that they regretted not having done so with the first baby. Forty percent of the unprepared group still felt that classes had nothing to offer and said that they would not go to classes next time either. Overall, about two-thirds of the 120 women planned to take some sort of classes with a second pregnancy and one-third did not.

Satisfaction With Medical Treatment

In the interview after the birth, women[2] were asked if they would go to the same medical attendant again for their next baby. Of the three women who had been attended by midwives, none had any complaints. Eleven women reported they would definitely change doctors before they had another baby, and nine others had some complaints about their doctors but were undecided about switching. The main complaints were that the doctor had given more medication than the woman wanted, making her feel that she had missed something, or that the doctor had kept her husband out of the delivery room although the couple had been told they could be together. Some saw the physician as distant and brusque during labor. Both husband and wife rated the wife's birth attendant on twenty semantic differential scales (Appendix A, table A.3) at every interview. This provided a more complete measure of how the couples perceived their obstetrician or midwife than was provided by their answers to interview questions. Although overt complaints or a wish to change doctors next time were not related to whether or not the woman experienced a Cesarean delivery, women's semantic differential ratings of their doctors after birth *were* significantly lower if a Cesarean operation had been performed.

On ratings before or after the birth, wives consistently saw the doctor or midwife in a more positive light than husbands did. In the latter part of pregnancy the attendant improved significantly in the eyes of the wife; women rated their doctor or midwife significantly higher when they were nine months pregnant than they had when they were six months pregnant. The wives'

---

[2]Husbands were not asked questions about physician, midwife, or hospital.

rating of the birth attendant also improved somewhat after the birth, as compared with before, but not enough to be statistically significant. Husbands' views of the attendant definitely improved after the birth, as compared with before.

The women generally complained about lack of information and guidance from the physician, and as discussed in chapter 3, they were forced to seek information about childbirth from other sources. In answering an opinion item (Appendix B, opinion item 31), 99 percent of them thought that women should feel free to ask the doctor questions and get explanations, even though they themselves were able to procure little information this way. But despite the women's desire for information and their view that this was a legitimate desire, their physicians' failure to meet this need apparently did not diminish physicians in their eyes over the latter part of pregnancy. Further, the physician's discharge of his / her primary task—delivering the baby—enhanced his / her status in the eyes of the husbands and in the eyes of many, but not all the wives.

Husbands and wives take a somewhat different perspective on drugs administered in labor and delivery; many wives were of the opinion they had been given too much medication, but most husbands were not.

Forty-two percent of the women wanted less potent medication, or none, with their next baby. (In addition, 7 percent had no drugs this time and wanted no drugs next time. Another 2 percent had only local infiltration, which they considered "no medication," and wanted no medication next time.) Eight percent wanted more next time. Forty-one percent were content with the amount of medication they had received during labor and delivery.

From 86 percent to 88 percent of the women, depending on which interview is chosen, feel that women should have some say about the drugs they are given in labor and delivery (opinion item 30). Before the birth, a majority (63 percent) believed that putting the mother to sleep during delivery could hurt the baby (opinion item 42). After the birth, fewer women (56 percent) held that view. This change occurred in women who had been put to sleep and who, naturally, did not wish to entertain the thought that their babies had been harmed in the process.

Husbands did not see drugs in quite the same light, although 88 percent also felt that women should have some say about what drugs are given to them and 60 percent to 65 percent (opinion item 42) believed that putting the mother to sleep during delivery could hurt the baby. Most husbands (79 percent) thought that their wives had received just the right amount of drugs with this delivery. Only 16 percent thought that their wives had received more medication than needed. The rest (5 percent) thought not enough drugs had been used.

The lack of correspondence in this sample between pain anticipated and actual pain is puzzling. (Only 16 percent reported in retrospect that they experienced the amount of pain they foresaw.) One reason for this inconsistency, pointed to in chapter 4, may be the high rate of obstetric intervention. There was a very small and nonsignificant correlation between wives' total

worry scores measured before birth and whether wives reported more pain than they expected ($r = .15$, n.s.). There was no correlation between such pain and husbands' worry scores. The almost total lack of relationships between traditional psychological test measures and pregnancy or childbirth events was not expected. However, the psychological tests were developed for purposes other than measuring variables related to pregnancy and birth.

There is also evidence that preparation is most effective for women who experience a delivery with little obstetrical intervention, but that for women experiencing complications, preparation loses all or part of its effectiveness. Because various kinds of intervention including Cesarean deliveries are so common, it may be advantageous (as pointed out in chapter 4) to expand the topics covered in childbirth-preparation classes to include coping with a surgical delivery—as is now being done in some places. This approach might mitigate some of the stress of complicated deliveries.

When asked whether they would go to the same hospital for their next baby, nine women reported that they were *very* dissatisfied and would not return again to the same hospital. Six others were critical, but less so. Most of the complaints about hospitals had to do with events after birth: not seeing the baby enough, rooming-in not allowed, husband could not visit long enough, and the like. Not many of the women were aware of the further room for improvement that exists in hospital care during labor and delivery, as seen in the failure to allow 47 percent of the women to hold their babies in delivery or recovery.

Interestingly, all five of the women who delivered at home planned home deliveries for the second baby.

Forty-eight percent of all the women expressed a desire prior to the birth for rooming-in. This was considerably more than the hospitals were prepared to handle, for only 31 percent of the women (including the five who delivered at home) had either modified or full rooming-in (with modified rooming-in the baby is in the room part of each twenty-four hours and in the nursery the other part).

In the nine-month interview 52 percent of the women intended to have nursery care; only four changed their minds and had rooming-in (two of them had rooming-in near the end of their hospital stay, and the other two had rooming-in for a few hours a day only).

The difference between desires and / or forecasts of women for rooming-in and what later transpired is large and significant ($\chi^2_1 = 10.24$, $p < .01$), especially in view of the fact that only sixteen of the thirty-seven women classified as having rooming-in had full rooming-in. None of the mothers who had full or modified rooming-in would change to nursery care with the next baby, but there were seventeen women who had nursery care and wanted rooming-in next time. Sixty-six women (55 percent of the whole sample) had nursery care and would not change.

Women's attitudes about rooming-in are reminiscent of other contradictory patterns noted earlier. That is, in some ways these women strongly favor

progressive obstetrics as practiced in the seventies—a large percentage of the women wanted to experience childbirth fully without drugs (48 percent said they wanted to be awake and feeling everything), and 94 percent wished to have their husbands present during labor. In rooming-in, however, their behavior is "reactionary," because over two-thirds of the women in the sample permitted themselves to be separated from their babies after birth, allowing the baby to be placed in the hospital nursery. Even those who had rooming in did not, in many instances, have full rooming-in. It is curious that many of the women were so willing to be separated from their newborns.

Separation from the baby is not entirely a consequence of hospital policy, as shown by women's answers to an opinion item (Appendix B, opinion item 45). After the birth 51 percent of the women and 42 percent of the men believed it was best for a new mother to get her rest and let the nurses take care of the baby while in the hospital. The percentage of women agreeing with this viewpoint after the birth actually increased (only 37 percent thought so before the birth). It seems paradoxical that most of the women wanted an active role during birth, and yet preferred to limit contact with the baby while in the hospital. The preparation process may be deficient in that it neglects early parenting—especially its emotional side.

There was also some increased sentiment after the birth for staying in the hospital longer (opinion item 46). Before the birth 92 percent of the women thought four days was enough, but afterward 16 percent of the women and 19 percent of the men thought a longer hospital stay would be better. Actually, a longer stay might be better if the time were used to let the new mother become used to her new responsibilities, but the drawback is the high cost of hospital care—which continues to rise. Most hospitals charge for two persons— mother and baby—at the full daily rate even when the mother is caring for her own baby.

RESUMPTION OF SEXUAL ACTIVITY

For the 104 women from whom the information was procured, the resumption of sexual intercourse after the birth occurred as follows: within three weeks of the birth (including five women who had Cesarean deliveries), 13 percent; during the fourth or fifth weeks after the birth, 24 percent; six weeks precisely, 35 percent; during the seventh, eighth, or ninth weeks after, 21 percent; ten weeks or longer, 8 percent.

HOW HUSBAND AND WIFE RELATED TO EACH OTHER

The strength and quality of the conjugal relationship could influence pregnancy and childbirth in myriad ways. One would guess that couples who get

along well together, who communicate well, and who are sensitive to each other's needs are in a favorable position to undertake a pregnancy. Indeed, we saw in chapter 3 that quality of communication between husband and wife apparently did influence wife's preparation, which was in turn associated with husband's participation in the birth event, and these two variables indirectly and / or directly affected the quality of the woman's and the man's birth experiences. Some of the positive effects of preparation probably come about because the wife's active preparation de facto involves the husband, i.e., acts to strengthen the couple's ties to one another. Also, since almost all women wanted their husbands to be present during labor and delivery, preparation effectively brought some couples closer together in a way that most already desired.

The sincerity of wives' strong desires for husbands' participation was borne out in answers to questions on this topic after the birth as well. Women's feelings about wishing their husbands to be present during labor and delivery did not change as a consequence of undergoing childbirth. Afterward, more of those whose husbands had been absent wished their husbands had been present than the reverse.

On the other hand, if a couple is well settled and enjoying their lifestyle, they may find the accommodations required by pregnancy burdensome and disruptive, even though they communicate well with each other. In fact, some 21 percent of husbands who were present during labor and delivery did not find the childbirth experience at all enjoyable. Furthermore, when asked after the birth what it was that made their marriage happy, over half the husbands (53 percent) and close to half the wives (43 percent) did not mention the baby at all or mentioned it very incidentally. Some men stated before the birth that they had little interest in their wives' pregnancies. In other words, for some couples pregnancy and childbirth may challenge rather than buttress the strength of the conjugal relationship.

There is a longstanding debate in the sociological literature concerning whether or not the presence of children increases or decreases the likelihood of divorce. The probability of divorce *is* less for parents of young children than for nonparents or for parents of older children, but the reasons parents of small children give for staying together hinge on the high costs of divorcing with preschool children rather than on the positive influence children have in holding a marriage together (Cherlin 1977). Ryder's (1973) report is consistent with this point of view. He found decreased marital satisfaction among women who had a child in the first year or two after marriage, compared to women who remained childless. But how the arrival of a first child affects the conjugal relationship probably depends on several things: the stress, including financial, imposed by the baby's birth; the baby's health and temperament; the amount of baby-sitting help available; and other demands on the couple, such as those stemming from the father's or the mother's job. The problem is exceedingly complex. A newborn baby can certainly produce stress in a

marriage, but so can failure to have a child if one is desired. Furthermore, a colicky baby can be a severe strain on a marriage, but a child can also enhance the quality of a couple's relationship in a way impossible to imagine for those who have not borne and nurtured a child. This viewpoint is consistent with Hoffman and Manis's survey data (1978b), and suggests that the quality of the marital relationship *changes* with the advent of a child.

There seems to be a stronger disposition on the part of today's young people to face up to the negative aspects of child care than was true of those a decade or two ago. The "me" generation can acknowledge that raising an infant might be tedious and unrewarding and above all, might seriously interfere with both self-development and the marital relationship. Since, according to the mother's report, all but four of the babies were at least partially planned, it seems likely that in this particular sample the bias, if any, is in the direction of the infant having a positive impact on the marital relationship.

As couples moved along in time over the period of this study (approximately a nine-month period beginning in the sixth month of pregnancy and continuing through the phone check six months after the birth), some questions were asked about the marital relationship itself. Both husband and wife answered several questions about how household chores were divided up. The reader will recall that during the pregnancy husbands appeared to help more with household tasks than previously reported by others. Other questions were asked about feelings and attitudes affecting the marital relationship—for example, how the wife viewed her mate in comparison to an "Ideal Man," how the husband viewed his mate in comparison to an "Ideal Woman," and how each viewed the other as parents. Questions before the birth about the couples' sexual relationship, the effect of pregnancy on sexual activity, and the question about resumption of sex all shed light on the couple's sexual adjustment.

Despite all this, there is not much evidence on marital quality for this set of respondents. Several questions were asked about the marital relationship after the birth, but not much variance was noted. Apparently the time when the interviews were held was too soon after the birth for marital stress to be acknowledged.[3] When asked about frequency of quarreling two to three weeks after the birth, for example, only nine women (7 percent) said that they quarreled often, and the rest said that they quarreled seldom (66 percent) or never (27 percent). Similarly, *no* husbands acknowledged quarreling often. These and other data indicate that a surface "honeymoon" period in the marital relationship followed the birth, with problems or adjustments postponed at least for the first few weeks. This honeymoon feeling is conveyed in the remarks of one woman, who said:

> I just can't put my finger on it. . . . Things are just going as smoothly as before the baby was born. You know, we share things with each other. If I'm upset, he'll just

[3]No questions were asked about the marriage at the six-month phone check.

listen to it. And when he's upset, I listen to him. . . . I guess part of it is the baby, because he's just a very nice baby—he's so special right now. And I'm pleased with the way D. is as a father, and he thinks I'm a good mother and that's kind of nice too.

There are hints here and there in the data, however, that the picture is not as rosy as it seems, as the following quotations suggest.

We've only had one quarrel since the baby was home, and that was just because I was blue and needed extra attention. And he felt like he's working real hard and I'm home all day not doing anything. He just didn't have any patience with me at all. [Laughs] But that's the only thing. Everything is fine. Except when the baby cries. He doesn't see why it should cry; it gets him mad. So I'm trying to keep it quiet when he's around. I think it's going to be hard for him: he can't stand the dog barking three times in a row. . . .

Oh, we don't quarrel. We don't fight. It's just silly things like my asking him to bring some paper towels up, and he says, "Can't I have two minutes' peace?" And that infuriates me, because I haven't had two minutes' peace since I *had* her. But, you know, I didn't say anything. I just wish I could have *one* minute's peace!

Furthermore, in a probe that inquired whether the couple ever disagreed about the baby or its care, answers contradicted those given to the frequency-of-quarreling question cited above. Even though 93 percent of the women said they seldom or never quarreled, over half (52 percent) said they did disagree about the baby!

The following quotations give the flavor of these kinds of disagreements.

He got mad because I'd wake him up each time I got up to feed the baby, and he doesn't sleep too well and he has things to do the next day.
[You woke him on purpose?]
No, no. Just when the bed would move when I got out, and the baby crying. So I learned to get out more carefully, and to go quick, and catch him on his first cry, so it doesn't wake my husband up as much.

We sit there and argue over should we pick her up or should we let her stay in bed and cry. Neither of us knows what to do. And we both realize that we don't know what we're doing, so there's nothing to really quarrel about.

It's not that we argue. It's just that I complain a lot.
[And what does he do?]
Listens. Listens and then says, "You're the one who wanted a baby."

The same hints of incipient stress are seen in other surveys. Feldman (as cited by Hobbs 1965) reported a "baby honeymoon"—couples are initially elated as a consequence of becoming parents, but stresses begin to be acknowledged after four to six weeks. The timing of the interviews after the birth was such in the present survey that stress was probably building up, but was temporarily being held in check.

COMPANIONSHIP AND SPARE-TIME ACTIVITIES

In the first interview during pregnancy, wives were asked how they spent their spare time and, in particular, with whom they spent it. The question was then coded for how much of the wife's spare time was spent with her husband. (By asking about spare time in general, the question did not lead the woman to report that she spent time with her husband.) There were a number of very small relationships between the number of activities wives shared with their husbands and things such as the degree to which the pregnancy was planned ($r = .15$), the level of the wife's sex drive at the time of the six-month interview ($r = .15$), and the level of the husband's sex drive as estimated by the wife at the six-month interview ($r = .16$). Apparently relatively high sex drive in one or both partners leads couples to spend time together, perhaps with the purpose of encouraging sexual activity. On the other hand, the argument can easily be turned around. If mates spend time together in recreational settings, this may lead to the kindling of sexual desires. (Two women even reported "making love" as one of their favorite spare-time activities.)

DIVISION OF LABOR

In division of household labor (see chapter 2), couples in this study were not as traditional in the assignment of tasks as other reports in the literature would have led one to guess. Also, there was considerable help given by husbands in the week immediately after birth, especially on the part of blue-collar husbands who took time off from work to stay with their wives after they came home from the hospital. Such a division of labor may signal recent trends among young married couples, and it is particularly noteworthy that the trend is found in both middle-class and lower-class couples. On the other hand, since almost all wives worked during pregnancy, it may have been only a temporary adjustment, with the husband assuming some transient responsibility for house chores until the wife resigned her job. By the second week home after delivery, most husbands were reported not to be giving much more help than was usual for them before childbirth. This observation is consistent with Lamb's hypothesis (1978) that having a child causes a shift toward more traditional sex roles.

There is a significant relation between division of labor around the house (as reported by the wife in her first interview, when stress of pregnancy was minimal) and several items involving husband's care of the baby. Husbands were asked how much they had held the baby in the preceding twenty-four hours, and their replies were coded from zero (did not hold at all) to 6 (held the baby four hours or more). The correlation between division of labor in the sixth month of pregnancy and the amount the husband held the baby was .34 ($p < .01$). Wives were asked how many times their husbands had diapered the baby since mother and child had returned from the hospital. Answers to this

question indicated a weak relationship between sharing of household chores in mid-pregnancy and the father's care of his newborn ($r = .19$, $p < .05$).

There is no significant relationship between division of labor (measured in pregnancy) and depression, or between a measure of couple communication and depression for women in either social class. These analyses controlled on prior preparation, father participation in delivery, the quality of women's birth experience, and the amount of baby's crying. In fact, only one significant predictor of depression was found, and it was characteristic only of lower-class women—the quality of women's birth experience. A differential effect by class underscores the question raised in chapter 5 about a hormonal basis for depression. This analysis also suggests that the character of the marital relationship measured during pregnancy does not predict occurrence of depression.

CHANGES IN ATTITUDES OF HUSBANDS AND WIVES TOWARD THEMSELVES AND EACH OTHER

THE SCALES

Semantic differential scales were used over the course of the study to assess the couples' attitudes toward each other, their babies, their parents, and their birth attendants and their attitudes toward themselves in various roles (as wife, as mother, as a woman in labor, as husband, as father, and so on). Each scale contained the same set of twenty bipolar adjectives (see Appendix A, table A.3). The scales were used in the hope of picking up changes in couples' attitudes as revealed in *differences* in ratings from one interview to the next.

To score a given concept—say "Myself"—averages were calculated for each of the twenty adjectives rated in two different interviews. If fourteen or more of these averages either increased or decreased, the concept was rated as "improving" or "declining," respectively. Otherwise, the concept was reported as "unchanged." (This amounts to applying a sign test to the direction of the differences between twenty adjective values on the same concept for two occasions.)

WOMEN'S VIEWS OF THEMSELVES IN VARIOUS ROLES

The women's views of "Myself" improved significantly between the six- and nine-month interviews; apparently as pregnancy progressed, women viewed themselves in a more positive light. However, women's opinions of themselves declined between the nine-month prepartum interview and the postpartum interview—they thought less well of themselves after birth as compared with before.

One of the roles women evaluated themselves in was "Self during Labor." Between the first and the second interview the women became more positive

about how capably they expected to behave during labor. After labor and delivery, however, their views of "Self during Labor" were much less positive. Apparently during labor many women found themselves unable to live up to the standards they had set for themselves.

Women's views of themselves as mothers also declined significantly from before the birth to afterward, while husbands' ratings of "Wife as Mother" went up after birth. Husbands' and wives' ratings of "Wife as Mother" during pregnancy were equivalent; thus a divergence between husbands' and wives' views on this concept occurred after the baby was born.

Another indication of the negative changes in women's views of themselves is that before delivery women rated themselves as mothers close to their ratings of "Ideal Mother."[4] Women rated themselves *below* their ideal after delivery, however. The only respect in which women's views of themselves improved from before the birth to after was in their views of themselves as wives. Perhaps producing a child certifies to a woman that she has fulfilled one of her most important wifely obligations, although no question specifically addressed this issue.

A natural question is whether the changes in women's views of themselves came about because of changes in their own personal evaluations or because they were being evaluated negatively by their husbands. Husbands rated "My Wife" just before the birth more positively than wives initially rated themselves, and husbands' views of their wives did not change from before the birth to after, so it seems unlikely that the change in wives' views is a consequence of a decline in husbands' evaluations. The more favorable view by women of themselves as wives postpartum—the only example in which women's views of themselves increased—agreed with their husbands' views of them all along.

Perhaps a certain euphoria characterizes women as childbirth approaches. They see themselves as doing well in labor and as ideal mothers. After the birth, however, they are fatigued, many are depressed, and the early weeks of child care test their mothering skills more than they have foreseen. The one role for which they do not rate themselves lower is the wife role, the role they have held all along and one which is not so threatened, perhaps because of the postpartum honeymoon. Women's deteriorating views of themselves over the period of study suggest a possible cause for postpartum depression.

WIVES' PERCEPTION OF HUSBANDS AND HUSBANDS' PERCEPTION OF WIVES

By contrast, between the six-month and nine-month interviews there is a definite increase in wives' ratings of their husbands, and a further increase approaching significance after the birth, as compared with before. Wives

[4]Both before and after delivery, their "Ideal Mother" significantly exceeded their rating of their own mothers.

viewed their husbands more favorably than their husbands viewed themselves, both before and after the birth. Wives' ratings of their husbands compared well with their rating of "Ideal Man," equaling or exceeding it. On the other hand, wives generally did not see their husbands measuring up as fathers to their "Ideal Father" ratings before the birth, although differences are a little short of significance. As was also true for their attitudes toward their own mothers, however, women's "Ideal Fathers" far outstripped their ratings of their own fathers. Husbands were seen as fathers in a much more positive light than the wives' own fathers.

When wives were asked after the birth to rate their husbands during labor, they rated them much more positively than husbands rated themselves during labor. As a whole, wives' views of "Husband as Father" did not change over the time of the study, although (as will be pointed out below) this may be true only for husbands who were with their wives in labor and delivery.

From the extraordinarily favorable views the spouses hold of one another as rated after the birth, one can conclude that the couple's relationship is in a honeymoon period like that previously described by Feldman (as cited by Hobbs 1965). Husbands either equaled or exceeded their wives' ratings of "Ideal Man," and they were rated more favorably by their wives from one interview to the next. Wives were consistently rated very favorably by their husbands. Further evidence of the honeymoon is the denial by both spouses of quarreling in the first few weeks after the birth, despite the hints here and there that more stress was experienced than couples were willing to admit.

VIEWS OF THE HUSBAND ACCORDING TO WHETHER HE WAS PRESENT DURING LABOR AND DELIVERY

In the second interview the wife was asked where she expected her husband to be while she was in labor. In only one case did the wife expect the husband not to be at the hospital, and only a small percentage (7 percent) of the women expected husbands to remain in the waiting room. A very large majority (93 percent) of women expected their husbands to remain with them during the entire first stage of labor or for some significant portion of it. When asked where the husbands would be during delivery, 78 percent of the wives expected their husbands to be *physically* next to them in the delivery room. The remainder (with the one exception) expected their husbands to be waiting elsewhere in the hospital during delivery. Even those who did not expect the husband to be present at delivery expressed a very strong preference for a companion to be in the labor room and for the husband to be that companion.

In retrospect, it can be determined how well the expectations of wives were fulfilled, and some of wives' ratings of their husbands appear to reflect how well husbands conformed to wives' expectations for labor and delivery. Separate tabulations of wives' ratings of their husbands were made according to whether the husband was present or absent during labor and delivery. If the

husband was present during labor (84 percent) and delivery (66 percent), the wife's view of her husband as a father was significantly more positive than was the case if her husband chose not to be present. However, if the husband was absent against his will, the wife's view of "Husband as Father" was not diminished. Thus, if the husband was there or wished to be there, the wife saw her husband as a better father.

The decision to be present during delivery may reflect basic differences in husbands. Henneborn and Cogan (1975) reported that husbands who chose to be present in delivery were more confident of themselves and of their skills than a group of other husbands who attended the same number of preparation classes, but who were absent from the delivery. In the present sample there are fathers who attended no classes at all, yet who were present for the delivery. Therefore, there could be great motivational differences among the fathers in the present study.

On the other hand, wives' views of "My Husband" were not affected by absence in labor or delivery. A husband absenting himself by choice from the childbirth event did not affect the wife's view of *her spouse as a husband,* nor was he rated higher as a husband if he wished to be present but was excluded.

The wife's ranking of the importance of self and of husband as compared to baby, work, relatives, and other sources of satisfaction both before and after the birth (see chapter 2) was also examined. In these tallies the wife's ranking of her husband did not change according to whether or not her husband was absent by choice in labor and / or delivery, but the wife's ranking of herself dropped more after the birth than other women's did if her husband chose not to be present. The inference may be that the husband's refusal to participate in delivery is interpreted by the wife as a denigration of her as a person. An alternative interpretation is that the wife who is less positive in her view of herself is insecure and does not encourage (or demand) that her husband take part in the birth. Women whose husbands stay away from delivery have considerably more negative views of themselves, perhaps because some husbands who are present in labor choose not to stay on into the portion of the birth event when they would be viewing their wives in positions that they might consider unattractive or embarrassing.

HUSBANDS' VIEWS OF THEMSELVES

Husbands, unlike their wives, did not suffer any loss of self-regard after the birth as compared with before; they rated themselves the same both times. The husbands rated "Myself during Labor" significantly lower than their wives rated them in that role, and the husbands' conception of "Myself as Father" deteriorated over the perinatal period. Husbands apparently found themselves not able to fill the father role as well as they earlier expected, even though their wives' views of them as fathers were more favorable than their own views both before and after the birth. As mentioned earlier, only fathers not present by choice (a small minority of the fathers who took part in the research) declined in their wives' views of "Husband as Father."

THE COUPLE AND THE CHILD

Among other things the conjugal relationship could be sensitive to are views the couple holds of each other as potential parents, whether or not those views are consistent with sex-role norms or with notions about "ideal parents" as seen by both members of the couple, whether or not each member of the couple does well during the crisis of childbirth, and how well the couple's views related to childbirth and early child-rearing actually agree. A closely related question is how the couple's relationship with each other helps or hinders them in caring for their newborn. It seems likely that a positive view of the spouse, or a close relationship between spouses, would enhance early parent-child relationships. (Research with older children suggests that a wife's positive feelings about her husband serve to facilitate sex-role identification in her son [Helper 1955; Rau 1960]). Such questions can be addressed in a very limited way on the basis of data procured in interviews after the birth event.

Preparation and Other Prepartum Events Related to Baby Care

The husband's attitude toward pregnancy (rated by him in the interview before the birth) was correlated both with wife's enjoyment of motherhood ($r = .27$, $p < .05$) and with whether the husband later mentioned the baby as a source of happiness in marriage ($r = .27$, $p < .05$). The husband's interest in pregnancy was also related to how much the husband later held the baby ($r = .31$, $p < .01$) and to whether he picked up the baby when it was crying ($r = .23$, $p < .05$).

Other provocative relationships exist. If the wife in the six-months-pregnant interview stated that she wished strongly for her husband to be present in delivery, the husband was considerably more likely after birth to report the baby as being a source of happiness in marriage ($r = .44$, $p < .01$). It seems that if husbands are involved in the pregnancy and birth experience from the beginning, having the baby is associated with more positive views of the marriage. The earlier analyses of husband-participation data suggest that motivation to participate and specific activities are both involved, but that emotional responsiveness rather than fatherly caretaking is at issue. In line with this, husbands' *actual* child-care activities do not relate to their wives' seeing the baby as a source of happiness in marriage.

Fatherliness

Shortly before the infant's arrival, men were queried about their own fatherliness ("Do you think of yourself right now as being a very fatherly, somewhat fatherly, or not very fatherly person?"—with answers coded 1, 2, and 3, respectively). The average score (1.8) is close to the middle category, with only one husband admitting that he saw himself as "not very fatherly."

When wives were asked before the birth whether or not their husbands were

fatherly, the average score turned out to be 1.59, about halfway between "very fatherly" and "somewhat fatherly." Wives apparently saw a father role as more suitable for their husbands than the husbands themselves did. There was no correlation between the ratings of fatherliness a husband assigned himself and his wife's rating of him on this trait.

Husbands who easily saw themselves in the parent role also tended to see their wives easily in a parent role ($r = .23$, $p < .05$). If a husband listed a large number of problems associated with his wife's pregnancy, he was apt to perceive himself as more fatherly ($r = .23$, $p < .05$) and his wife as more motherly ($r = .27$, $p < .05$). Perhaps the man who sees many problems associated with pregnancy is one who is sensitive to needs and problems of other persons around him. A sensitive man may actually be more fatherly (more nurturant), because the manifestations of fatherliness require sensitivity toward another person's needs for support.

MOTHERLINESS

The same questions were asked both men and women about motherliness. When husbands were asked whether they saw their wives as motherly or not, 68 percent of respondents saw their wives as "very motherly," and none saw his wife as not very motherly (average score of 1.32, with 1 = very motherly). There thus appears to be a tendency for these husbands to endow their wives with parental qualities more often than themselves.

Wives rated their own motherly qualities at 1.67 on the average. Four women actually admitted to being "not very motherly." Thus, the wives saw themselves as somewhat less motherly than their husbands saw them. Also, there is no correspondence between how women rated themselves on motherliness and how their husbands rated them. As was true for men, however, if women saw themselves as "motherly," there was a noticeable tendency for them to see their husbands as fatherly ($r = .47$, $p < .01$). In fact, this association is even stronger for women.

In sum, wives saw both themselves and their husbands as between "somewhat" and "very" motherly / fatherly. Wives did not perceive much difference, on the average, in the parental inclinations of either spouse. Husbands attributed more parent potential to their wives than to themselves and thereby tended to disagree to some extent with wives' ratings. But wives' ratings of husbands as "fatherly" did not correspond at all with husbands' ratings of themselves, nor did husbands' ratings of "motherly" correspond at all with wives' ratings. These ratings, all made before birth, suggest once more that the couples' expectations about child care or its demands are unrealistic.

Actually, it is not clear what meanings husbands attached to *fatherly* and *motherly,* because estimates of these traits do not correlate with later fatherly activities—helping with the baby, enjoying fatherhood, and the like—or with motherly activities—the mothers' statements about enjoying motherhood and

baby care. Wives were somewhat more accurate than husbands, but not much. Their "motherly" forecasts related modestly to their own later reported enjoyment of baby care ($r = .25$, $p < .01$) but not to other variables related to mothering. Wives' "fatherly" ratings did not relate to any later fatherly activities.

OTHER PRECURSORS OF FATHER INVOLVEMENT

When the new mothers were asked about their husbands' interest in the baby, there was not much difference of opinion: almost all saw their husbands as "very interested." This matter was probed further, however, by asking "How does he show his interest?" and a long list of ways fathers demonstrated interest in their newborns was obtained. This probe was coded for "father's actual interest in the baby." Scores ranged from 0 (no interest—3 percent) to 4 (extremely interested—12 percent), with an average of 2.4 (some interest and participation). As mentioned, both the husband and wife had been asked to rate the expectant father's "fatherliness" in the nine-month interview. Both the man's before-birth estimate of his own fatherliness and his wife's estimates agreed to some extent with "father's actual interest in the baby" ($r = .21$, $p = .06$, and $r = .29$, $p < .05$, respectively) but not with any other measure related to the father's activities with the baby or his feelings about it.

After the men and women had been asked to define *motherliness* and *fatherliness* by giving three adjectives that best described a "motherly" person and then a "fatherly" person, a congruence score was derived by determining how many of the adjectives were identical. A low congruence score would indicate that the respondent held a stereotyped sex-role ideology (i.e., fatherly = strong, responsible, and strict; motherly = loving, patient, and kind), whereas a high congruence score would indicate that the respondent pictured the important nurturant qualities to be the same whether the parent is male or female (i.e., motherly and fatherly both imply loving, strong, responsible). Only 6 percent of the wives scored 0 (none the same), and 55 percent scored 3 (all the same); the average score was 2.3. The father's proper role is seen by many present-day women as being one of participation in pregnancy, birth, and infant care. The women's congruence scores are further indication of these attitudes.

The men, however, had not abandoned traditional sex-role stereotypes as thoroughly as had the women: 10 percent of the husbands interviewed received a congruence score of 0, while only 38 percent scored 3. The male average was 1.9, lower than that of the wives.

Both the father's and mother's congruence scores were related to the father's actual interest in the baby ($r = .35$, $p < .01$, for fathers; $r = .21$, $p = .06$, for mothers). Thus, men in this sample who adhered to rigid stereotypes (nurturing an infant is unmasculine) did show less interest in their new babies, or less fatherly behavior.

If one parent enjoys parenthood, it appears easier for the other parent to do so also. There is a relation between the time the father spent with the baby in activities other than caretaking and whether the wife enjoyed motherhood ($r = .24$, $p < .05$), as well as with whether the wife enjoyed baby care ($r = .24$, $p < .05$).

Fathers with more education enjoyed fatherhood more ($r = .29$, $p < .05$), but there is no correlation between enjoyment of fatherhood and the men's job prestige. For women there was a small correlation between level of education and enjoyment of motherhood ($r = .19$, $p < .05$), and between educational level and when they felt like a mother ($r = .17$, $p < .05$).

Wives' previous baby-care experience was strongly related in a *negative* was to father's enjoyment of parenthood ($r = -.42$, $p < .01$). Before the birth there was a relation between a husband's experience with newborns and his wife's confidence in her own ability to care for a baby ($r = .22$, $p < .05$).

The finding that a wife's previous experience is negatively correlated with her husband's enjoyment of parenthood seems curious, but in chapter 7 we will see that men's parenting apparently has different sources according to social class. The women who had previous baby-care experience (defined as having full responsibility for an infant under six weeks of age) were more often lower class and less well educated.

One interpretation that knits together these various observations is that the lower-class mother wishes to dominate in setting parenting styles. Her own previous experience helps legitimate this, while previous experience of her husband has the opposite effect. Some evidence in support of this view will be given in chapter 7.

NUMBER OF CHILDREN WANTED AND PLANNED

There was good overall agreement ($r = .64$, $p < .01$) between spouses at the time of the first interview on the degree to which the current pregnancy was planned and also good overall agreement on the number of children husbands and their wives saw as desirable. Agreement within couples before the birth on the number actually planned was also good ($r = .65$, $p < .01$), but the agreement on this topic was less after the birth ($r = .39$).

Before the birth, nine women (8 percent) wanted only one child. Two or three weeks after the birth there were thirteen women who wanted only one child. Of these, eight were women whose minds had already been made up (one of the "sures" beforehand changed her mind to "not sure"), but five other women who had planned more than one child before the birth changed to "no more" right after the birth. In one woman's case, the husband left when the baby was two weeks old. In two other cases, the decision was directly attributable to a terrible childbirth experience. In a fourth case the woman developed thrombophlebitis after the birth and was advised by her doctor to

avoid a second pregnancy. The fifth woman developed a profound dislike of motherhood and baby care.

Even among the women who did not change their minds about having more children there was a decided shift toward waiting longer before having the next baby. Before the birth over half the women (55 percent) who wanted another child wanted it in less than 2½ years. Shortly afterward, only 37 percent wanted another child that soon. The number changing to a longer child-spacing interval was large and significant ($\chi_1^2 = 10.67$, $p < .01$).

The social-class difference in conception timing noted for the first pregnancy continued in planning for a second. While intentions expressed by the wife in the interview held two to three weeks after the birth indicated that there was no average difference by class in when the next child was wanted, by the six-month phone check twice as many lower-class as middle-class women were already pregnant with a second child (eight vs. four). Also, by the six-month phone check, more than twice as many of the women who wanted no more children were lower-class as were middle-class.

Husbands' views about children changed in the opposite direction. Before the birth, seven of the husbands (12 percent) who were interviewed wanted only one child. After the birth only four (7 percent) still felt that way. After the birth the husbands continued to favor the same child-spacing interval on the average that they had favored before birth. For men, changes in child-spacing preference were few and occurred equally in both directions—some wanted a longer interval, but an equal number wanted a shorter interval. Thus, some disagreement about child spacing developed, with wives coming to prefer longer intervals. The disagreement within couples on this topic after the birth is significant ($\chi_1^2 = 4.26$, $p < .05$). The husband's and the wife's desire for further children thus appears to have been differently affected by the birth event and the early weeks of the baby's life.

The women differed from their husbands both in how childbirth affected their own self-images and in their desires to delay having a second child. What may be the sources of these feelings? For one thing, the babies apparently did not live up to the mothers' expectations. There were significant decreases in ratings of "My Baby" after birth as compared to before, and mothers who had undergone a Cesarean delivery rated "My Baby" significantly lower than other mothers. Also, women were less positive in their views of the baby when they first saw it than their husbands were, and it took some women several months to start "feeling like a mother." Both parents underestimated the difficulties of caring for a young infant beforehand, but since it is the mother who bears most of the unexpected burden, it appears that her views of parenthood respond more strongly.

At the six-month phone check, respondents were again asked if they planned to have another baby and, if so, when. Twelve of the thirteen women who had said "no more children" immediately after the birth still held to that view. In addition, seventeen more women (altogether 24 percent of the sam-

ple!) were now seriously contemplating having only one child. At the other extreme, twelve women (10 percent) were already pregnant again. When asked in the six-month phone check, thirty-two percent of the sample planned to have their second child before the first child was 2½ (down from 37 percent with such plans three weeks after birth). There were many shifts in plans, but the big difference from before to after birth is in the change from desiring two or three children to desiring only one.

OPINIONS RELATED TO CHILDREN AND CHILD REARING

Men and women in the sample were asked their opinions on a number of issues related to children or child-rearing. (See Appendix B, especially section V.) Unless specifically stated, there are not significant differences in opinions by social class.

Almost all the women (96 percent) and men (95 percent) believed that the most important quality in a father is the warmth and interest he shows in his children. The role of father as breadwinner was the other choice in this item (Appendix B, opinion item 2). It is unlikely that the breadwinner role is seen as unimportant, however, even though "father warmth" was chosen at the expense of "father provider." The largest source of concern about childbirth for men in this sample was finances. Also, in Yankelovich's (1974:98) survey "good provider" was cited as the *most* important quality noncollege respondents look for in any man (77 percent) and was the third most important quality mentioned by respondents attending college (56 percent).

Only 28 percent of the women in this sample believed that fathers are stricter with children than mothers, a view that is counter to that of children generally (see Becker (1964:172). Most children see fathers as more strict than mothers. Of the husbands in this study, 57 percent thought fathers were more strict (opinion item 1).

In chapter 1 it was pointed out that new fathers might experience role strain because, although young men in the seventies are expected by their wives to take an active part in the care of infants, their earlier life experiences do little to prepare them for an active father role. An indication of the divergence between wives' expectations and husbands' inclinations is contained in replies to two opinion items. Some mild disagreement is revealed in answers to a question about when fathers get interested in their children; more women than men (83 percent vs. 78 percent when asked before the birth, and 81 percent vs. 72 percent when asked after the birth) believed fathers are just as interested in their children when they are babies as when they are older (opinion item 8). There was greater disagreement about whether new fathers would like to hold their babies right away when they are born or would be content to wait until they get home (opinion item 7). More wives than husbands (81 percent vs. 67 percent or 87 percent vs. 68 percent, depending upon when the ques-

tion was asked) believed fathers would resent not being able to hold their newborn child.

Furthermore, as noted in chapter 4, there was a difference in opinion by social class among fathers. A majority of middle-class fathers (59 percent) believed new fathers would like to hold and touch their babies right away, whereas 77 percent of lower-class fathers believed men would rather wait (χ_1^2 = 3.63, $p \cong .055$).

At the time of the nine-month interview, some women (37 percent) were of the opinion that newborns are better cared for in the hospital nursery than by their own mothers (opinion item 45; a question not asked of husbands before the birth). This belief is one that might be altered as a consequence of the childbirth experience. In this sample, there was actually an increase in the number of women endorsing this view after the birth (51 percent). The majority of babies (69 percent) *were* cared for in the hospital nurseries, and most people would not want to change to rooming-in with a second child (55 percent of the total sample had nursery care and would choose it again). In line with cognitive dissonance notions, changes in women's opinions to agree with what they actually did are to be expected, but it may just be that women found childbirth a more tiring experience than they anticipated.

Women in this sample reflected the general permissiveness toward toilet training found in both middle-class and blue-collar parents since World War II, for only a small minority (15 percent) thought children could be toilet trained by eighteen months of age (opinion item 57). Of the small group of women who held this view, twice as many were lower-class. Husbands' opinions on this matter were not sought.

Permissive attitudes toward feeding were less prevalent—at the time of the first interview 29 percent of women subscribed to feeding babies on schedule rather than on demand, and fewer (17 percent) subscribed to that opinion after the birth (opinion item 50). But this apparent change in opinion about feeding schedule is not related to what the women actually did. After the birth 26 percent were actually scheduling feedings rigidly, and of the women who had intended to feed on demand before the baby was born (46 percent), almost half switched to "semischeduled" feeding. Only 26 percent actually reported demand feeding. (There was no difference in women's opinions on feeding according to social class.) The inconsistency in feeding behavior is also reflected in answers to more detailed questions about feeding schedules. Women were asked, "Are you feeding the baby on a schedule or on demand?" and probes followed about how often the baby ate: "What do you do if he cries sooner?" and so forth. These detailed replies were coded for what the mother actually did, which was not necessarily what she *said* she did. For instance, many women replied, "demand" to the original query, and then under the probes revealed that they permitted their babies to eat fifteen minutes early sometimes, if the baby cried really hard, (i.e., on a 3 ¾ to 4 hour schedule). Other women interpreted anything closer than four hours as "demand," even a rigid three-hour schedule or a semischeduled regimen such as

"three to four hours." Many women, in order to hold the pretense of demand feeding, simply interpreted cries that occurred too "early" as not being for hunger, even when the baby showed clear signs of hunger such as rooting and sucking fingers vigorously.

Men overall were about as permissive as women about feeding on demand—25 percent thought babies should be fed on schedule (opinion item 50). However, this item revealed one of the few strong differences in men's opinions by social class—of the men who believed babies should be fed on schedule, 86 percent were lower class ($\chi_1^2 = 7.23$, $p < .01$).

A preference for more regular feeding inconsistent with general attitude may reflect the degree of inconvenience that need feeding confers upon the mother. To feed a baby whenever he / she is hungry places a mother completely at the service of her infant. Toilet training is quite a different story. With automatic washers, diaper services, and disposable diapers, the burden of caring for diapers is almost negligible. More husbands than wives favored scheduled feeding (33 percent before the birth and 25 percent afterward), and the shift toward more scheduled feeding could have been prompted by husbands' preferences also.

Before the birth, only a minority of the women (29 percent) saw no harm in letting a six-month-old baby have a bottle in the crib rather than being held, and even fewer were of this opinion after birth (12 percent) (opinion item 53). Thirty-nine percent of husbands, on the other hand, believed it was all right for a baby not to be held while being fed. The fathers appeared to have little appreciation of infants' psychological needs, perhaps as a consequence of their lack of experience with infants.

Views about demand feeding are obviously related to views on whether a crying baby should be attended to. Close to 32 percent of the women believed that a baby will be spoiled if responded to every time it cries, and the number of women who endorsed this view did not change over the period of study (opinion item 49). Some men's opinions on this matter did change, however. Before the birth almost half of the men (42 percent) saw spoiling as a consequence of consistent responses to crying, but after the birth fewer (30 percent) held this opinion.

Men held more conservative opinions than women on how long a child should be breast-fed. Well over half the women (58 percent before and 55 percent after the birth) felt that it was all right for a one-year-old to be breast-fed still (opinion item 54), whereas only 26 percent of men felt this way (answers procured after the birth only).

Men held slightly less conservative opinions on whether babies should sleep in the same bed with their mothers occasionally. For this item mothers' opinions became more conservative over time. Before the birth 21 percent of mothers and 15 percent of fathers believed young babies should *never* sleep in bed next to their mothers, and afterwards 32 percent of the mothers and 18 percent of the fathers subscribed to that opinion (opinion item 51).

Views on when parents start to love their children do not agree very well

with when the mothers themselves reported first feeling like mothers. Many women (62 percent or 64 percent, depending on the interview) believed that most mothers already love their babies during pregnancy (opinion item 48), whereas it was close to six weeks on the average before women "felt like mothers." This inconsistency may be another example of women voicing sentiments they perceive to be socially desirable rather than those they actually feel. Fewer fathers (47 percent) felt that mothers already love their children during pregnancy.

OPINIONS ABOUT SEX AND SEX ROLES

Overall, there was good agreement between men and women respondents on whether men and women want to have sex during a woman's menstrual period as much as at any other time of the month: exactly 70 percent of both sexes did not think so (Appendix B, opinion item 18). Also, there was good overall agreement between men and women that there are more important things in a good marriage than sex (71 percent of women and 72 percent of men subscribed to that view; opinion item 20), and that a woman should not feel a duty to have sex whenever her husband wants it (90 percent of women and 93 percent of men: opinion item 21). Only 16 percent of the women and 7 percent of the men thought that men are much more interested in sex than women are (opinion item 19).

A majority of the women (59 percent) thought that pregnant women *can* safely have sexual intercourse right up until labor starts (opinion item 24). As reported in chapter 3, one-third of the women planned to continue right up to the end,[5] but more continued than had planned to. When pain was not experienced, these women's actions appeared to match their opinions.

Men and women also agreed rather well on items related to breast-feeding. Over 80 percent of both men and women thought that a woman could breast-feed her hungry baby in public as long as she did it inconspicuously, and this opinion did not change over the period of the study for either sex (opinion item 23). However, of the men who disagreed, 82 percent were lower-class. (There was no interaction with class for women on this item.) More women than men believed breast-feeding is very pleasant for the mother (91–92 percent vs. 82 percent), and women's opinions on this matter did not change after the baby was born (opinion item 22). It is surprising that such a large majority of the women saw breast-feeding as pleasurable for the mother, yet only two-thirds of them planned to breast-feed.

At present, ideas about sex roles are undergoing rapid change in the United States. A recent national survey (Yankelovich 1974:98) found that 55 percent of noncollege women and 61 percent of college women agreed that "men and women are born with the same human nature; it's the way they're brought up that makes them different." A minority saw keeping feelings under control as

---

[5] Husbands reported that only one-fifth were "not stopping."

a "very important quality in a man" (43 percent and 24 percent). Also, a surprising percentage of Yankelovich's respondents saw as a "very important quality" a man's willingness to do household chores (29 percent and 35 percent). Opinions about sex-role standards expressed by respondents in the present study likewise indicated a broad conception of both men's and women's roles.

With one or two exceptions, women's ideas about sex roles are more liberal than men's in this study. The difference observed here between the opinions of the sexes is likely to be smaller than the true difference, however, because the male respondents in the present study were probably self-selected to be more open-minded than the nonrespondents. In what follows, sex-role opinions where the differences between men and women are slight will be discussed first.

About 60 percent of both sexes repeatedly endorsed the statement that a woman's personality suffers if she is involved only in household tasks and child care (opinion item 12). For women (but not for men) there was a significant interaction with class, because 74 percent of middle-class vs. 45 percent of lower-class women endorsed the statement ($\chi_1^2 = 9.20, p < .01$). Yet a majority of both men and women (58 percent and 52 percent, respectively) believed that most men would prefer that wives *not* have a job outside the house (opinion item 14). In other words, a majority see a woman's psychological well-being as inconsistent with her husband's desires. Replying to a rather abstract item on discrimination in the marketplace, however, almost all men and women (over 90 percent) believed that married women have as much *right* to jobs as men (opinion item 16). These conflicting opinions are one expression of the ambivalence respondents felt about women's work roles.

A large proportion of both men and women (over 70 percent) believed that men prefer their first child to be a son (opinion item 3), and the men in this sample actually conformed to this opinion; 71 percent did want a son, and those who were disappointed in the baby's sex were almost exclusively fathers of daughters. However, most people would probably like both sexes as long as they have at least one boy (see Hoffman and Manis 1978b), and most fathers would be likely to prefer a girl next, given a boy first. Unfortunately, we did not ask a question about sex preference for additional children. Even though the women correctly perceived their husbands' preference for a boy baby, they themselves wanted girls almost as much as boys, and 77 percent believed that most women do not care about the sex of the first child (opinion item 4). The women's receptiveness to a baby of either sex is also borne out by their ratings of "My Baby, If Boy" and "My Baby, If Girl," procured from the women before they gave birth. Women rated their unborn child, pretending it was one sex or the other. Altogether babies of both sexes were rated just as positively on the set of twenty descriptive adjectives (Appendix A, table A.3).

Before the birth, a majority of women (52 percent) believed that raising

children and keeping house is more interesting than the work most men do, and afterwards 62 percent reported this belief (opinion item 13). Most men (68 percent) saw men's work as more interesting. On this item there is an interaction with class for women, but not for men; of the women who saw men's work as more interesting, 64 percent were middle class and 36 percent lower class ($\chi_1^2 = 5.00$, $p < .05$). Psychological theorists would predict such differing views; they lead to consistency between attitudes and required behavior. People often get to like doing what they must do (the functional autonomy of motives).

Two items dealing with outside recreation received somewhat different answers from men and women. A majority of women (55 percent) and a larger majority of men (75 percent) believed that a married man should plan his social life to include his wife and not "have at least one night a week out with the boys" (opinion item 10). All of the husbands and 92 percent of the wives believed that a woman needs some time away from a small baby, even if it means the husband has to baby-sit (opinion item 11).

Most of these couples subscribe to an egalitarian outlook, one that is not hard to implement as long as there are no children. However, both in chapter 2 and in the opinion items just reviewed, there is evidence of some conflict in views. In particular, couples hold different views about women's working and about the nature of women's work, and women have a less stereotyped view than men of men's sex roles. These differences are not critical for a couple with no children, but their importance increases greatly after the birth of a child. This observation suggests that Lamb's hypothesis (1978) about the arrival of a child moving couples toward more traditional views could be instead activation of views held all along. Rather than changing views, the child's arrival makes them more salient.

The conflict expressed by persons in this sample reflects conflict experienced in society more generally. It is now estimated that over half the mothers in the country work, but society has not come to terms with mothers of young children working unless financial pressure is severe. In a recent survey of parents, 69 percent thought that children of working mothers are worse off. Only working mothers split evenly on this question (Yankelovich 1977). One can begin to see change in the couples in the present study along these lines—after becoming parents, their ideas become more conservative.

SUMMARY

The fact that the conjugal relationship was apparently in a honeymoon phase in the first few weeks after the birth prevented drawing much in the way of conclusions about the couple's marital relationship over that period.

Disagreement between spouses on the number and timing of future children increased from before the birth to after it. Hints of maternal stress are also available from data on resumption of work, because some of the women tried working and stopped, and far fewer women returned to employment full-time

than had planned to do so. The wives' views of husbands as fathers turned out to be contingent on husbands' presence in labor and delivery or husbands' *desire* to be there. There was also increased disagreement after the birth on some of the child-rearing and sex-role opinion items.

The data leave little doubt that the birth and first few weeks of the infant's life are times of considerable stress, especially for the couples with surgical delivery. For one thing, pain at the birth itself was not in line with women's expectations and turned out to be more severe than either they or their husbands had anticipated. The women received more medication in delivery than they wished, and its effectiveness in reducing pain is doubtful. There were considerably more obstetrical procedures carried out than were expected, with adverse effects into the weeks well after the birth. For these forms of stress, preparation afforded no protection that could be detected. In particular, the women who experienced various kinds of intervention appeared more vulnerable to tiredness and depression.

There is very little preparation of any kind for the rigors of early infant care. The couples in this study, like those in Fein's study (1974), were unprepared for the amount of work required of them in the early weeks of their infants' lives. Most preparation classes do not devote much attention to infant care, and the couples had little exposure to infants or knowledge of baby care from earlier life experiences. They also tended to underrate beforehand the value of knowing about infant care, so they apparently sought out little information during the pregnancy. The fruits of this are seen in the couples' earliest reactions to their babies—many were not emotionally prepared to welcome an infant. Perhaps for this reason, it took some of them considerable time to feel comfortable in their new parental roles. Many tended to be unaware of, or unresponsive to, the infant's emotional needs, first in the hospital and then later at home.

The parents in this study who were more successful at parenting are those who seem more flexible—they divided tasks and were less fearful of or threatened by the pregnancy. Some of the prior life experiences of the lower-class men and women (in terms of caring for babies) seemed to hinder more than help, especially as related to father's enjoyment of his baby and "fathering."

Considering all the effort invested in well-baby clinics and other facilities designed to improve the physical health of children, it is truly astounding that society has so far provided so little to assure the psychological and social health of neonates and their parents. Informal family supports did exist for some couples in the way of help from relatives when arriving home from the hospital, and the importance of such help is dramatized by the fact that many mothers became depressed when left on their own. Furthermore, the early data on women's returning to work suggest the extent to which lack of institutional child-care facilities and rigidity of work schedules place stress on first-time mothers.

7 | EARLY PARENTING

A particular focus of this book are the possible links for both mothers and fathers between pregnancy, childbirth, and early parenting. A longitudinal study can be of help in determining the respective roles of prenatal experience and birth experience in shaping later events. It was shown in chapter 5, for example, that feeding behavior was apparently not affected by women's birth experience. Prenatal preparation, on the other hand, did seem to have positive impact on middle-class women's persistence in breast-feeding, net of prenatal motivational factors. In this chapter possible explanations of early parenting behavior are the main topic of interest; the couples' readiness for parenthood in terms of preparation level and the influence of social class occupy a prominent place in the analyses. Some attention is also given to parents' roles vis-à-vis one another in early parenting. Except for work by Parke and his colleagues (1972), this topic and the effects of social class on early parenting have not been extensively researched.

To understand possible effects of preparation and of social class on parenting, a number of analyses will be presented that highlight mothers' and fathers' emotional responsiveness to their infant as possible consequences of preparation and previous experience in caring for young babies. Most analyses are performed separately by social class. Since preparation encourages father presence in delivery, we will first examine fathers' reactions to their infants according to whether or not the father participated in delivery.

FATHER'S REACTION TO THE BABY ACCORDING TO THE FATHER'S PARTICIPATION IN DELIVERY

In chapter 4, structural models revealed that husband participation was a strong determinant of the quality of each spouse's birth experience. In fact, father participation was a major factor affecting both partners' birth experi-

ence.[1] A further question involves the extent to which the father's participation in the birth event may shape early father-child relations. Is early fathering enhanced if the father takes an active role in birth? Scientific evidence on this point is meager as yet. In a study of thirty English first-time fathers, Greenberg and Morris (1974) did not find such an effect,[2] and the evidence presented by Peterson, Mehl, and Leiderman (1979) does not make it entirely clear whether the father's participation reflects prior motivation or effects of delivery experience on father-infant attachment.

Possible effects on parenting of the father's participation in delivery could be checked in two ways, first by tallying fathers' behavior and feelings toward infants according to whether fathers were present or absent during delivery, and second by estimating models where the degree of participation in labor and delivery is related to measures of fathering. These possibilities will be taken up in turn.

PRESENCE OR ABSENCE DURING DELIVERY

The early caretaking and emotional reactions of fathers were tallied for three groups of fathers: (1) those absent from delivery by choice, (2) those absent against their will, and (3) those present. Available for examination are both fathers' and mothers' replies to many items concerning early fathering, including the extent of caretaking by fathers (diapering, bathing, and the like) and fathers' emotional responses to their babies. (See table 7.1. Feeding is not included there because most interviewed fathers were fathers of breast-fed children.)

As judged from fathers' reports, in every instance except two (how long the husband held the baby on the previous day and how soon the man felt like a father), fathers who were present in delivery scored higher on fathering measures than fathers who were absent by choice. But fathers absent against their will scored higher than fathers who were present (minor exceptions are the father's helping with bathing, how long the father held the baby on the day preceding the interview, and whether the baby was mentioned as a source of happiness in the marriage). Although most differences between groups do not attain statistical significance, the pattern of the differences is rather consistent across the three groups—excluded greater than present greater than absent by choice. That is, fathers who were present at the birth changed more diapers, engaged in more activities with their babies, and scored higher on most other measures than fathers who were absent, but fathers who were excluded

---

[1]In line with current social trends, an overwhelming majority of couples in this sample (84 percent) were together for at least part of the time during labor. Only fourteen husbands (12 percent) were not present during labor by choice, and five others (4 percent) wanted to be there but were excluded unexpectedly. Fewer husbands (66 percent) were present at delivery; 7 percent were excluded, and 27 percent were not present by choice.

[2]Their questionnaire perhaps did not probe deeply enough—for example, fathers were not asked what the baby looked like or about feelings about the delivery itself, in contrast to feelings about the infant.

TABLE 7.1. Relation between early fathering and father's presence in delivery

	Father absent by choice			Father present			Father absent involuntarily				
	N	Mean	SD	N	Mean	SD	N	Mean	SD	t-value[a]	t-value[b]
As reported by fathers											
When first changed diaper 3 = 8 to 14 days 4 = 4 to 7 days 5 = 0 to 3 days	13	3.77	1.42	40	4.22	0.97	4	4.50	0.58	1.30	0.55
Bathing baby 1 = never 2 = helped with bathing 3 = bathed baby without help	13	1.69	1.03	40	1.98	1.00	4	1.75	0.96	0.88	0.96
Response when baby cries 2 = other things first, but then lets baby cry regularly 3 = other things first, but lets baby cry occasionally 4 = somewhat solicitous, let cry not mentioned	12	2.42	1.38	39	3.18	1.14	4	3.25	0.50	1.92†	0.12
Number of activities with baby 2 = 1 activity in addition to caretaking 3 = 2 activities in addition to caretaking	13	2.92	1.12	39	3.21	1.26	4	3.25	0.96	0.72	0.07
Picks up baby when cries 2 = if wife asks or wife is busy 3 = picks up on his own	13	2.38	0.87	40	2.88	0.46	4	3.00	0.00	2.63**	0.53
How long held baby on previous day 3 = 1 or 1.5 hrs. 4 = 2 or 2.5 hrs.	13	3.15	1.40	38	3.03	1.36	4	3.00	0.82	0.29	0.04

(continued)

195

TABLE 7.1—Continued

	Father absent by choice			Father present			Father absent involuntarily			t-value[a]	t-value[b]
	N	Mean	SD	N	Mean	SD	N	Mean	SD		
What baby looked like at first view 3 = neutral 4 = mild positive	13	3.38	1.76	40	3.88	1.44	4	4.25	1.26	1.01	0.50
How felt about baby at first view 3 = neutral 4 = mild positive	13	3.77	1.17	37	3.95	0.97	4	4.75	1.26	0.49	1.53
How father felt about act of holding baby first time 3 = neutral 4 = mild positive	13	3.23	1.23	39	4.26	1.31	4	4.50	1.73	2.47*	0.27
How father felt toward baby on holding for first time 4 = mild positive 5 = definitely positive	13	4.23	0.60	35	4.31	1.21	2	5.00	1.41	0.32	0.78
Enjoyment of fatherhood 1 = not speak about baby 2 = mentioned baby abstractly 3 = mentioned baby secondarily	13	2.15	0.69	40	2.35	1.00	4	2.75	1.50	0.79	0.73
Baby mentioned as source of happiness in marriage 2 = mentioned secondarily 3 = mentioned primarily	12	2.33	0.49	39	2.51	1.05	4	2.50	1.00	0.82	0.02
How father feels when baby cries 2 = accept it—"that's what babies do" 3 = some concern, but some neutral or negative feelings 4 = mild concern	13	2.85	1.34	36	3.19	1.04	3	4.00	1.00	0.85	1.30
When felt like father 4 = during third week 5 = during second week	13	5.46	2.57	39	4.85	2.44	4	5.25	2.22	0.78	0.32

As reported by mothers

	N	Mean	SD	N	Mean	SD	N	Mean	SD	t^a	t^b
Total number of diapers changed since return from hospital	33	8.33	11.21	79	14.96	20.26	8	23.38	20.96	1.77†	1.12
Bathing baby 1 = never 2 = helped with bathing	33	1.52	0.80	79	1.54	0.76	8	1.88	0.99	0.18	1.13
Picks up baby when cries 2 = if wife asks 3 = on his own	33	2.88	0.33	79	2.76	0.49	8	3.00	0.00	1.29	1.39
How long held baby on previous day 3 = 1 or 1.5 hrs. 4 = 2 or 2.5 hrs.	33	3.15	1.58	76	3.32	1.39	8	3.00	0.00	0.56	0.60
Wife's opinion of husband's interest in baby 1 = very interested 2 = somewhat interested	33	1.09	0.29	79	1.15	0.39	8	1.00	0.00	0.80	1.08
Wife's rating of quality of husband's interest 2 = some active interest 3 = more interest and participation	33	2.48	1.00	79	2.27	0.93	8	2.88	0.64	1.11	1.81†

†$P(t) < .10$, two-tailed.
*$P(t) < .05$, two-tailed.
**$P(t) < .01$, two-tailed.
^{a} t-tests run between ''Father absent by choice'' and ''Father present.''
^{b} t-tests run between ''Father present'' and ''Father absent involuntarily.''

against their will rather consistently exceeded fathers who were present. Consistency of the patterns (ten of fourteen triplicate rankings followed that pattern) suggests that the father's general disposition to take an active role in fathering, rather than whether or not the father was present at delivery, explains these fathers' behavior. Those who were barred give somewhat stronger evidence of later nurturing and enjoyment of the baby than those who were present.

On the other hand, the data derived from wives' reports on the three groups of fathers contained in the same table are not very clear in this regard. With *all* excluded fathers taken into account, patterns are mixed.

EXTENT OF HUSBAND'S PARTICIPATION DURING DELIVERY

A different kind of evidence on the issue is provided by modeling fathering as a consequence of three variables: the strength of the husband's prepartum desire to take part in delivery, the father's level of preparation for childbirth, and the extent of husband's participation in delivery (scaled as a continuous variable evaluating how much the husband helped in delivery).[3] In a multiple regression analysis with father caretaking behavior as the dependent variable (measured by a summative index of child-care activities: bathing, response to crying, number of activities with the baby, whether the father picked up the baby when it cried, diapering, and how long the father held the baby), and with the father's prepartum estimate of the importance of father presence in delivery, father's preparation level, and degree of participation in delivery as three independent variables, only 4 percent of the variance in the index of fathers' child-care activity was explained. A parallel analysis of wives' ratings of husband's caretaking behavior with the same predictors explained only 2 percent of the variance. In terms of father caretaking, then, neither the degree of father participation in delivery nor prepartum preparation appear to be relevant.

Somewhat different findings emerged from an analysis of fatherhood feelings that sought to predict "fatherly feelings" (how the father felt about the baby the first time he saw it, how he felt about holding the baby for the first time, how much he enjoyed fatherhood in the hospital and at home, whether he mentioned the baby as contributing to marital happiness, how soon he felt like a father). Again, taking husband's prepartum estimates of the importance of husband's presence in delivery, husband's preparation level, and the extent of father's participation in delivery as predictors (excluding husbands who were barred against their will), a multiple regression analysis accounted for 16.9 percent of "fatherly feelings," and the level of father's participation in delivery contributed significantly to this prediction. Neither fathers' estimates of the importance of being present in delivery nor preparation level made a

---

[3]These analyses obviously did not include fathers who were excluded from delivery against their wishes. All others were rated on a scale from 0 (absent by choice) to 6 ("helped a lot").

significant contribution, but including them effectively controls on these sources of variance.

In interpreting these regression analyses, a number of facts must be weighed. First, a small amount of variance in fatherhood feelings is being accounted for. Second, there is no direct way to measure how much participation net of motivation affects fatherly feelings, because there are no men in this study who did not wish to help, but who were compelled to. However, by including the husband's prepartum estimate of the importance of husband's presence in delivery, the analysis does provide at least a partial control on motivational factors.

Altogether the effect of husband participation seems best interpreted as a consequence of *both* motivation to participate and the effect that actual participation had. The previous analysis of responses of husbands who were barred from delivery suggests that motivation rather than undergoing the actual experience can be an important causal element for some fathers. The regression analysis suggests that husband participation has less influence on caretaking behaviors than on fatherhood feelings, and that degree of participation has some effects net of prenatal factors. These ideas will be extended further in more detailed analyses of fathers' emotional responsiveness later in this chapter (table 7.8 and figure 7.2).

EARLY PARENTING AS RELATED TO PREPARATION LEVEL

Table 7.2 provides a summary according to preparation level of the responses of both parents to the infant in the first few weeks after birth.[4] Since the sample is constructed so that there are equal numbers of middle- and lower-class persons in the three major preparation categories (1 to 3, 4 to 5, 6 to 7), social class does not affect differences according to preparation level.

The most highly prepared mothers differ from those with intermediate preparation. Feeding according to need was a variable that was significantly more positive among the highly prepared women. In addition, how the mother felt on first holding the baby, differences in contact in the first three days, and how the mother felt when the baby cried were borderline. There were three differences favoring mothers with intermediate levels of preparation compared to women with little or no preparation—the mother had a more positive opinion of the baby's appearance the first time she saw it, she felt like a mother sooner, and had more contact (the latter two borderline). On the other hand, women at the lowest levels had babies who cried the least, and they were more positive in their feelings about caring for a newborn compared to both other groups. Mothers' responsiveness to baby's crying was mixed

---

[4]Feeding mode and duration were discussed in chapter 5.

TABLE 7.2. Comparison of parenting by preparation level[a]

	Level 1 to 3			Level 4 or 5			Level 6 or 7			t-value[b]	t-value[c]
	N	Mean	SD	N	Mean	SD	N	Mean	SD		
For mothers											
How felt about holding baby first time	34	3.76	1.48	31	3.81	1.54	52	4.35	1.37	0.11	1.66†
3 = neutral											
4 = mild positive											
5 = definitely positive											
Opinion of baby's appearance, first glimpse	35	2.71	1.43	32	3.47	1.24	53	3.87	1.49	2.30*	1.27
2 = mildly negative											
3 = neutral											
4 = mildly positive											
Average daily number of hours baby with mother in first three days	34	4.32	4.23	32	6.62	6.29	53	9.58	7.04	1.75†	1.95†
Feeding according to need	35	1.71	0.67	32	1.91	0.64	53	2.25	0.73	1.20	2.17*
1 = rigid schedule											
2 = semischedule											
3 = need feeding											
Number of feedings per day	35	3.49	1.07	32	3.84	1.25	53	4.06	1.29	1.26	0.75
2 = 5 feedings											
3 = 6 feedings, or every 4 hrs.											
4 = 7 feedings, or every 3.5 to 4 hrs.											
Baby crying	35	3.89	1.30	32	3.28	1.25	53	3.68	1.24	-1.94†	1.43
3 = 2–3 hrs. daily											
4 = 1–2 hrs. daily											
Typical response to baby's crying	35	3.09	1.38	32	2.72	1.20	53	3.15	1.23	-1.16	1.58
1 = let cry, first response											
2 = other things, but let cry regularly											
3 = other things, but let cry occasionally											
4 = somewhat solicitous, crying not mentioned											

	N	Mean	SD	N	Mean	SD	N	Mean	SD		
Feelings when baby cries 2 = neutral, doesn't bother her 3 = some concern for baby, some neutral or negative feelings	35	2.80	1.35	32	2.50	1.14	53	3.00	1.37	−0.98	1.73†
How feels about caring for a newborn 3 = strong ambivalent 4 = mild ambivalent 5 = mild positive	35	4.60	1.26	32	3.62	1.45	53	4.30	1.37	−2.94**	2.16*
Baby mentioned as a source of happiness in marriage[a] 2 = mentioned secondarily 3 = mentioned primarily	35	2.66	0.84	32	2.44	0.80	53	2.68	0.94	−1.10	1.22
When felt like a mother[a] 3 = 2nd month 4 = 1st month 5 = 1 to 3 weeks	34	3.70	1.85	31	4.65	2.30	52	4.96	2.52	1.82†	0.57
For fathers											
Opinion of baby's appearance, first glimpse 3 = neutral 4 = mild positive	14	3.29	1.73	16	3.81	1.38	27	4.04	1.43	0.91	0.51
How felt holding baby first time 3 = neutral 4 = mild positive 5 = definitely positive	14	3.21	1.31	15	4.27	1.39	27	4.33	1.27	2.10*	0.16
Baby crying 3 = 2 to 2.5 hrs. daily 4 = 1 to 1.5 hrs. daily 5 = 30-59 minutes daily	7	3.71	1.98	6	4.50	2.34	10	4.00	1.49	0.66	0.53
Typical response to baby's crying 1 = let cry, first response 2 = other things first, but let cry regularly 3 = other things, but let cry occasionally 4 = somewhat solicitous, let cry not mentioned	13	2.08	1.12	16	3.31	1.30	26	3.31	0.93	2.71*	0.01

(*continued*)

TABLE 7.2—Continued

	Level 1 to 3			Level 4 or 5			Level 6 or 7			t-value[b]	t-value[c]
	N	Mean	SD	N	Mean	SD	N	Mean	SD		
How feels when baby cries	14	2.79	1.31	15	3.67	1.05	23	3.04	0.98	2.01†	−1.87†
2 = neutral											
3 = some concern, some neutral or negative feelings											
4 = mild concern for baby											
Picks up baby when cries	14	2.21	0.98	16	2.94	0.25	27	2.96	0.19	2.87**	0.37
1 = not mentioned, or tells wife											
2 = if wife asks or wife is busy											
3 = picks up on his own											
Total number of diapers changed since return from hospital	14	15.71	19.11	16	23.50	21.50	27	20.89	22.15	1.04	−0.38
Attending to baby at night	14	1.43	0.51	16	1.75	0.45	27	1.74	0.45	1.83†	0.07
1 = never or only once											
2 = occasionally, even if only 2 or 3 times											
Extent of holding baby in previous 24 hrs.	14	2.79	1.48	15	3.13	1.46	26	3.15	1.19	0.64	0.05
2 = 30-59 minutes											
3 = 1-1.5 hours											
4 = 2-2.5 hours											
When felt like a father	14	5.43	2.88	16	4.88	1.96	26	4.88	2.50	0.62	0.01
4 = before end of 3rd wk.											
5 = before end of 2nd wk.											
Enjoyment of fatherhood	14	1.86	0.66	16	2.50	0.97	27	2.48	1.05	2.09*	0.06
1 = baby not mentioned											
2 = spoke of baby abstractly											
3 = enjoyed baby, but not "nicest thing" about first few days at home											

Baby mentioned as source of happiness in marriage
  2 = mentioned secondarily
  3 = mentioned primarily
	13	2.23	0.60	16	2.62	0.88	26	2.50	1.11	1.37	0.38

Number of activities with baby
  2 = one activity in addition to caretaking
  3 = two activities in addition to caretaking
	14	2.71	1.14	16	3.50	1.32	26	3.15	1.12	1.74†	0.91

† $P(t) < .10$, two-tailed.
* $P(t) < .05$, two-tailed.
** $P(t) < .01$, two-tailed.
[a] See Appendix C for definitions of various preparation levels.
[b] t-tests run between levels 1 to 3 and levels 4 or 5.
[c] t-tests run between levels 4 or 5 and levels 6 or 7.
[d] Data obtained at six-month phone check.

across levels, with mothers at the lowest level more responsive on the average than mothers at intermediate levels. The relation between preparation and mothering is thus fairly complex, especially in terms of possible benefits conferred by intermediate levels of preparation.

For fathers the picture is more unitary. For them the highest levels of preparation are not associated with higher values on the various parenting indices. For example, in only one instance (feelings about baby's crying) is the difference between fathers with high levels of preparation and those with intermediate levels significant, and the difference is in a negative direction. There are many instances, however, in which fathers with intermediate preparation registered higher values on parenting than those with little or no preparation. These include: how the father felt upon holding the baby for the first time, three measures of responsiveness to crying, whether the father attended to the baby at night, and enjoyment of fatherhood. In addition, there are no significant reversals between these levels, as was the case for mothers.

Data pertaining to fathers in table 7.2 suggest that some form of father preparation is associated with higher quality parenting, but—as was true for the fathers' reactions to delivery (table 4.7)—the highest levels of preparation do not seem to confer benefits beyond those conferred by an intermediate level.

In sum, with social class balanced, there appear to be associations between preparation level and some indicators of parenting. Relations are complex, however, and a number of other variables, such as previous baby-care experience or quality of parents' birth experience, are neglected here. More extensive analyses will therefore be undertaken later in the chapter.

EARLY PARENTING AS RELATED TO SOCIAL CLASS

As mentioned, couples were selected in such a way that social-class groups have almost the same distributions according to preparation level (see Appendix A). To explore whether parenting differs by social class (with preparation balanced), average values for a number of parenting variables were calculated for couples in the two classes, and differences between averages were tested. Fortunately, there was only a small and nonsignificant difference in the sex-ratio of babies according to social class (57 percent boys, lower class, 48 percent boys, middle class). Thus, social class comparisons are approximately balanced by sex of baby as well.

Differences by social class in either maternal or paternal behavior toward the infant or in parental feelings about the infant are small and, in all cases but two, not statistically significant (table 7.3). The two exceptions are that lower-class mothers are somewhat more pleased about the sex of the baby than middle-class mothers, and middle-class fathers spontaneously mentioned the baby more often in answering a question about enjoying fatherhood. (The

TABLE 7.3. Comparison of parenting by social class

	Middle class			Lower class			
	N	Mean	SD	N	Mean	SD	t-value
For mothers							
Baby crying	60	3.65	1.19	60	3.62	1.35	0.14
3 = between 2 and 3 hrs. daily							
4 = between 1 and 2 hrs. daily							
How felt about baby at first view	59	3.63	1.34	57	3.84	1.19	0.91
3 = neutral							
4 = mildly positive							
How felt about sex of baby	58	2.47	0.94	60	2.82	0.83	2.15*
2 = didn't care							
3 = pleased							
Feeding flexibility	60	2.02	0.62	60	1.98	0.81	0.25
2 = semischedule							
3 = need							
How rested mother felt	60	2.98	0.72	60	3.07	0.82	0.59
three weeks postpartum							
2 = quite tired							
3 = somewhat tired							
Enjoyment of motherhood	59	2.32	1.01	60	2.43	1.21	0.54
2 = spoke of baby abstractly							
3 = enjoyed baby, but not the							
"nicest thing" about first							
few days at home							
How feel about caring for newborn	60	4.05	1.47	60	4.37	1.33	1.24
4 = mild ambivalent							
5 = mild positive							
How feel when baby cries	60	2.80	1.41	60	2.82	1.21	0.07
2 = neutral							
3 = some concern, but also							
neutral or negative feelings							
For fathers							
How felt about baby at first view	28	3.71	1.49	29	3.86	1.53	0.37
3 = neutral							
4 = mild positive							
Enjoyment of fatherhood	28	2.64	1.03	29	2.03	0.82	2.47*
1 = not speak about baby							
2 = mentioned baby abstractly							
3 = mentioned baby secondarily							
How felt about sex of baby	27	2.37	1.01	28	2.68	0.86	1.22
2 = didn't care							
3 = pleased							
Baby mentioned as a source of	26	2.62	0.94	29	2.34	0.94	1.07
happiness in marriage							
2 = mentioned secondarily							
3 = mentioned primarily							
When felt like father	27	4.81	2.70	29	5.20	2.18	0.60
4 = during third week							
5 = during second week							

(continued)

TABLE 7.3—*Continued*

	Middle class			Lower class			
	N	Mean	SD	N	Mean	SD	t-value
How long held baby on previous day 3 = 1–1.5 hrs. 4 = 2–2.5 hrs.	26	3.11	1.34	29	3.00	1.34	0.32
Number of activities with baby 2 = one activity in addition to caretaking 3 = two activities in addition to caretaking	27	3.30	1.14	29	3.00	1.25	0.92

NOTE: There were no differences in feeding mode or duration.
*$P(t) < .05$, two tailed.

question was: "What was the nicest thing about the first few days after your wife returned from the hospital?") On all other variables, differences are small. Given that many differences were tested and that a few would be expected to differ by chance alone, the best conclusion seems to be that in this sample the *average* responsiveness of parents to the baby and other measures of parental behavior do not differ by social class. More comprehensive measures of parenting also show negligible differences according to social class (tables 7.4 and 7.8).

It is rather surprising that averages of parental behavior are so similar by class. This may be at least partly a consequence of the forced equivalence on preparation level. (Lower-class parents who take preparation classes may be more like middle-class persons than other lower-class parents.) In the earlier analyses of feeding behavior (tables 5.5 and 5.6), however, although feeding mode and duration were equivalent, structural models revealed strong class differences. To explore whether there are analogous structural differences in explanations of parenting behavior, more elaborate analyses will now be undertaken.

A MODEL FOR MOTHERING BEHAVIOR

To explore the possibility that structural relations linking parenting to other variables may differ by class, a model for mothering will be proposed in which several prepartum variables are linked to birth-event variables, and then mothering will be examined as it responds jointly to feeding, birth event, and several variables measured during pregnancy. The model will be estimated separately by class.

Mothering was measured by combining seven variables into a scale that rated the mother's responsiveness to the baby (how the mother felt on first

holding the baby, need or scheduled feeding, a number of measures related to crying, and when the woman felt like a mother). (See Appendix C.)

A number of the variables in the mothering model are included mainly for purposes of control. One of these is previous baby-care experience (measured by asking the mother about her previous experience with babies under six weeks of age and how confident she felt in her ability to care for a newborn). Previous experience with babies might make the birth experience less threatening (a hypothesis explored earlier to some extent), but more importantly here, such experience could have taught women how to parent. Another variable requiring control is prepartum plans (women were asked during pregnancy whether they intended to breast-feed or bottle-feed, to have nursery care or rooming-in, and how important they felt such decisions were). Before the birth most women had decided whether or not to breast-feed and whether or not to have rooming-in. These decisions can serve as a proxy for preexisting and possibly powerful psychological traits characterizing the women before the birth that could affect mothering later.

A number of other variables are included in the model mainly to explore possible structural relationships. For example, the woman's birth experience and feeding behavior are included because a woman's sensitivity to the needs of her child may be contingent on these variables.

RATIONALE FOR THE MOTHERING MODEL

Both preparation (WPREP) and previous baby-care experience (PREBY) could affect feeding behavior in the first month (EFDBE) and mothering behavior (MOTH) directly. Some preparation classes cover aspects of infant behavior, and in Lamaze classes mothers are strongly encouraged to breast-feed. Baby-care experience would be expected to affect mothering behavior for obvious reasons, and could affect feeding behavior if, in caring for other newborns, the respondents had previously observed successful (or unsuccessful) breast-feeding.

Preparation and previous baby-care experience might also affect average contact between mother and child in the first three days (CONT) and the mother's attitude on first seeing the baby (FSVIEW). Preparation classes educate women about what to expect in the first few days after birth, and some classes encourage women to have close contact with the young infant. Previous baby-care experience could make the mother seek (or avoid) such contact or could cause her to select rooming-in and / or breast-feeding, each of which would increase contact.

The effect of preparation on women's attitudes at first view has already been mentioned. Previous experience with infants could lead the mother to have realistic expectations about the baby's appearance, and could therefore lead to a more positive initial reaction to the baby.

The effects of preparation on the woman's birth experience (BESCL) and on level of awareness (AWARE) have been analyzed in detail above, and the

possible effects of previous baby-care experience making the birth event less threatening have also been alluded to earlier.

As already mentioned, prepartum plans (PREPL) are included mainly for control purposes. Whatever is planned ahead of time and the reasons for these plans represent *previous* commitments or dispositions. It is of great interest to separate out these effects, which may reflect underlying psychological traits present before the birth, from effects that can be strictly attributed to preparation per se, events at birth, or other, later-acting variables. Such plans and / or the psychological traits for which they stand could have direct effects on every subsequent variable in the model, but especially on feeding and mothering behavior.

Awareness and the quality of the mother's birth experience might affect the mother's attitude on first viewing the baby for reasons outlined earlier in rationales for the feeding models (chapter 5, table 5.4). Mothers who remain relaxed during labor and who cooperate with those caring for them are more likely to be pleased with their infants at first sight (Newton and Newton 1962). For similar reasons, contact may respond to the nature and quality of the birth event. If the woman has a Cesarean delivery, for example, she may have, or prefer to have, little early contact with the baby. The mother's early feeding behavior could be affected by the nature of the birth in the manner suggested already in discussion of the 1965–69 data. Although no significant effects of this sort were observed in prior analyses, this path will be maintained here to increase comparability with earlier analyses and to provide a complete picture according to social class. Finally, the nature of the birth event could affect mothering, because a woman with a difficult delivery might "blame" the baby, while a woman with a very positive birth experience might react by becoming more enthusiastic about the baby.

The woman's initial psychological reactions to the baby (attitude on first view) could be the product of many precursors, as already mentioned, and could affect later events. A woman who initially responds positively to her infant may stimulate her baby to react positively as well, and pleasant initial contact may lead to more extensive contact. Also, a positive initial reaction might lead a woman to enjoy feeding, and therefore to persist at it. A more positive attitude toward the baby would also be expected to lead to higher quality mothering—a woman who is positively disposed toward the baby initially may be more responsive to its needs and thereby respond to it more sensitively.[5]

Since this research began, Klaus, Kennell, and their co-workers (see Klaus and Kennell, 1976b, for citations, especially chap. 3) have asserted that close contact between mother and child in the hour following birth is essential to the child's future health and well being. They believe that there is a "maternal

[5]A variable measuring the seriousness of depression was incorporated in exploratory analyses of the mothering model. Depression did not explain significant variance in mothering for women of either class. The depression variable was therefore eliminated from the final model.

sensitive period'' (p. 50). In several experimental studies they cite, in which the amount of contact between mothers and infants varied, mothers who had early contact—especially in the first hour after birth—turned out to be more responsive to infants when they cried, to be more likely to continue breast-feeding or to feed babies longer at night, to kiss babies more, and generally to show more attachment behaviors. Presumably, early close contact leads to stronger, and perhaps a different quality of, attachment. For this reason, ''contact'' was included as a variable in the mothering model, following the variable that measures the woman's initial reaction to her baby. In this model contact is measured as the average number of hours per day the mother and baby spent together daily in the first three days after birth.

If Klaus and Kennell (1976b) are correct, contact could lead to better parenting on the basis of hormonal or biologically programmed effects. An alternative and simpler explanation is that more early contact may permit time for the woman to learn how to breast-feed. Contact could lead to better mothering not only because of a maternal sensitive period but because mothers with early contact breast-feed early and / or because women who have early contact actually care for their babies at an early age and learn to interpret the baby's signals.

Finally, first-month feeding behavior appears in the model. It appears partly as a control—feeding choice overlaps contact to some extent. Women who breast-feed are likely to have more contact. But breast-feeding per se could also lead to better mothering, all else held constant, for reasons given previously.

ESTIMATING THE MODEL FOR MOTHERING

The rationale outlined above led to a recursive model with preparation, previous baby-care experience, and prepartum plans as exogenous variables. Because social class has earlier been shown to affect the structure of feeding models, the mothering model was estimated separately for women of the two social classes, even though the average value of mothering was almost the same for women of both classes (26.09 vs. 26.92). (See table 7.4).

To facilitate the discussion, figure 7.1A reports structural coefficients exceeding 1.5 times their standard errors for the sample of middle-class women, and Figure 7.1B gives the same information for lower-class women. Omitted paths—those with size not exceeding at least 1.5 times their standard error— were estimated, but were left out of the figures for reasons of clarity. Full numerical information is given in table 7.4. The model will be discussed mainly in terms of the light shed on structural relationships, and there will be no attempt to make an exhaustive analysis of all indirect effects.

The structure of the mothering model looks different according to class. Most striking is that both awareness and the quality of the mother's birth experience appear to affect mothering directly for middle-class women (.995

TABLE 7.4. Model for predicting mothering behavior by social class

Dependent variables, middle class

Independent variables	Level of awareness (AWARE)		Woman's birth experience (BESCL)		First view (FSVIEW)		3-day contact (CONT)		Feeding, first month (EFDBE)		Mothering (MOTH)	
	Metric coefficients	Standardized coefficients	Metric coefficients	Standardized coefficients	Metric coefficients	Standardized coefficients	Metric coefficients	Standardized coefficients	Metric coefficients	Standardized coefficients	Metric coefficients	Standardized coefficients
Preparation level (WPREP)	.501	.488*	.365	.131	.040	.054	−.065	−.020	.203	.215†	−.488	−.164
Mother's previous experience (PREBY)	.214	.126	.807	.174†	.200	.162	−.349	−.066	−.116	−.074	.855	.173
Prepartum plans for care (PREPL)	.186	.225†	.147	.066	−.052	−.087	1.278	.499*	.446	.589*	.296	.124
Awareness level at birth (AWARE)			1.478	.544*	.257	.357†	.953	.306†	−.124	−.135	.995	.344†
Woman's birth experience (BESCL)					.031	.117	.007	.006	.068	.201	.326	.306†
First view (FSVIEW)							.521	.121	−.034	−.027	.449	.112
3-day contact (CONT)									−.046	−.156	−.133	−.142
Feeding, first month (EFDBE)											.569	.180
Variance accounted for	36.5%		47.0%		24.9%		50.8%		41.0%		45.7%	
Constant term	0.382		7.176		0.857		3.464		2.497		12.488	

Correlation coefficients (listwise present)
N = 54

	WPREP	PREBY	PREPL	AWARE	BESCL	FSVIEW	CONT	EFDBE	Mean	SD
WPREP									4.89	1.98
PREBY	−.029								4.41	1.19
PREPL	.328	−.132							0.12	2.46
AWARE	.558	.082	.368						3.80	2.03
BESCL	.451	.206	.286	.655					18.15	5.52
FSVIEW	.272	.226	.074	.445	.384				3.46	1.46
CONT	.352	−.078	.624	.531	.373	.276			7.31	6.32
EFDBE	.364	−.122	.578	.233	.294	.032	.289		3.33	1.86
MOTH	.247	.267	.285	.529	.571	.352	.244	.303	26.09	5.89

Dependent variables, lower class

Independent variables	Level of awareness (AWARE)		Woman's birth experience (BESCL)		First view (FSVIEW)		3-day contact (CONT)		Feeding, first month (EFDBE)		Mothering (MOTH)	
	Metric coefficients	Standardized coefficients	Metric coefficients	Standardized coefficients	Metric coefficients	Standardized coefficients	Metric coefficients	Standardized coefficients	Metric coefficients	Standardized coefficients	Metric coefficients	Standardized coefficients
Preparation level (WPREP)	.380	.383*	−.242	−.082	.166	.210	−.588	−.177	.188	.205†	−1.045	−.369*
Mother's previous experience (PREBY)	.076	.047	.477	.100	−.073	−.057	.592	.110	−.100	−.068	−.415	−.091
Prepartum plans for care (PREPL)	.135	.173	.101	.043	.096	.154	1.394	.531*	.570	.791*	−.397	−.178
Awareness level at birth (AWARE)			2.203	.743*	−.145	−.182	1.090	.325*	−.061	−.066	.276	.097
Woman's birth experience (BESCL)					.116	.433*	.132	.117	−.011	.034	.212	.220
First view (FSVIEW)							.676	.161	−.094	−.082	.961	.268*
3-day contact (CONT)									−.022	−.078	.177	.208
Feeding, first month (EFDBE)											1.949	.628*
Variance accounted for	24.7%		53.9%		23.8%		61.3%		69.1%		54.1%	
Constant term	1.915		8.227		1.534		−1.707		3.565		17.616	

Correlation coefficients (listwise present)
N = 51

	WPREP	PREBY	PREPL	AWARE	BESCL	FSVIEW	CONT	EFDBE	Mean	SD
WPREP									4.61	2.06
PREBY	−.027								4.92	1.28
PREPL	.520	.012							−0.15	2.61
AWARE	.472	.039	.373						4.02	2.04
BESCL	.288	.132	.279	.724					18.29	6.06
FSVIEW	.330	−.011	.315	.285	.397				3.47	1.63
CONT	.336	.148	.645	.574	.527	.408			7.43	6.86
EFDBE	.543	−.073	.805	.279	.183	.199	.437		3.31	1.88
MOTH	.150	−.068	.452	.384	.454	.416	.512	.503	26.92	5.84

†Coefficient 1.5–1.99 times its standard error.
*Coefficient 2.0 or more times its standard error.

FIGURE 7.1. Estimated model for mothering: (*A*) middle class, (*B*) lower class. All parameters in the fully recursive model were estimated. Only those exceeding 1.5 to 1.99 times their standard error (_ _ _) or 2.0 or more times their standard error (———) appear.

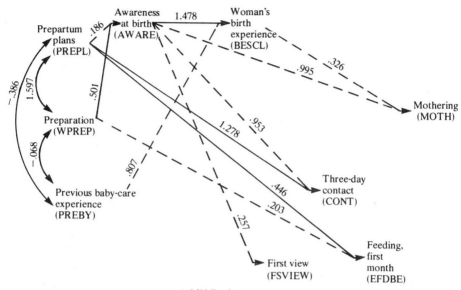

A. Middle class

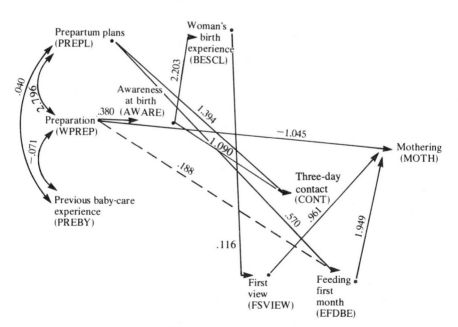

B. Lower class

and .326). The middle-class woman's attitude on first seeing the baby is also affected by awareness (.257), but no further significant-sized effects follow. In particular, the middle-class woman's attitude on first view does not play the mediating role between the birth event and mothering that it does for lower-class women. Mothering of middle-class women as estimated in this model, in fact, is not significantly affected by *any* of the variables subsequent to birth (first view, contact, or feeding), and the variables prior to birth operate by way of awareness and birth experience. The birth variables therefore appear critical for mothering of middle-class women, even though in analyses in chapter 5 these same variables had trivial impact on women's feeding behavior.

For lower-class women, by contrast, first view and feeding affect mothering directly and substantially (.961 and 1.949), while preparation has a strong negative direct effect (−1.045). Awareness has only an indirect effect through birth experience and first view (2.203 × .116 × .961 = .246), approximately half as large as the one indirect effect of awareness mediated through birth experience (1.478 × .326 = .482) for middle-class women. For lower-class women, feeding behavior has a strong direct effect on mothering and effectively mediates whatever effects prepartum plans may have. It appears that, with the amount of early contact controlled, the experience of breast-feeding in itself acts to make these lower-class women more responsive to their infants. It also appears that for lower-class women the overall effect of preparation on mothering may not be as negative as the direct path (−1.045) suggests. Preparation has a positive effect mediated through feeding (.188 × 1.949 = .366). Also to the extent that preparation affects plans rather than the other way around, there could be a positive effect mediated by plans.

For middle-class women preparation has sizeable effects on birth experience through awareness and has borderline direct effects on feeding behavior in the first month, duplicating what was seen in earlier analyses. For lower-class women the sizeable effects of preparation on birth experience through awareness are also repeated, but effects of awareness and birth experience on mothering are all indirect. (The borderline effect of preparation on feeding for lower-class women here and not seen earlier is apparently a consequence of using "prepartum plans" concerning baby care in this model rather than the "wife's prepartum feeding intentions" (WFIN), the variable used in the feeding models of tables 5.5 and 5.6. See appendix C.) As would be expected, prepartum plans for women of both classes strongly affect contact and feeding. For women of both social classes, however, contact (average number of hours per day in first three days) has negligible effects on either feeding or mothering, and for middle-class women, preparation has mainly indirect effects on mothering.

The remaining finding of note is that previous baby-care experience has a positive indirect effect through birth experience (.807 × .326 = .263, borderline) on mothering for middle-class women, but no significant effects for lower-class women.

To sum up: the structural relationships explaining mothering look different by social class and are rather complex. Why feeding behavior does not affect mothering for middle-class women is puzzling. As far as we can tell, it is not a consequence of restriction on the range of the relevant variables or on other statistical artifacts, for there were no differences by class in either early feeding behavior or its persistence. For lower-class women, feeding behavior and other postpartum events seem to play a critical role in predicting mothering, and the birth event itself has only indirect impact. For both groups, however, net of direct influences of the prepartum variables, events at the birth or shortly thereafter seem to influence mothering behavior. This is an important finding, for it argues that the quality of women's birth experience and early contact with the infant could have far-reaching effects for family relationships. Surely attention to quality of women's birth experience is justified on grounds involving the woman alone, but if women's birth experience has long-range effects on other family members, it is an aspect of birth management that should command substantial attention.

MATERNAL SENSITIVE PERIOD

The model shown in figure 7.1 was estimated with early mother-infant contact measured in three different ways: by the number of minutes mother and infant spent together in the first hour after birth, by the number of hours that mother and baby were together in the first twelve hours after birth, and by the average number of hours spent together per day in the first three days of the baby's life. For each measure, contact had no significant effects on either feeding behavior or mothering. The absence of such effects could be taken as evidence against Klaus and Kennell's (1976b) notions concerning the importance of early contact and could call into question the idea of a maternal sensitive period shortly after childbirth.

Before commenting further, however, we must point out that even though contact was incorporated in the model using three alternative measures, these measures are not formulated in terms entirely compatible with detecting a maternal sensitive period. If only a few mothers have *significant* contact during the first hour (more than a few minutes), when these mothers are pooled with the total sample in a structural analysis, any relationship between contact and subsequent mothering could be obscured. If the sensitive-period hypothesis is correct but only a few minutes' contact or no contact at all is experienced by most women in the sample, then minutes of contact in the first hour for all women in the sample is not a measure very well suited to test the Klaus-Kennell hypothesis.

For these reasons, we examined possible effects of contact on mothering and on the two measures of feeding behavior in several other ways. In these additional analyses we defined two dummy variables, one to measure early contact and the other to measure "immediate feeding." The first was scored 1

if the woman had thirty minutes or more contact with her infant in the first hour after birth, otherwise 0. The second was scored 1 if a woman breast-fed her baby within the first hour after birth, otherwise 0. (These two groups overlap, and nine women did both.) Only two women who were bottle-feeders from birth had contact lasting over thirty minutes. To keep the analysis as clear as possible, these two bottle-feeding women are excluded, and only breast-feeders will be considered in what follows.

A word is needed about the possible confounding between contact and breast-feeding in the first hour. Winters' findings (1973) relate *only* to feeding (six women, randomly chosen, breast-fed right after birth, six others breast-fed for the first time sixteen hours after birth), and DeChateau's experiment (1976) involved suckling within the first hour as well as early contact. Klaus and Kennell (1976*b*) cite both experiments in support of their hypothesis, although their own experiment (Kennell et al 1974) involved only bottle-feeders. The possibility exists that very early feeding could be a critical mechanism promoting bonding. Put differently, an analytic distinction can be made between "contact," "contact with feeding," and "early feeding" not associated with lengthy contact. The present data offer some ways to resolve this ambiguity.

Table 7.5 summarizes the means and standard deviations of feeding behavior in the first month, feeding persistence, and mothering according to whether or not feeding was immediate and whether or not mothers had contact of thirty minutes or longer in the first hour after birth. These tabulations show negligible differences in feeding behavior in the first month. However, there appear to be differences in the means of both feeding persistence and mothering that are associated with whether or not mother and infant had significant contact within the first hour. Analyses of variance indicate that only the differences in mothering behavior are large enough to be significant ($F_{1,71} = 10.450$, $p < .01$). Whether or not the infant was fed within the first hour seems of little consequence. In short, if interaction of mother and infant within the first hour after birth does have effects, such effects appear to be linked with contact rather than with feeding per se in the first hour. Thus, these tabulations are consistent with Klaus and Kennell's hypothesis.

In the present sample, however, women are not randomly allocated to a "contact" vs. "no contact" condition. In fact, women in this survey who attended preparation classes or had firm plans to breast-feed before birth probably would be more likely to have extensive early contact. The association between early contact and higher scores on mothering in table 7.5 could therefore represent a spurious association that is the consequence of preexisting differences among the women.

To control preexisting differences, two regression models were run (for breast-feeders only) that included the same prenatal variables as the previous models (table 5.5 for women's feeding behavior and table 7.4 for mothering) but with "contact" now included as a dummy (zero-one) variable. The criti-

TABLE 7.5. Average scores on early feeding behavior, persistence in breast-feeding, and mothering for combinations of "contact in first hour" and "first feeding" (breast-feeders only)

Feeding, first month

Timing of first feeding

Contact in 1st hour	Within 1st hour	After 1 hour	Total
30 min. or more	Mean = 4.67 SD = 1.00 N = 9	Mean = 4.40 SD = 1.34 N = 5	Mean = 4.57 SD = 1.09 N = 14
Less than 30 min.	Mean = 4.64 SD = 0.81 N = 11	Mean = 4.47 SD = 1.07 N = 53	Mean = 4.50 SD = 1.02 N = 64
Total	Mean = 4.65 SD = 0.88 N = 20	Mean = 4.47 SD = 1.08 N = 58	Mean = 4.51 SD = 1.03 N = 78

Feeding persistence

Timing of first feeding

Contact in 1st hour	Within 1st hour	After 1 hour	Total
30 min. or more	Mean = 5.89 SD = 2.26 N = 9	Mean = 5.80 SD = 2.28 N = 5	Mean = 5.86 SD = 2.18 N = 14
Less than 30 min.	Mean = 5.00 SD = 1.90 N = 11	Mean = 5.08 SD = 1.94 N = 53	Mean = 5.06 SD = 1.92 N = 64
Total	Mean = 5.40 SD = 2.06 N = 20	Mean = 5.14 SD = 1.96 N = 58	Mean = 5.21 SD = 1.98 N = 78

Scores on mothering

Timing of first feeding

Contact in 1st hour	Within 1st hour	After 1 hour	Total
30 min. or more	Mean = 31.88 SD = 3.94 N = 8	Mean = 33.20 SD = 6.38 N = 5	Mean = 32.38 SD = 4.81 N = 13
Less than 30 min.	Mean = 26.45 SD = 5.73 N = 11	Mean = 27.20 SD = 5.40 N = 50	Mean = 27.07 SD = 5.42 N = 61
Total	Mean = 28.74 SD = 5.65 N = 19	Mean = 27.75 SD = 5.70 N = 55	Mean = 28.00 SD = 5.67 N = 74

NOTE: Bottle-feeders are excluded. See Appendix C for definitions of all variables.

cal parameters are summarized in table 7.6. When social class is not taken into account, these regressions show no significant effects of the contact dummy variable on mothering, feeding in the first month, or feeding persistence. Since earlier both mothering and feeding were sensitive to social class, however, the analyses involving contact were also carried out separately by class. (There are thirty-seven middle-class women, of whom eight had significant contact, and thirty-three lower-class women, of whom five had significant contact.) In these separate analyses, the sizes of the parameters for women in the two classes look different, but only the parameter for feeding behavior in the first month for middle-class women reaches a borderline level of significance. The effect, however, is in a counterintuitive direction—more contact produces earlier cessation of feeding—and the lack of a similar effect in the models for feeding of middle-class women (the coefficient $-.482$ is not significant) suggests that the effect is spurious.

The suggestive differences in women's maternal behaviors according to contact that appeared in the cross-tabulations of table 7.5 thus disappear when control variables are introduced. The implication is that *prenatal* variables account for "effects of contact" in our data. To the extent that differences associated with contact do appear in the present data, the effects must be attributed to prenatal variables rather than to contact per se in this sample of women.[6]

The feeding model (table 5.5) was also estimated with a variable inserted to represent women's feeding experience during the first two postpartum days. (including how soon and how long the women breast-fed for the first time, when the milk came, whether a nurse helped with early breast-feeding, and how many times the women breast-fed in the first forty-eight hours). Feeding experience in the first two days had no appreciable effect either on women's feeding behavior in the first month or on their feeding persistence.

The picture is certainly complex. For breast-feeders—or for women with certain predispositions (planning to breast-feed, etc.), as all women in these analyses were—early contact may not be important. The maternal-sensitive-period hypothesis may hold true only for women like those Klaus and Kennell studied—lower-class bottle-feeders. In the mothering model, first view—another kind of variable related to early contact—was significant only for lower-class women, again a suggestion that contact and class interact.

In sum, the confirmatory pattern in table 7.5, followed by the disconfirmation in table 7.6 when the full set of variables is included, poses some challenge to the Klaus-Kennell hypothesis. Hopefully, further work can resolve

[6]For completeness, parallel models were run with the feeding dummy variable inserted in the same position as the early-contact dummy variable. For the total sample it turned out that women who fed in the first hour after birth had (borderline) *lower* scores on maternal responsiveness. Again, however, when the sample is divided by social class, effects look different. No effects reach even borderline significance, although maternal responsiveness is depressed for middle-class women and not for lower-class women.

TABLE 7.6. Metric coefficients linking contact to dependent variables for breast-feeders

Independent variable: contact dummy	Dependent variables			
	Model for feeding behavior (table 5.5)		Model for mothering (table 7.4)	
	Feeding, first month[a]	Feeding persistence[a]	Feeding, first month[b]	Mothering[b]
Classes combined	−.193	−.086	−.404	2.374
Middle class	−.482	.156	−1.211†	3.970
Lower class	.137	−.008	.343	−.973

NOTE: See Appendix C for definitions of all variables.
†Coefficient 1.5−1.99 times its standard error.
[a] The equations for estimating feeding behavior were the same as those summarized in table 5.5 except that contact was added as an endogenous variable prior to the feeding variables.
[b] The equations for estimating mothering and feeding behavior in the first month were the same as those summarized in table 7.4 except that the dummy contact variable was substituted for 3-day contact.

these questions. A troublesome fact for a maternal-sensitive-period hypothesis to explain is the rather different size of parameters associated with contact—including opposite signs—that emerged in our data when separate models were run for women of both social classes. A biologically based explanation should be insensitive to class. Both Leiderman and Seashore's (1975) and Whiten's (1977) observational data also raise questions about effects of early contact, because effects observed early disappeared in later months.

CRYING

The social-class differences in the structural relationships between feeding and mothering, as noted earlier, are puzzling and did not appear to be the consequence of statistical artifacts. Also, the reactions of middle-class women to crying appeared to be very different from those of lower-class women, even though the average amount of crying per day—as reported by women in the interview two to three weeks after confinement—was almost identical for the two social class groups (3.65 vs. 3.62 where 4 = 1 to 1.5 hrs. daily and 3 = 2 to 2.5 hrs. daily). For this reason, further analysis of the part of the structural model for mothering that involved crying was undertaken.

The mothering scale was defined as the sum of seven variables—one of which was crying, on the assumption that less crying implies better mothering. To elucidate the possible structural relationships among these seven variables, crying was taken in a separate analysis as a predictor of four of the variables (items 2, 4, 5, and 6 of the mothering scale, which involve feeding

TABLE 7.7 Metric coefficients linking first-month feeding behavior and crying to maternal responsiveness

	Dependent variable Maternal responsiveness	
	Middle class	Lower class
Independent variables		
Feeding, first month (EFDBE)	.574*	1.020*
Crying	−1.187*	−.283
Variance accounted for	49.5%	39.0%

NOTE: Other independent variables are the same as in figure 7.1.
*Coefficient 2.0 or more times its standard error.

schedule, attitude toward newborns, and responsiveness to crying). In other words the mothering scale, which is the ultimate endogenous variable in the mothering model, was replaced by two variables in sequence, the first being crying and the second being a scale of maternal responsiveness consisting of the four items mentioned above. This revision allows direct exploration of the relation between crying and maternal responsiveness. The fully recursive model shown in figure 7.1 was then reestimated, with crying following feeding in the model, and the four-item maternal responsiveness measure following crying.

Separate analyses by social class of this expanded model revealed that crying was not explained to any significant degree by prior variables in the model. The overall F-values were nowhere close to significant. Also all variables prior to crying except feeding had almost identical effects to those already reported in figure 7.1 and so require no further discussion here. However, study of crying per se revealed the sharply different patterns of maternal responsiveness by social class shown in table 7.7.

For women of both classes, responsiveness is negatively related to crying—the more the baby is reported to cry, the less likely the mother is to rate high on responsiveness,[7] but the effect is large and significant only for middle-class women. Furthermore, with crying as a separate variable in the model and therefore controlled, a significant connection emerges between feeding and maternal responsiveness for middle-class women. The relationship between feeding and maternal responsiveness of lower-class women does not appear to be much affected by crying. The significant strong link for lower-class women between feeding and mothering seen in the mothering model (figure 7.1B) when crying was not included as a separate variable is repeated here. (In both analyses the standardized effect was by far the largest

[7]In some explorations of the extent of reciprocal causation between crying and mothering, the effect appears to be mainly in the direction used in the model—crying affecting maternal responsiveness rather than the reverse.

in the set.) Furthermore, the path from crying to maternal responsiveness is not even of borderline significance for them. The maternal responsiveness of middle-class women, on the other hand, is affected by feeding in a contingent manner, because a significant path from feeding to maternal responsiveness appears only when crying is separated out. Furthermore, middle-class women's responsiveness is strongly affected by crying (the large and significant path from crying to responsiveness of -1.187).

The present analysis makes somewhat clearer the chapter 5 findings on parental responsiveness based on analysis of thwarted breast-feeders, and also clarifies the possible source of a class-related difference in the link between feeding and parenting. In future work it would be highly desirable to explore these connections in more detail. The analysis here must be interpreted cautiously, because the measure of crying has serious limitations. Parental recall of crying time in this study was unaided by diary keeping and uncorroborated by other checks. It may therefore be prone to error, particularly because with no forewarning that a question on crying would be asked, it may be difficult for mothers to report accurately. The class differences in reactions to crying could therefore represent class differences in accuracy of recall or in accuracy of time estimates, with middle-class mothers being more accurate. If this class difference in women's responses to infant crying is valid, however, it falls in line with Kohn's notions (1969) of middle-class emphasis on control. It could indicate that middle-class women become particularly disturbed when they cannot control crying, whereas lower-class women do not.

A MODEL FOR FATHERING BEHAVIOR

Parke (1974) describes very active fathering behavior when infants are two to four days old, and among the parents he observed, the father played the more active role when both parents were present. In his research fathers' activity with the baby did not seem to depend on whether or not fathers had been present at delivery. This observation is not necessarily inconsistent with our own, because we observed that some fathers were very active after being barred from delivery. In our sample both fathers and mothers also report large amounts of father-baby interaction in the first few weeks of the infant's life.

In order to clarify further the nature of early responses to infants by fathers, a model for fathering was developed that resembled as closely as possible the model for mothering. There must be differences between mothering and fathering because fathers are not directly involved in breast-feeding and for them hormonal explanations of parent behavior seem less likely (although certainly not impossible).[8] Furthermore, their early contact with the infant is

---

[8] Lind (1973) suggests that there may be a "paternal sensitive period" like that Klaus and Kennell (1976b) postulate for mothers.

much more limited if the baby is born in a hospital, because unless there is rooming-in, the father may have no direct contact with the baby—except for a few minutes right after delivery—until mother and baby return home.

Another possible difference between mothering and fathering could be that, since the mother spends much more time with the baby, especially in the earliest days, fathers model their nurturant behavior along lines suggested by their wives' nurturant behavior. For example, a father who observes his wife letting the baby cry may do the same. Or a father who observes his wife responding solicitously may develop a solicitous attitude himself. There is also reason to see fathering as responsive to mothering (rather than the other way around) because the women in this sample *had* more baby-care experience than the men and were seen by their husbands as competent and knowledgeable as far as infants were concerned (although most of them actually were not).

In view of earlier findings, models were estimated separately for men in the two social classes. The case base available for estimating fathering models is marginal, because only fifty-seven fathers were interviewed after the birth event and there is the usual loss of cases in a listwise analysis. In addition, because most of the interviewed fathers were fathers of breast-fed children, only data for breast-feeders are included. The small size of the ultimate sample (forty-seven fathers) makes conclusions suggestive at best.

Initially, a fathering scale was created to match as closely as possible the mothering scale used in the model developed in the previous section. However, inclusion of a variable indicating when the respondent "first felt like a father" decreased the reliability of the fathering scale, because the item on timing of fatherly feelings correlated negatively with the other items. The final fathering measure is based on four variables, all of which measure in one way or another the father's reaction to holding his baby or his responses to crying. (Full information on the components of the fathering scale is provided in Appendix C.)

Rationale for the Fathering Model

The rationale for the fathering model follows the same lines as the rationale for the mothering model, and to the extent it is the same, that rationale will not be repeated. In particular, preparation level (WPREP), father's previous baby-care experience (PREEX), the quality of the man's birth experience (MBESCL), and the father's attitude toward the baby as measured by his description of what the baby looked like when he first saw it (FFSVI) are presumed to act upon fathering (FATH) for the same reasons they are assumed to be determinants of mothering.

In preliminary trials of various models, rooming-in intentions (secured during pregnancy) were inserted into the fathering model to parallel the prepartum-plans measure used in the mothering model on grounds that plans

for rooming-in might serve as a proxy for the father's positive disposition toward his unborn infant. Such a measure would be poor at best, however, because many couples did not have the option of selecting rooming-in, and rooming-in in any case is probably more responsive to the mother's desires than to the father's. For these reasons, it was hardly surprising that rooming-in plans did not relate to any of the other variables included in several exploratory versions of the fathering model, and so the variable was eventually dropped.

Also in preliminary analyses, actual rooming-in (after birth) was included as a proxy for father contact with the infant. A father whose child is cared for in the hospital nursery is not allowed to handle his baby whereas a father whose baby is in the mother's room can help in the early care of the baby. But actual rooming-in, like planned rooming-in, failed to relate to any of the other variables in the fathering model, and probably for similar reasons. It was eventually dropped as well.

Thus, there are no variables in the fathering model paralleling prepartum plans, feeding, or contact in the mothering models; all fathers included had breast-fed children, and the fathering scale is based on fewer variables.

In models for the man's and the woman's birth experience in chapter 4, a measure of father participation in delivery (HPART) based on information secured from wives was used rather than a measure based on fathers' own replies, because the case base was thereby increased and the two variables behaved in the same way with other related variables. In the present model—again, so that more cases could be included—the measure of father participation in delivery based on mothers' replies was used.

ESTIMATING THE MODEL FOR FATHERING

A recursive model is posited, with preparation and previous baby-care experience as exogenous variables (see figure 7.2). The model was estimated separately for the two social-class groups. As before, to facilitate discussion, figure 7.2 displays only the structural parameters that exceed 1.5 times their standard errors, although all parameters were estimated (see table 7.8). The model will again be discussed mainly in terms of major structural relationships, with no attempt made to assemble an exhaustive catalogue of all the indirect effects. A further caveat is that the number of cases per class is very small for an analysis of this kind.

Models estimated for men of each class explain considerable proportions of variance in fathering—63.4 percent for middle-class fathers, 49.4 percent for lower-class. For men of both classes, fathering responds positively to the quality of the birth experience and negatively (not significantly for lower-class fathers) to the father's first view of the infant. However, the parallel diagrams of figure 7.2 do suggest some structural differences in the determinants of fathering according to class. Men of the two classes respond very differently to previous experience with newborns. Previous experience with infants ap-

FIGURE 7.2. Estimated model for fathering: (A) middle class, (B) lower class. All
parameters in the fully recursive model were estimated. Only those exceeding 1.5 to
1.99 times their standard error (_ _ _) or 2.0 or more times their standard error (_____)
appear.

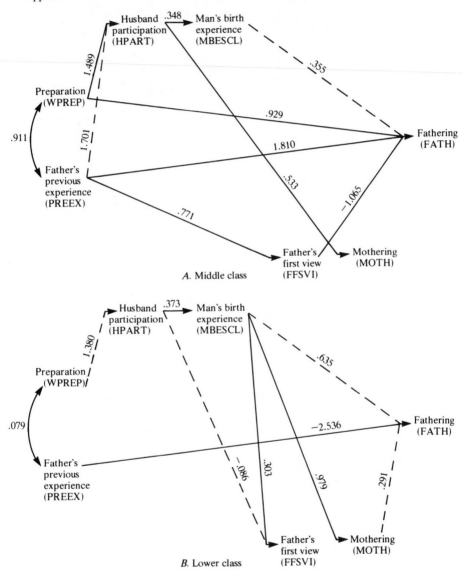

A. Middle class

B. Lower class

pears to directly enhance fathering for the middle-class men (1.810) and to
directly depress it for lower-class men (−2.536). (In each instance the standardized coefficients are among the largest directly relating prior variables
to fathering.) Participation has no direct significant effect on fathering for
men of either class, and its indirect effects on parenting are transmitted mainly

TABLE 7.8. Model for predicting fathering behavior, by social class

	Dependent variables, middle class									
	Husband participation (HPART)		Man's birth experience (MBESCL)		Father's first view (FFSVI)		Mothering (MOTH)		Fathering (FATH)	
	Metric coefficients	Standardized coefficients	Metric coefficients	Standardized coefficients	Metric coefficients	Standardized coefficients	Metric coefficients	Standardized coefficients	Metric coefficients	Standardized coefficients
Independent variables										
Preparation level (WPREP)	1.489	.493*	.384	.195	.051	.069	−.576	−.235	.929	.523*
Father's previous experience (PREEX)	1.701	.282†	.176	.045	.771	.526*	.278	.057	1.810	.510*
Husband participation (HPART)			.348	.536*	.071	.291	.533	.656*	−.203	−.345
Man's birth experience (MBESCL)					−.060	−.162	−.091	−.073	.355	.392†
Father's first view (FFSVI)							.303	.091	−1.065	−.440*
Mothering (MOTH)									.089	.123
Variance accounted for	43.0%		48.2%		45.0%		33.7%		63.4%	
Constant term	6.617		.269		−1.271		16.895		7.112	

Correlation coefficients (listwise present)
N = 23

	WPREP	PREEX	HPART	MBESCL	FFSVI	MOTH	FATH	Mean	SD
WPREP								5.09	2.17
PREEX	.385							5.00	1.09
HPART	.602	.472						22.70	6.56
MBESCL	.535	.373	.674					11.00	4.26
FFSVI	.360	.629	.471	.267				.378	1.59
MOTH	.176	.306	.536	.290	.332			27.61	5.33
FATH	.585	.455	.333	.547	.052	.154		18.61	3.86

Dependent variables, lower class

Independent variables	Husband participation (HPART)		Man's birth experience (MBESCL)		Father's first view (FFSVI)		Mothering (MOTH)		Fathering (FATH)	
	Metric coefficients	Standardized coefficients	Metric coefficients	Standardized coefficients	Metric coefficients	Standardized coefficients	Metric coefficients	Standardized coefficients	Metric coefficients	Standardized coefficients
Preparation level (WPREP)	1.380	.339†	-.048	-.024	.043	.055	-.075	-.028	.533	.236
Father's previous experience (PREEX)	-1.154	-.135	.154	.036	-.204	-.124	1.411	.253	-2.536	-.532*
Husband participation (HPART)			.373	.751*	-.086	-.446†	-.172	-.263	-.228	-.409
Man's birth experience (MBESCL)					.303	.785*	.979	.747*	.635	.567†
Father's first view (FFSVI)							-.917	-.270	-.781	-.269
Mothering (MOTH)									.291	.341†
Variance accounted for	12.9%		54.8%		31.6%		31.3%		49.4%	
Constant term	20.011		2.812		3.128		16.408		21.270	

Correlation coefficients (listwise present)
N = 24

	WPREP	PREEX	HPART	MBESCL	FFSVI	MOTH	FATH	Mean	SD
WPREP								4.83	1.81
PREEX	.051							4.96	0.86
HPART	.333	-.117						20.96	7.36
MBESCL	.228	-.053	.739					11.17	3.66
FFSVI	.079	-.111	.167	.475				3.92	1.41
MOTH	.046	.273	.205	.404	.010			26.79	4.79
FATH	.196	-.379	.175	.356	.013	.350		18.33	4.09

†Coefficient 1.5–1.99 times its standard error.
*Coefficient 2.0 or more times its standard error.

225

through birth experience. The conclusion is, therefore, that participation appears to affect the man's birth experience in a positive fashion and shapes fathering mainly through that route. The actual experience of sharing delivery transmits positive effects of preparation for men of both classes. Aside from effects transmitted through participation, preparation of lower-class men has negligible impact on subsequent variables. For these men, however, positive indirect effects of preparation through participation partly offset the negative direct effect of previous baby-care experience.

These findings on the man's birth experience are consistent with an analysis by Peterson, Mehl, and Leiderman (1979) showing that the man's birth experience was the strongest predictor (among labor length, the birth environment, a "disappointment" factor, and parity) of father attachment in a group of forty-six middle-income couples followed for the same period of time as couples in our study. Apparently a "prenatal attitude variable" did not account for appreciable variance in their data, so there was some control on effects of prior motivation.

For lower-class men, mothering exerts a borderline effect on fathering. The effect of mothering on fathering is close to zero for middle-class men. This pattern, coupled with the reversed effect between social classes of the man's previous experience with newborns, suggests that middle-class fathers may use their own experience directly as a resource for early fathering, while lower-class men seem to be hindered by their previous experience and may turn to their wives for models of parenting behavior.

Effects of the quality of the man's birth experience upon fathering, while positive for men of both classes, look somewhat different. Fathering of lower-class men responds directly to a greater degree than that of middle-class men (.635 vs. .355) and whereas no indirect effects emanate from birth experience for middle-class men, for lower-class men there are effects from birth experience through mothering that are sizeable (.979 × .291 = .285). Other major differences by class are the strong direct effect of preparation for middle-class men compared to the absence of such an effect for lower-class men, and the modest and borderline effect of mothering for lower-class men. To the extent these small samples can be trusted, spouse's behavior seems more critical for the parenting of the lower-class man than for the middle-class man. Furthermore, in several different analyses with varying sets of predictors, the class differences in fathering models involving mothering were similar to those seen here.[9]

The actual amounts or averages of parenting behavior, as shown in table

---

[9]The positive impact of husband participation and men's birth experience on mothering seen in these models should be discounted. Since men's birth experience is closely related to women's birth experience and women's experience is not included in the model, effects of men's birth experience on mothering are spurious. The partial correlations between men's birth experience and mothering, net of women's birth experience, are small and not significant for men of either class ($r = -.24$ and $+.14$ for middle- and lower-class men, respectively).

7.8, do not differ by social class, but the present model suggests that the parenting behavior of the men may be explained by somewhat different processes according to class. Additionally, these different processes parallel to some degree differences by class seen in the mothering models.

SUMMARY

In this chapter parenting was explored in several ways. Average differences in parenting behavior between the two social classes are negligible, but the explanations for (similar) behavior do appear to differ according to class.

For men of both classes the role of father participation in labor and delivery is to enhance the quality of men's birth experience, suggesting that Janis's stress theory (1958) is useful in interpreting fathers' reactions to the birth event in the same way it was for mothers. Men who take an active role have a higher-quality birth experience. Furthermore, although prepartum variables could not be controlled as well for fathers as for mothers, analyses with father's estimates of the importance of his presence in delivery controlled suggest that participation has effects net of motivation. The man's birth experience appears to be a factor in enhancing early fathering, and father participation in delivery seems to transmit some effects of prenatal factors on parenting.

As for the parents' reactions to their babies, the mechanisms producing these reactions look different according to class. In particular, whereas earlier analyses of feeding behavior did not point to the woman's birth experience as a predictor, the model for mothering suggests that for women of both classes birth experience may transmit effects of prior variables to mothering. For middle-class mothers variables measured in pregnancy appear to affect mothering mainly through awareness or quality of the birth experience. Lower-class women's responsiveness to their infants appeared to be affected indirectly by birth experience through variables operating after the birth, such as feeding and psychological factors measured by their reactions on first view. Lower-class women's mothering responded directly to feeding, but for middle-class women a similar (and much smaller) effect was contingent on crying.

The influence on parenting of variables measured in pregnancy appears to be of considerable consequence, and such variables (particularly previous baby-care experience) play somewhat different roles for men of one social class as compared with those of the other. The analyses also point to the role of birth experience in shaping men's parenting. Enhancing the quality of the man's birth experience, like enhancing the woman's, can serve as a goal in itself, but its importance is even greater if it affects later family relationships.

Preparation seems to affect the birth event in a positive fashion for middle-class women and thus to contribute indirectly to higher quality mothering, but

its effects for lower-class women's mothering are mixed. Preparation has direct effects on fathering only for middle-class men.

The negative direct effects of preparation on mothering for women of both classes are perplexing. One explanation could be that the kind of woman who vigorously pursues all avenues of information and who wishes to be in active control during birth is at a psychological disadvantage in very early parenting. That is, the woman's early mothering is here measured by the extent she is completely at the beck and call of her infant. Mothers who are highly prepared have actually received little information about baby care and may find an unremittingly subservient role hard to deal with.

Some question is raised about effectiveness of early contact. When women who had thirty minutes or more contact with their infants in the first hour after delivery were compared with other women who had less contact than that, simple associations between contact and mothering looked positive net of effects of feeding in the first hour. When a dummy contact variable was inserted in the full mothering model (or the full feeding model), however, effects of contact disappeared. Also social-class patterns in the parameters related to contact seem inconsistent with a biological explanation.

Fathering models suggest structural differences by social class, but the small number of cases make conclusions very tentative. For the lower-class man, the parental responsiveness of his wife appears important. Another notable structural contrast by class is the apparent positive effect of previous baby-care experience for the middle-class man and the emergence of a large negative effect associated with previous baby-care experience for the lower-class man. Delivery experience of men of both classes seems to affect their parenting positively, and preparation of lower-class fathers is effective mainly through delivery participation.

Much further work will be required to explore these leads on class differences in parenting behavior, but it is tempting to rationalize the major points in terms of sociological concepts about the nature of social-class differences. The major theme of such differences (e.g., Kohn 1969) is that middle-class persons value self-direction and autonomy, while lower-class persons value conformity. In Kohn's analyses, the same kinds of parenting behaviors were manifest by parents regardless of social class, but reasons for the behavior differed by class. In the present data, findings are similar, because parenting behavior is the same, but its causes appear to differ by class. Middle-class parents seem to be more emotionally responsive to infants the more they are in control. For middle-class men, both preparation and previous experience, which can be seen as allowing "control," are strong direct positive influences. Previous experience acts in the opposite direction for lower-class men. For lower-class parents, patterns involve responding to direction by others. In the present data the lower-class women respond more directly to feeding; the lower-class men respond to "direction" by the spouse.

8 | AN OVERVIEW

INTERPRETATION

Pregnancy, birth, parenthood—reproduction is still the norm for the large majority of adults in the United States, but there is little scientific information to guide couples through this critical stage in their lives. Freud's idea of the mother-infant relationship, the prototype of all human dependency ties, has received wide acceptance. Only in the last few decades, however, has the nature of mother-infant attachment undergone serious empirical scrutiny. Still shrouded in mystery are such topics as social relations of a couple during pregnancy, the stress both parents face at the birth, the dynamics of interaction between new parents, and the actual process by which the first child is integrated into the family.

Wildly changing fads in child-rearing patterns over the present century testify to a collective ignorance concerning the dynamics of early family formation. Perhaps over-impressed with the medical mystique that has surrounded birth, social scientists until recently joined the rest of society in assuming that pregnancy, birth, and parenting were natural events that would take their course. Perhaps so. But the current generation of new parents is now forcing a reappraisal of this policy of benign neglect. No doubt in part because they lived through the tumultuous sixties, they seem less willing than their parents to accept statements from "authorities" about how to handle major events in their lives.

Certainly birth is a major event in several people's lives. At the moment of birth a child and its parents start a lifelong relationship. Once that relationship begins, it touches every aspect of the lives of all three. And, unlike the marital relationship, the parent-child interactive drama is seldom terminated—it goes on as long as life itself.

A married couple changes into a family when the first child arrives. One of the family's major functions is to provide for the socialization of children. Yet research on the family and the study of the developing child are seldom

pursued together. Except for research on divorce or father absence, there are few bridges between sociology of the family and developmental psychology. The joint research on families and developing children that does exist, however, underscores the importance of the transitions between pregnancy, birth, and early parenthood for father, mother, and child (Henneborn and Cogan 1975; Macfarlane 1977: and references cited therein). Early parent-child relationships evolve from a time starting prior to birth. And family processes set in motion early can have far-reaching effects. For example, premature babies or those with neonatal problems are more often the targets of child abuse than are other infants (Elmer and Gregg 1967; Klein and Stern 1971; Lynch and Roberts 1977). (See also Rogerson and Rogerson 1931.) Our inquiry therefore began early in the family's life and tried to integrate the two research traditions.

Some of the key findings of the research will be summarized and placed in perspective in this chapter, but before undertaking this overview, a word is needed about what an observational study like ours could reasonably be expected to accomplish, and what its advantages and limitations are.

The research had two major purposes. The first was to provide a rich description of a set of couples as they became first-time parents. This was necessary because social conditions influencing family formation changed very rapidly in the 1970s, and how emergent families reacted to these dramatic social changes has yet to be thoroughly documented. The second purpose was to examine associations among the variables that linked pregnancy, the birth crisis, and then the ensuing period of early parenthood. Little prior research has focused on *both* parents or has tied events in pregnancy and childbirth to subsequent family functioning. Since the research was exploratory, the analysis is not likely to provide final answers. On the other hand, the richness of the data and the longitudinal nature of the study promised insights on a number of important issues.

We assume that there are strong similarities in the basic ways couples and families cope, and that families satisfy basic needs for most people. Spouses depend on each other; they must cooperate if the family is to survive. The birth crisis is a threat most couples face. The way this crisis is met is not exactly the same from one couple to the next, but the gross outlines of family functioning over the perinatal period, and the ways in which young families respond to the early demands of infants, are probably similar. If preparation in pregnancy or previous life events affect birth experience for this group of couples, it is reasonable to assume similar effects for other couples. But to have any hope of success the inquiry had to be careful and deep. We therefore chose to focus on a small sample of couples picked to allow careful study of critical factors such as social class and the amount of preparation couples had before the birth and then to inquire searchingly into how these factors and others might shape their subsequent lives.

Also, after weighing the scant evidence at hand, we made some assump-

tions about early parenting. We assumed that good early parenting is mainly the parents' ability to be emotionally responsive to the baby (see Klopfer 1971). We therefore looked for relationships between breast-feeding and early parenting and at indicators of paternal and maternal responsiveness as related to other factors. These assumptions are not particularly risky, because if such relationships are absent or negative, estimates of the models we propose would reveal that fact.

CONCEPTION CONTROL

For interpreting this research, good conception control is a trend deserving special notice. It is a pervasive influence affecting all young adults today. Besides reducing the number of unwanted children, it affects rates of cohabitation among young people and the rising age at first marriage. With ready contraception and abortion backup, couples can choose whether or not to become parents. Many of the couples in this study, in contrast with families of earlier decades, lived together before marriage and later decided when to have a child. Childbearing was postponed at least for a time.

Choosing exactly when to have a child probably has many ramifications, the prime one being emotional. Voluntary parenthood is much different from accidental parenthood, especially for the woman. For example, Miller (1978) found that women with unplanned pregnancies did not adopt a new identity based on pregnancy, and Landis (1952) noted greater emotional upset in the first trimester as compared to women who had intended to conceive. Postponement of pregnancy until a couple is ready may have consequences for the father as well, and for marital satisfaction (Christensen 1968). For relatively settled couples, the nature of the birth crisis may not be the same as for couples who are less settled, because older, more affluent parents may experience less stress than younger, impecunious ones. It also seems likely that planned births would lead more often than unplanned ones to happy children and happy parents. Miller's data (1978), for instance, indicate that fully intended pregnancies result in fully wanted children at six months of age.

Our sample may be rather typical of present-day couples as far as planning goes, but it differs markedly from samples procured in previous decades. Data on a national sample surveyed in 1971–75 revealed that of white women married at least thirty months, 5.1 percent experienced a pregnancy when birth was not wanted at all (U.S. Bureau of the Census 1979). This figure cannot be directly compared to our sample, with its rate of 3.3 percent or 6.7 percent[1] completely unplanned pregnancies, because 11 percent of our women acknowledged an abortion at some time in the past. But the rates do suggest that women in our sample are not atypical in their conception histories compared to other, similar women in the early seventies. Such conception control contrasts sharply with that seen earlier. A report by the Foundation for Child

[1]Depending on whether one credits wives' replies or husbands'.

Development (1977:19) based on a national sample of children born between 1964 and 1969 states that "less than half of the youngsters in the survey were the result of a planned pregnancy, in the sense that the mother 'wanted to become pregnant at that time,' " and Russo (1979) suggests that 20 percent of pregnancies were unplanned in the sixties. In previous research on birth, the ratios of planned to unplanned children were certainly different from those found now.

Although it is impossible to tell exactly how different present rates of accidental pregnancies are from those of earlier decades, implications are far-reaching. In earlier decades, there was a strong association between conception control and socioeconomic status, for example, and average family size was larger. Preparation classes may then have attracted mainly couples with planned pregnancies. For these reasons conclusions from the present research about how social class and preparation affect the quality of life in young families—drawn from a sample interviewed recently and for which almost all pregnancies were planned—need not agree with conclusions drawn earlier, when the ratio of planned to unplanned pregnancies was so different, or with present-day findings for families whose children are unplanned.

ADVANTAGES AND LIMITATIONS OF THE RESEARCH

The advantages and limitations of this research are matched to its strategy. It is developmental both from the standpoint of individuals, because each member of the family is developing, and from the standpoint of the family, because the family develops as it moves from a twosome to a threesome. This approach joins together ideas of actors with individual age and sex roles, stages of the life cycle, the family's developmental needs and tasks, and the family as a set of mutually contingent roles (see Hill and Rodgers 1964). The imperatives of human development *and* of previous life history are assumed to shape each individual's development, and the family is assumed to be a social organization whose functioning relates to the dependencies and complementaries among its constituent members.

One important advantage of this research for studying family dynamics is that pregnancy lasts for nine months and has a predictable outcome. It would be much harder to study other kinds of family crises, say divorce, because it is impossible to predict when a divorce will occur or even *if* it will occur. Collecting data before a crisis is essential, because a crisis often causes people to change, and people change in ways of which they are not necessarily consciously aware. Therefore, it may be impossible afterward for them to recall events or exact states of mind before a crisis. For example, evidence of change in women's views of themselves was uncovered over the course of this study, but it is doubtful if the women could have reported these changes directly. They probably were unaware that their self-images were altered after childbirth. (Other research also indicates that attitudes change significantly as

a consequence of delivery [Zemlik and Watson 1953], and that even attributes supposedly as stable as IQ scores change [Breen 1975:19].)

Studying a first birth has another strategic advantage. Families experiencing this crisis can be demographically similar. Most are relatively young and have the same number of members. Other family research is plagued by the need to allow for large differences in family size or age composition, which can be extremely difficult to evaluate.

The longitudinal nature of this research offers a third advantage, in that causal inferences are made more secure. No design can guarantee correct causal inferences, of course, but besides guarding against bias in recall (as mentioned above), a longitudinal design imposes a temporal ordering. Measurements taken in pregnancy precede measurements taken after childbirth, so the possibilities for assigning causes are limited. A cause must precede its effects, and an event after childbirth cannot be taken as a cause of an event in pregnancy. A panel study is no passport to the correct assignment of causal priorities, but its temporal structure prevents some kinds of errors and removes some ambiguities.

A further advantage is that the couples observed were not picked for study because they had a problem or because they were all hospitalized in a single medical facility. The findings may therefore have more relevance for normal families than family research undertaken to study some problem or done with the cooperation of one particular hospital or group of physicians.

A final major advantage is the structure of the sample. By assuring an equal number of middle-class and lower-class respondents and by stratifying on preparation level within social class, the sample offers a way to study other variables, with these two factors either held constant or balanced. Although we guessed before the research was begun that social class and preparation would prove to be important explanatory variables and that such a sampling design would be advantageous, it has turned out in retrospect to be even more advantageous than we foresaw. In particular, social class appears to be associated with the dynamics of early parenting in much the way Kohn (1969) deduced it affected the rearing of older children. What parents actually do with their children does not differ by class, but the apparent causes for those actions differ markedly.

Any research involves trade-offs, however, and this research has its drawbacks.

One limitation is that the persons who took part in the research were, of necessity, volunteers. (A few lower-class women received small payments after the third interview.) It is not clear how volunteering may affect the findings. Couples who were having marital difficulties during pregnancy would probably not volunteer to take part in a study of this kind, however, or those who did volunteer may have been especially eager to seek out information about childbirth and parenting.

Another limitation is that not all fathers were interviewed. Fathers partici-

pated selectively. Some refused to be interviewed. A careful analysis to see whether fathers who agreed to be interviewed were different from fathers who did not (see table A.4, Appendix A) revealed that except for differences associated with questions about breast-feeding, the respondent and nonrespondent fathers did not differ much. On the other hand, such comparisons are based on information furnished by wives, with all of the drawbacks that secondhand information implies.

Another caveat is that the time span of the research is relatively short, whether in terms of a baby's childhood or a couple's marriage. There are data for the last three months of pregnancy and on into the first few weeks of the baby's life, with some limited information from a telephone interview with the mother when the baby was six months old. How men and women rate childbirth very soon after the event does not necessarily reflect the way in which they would view childbirth later on. Important changes in outlook do occur, for we observed that a number of women's views about never having another child changed considerably in just the first six months after the birth. The present data are rich, but they cover a short period.

There are also limitations on sources of information. All information on the women's physiologic or medical status was derived from interviews. No hospital records were consulted. Strong efforts were made to ensure reliability of data on delivery and related matters, but the information has all the drawbacks of self-report.

A major limitation is that the sample is not representative. A purposive sample is especially problematic for estimating averages or relative frequencies because measures of location can be badly biased by nonrepresentativeness. For this reason it would be extremely hazardous to generalize findings concerning averages from this group to any wider universe. The number of children desired by these men and women, for example, may not be at all typical of the number desired by other American couples. On the other hand, when the sample could be checked against census data or other national benchmarks, it seemed to be reasonably typical in terms of demographics for other white American couples having a first child (chapter 2 and Appendix A). Also, comparisons with national polls (cited throughout the book) suggest that the opinions and attitudes of the panel are fairly typical of those expressed by other young adults in the mid seventies. These equivalences, however, are entirely a matter of judgment.

Fortunately, nonrepresentativeness is usually not as serious a threat to measures of relationship as it is to measures of location, so purposive samples have an honorable history in exploratory research. (Covariance measures are thought to be relatively robust in respect to sampling bias.) We are inclined to believe that the associational relationships uncovered in this research have some validity. For example, women in this sample who were breast-fed as infants more often chose to breast-feed their own infants. Husbands who participated in delivery apparently improved their wives' birth experience.

One would expect these and similar associations to hold for other, similar women. The basic trade-off was between breadth of coverage and depth. We did not believe that the dynamics of early family formation could be understood unless respondents revealed a great deal of intimate detail about their past history and present circumstances, and unless the family could be studied as a unit. Given our goals, our choice had to be a carefully chosen, relatively small sample of volunteers. As a matter of fact, compared to other research of this genre, our sample is quite large, however.

CURRENT SOCIAL CONDITIONS AND BIRTH

Today over 40 percent of marriages end in divorce. Yet despite the strain in contemporary families, people still value and want family relationships (Douvan 1978) and see emotional benefits as the primary reason for having children (Fawcett 1978). The most dramatic change in American marriage during the twentieth century is not in the proportion of those marrying or divorcing but in what husbands and wives do and in the number of years they spend with and without one another and with and without children (see Bane 1976). The patterns and quality of marital life are different from what they were a generation ago. Says Bernard (1975:233): "If we had a Richter scale for societal, as well as for earthquakes, the present societal quake would surely register 8." At no point in the life cycle are changes more profound than during the period around the birth of the first child. Curiously, however, birth provoked little interest among social scientists until recently. Nevertheless, this important family event brings many recent social changes into focus—women's reduced fertility, women's increased labor-force participation, the blurring of sex roles, and the increased salience of the quality of life as a goal in itself.

Birth has great social significance, and therefore its meaning changes as society changes. For this reason research on emergent families that may have accurately reflected attitudes or customs ten or fifteen years ago is dated in important ways today. Evolution in the social aspects of birth can be seen in respect to conception control, the personalization of birth, the rate of breast-feeding, and particularly in the strong impetus toward father participation.

Most couples are now more interested in the quality of their childbirth experience and in sharing that experience. Prospective fathers want an active role in birth and early parenting. It is not just that couples now plan to have fewer children or to space them differently. Rather, they approach the whole matter of birth from a new perspective. In the 1930s couples also wanted fewer children—economic conditions forced couples to limit family size. But the self-imposed limitations of today are of a different sort: couples are now concerned about overpopulation in relation to the environment, the quality of their own lives, and the high divorce rate. Also, because young marrieds

can now choose whether or not to become parents, their reasons for under-taking parenthood vary. For each couple the role conflicts and psychological problems associated with parenthood are therefore somewhat different, if only because some postpone parenthood longer than others.

PERSONALIZATION OF BIRTH

People in the seventies saw the quality of mothers' and fathers' birth ex-periences and the gratifications parents experience in early parenting as ends in themselves. Young couples increasingly wished to experience a more natural labor and delivery and to have the father and possibly close friends present when the birth occurred. They questioned the quality of parents' emotional experience in old-fashioned hospital obstetric units, and many wanted extended contact with the baby right after the birth. Couples shopped for progressive physicians and hospitals where they could receive the type of care they desired. Because this type of supportive environment can be hard to find in hospitals, some couples are now opting for home births or for delivery at a "birth center." There are now doctors and nurse-midwives, particularly in large cities or rural areas, who are willing to attend home deliveries. The home-birth movement began with those living in communes on the West Coast, was picked up on the East Coast, and now more and more includes run-of-the-mill Americans (Mehl 1978).

A closely related trend in the seventies was the changing notion of woman's role in childbirth. Feminists persuaded more and more women that it is impor-tant to control their own bodies. Just as feminists strongly support a woman's right to abortion, they also insist that women should be allowed to maintain control over the events of labor and birth. In particular, feminists challenge what they see as the devaluation of female patients at the hands of the (usually male) obstetrician, and these views are percolating to people at all levels of society (Corea 1977).

A large proportion of women in this sample wanted to take an active role in childbirth. Many wanted a birth with little or no medication so that they could be fully conscious when their infants were born. They wanted to give birth rather than to be delivered. Although less than a quarter of these women went through childbirth with little or no medication, close to 50 percent of them were ready to do so. Natural childbirth has been talked about for three dec-ades, so it is not a new idea; yet the women in this study who had wishes along these lines were often ahead of the styles of medical care prevailing in the urban areas where they lived in the seventies.

Serious questions are now being raised about the medical management of childbirth in the United States. The women in our study were relatively conservative on these issues compared to other young women, but they ex-pressed considerable dissatisfaction with the amount of information given by their physicians during pregnancy and also were unhappy when they received more medication than they wanted during delivery.

There is enormous variation in facilities presently available for helping couples experience the kind of birth they wish. The experience of most women is not mirrored at all well by what happens in a few high-quality hospitals, the kinds of hospitals where most obstetric research is carried out. Because of this, the couples who took part in this research were recruited from many sources, and the quality of their birth experiences did vary greatly. Although scientific justification supporting the personalization of birth was not available to inform these couples as they undertook parenthood, the present research suggests that there *are* important effects if parents share a delivery with little or no medication.

The majority of the couples in this sample viewed pregnancy and childbirth as a *joint* undertaking; many seemed to form an alliance that strengthened both husband and wife as they undertook this new challenge. The analyses of husband's and wife's birth experiences indicated that each was a strong influence on the other. The man's participation improved the quality of the woman's birth experience, and the woman's birth experience was a strong predictor of the man's birth experience. Husband's support during labor and delivery was a critical factor from the wife's viewpoint. The tenor of the times encouraged a joint approach to birth, and these couples' eagerness to share the experience—noted even among those who came from working-class backgrounds and some who did not attend preparation classes—is truly remarkable considering how recently birth customs have changed.

About two-thirds of the fathers in this study witnessed the birth of their children. Such a high rate of father participation is in sharp contrast to rates in the previous decade, when fathers were often actively barred from labor and delivery suites and fainted in the waiting room when given news of the birth (Shereshefsky and Yarrow 1973). In this respect, these couples' birth experiences in the seventies differed greatly from couples' experiences in earlier decades. In Shereshefsky and Yarrow's study, *no* fathers attended delivery. Not long ago it was assumed that a husband witnessing the delivery of his wife would experience "revulsion" and that she could never regain her sexual prestige with him (Stewart 1963:1066–67). The quotes from fathers interviewed in this research indicate how far off target such assumptions would be today. In the present study, wives looked forward enthusiastically to their husbands' sharing the birth with them, and afterwards their enthusiasm was undiminished. Furthermore, the majority of fathers enjoyed being present in delivery, and the level of their participation was reflected in their enjoyment of the birth event. Actually of all the findings, those that most capture the social climate of birth in the seventies pertain to the father.

The fathers' active involvement in pregnancy and childbirth apparently had two outstanding consequences, one affecting quality of life for the man himself and the other affecting his and his wife's early parenting.

The first point requires little elaboration. Some of the men in this study rated being a participant in the birth of their first child as the most thrilling and profound event in their lives so far (see direct quotes in chapter 4; also

Grossman 1978). These included a few men who had not planned to attend, but who were invited into delivery at the last minute.

The effect of husbands' involvement prior to and during birth on parenting is more complex. In this study, if a wife stated at the sixth month of pregnancy that she wished her husband to be present in delivery, the husband was more likely later to report the baby as being a source of happiness in marriage ($r = .44$). Also, provocative relationships were uncovered between wives' attitudes toward their husbands as fathers and the husbands' degree of participation in pregnancy and delivery. The women's views of their husbands as fathers differed depending on whether their husbands were present during delivery (or whether the husbands *wished* to be present). If husbands stayed away from delivery by choice, their wives' views of them as fathers were lower.

Similar conclusions can be drawn from the mothering and fathering models. Men's participation in the birth was a key element in improving women's birth experience and in helping women do without medication. For middle-class women, awareness at birth acted directly and indirectly on parenting, while for lower-class women awareness had sizeable indirect effects on parenting. The structural patterns between men's birth experience and fathering seemed to show particularly strong effects for lower-class men. Preparation during pregnancy seemed to affect fathering positively *through* birth experience for men of both social classes. For lower-class men this is the only route by which preparation had significant impact on fathering.

These findings about father involvement are consistent with other reports. The father's regard for the mother has been found related to her feeding competence and her ability to provide good mothering (Pedersen and Robson 1969), and Grossman (1978) concluded that much of the father's early parenting activity is closely linked to the mother-father relationship. On the other hand, findings about husband involvement in the present study differ completely from findings for young black unwed mothers in Furstenberg's analysis (1976). He found that success of black adolescents at the maternal role was not different according to whether or not the baby's father lived with the family. In fact, Furstenberg found little support for the contention that the absence of the father from the home adversely affects the mother's adaptation to parenthood. But in the case of both Furstenberg's families and the families studied by us, birth is not a mother-infant dyadic affair. It is a truly social affair. Furstenberg's young mothers leaned on relatives other than husbands, while husbands and wives in this study leaned mainly on each other. The birth event cannot be isolated from its overall social context. In particular, in order to understand its effects on family functioning, birth must be viewed in social perspective both before and after it occurs. To study only mothers and / or infants slights the full range of facts.

In sum, there seems to be substantial evidence supporting need for the personalization of childbirth. A woman's emotional state can be an important

determinant of the physical stress of delivery (Robertson 1939). If husbands are made a part of the pregnancy and birth experience and / or wish to take part, they can enhance their own potential and their wives' potential as parents, and they have more positive views of the child later on. Statistical controls make it reasonable to conclude that the quality of the birth event per se exerts some important influence on early family relationships in addition to that exerted by factors present earlier or that effects of the earlier variables are mediated by birth experience. The mothering models include prepartum baby-care plans and therefore control on predispositions present before the birth. The fathering model controls on preparation, which is an indicator of prior interest, as well as on previous baby-care experience, and earlier analyses indicated that paternal responsiveness responded to participation net of father's psychological predisposition. Other preliminary reports now appearing suggest in addition that the mother's adaptation to labor and delivery predicts the physiological functioning of the infant (Eichler et al. 1977).

The quality of a couple's birth experience is an important goal in itself. Sharing the birth experience may also benefit the marital relationship, although we could procure little data bearing directly on this point in the short time span available. Our data, however, leave little doubt that the birth event possesses unique significance for both members of the couple *and* for their relationship with the baby.

Sex Roles

A particularly strong trend during the seventies was society's movement toward less stereotyped sex roles, especially for women (see Thornton and Freedman 1979). Broader sex roles encouraged women to work outside the home, and all but a handful of the women in this sample were working when they became pregnant. Exactly half of them continued working to the end of pregnancy.

Men were also experiencing societal pressure toward less stereotyped sex roles, whether in terms of hairstyle, dress, spare-time activities, vocational choice, or family obligations. But liberation of men is still on the social frontier. Most men are still not able to choose whether or not to devote themselves to full-time money-making jobs, and most cannot choose full-time child care easily (see Fein 1978).

Some of the blurring of men's sex-role obligations is in the domain of parenting. It is as common now to see a young father taking a toddler to the store as it was in decades past to see a young mother in this role. It is less common for young men to assume full-charge care of very young infants, but the data in this study indicate much sharing in the nurturance of young babies. A few weeks after the birth, for example, fathers were holding their babies for more than one hour per day, and the majority got up with babies in the night.

Many men were actively interested in the pregnancy and attended prepara-

tion classes. This interest had implications for later events. A man's interest in his wife's pregnancy was modestly correlated ($r = .31$) with how much he held the baby in the first six weeks of its life, and also with whether he picked up the baby when it cried ($r = .23$) (chapter 6). Also, the husband's attitude toward the pregnancy was related to his wife's enjoyment of motherhood—the happier he was about the pregnancy, the more she enjoyed the first few weeks of the baby's life ($r = .27$) (chapter 6).

Blurring of sex roles appeared to have a number of other associations with parenting. There was a correlation between division of household labor in the sixth month of pregnancy and the husband's care of his new baby. Men who helped more around the house during pregnancy tended to be those who diapered the baby ($r = .19$) and held it ($r = .34$) more often, for example. Division of labor in pregnancy was also associated with measures of father's interest in the baby ($r = .33$). Young men's sharing in household chores may make it easier for them to adopt a more active father role, at least when the child is a young infant.

It seems likely that couples' attitudes toward appropriate sex-role behavior would differ by class and affect early parenting behavior. Although there was no social-class difference in division of labor, there were hints here and there that the lower-class couples held more rigid sex-role stereotypes, for example, in their inhibitions about breast-feeding. The lower-class mother's apparent influence upon the father's early parenting can be taken as further evidence of less flexible roles. The *average* amounts of fathering activity did not differ by social class, but there were strong indications that father behavior has different roots in the two social classes. For the middle-class families, preparation and previous experience had positive effects on parenting, and the baby did not appear to be viewed as the "mother's property." For the lower-class families, the influence of mothering on fathering, together with the negative effects of fathers' previous baby-care experience on fathering, strongly suggested that baby care was controlled by the mother.

But irrespective of class, the young men expressed opinions consistent with an active father-role—78 percent of the young fathers said before the birth that men are just as interested in their children when they are babies as when they are older (Appendix B, opinion item 8). Young men in the sample apparently also reacted to their wives' expectations—96 percent of the women believed the most important quality in a father is the warmth and interest he shows in his children (Appendix B, opinion item 2). Even the most traditional of the couples in this panel gave evidence of remarkable shifts in sex-role attitudes and behaviors compared with young families of a decade ago.

SUMMARY

Much has been written about the breakdown of sex-role stereotypes. Less visible social changes have probably had even more influence on people

starting families. Couples, more and more dissatisfied with other people taking charge during childbirth, are actively seeking personalized and more satisfying birth experiences. Many women want an active role in the birth; some are achieving it.

Our data provide some scientific justification for seeking a good birth experience. In the present study parents' birth experiences apparently affected their later emotional responsiveness to their infants. There are also suggestions that husbands' participation affected wives' views of themselves, wives' views of their husbands as fathers, and wives' parenting behavior. Mehl (1978:114) also offers evidence of this kind. He found that as couples become "more involved in taking control for and planning their own birth experience, in educating themselves for childbirth, and in preparing for the actual delivery," the impact of other things, such as the couple's personalities and how they themselves were reared, diminished.

CHANGES IN MEDICAL MANAGEMENT OF BIRTH

A trend related to the personalization of birth is young people's skepticism about the value of medical interference in the birth process (see Corea 1977 for citations). When this century began, most babies were born at home. Infant mortality rates were high. Partly as a consequence of improved public health but also as a consequence of urbanization, as the century progressed, more and more children were delivered in hospitals. (By 1975, 99 percent of all babies in the country were delivered by physicians in hospitals [Querec 1978].) But with Read's "natural childbirth" in the fifties, and then with the Lamaze method (sometimes called *psychoprophylaxis*), which came into vogue in the sixties, there has been a decline in the medical mystique surrounding birth.

No one would doubt that some Cesarean deliveries are mandatory or that some obstetrical crises call for medical intervention, but serious questions are being raised by lay persons (Haire 1972) and by medical practitioners (Banta and Thacker 1979; Haverkamp et al. 1976; Lee and Baggish 1976) about routine use of procedures such as fetal monitoring. Also, the impressive mortality statistics for other Western countries where most births occur outside hospitals are thought-provoking. In Holland, for example, a large percentage of births occur at home, and Dutch infant and maternal mortality rates are among the lowest in the world (Richards 1978:67). The physiology of birth is still imperfectly understood, but given a process so delicate and fine tuned, many thoughtful physicians believe that nature should be interfered with as little as possible (Klaus and Kennell, 1976b; Macfarlane 1977:125; Richards 1978). Furthermore, the fear of malpractice suits as a consequence of failure to interfere with the birth process seems unfounded (Baier, n.d.).

CESAREAN DELIVERY

The number of mothers undergoing Cesarean delivery in the United States has skyrocketed in the seventies (Gibbons 1976; Klassen 1975). In line with this, although the women in this sample were judged to be in excellent health and, except for one, were not expecting operative delivery, they experienced a high rate of Cesarean delivery (17 percent). They also experienced many other less dramatic obstetrical interventions.

It is not possible to judge the accuracy of a medical decision without appraising all its aspects. This study is particularly limited in that respect, because all data were drawn from interviews with parents, and no data were procured from hospital charts or other medical records. On the other hand, some troubling facts turned up. The women admitted to hospitals at night received different treatment from those admitted in the daytime; fewer procedures were undertaken and there was less medical interference when women were admitted at night. The difference from day to night in the number of operative deliveries is statistically significant. Of twenty operative deliveries, sixteen occurred between 8 A.M. and 8 P.M. (An analysis of the times of surgery makes it unlikely that cases admitted in the night were being held over until daytime for operation.) Also, labor times for women admitted to the hospital in the daytime were significantly shorter than labor times for those admitted at night.

The attention attracted by increased national rates in Cesarean deliveries has so far been astonishingly small, in part because obstetrical surgery rates are not included in reports that summarize national rates for surgery. But in 1971 in the Netherlands—where mortality connected with births stands at one of the lowest figures in the world—the rate of Cesarean delivery was 2.0 percent, compared to 6.9 percent in the United States (Kloosterman 1978), and the U.S. rate has probably at least doubled since then.[2]

The full costs of surgical deliveries in terms of family functioning apparently have never been calculated. In our data, psychological costs both immediately and over the longer term appear to be substantial. On almost all measures of individual functioning through the six-month postpartum phone check, women who experienced an operative delivery were at a disadvantage. And since father participation in delivery and father's birth experience are prejudiced by surgical delivery, there are probably social costs as well. An additional cost will be borne by many of these women in the future, because having a first delivery by operation often leads to future deliveries being handled in the same manner.

Babies delivered vaginally travel down the birth canal, and the full significance of that natural mode of entry into the world is not yet completely understood. Many profound physiological changes occur in the infant as birth is occurring; these changes may be stimulated or modulated by unknown

[2]Other Maryland women not in this study, with Blue Shield insurance, were reported as experiencing surgical delivery at rates as high as 35 percent in March 1976 (Beall 1977).

factors that come into play as the baby is being born. Serious thought is in order when the rate of Cesarean delivery—which held steady at around 5 percent for decades—has suddenly doubled, tripled, or risen even higher for some groups of women in the late seventies, particularly since Gibbons's analysis (1976) for Baltimore first-time mothers reveals that the change in rate is not connected with demographic changes in the population.

Young couples are also concerned about the potential threats to health posed by other kinds of medical intervention, such as induction of labor or the use of fetal monitoring. The *lower* rates of obstetrical intervention in countries that have better infant mortality rates is especially thought-provoking.

MEDICATION

Another medical change affecting young couples' views of birth in the seventies was the growing body of evidence that *all* drugs given during labor and delivery, even local anesthetics, have potentially negative effects on the newborn baby. Many studies show ill effects—including depression of the infant's early sucking and breathing reflexes—for infants born to mothers given even small amounts of medication or local anesthetics (see chapter 4 for citations). Thoughtful people are concerned about the potential effects of drugs or other compounds that have not yet been documented. For example, only recently has the negative impact on pregnant women of small amounts of alcohol ingestion and environmental air pollutants attracted attention in the press. Women who might laugh at feminist ideas about controlling their own bodies are still aware of, and worried about, how drugs and other artificial substances may harm their babies. Naturally, they wish to avoid these possible dangers.

Many women in this sample, particularly those who were the best prepared, wished to have minimal medication. In fact, of the 100 women who delivered vaginally, 50 wanted to be awake and feeling everything. Only 27 of these fulfilled their desires (table 4.3). Our analysis of the relationship between medication and pain suggests, furthermore, that medication was not very effective in controlling pain and agrees with the report of Klopfer et al. (1975). The analysis also reveals that the women who were fully conscious and who reported little or no pain in the second stage of labor were those who were best prepared.

Medication given the mother during delivery was apparently linked directly to middle-class woman's parenting two to three weeks later and indirectly to lower-class women's parenting. It also appeared to directly affect the average amount of time all mothers and babies spent together daily in the first three days net of prepartum plans.

The overall amount of medication used with this group of women, who were delivered in many kinds of hospitals, exceeds the amounts reported for patients in large teaching hospitals (see Norr et al. 1977). Medicated patients may be easier to deal with, or perhaps in some instances medical personnel are

THE FIRST BIRTH

simply behind the times in obstetrical knowledge. In either case, the histories of the women in this sample suggest that the use of obstetrical medication generally needs some reexamination. It is particularly noteworthy that the *main* complaint women voiced about their doctors here had to do with excess medication and that the three women who were attended by midwives had no such complaints.

BREAST-FEEDING

Another trend in the seventies was a turnabout in attitudes of medical personnel toward breast-feeding. There were all along some thoughtful practitioners who favored breast-feeding in the fifties and sixties, but many did not encourage it, particularly if the parturient woman had reservations about it. Moreover, since it can be difficult for a woman to learn how to breast-feed, nurses in obstetrical wards often discouraged breast-feeding on practical grounds. It was easier for them to feed the babies formula themselves in the nursery than to try to help women establish breast-feeding. For these and other reasons, the incidence of breast-feeding in the United States dropped steadily: in the late thirties, the rate was about 77 percent (Hirschman and Sweet 1974); in 1946, 65 percent (Bain 1948); in 1956, 37 percent (Meyer 1958); and in 1966, 27 percent (Hirschman and Sweet 1974). (See also Hill 1967.) However, there may now be a return to breast-feeding. In a 1978 survey, 47 percent of new mothers were breast-feeding when they left the hospital, and 35 percent of them were continuing two months later (Sauls 1979). (See also Hirschman and Hendershot 1979).

We see two major causes for changes in breast-feeding rates. One is its promotion by the medical profession because of health advantages for mother and infant. It is now recognized that human milk promotes optimal growth and development in infants (Jelliffe and Jelliffe 1978). Human milk is more digestible and less allergy-provoking than other foods, and in addition it provides immunities and specific antibodies (Gerrard 1974; Harfouche 1970). Breast-feeding also benefits the mother, in that it hastens involution of the uterus and provides some protection against pregnancy (Harfouche 1970). The other cause is the increased social acceptability of breast-feeding in the United States. While some of this acceptability may be a consequence of awareness of the health benefits of breast-feeding, at least part of it is related to the women's movement.

The couples in this survey exemplified current life styles in their dedication to natural feeding of babies. Attitudes toward breast-feeding were highly positive among those fathers who agreed to be interviewed, and 68 percent of the women indicated during pregnancy that they planned to breast-feed. It is probably no accident that the women who wanted to take an active role in childbirth also wanted to breast-feed. The two go hand in hand. Childbirth preparation classes emphasize both. Also, feminists urge women to value their bodily functions, one of which is lactation. The sexual component of

breast-feeding, long ignored by both men and women, is now more generally acknowledged. Conception planning probably affected breast-feeding too, for much higher rates of breast-feeding are found for planned babies, as compared with unplanned (Hubert 1974).

This study documents some of the psychological advantages of breast-feeding as well. For women of both social classes (with amount of infant crying included as a control) feeding seemed to have positive effects on maternal responsiveness net of other predictors. Although the analysis of thwarted breast-feeders was not definitive, estimates of the mothering model suggest that breast-feeding may enhance both mothering and fathering for lower-class couples. Breast-feeding may have additional effects, in that it promotes early contact between mother and child. Also, if husbands have strong opinions on feeding mode, it may increase husband-wife solidarity.

Nonetheless, a sizeable fraction of the women in this sample who tried breast-feeding gave it up quickly. (Newton [1971:994]) would characterize these women as "token breast-feeders.") The outside employment of women appeared to be no barrier—probably because most women with outside work during the first six months of the baby's life were employed only part-time—but it was mostly the Lamaze-trained women who persisted. Middle-class women's persistence in breast-feeding responded to prior preparation, and under present conditions it is probably more critical to understand why women persist than why they start.

SUMMARY

The past decade saw profound changes in the medical management of birth—decreased use of general anesthesia, encouragement of breast-feeding, fetal monitoring, and increased rates of surgical delivery. The encouragement of breast-feeding now provided by most hospitals and medical personnel may partly account for the high rate of breast-feeding by women while still in the hospital. The full consequences of all the changes are hard to assess, but some trends, especially the sharp increase in surgical delivery, are disturbing. To the extent this survey is representative, changes in obstetric medication have not yet been as widely adopted as one would hope. In addition, our data contradict the assumption that women's birth experience will be improved as a consequence of increased medication. This topic deserves further study.

THE INFLUENCE OF LEVEL OF PREPARATION FOR
CHILDBIRTH

Our earlier cross-sectional survey of 269 new mothers suggested that preparation in pregnancy affected the nature of the mother's birth experience and her reaction to her newborn (Doering and Entwisle 1975). Mothers with a

good birth experience seemed at an advantage, in that they had more positive responses to their children right away and breast-fed them longer. This earlier work indicated that training during pregnancy appeared to add something unique over and above the positive motivational factors that led women to seek out preparation in the first place. These conclusions, however, were made insecure by the retrospective nature of the data and by the fact that considering the complexity of the issues, relatively few variables were included.

The conclusions of the earlier study generally hold up under the more extensive analysis undertaken in this book, although conclusions about the exact ways in which childbirth preparation affects breast-feeding are modified. Investigation of social-class effects in the present study also qualifies some of the conclusions reached earlier. In both studies and irrespective of social class, preparation acts to increase women's level of awareness at birth and improves the mother's birth experience. Preparation's effects on feeding, however, depend on social-class level. Since the models for feeding (chapter 5) and those for mothering with feeding inserted (chapter 7) all control on feeding intentions beforehand, the influence of preparation in the present study is evaluated net of psychological predispositions that may differentiate breast-feeders from bottle-feeders ahead of time. In other words, effects of preparation are rather well shielded from confounding with effects of other prenatal variables that could readily account for positive effects. In the earlier study with all data gathered retrospectively, this kind of controlled analysis was not possible, so inferences were less secure. The present study not only adds a number of new conclusions about preparation but points to possible negative effects of preparation for lower-class women as well.

A new dimension is added by studying the father's preparation. The men in this study experienced varying degrees of preparation, with levels almost exactly correlated to those of their wives. Preparation led men to fuller participation in the birth, which helped them cope with the birth crisis and accentuated their contribution to the quality of their wives' birth experience. It also had indirect effects, since the quality of men's birth experience predicted early fathering. For some of the men (middle-class), apparently preparation even had some direct positive effects on fathering apart from birth experience.

Women's preparation helped them have a positive birth experience, but husbands' participation made a *separate* contribution to the quality of women's birth experience. Similar conclusions about beneficial effects of husbands' participation on wives' birth experience were reached by two other research teams recently (see Henneborn and Cogan 1975 and Norr et al. 1977). But father participation may be efficacious partly because of psychological factors correlated with the father's *wish* to participate. Our analyses suggested that the father's psychological state (the wish to participate) does affect the woman's view of her husband as a father and the husband's fathering activities apart from participation. On the other hand, partici-

pation may add something unique, because with some control on prepartum dispositions, men who were present at delivery and who took a more active role enjoyed more benefits than those who were present but did little. One very important consequence of preparation is that it encourages men to be present at the birth.

The motives leading women to seek childbirth preparation remain rather obscure. There is evidence of a strong association between preparation classes and women's preference for an active role in labor and delivery. Since these role preferences preceded taking classes, the inference may be that role preferences lead to childbirth preparation. There are hints that lower-class women who already wanted to breast-feed sought out classes. For lower-class women the husband's attitude in favor of preparation may also play a critical role. Little is presently known about lower-class couples and childbirth preparation, for until lately, classes attracted mainly middle-class couples.

Childbirth preparation may be of less benefit for lower-class couples, as illustrated by the negative direct link between preparation and mothering and because their breast-feeding persistence was not affected by preparation. The reasons for these negative effects are not clear. But feeding seems to play more of a role in mothering for lower-class women than for middle-class women, so the small direct benefit of preparation for lower-class women's early feeding behavior cannot be discounted. Weighing all the effects of childbirth preparation, especially on parents' childbirth experience, leads to the conclusion that effects are, at worst, neutral, even for lower-class couples.

One implication of the negative or minimal longer-term effects of preparation for lower-class men and women is that preparation classes may not be geared to their needs. Teachers of preparation classes are drawn from middle-class backgrounds. For this reason, they may fail to understand the problems of lower-class people, and they may fail especially to communicate with them in terms of infant feeding and parenting. The assumptions of middle-class trainers about the interpersonal dynamics of lower-class marriage could even be such as to create obstacles for lower-class couples.

Previous baby-care experience apparently leads the lower-class father to be less responsive to his infant—perhaps because his being responsive is emotionally threatening to his wife. Higher levels of father preparation could have negative effects for the same reason. A father made "overresponsive" by preparation could be a problem for a lower-class woman who believes it is her prerogative to assume the major burden of infant care. An alternative possibility is that the previous experience of middle-class men may have been extrafamilial (in connection with medical work, for example), whereas that of lower-class men may have been intrafamilial (caring for younger siblings while his mother worked). If so, previous experience of lower-class men could be of a very different quality (negative), derived from situations where the man had very little choice in whether or not he interacted with an infant or in the nature of the interaction. These topics call for additional research.

Effects of preparation classes reached a ceiling for men, but prepared husbands scored higher than those with little or no preparation on several measures of fathering. Perhaps the type of preparation class attended is less important for men than women because Lamaze classes give explicit instruction that will help women give birth—in breathing techniques, for example. For men, this explicit instruction is not so directly relevant to fathering because their participation is more in psychological than in physical terms. Father preparation has not received much attention, but it may be just as important as mother preparation for early parenting, particularly since father's participation in delivery apparently can have some positive effects on women's parenting. To our knowledge, father's preparation up to now has been interpreted only as an effect on the wife's childbirth experience.

The decision to breast-feed and persistence at it appear to be major positive consequences of preparation for middle-class women. Their feeding persistence responded directly and indirectly to preparation. Women with little preparation gave up breast-feeding easily. For middle-class women, acceptability in the husband's eyes and his early encouragement appear to be strong determining factors in early breast-feeding success, but preparation exerted significant influence in addition with women's prepartum intentions controlled.

Uniqueness of Influence of Preparation

What influence should be uniquely attributed to preparation in our analyses? Women who go to the trouble of seeking out the most comprehensive kinds of classes (Lamaze) may be exactly the ones who would cope well with childbirth and breast-feeding without attending classes. The women in this sample who were more highly prepared did have lower worry scores, and they therefore might have been less anxious even with no preparation. The models, however, include plans for rooming-in and plans for breast-feeding and so reduce much of this ambiguity. People who have firm intentions to breast-feed before the baby is born, for example, are those who would be expected to have strong predispositions about mothering. When effects of preparation are estimated *net* of prenatal plans, and preparation still remains efficacious, this suggests that the positive effects of preparation are not entirely attributable to preexisting differences among the women.

For men, similar arguments hold, although the analyses were more limited because of less adequate control on prenatal factors. In particular, prenatal plans are better proxies for mothers' dispositions than for fathers'. But preparation had positive effects on birth experience via participation for fathers, and the percentage of fathers who attend delivery is far higher for those who enroll in classes. Without preparation, it is likely that appreciably many fewer men would choose to be present or would realize that this option exists.

Two other studies[3] specifically test the importance of motivation and / or self-selection vs. training. Both support the conclusion that preparation by itself confers benefits regardless of personality factors.

The first (Huttel et al. 1972) was carried out in a clinic in Hamburg, Germany. Seventy-two women having a first child were randomly assigned to an experimental (prepared) group or a control (not prepared) group. None of the women or their husbands had ever heard of preparation for childbirth, nor had it been practiced previously in any hospital in their city. Significant differences favoring the prepared women were found in length of labor, amount of medication required, the woman's control during labor and delivery, and in her positive feelings afterward. In this research, since preparation was controlled by random assignment, clearly motivation or personality factors are ruled out.

The second study, by Enkin and his colleagues (1972), involved a carefully controlled test of motivation using a different strategy. Because of the growing popularity of preparation classes, they formed a comparison group of women who wanted training but who could not be accommodated in the overcrowded classes. Thus, they had a group of women who were both unmotivated and unprepared, another group who wanted to take classes but were prevented, and a third group consisting of women who wanted preparation and received it. There were twenty-eight women in each group, carefully matched for background factors such as age, number of children, and education. Significant differences between the prepared group and the two unprepared groups were found in use of medication and forceps, as well as in the women's positive emotions toward their birth experiences. Differences between the two unprepared groups were small but in the expected direction, showing that motivation mattered slightly, but that actual preparation was responsible for most of the differences. All told, there seems little doubt that preparation is effective in itself.

In the present sample, further light was shed on the mechanism by which preparation achieves its effect. Its effectiveness cannot be attributed to reducing pain directly. It may seem contradictory that others have reported a significant connection between Lamaze preparation and less pain, but the explanation is that the structural relation between preparation and delivery experience

[3]Another study involving thirty counseled vs. thirty control couples (Shereshefsky and Yarrow 1973) was not made available to us prior to starting our research. This study consisted of biweekly counseling of wife and monthly counseling of husband (where counseling was "basically . . . ego-supportive": p. 123). The outcome was equivocal. Although "the degree of change in the control group, compared to its own baseline, is generally lower than that of changes in the counseled group" (p. 153), the changes did not attain significance. Too few data are reported to allow us to compare this study with other research, and the verbal summaries of "change" (pp. 153 ff.) in particular cannot be compared with other reports. For example, on p. 156 no significant differences are reported for any of eight "super-factor" scale means, but it is stated that counseling had some positive effects in adaptation to pregnancy, labor, and delivery.

was not fully specified in the other research. Women's level of awareness was not included in other studies. If awareness is taken as the major manifestation of ability to cope with pain, our data are also consistent with the idea that preparation affects pain. This line of reasoning could apply to such studies as Chertok's (1959), relating preparation and pain, in which preparation provided more pain relief than did drugs. In this regard, the positive and large partial correlation between level of awareness and quality of women's birth experience with pain controlled is instructive (chapter 4). Other evidence in this study also casts doubt on the idea that reduced pain is a major consequence of preparation and / or that pain reduction is the main reason for a positive birth experience. Effects of preparation appear to be nil for women who have Cesarean deliveries. For these women, level of awareness and participation are low even though the birth itself is pain-free.

The structural models developed in chapter 4, together with Janis's theory (1958) accounting for how preparation may shield persons from stress, suggest that active control is the major benefit conferred by preparation. Active measures mothers and fathers take themselves appear to make the birth a more satisfactory experience. This rationale is made more persuasive by noting that birth experience per se appears to play a more direct role for middle-class parents than for lower-class, and being in control is often cited as the kernel of the middle-class value system.

Our models call into question reports that attendance at preparation classes does not help in the adjustment to parenthood (Parke and O'Leary 1975, Wente and Crockenberg 1976). Also, the models for early parenting, which include a number of variables measured during pregnancy, suggest that other recent reports of no impressive relationships linking events in pregnancy, labor, and medication with the baby's behavior have failed to ask the right questions or have not made a sensitive enough analysis (e.g., Yang et al. 1976). Preparation or other events prior to birth may affect the baby's behavior mainly by way of affecting early parenting behaviors, and if quality of parenting is not taken into account, explanations of the baby's behavior may remain obscure. Although we had no direct measures of the baby's behavior in the present study, there were differences in parenting associated with preparation for both middle-class mothers and fathers.

THE INFLUENCE OF SOCIAL CLASS

Social class was a second basic parameter in the design of this research. There is an enormous literature on social class and child socialization, but only a handful of studies on early parenting include social class. In this study, average behavior of parents is approximately the same by social class. (Some of this equivalence is probably forced by selecting people of similar preparation levels, in each class.) Lower-class fathers were present as often in deliv-

ery as middle-class fathers. Just as many lower-class women undertook breast-feeding as middle-class women. On all indications of parental responsiveness, the two classes were equivalent. Lower-class fathers were as active in caretaking and as emotionally involved with their infants as middle-class fathers. Superficially, it is impossible to distinguish early parenting by class in this particular sample.

On the other hand, in every instance where models were estimated separately for parents of the two classes (feeding models, mothering models, fathering models), the differences in structure by class—the apparent reasons for their behavior—were impressive.[4] Some of these structural differences point to variation by class in spouses' roles vis-à-vis each other. Relationships between parents seem to differ by class in several respects: middle-class women's early breast-feeding success was sensitive to their husbands' opinions and attitudes; lower-class men's fathering responded to wives' mothering; and middle-class women's birth experience had direct effects on mothering, whereas only indirect effects appear for lower-class women. The overall pattern suggests that in the lower-class family the mother sets the parenting style, but in the middle-class family the father retains more control. Other differences point to varying effects by class of prenatal influences, the prime example being the reversed effect by class that previous baby-care experience has on fathering, with lower-class men apparently hindered by such experience.

Previous research on child socialization points to the importance of parental values in producing social-class effects. Kohn's classic work (1969) reveals that middle-class and lower-class parents use similar sanctions—parents of both classes use physical punishment to about the same extent, for example. But middle-class parents punish children for losing control of themselves, while lower-class parents punish for wild play. Kohn explains these class differences in child-rearing practices in terms of fathers' job conditions. Lower-class parents hold jobs where performance demands conformity, so these parents try to instill conformity in their children. Middle-class parents hold jobs requiring flexibility, where it is important to be self-directed. Therefore, middle-class parents, according to Kohn, use child-rearing methods that encourage children to value self-direction and responsibility.

Kohn's basic conclusions, if correct, should apply as much to young babies as to older children. In what ways could class-related value differences be manifest in very early child-care techniques? One possibility is breast-feeding, because of its relation to sex roles and sex-role stereotypes. Middle-

---

[3]The fact that these structural differences by class are so pronounced is something of a drawback to the analysis, in fact, because models involving fathering must be estimated separately by class. With fifty-seven fathers responding after the birth event, and with the inevitable reduction in cases in a listwise analysis, the number of cases is marginal for estimating structural models separately for men of the two classes. We analyzed the data as fully as possible, however, since our work is mainly exploratory.

class women may be less responsive to pressure to conform to current stereotypes of proper feminine behavior. The parents' relations with one another might also reflect social-class differences, with more conformity to sex-role stereotypes among lower-class husbands. A third possibility deals with the way parents handle the birth crisis. The birth event provides an opportunity to take responsibility, and parents could derive differential benefits from remaining in control. Another control opportunity is for the father to be self-directed in his parenting rather than conforming to maternal standards.

In chapter 4 it was seen that the woman's birth experience responded strongly to awareness at birth, and this link was interpreted in terms of Janis's stress theory. Irrespective of class, women who remained in control reported higher-quality birth experiences. But further analysis indicated that only for middle-class women did mothering respond directly to the birth experience. Direct effects of the birth experience on parenting were not seen for lower-class women. Rather, their mothering responded to reaction at first view and to feeding, two effects linked to the infant. The lower-class mother apparently modified her behavior in response to demands or perceptions of another individual, i.e., the baby. She is other-directed in this sense and "conforms," if you will, along lines that appear compatible with Kohn's notions.

This interpretation of class-related differences in parenting can be extended to fathering as well. Whereas middle-class fathers seemed to use their previous baby-care experience in a positive fashion and to be directly affected by their own preparation, presumably because these factors reflect control and responsibility, lower-class men seemed instead to be affected by their wives' behavior. They conformed to their wives' parenting style and were apparently impeded by their own previous experience.

Altogether our analyses—plus Furstenberg's (1976), which shows that solo black mothers are only minimally affected by father absence—suggest that the dynamics of early parenting may be highly responsive to social class. Differences turned up in unexpected places, for ahead of time it seemed likely that sex of the baby might affect parenting of lower-class couples more than that of middle-class couples, but it did not. We are particularly impressed that the social-class effects discovered in the data reflect deep causes consistent with Kohn's theory of class values and that relatively few effects reflect superficial causes such as the more rigid sex-role stereotypes often cited as typical of a lower-class outlook. Furthermore, the fact that members of the two social classes were selected to be equivalent with respect to preparation probably attenuates rather than exaggerates any social-class effects.

THE BIRTH AS CRISIS

There is a long-standing debate in the sociological literature on whether birth is or is not "a crisis" (see Hobbs and Cole 1976 and references cited therein). Some researchers think the evidence argues for a crisis (Dyer 1963,

LeMasters 1957). Others say not (Lamb 1978). This debate seems rather pointless, however, unless *crisis* is carefully defined. With the arrival of a first child, new role obligations must become established; the routines for child care must be worked out, and in this sense a first pregnancy and birth is certainly a critical turning point. Subsequent children add to the load, but the major social reorganization of the family and redefinition of the self is forced by the first birth. The first birth also often represents a couple's first brush with hospitalization or health problems of any magnitude. But does this generate a crisis?

Crisis implies a threat or test. Birth appears to have elements of threat along two main dimensions: one medical or physiological, the other sociopsychological. The anatomy of the birth crisis can be outlined under these two major rubrics.

I. Physiological crisis linked to physical separation of mother and child
   1. Stress of the birth event (operative delivery; other obstetrical procedures, including medication)
   2. Late arrival of child in comparison with due date
   3. Ill health of either mother or child in perinatal period, including mother's depression and exhaustion
   4. Establishment of breast-feeding

II. Social crisis linked to family equilibrium
   1. Assumption of new role for both parents, with need to care for a helpless person and to integrate that third person into the preexisting social group
   2. Disruption of couple's marital relations, sexual and otherwise
   3. Resignation of wife from work force, at least temporarily
   4. Test of financial solvency of family unit
   5. Assorted other events—moving, changing jobs, etc.—and new relationships with kin, which are forced by infant's arrival

Among the couples included in this research, there were enormous differences in the birth crisis in terms of the threats posed by factors listed under the first major heading. The physiological stress at the time of birth varied enormously, from difficult operative deliveries to simple vaginal births without medication. Twenty women experienced Cesarean deliveries, and fourteen others had a variety of serious delivery complications. All but 7 percent of the women received some kind of medication during labor or delivery, and for many women there was a large discrepancy between the amount of medication they received and the amount they desired.

A tally of time of birth in relation to expected due date revealed that 5 percent of the infants were more than three weeks late, and another 7 percent were over two weeks late. Being overdue apparently dampened women's perception of their birth experience and was weakly associated with depression.

There was some serious ill health of mother and / or child. Two women had
to be rehospitalized with thrombophlebitis soon after delivery; one baby was
born very prematurely, one had a cleft palate, and one has a serious leg
deformity. Some women had to abandon breast-feeding for health reasons. In
addition, 81 percent of the women reported depression at some time in the
first few weeks after childbirth.

Although in the sixth month 68 percent of the couples had planned on
breast-feeding, a few changed their minds immediately (two because of Cesarean deliveries), so only 65 percent actually began to breast-feed. By the time
the infant was one month old, another 16 percent had stopped breast-feeding.
Thus, 19 percent of the total sample were unable to establish what might be
termed "successful breast-feeding," and for some women ceasing to breast-
feed was a great disappointment.

Even the *average* women in this study saw the birth event in retrospect as
being considerably more stressful in physical terms than she had thought it
would be beforehand. After the birth far fewer women than before subscribed
to the view that nature intended childbirth to be painless. Also, a number
would have liked to stay in the hospital longer and would have been pleased to
have more help when they got home. For some the physiological stress was
severe.

There seemed to be less variation among couples in the degree of stress
listed under the second major rubric. All women had to leave the work force,
at least for a time. All couples discontinued sexual intercourse for some
period. All couples had to integrate the child into the family. About two-thirds
of the fathers offered social support (by being present in delivery), and even
more were present during labor. By taking an active role in early parenting
and helping with child care, almost all fathers gave support. There was no
deterioration in couples' views of their mates or marriages in the first few
weeks after the birth.

A major source of social stress for these couples, however, was their
inexperience in caring for young infants. Most couples had been overoptimis-
tic about infant care. This finding is in accord with LeMasters' report (1957)
that in thirty-eight of forty-six couples he observed, a crisis was precipitated
because the couples romanticized parenthood, and also with Hubert's observation (1974:55): "[not] all first pregnancies are a nightmare . . . . but [parents']
ideas and expectations are very confused, and their experience as a result is
often surprised and unpleasant." In this study the first two or three weeks
home from the hospital found a large majority of wives continuously tired. At
two to three weeks of age the average infant was crying over one and one-half
hours daily.

Birth *is* a change for all couples, in the sense of being a social turning
point, but the social forms of stress stretch out over time. It seems likely on
this account that a crisis occurs mainly for parents who are unlucky enough to
experience severe stress of a medical sort. An operative delivery is sudden,

and health problems with infants can occur suddenly. The social readjustments required by birth, on the other hand, are more gradual, so it seems reasonable to think of the social integration of the child and the consequent role integration of parents, not as a crisis, but as a fairly lengthy transition period. And some social supports exist to aid in this transition. The majority of babies stayed on in the hospital nursery. The mothers had extra help on returning home. But with the passage of time, the baby's demands became more salient. The woman's depression appeared to be triggered by assuming full responsibility for the infant, and later the woman's return to work depended on whether or not she could manage child care along with the job.

The two factors hypothesized to be important in understanding couples' reactions to birth—social class and prior preparation—are rather specific to particular aspects of the crisis. For example, preparation and social class apparently did not affect most of the sources of physiologic stress: the severity of delivery complications, late arrival of infants, depression, or ill health of mother or child—although preparation did affect the need for medication and some women's success in breast-feeding.

Preparation and social class both affected the social integration of the child, however. Models for mothering and fathering revealed that preparation during pregnancy, or prior to it, was associated with couples' later parenting but that the response to preparation depended on social class. Social class apparently also has strong effects on the parents' roles vis-à-vis one another.

The full magnitude and complexity of the birth crisis deserve much further work. The postpartum honeymoon, when the new parents see each other through a rosy haze and when each unrealistically idealizes the other as mate and parent, might seem at first to be a blissful state. It could be interpreted either as an absence of stress or as evidence of effective coping. But it may signify stress so intense that most couples do not face it: put simply, the honeymoon may be an unconscious cover-up. New parents are experiencing many new demands and self-doubts that are hard to face. Paradoxically, such a honeymoon may be dysfunctional, because by denying problems, couples necessarily postpone resolving them. Additionally, assessments of stress are probably biased downward. People are reluctant to admit that they are having trouble with their mates or are inept at comforting their own child.

Some kinds of stress at the time of the birth appear to be accentuated by current life conditions, even though (as noted earlier) other forms of stress such as having unwanted children are currently reduced. A particular example is women's outside employment. The high cost of living, tacked on to a continual spiral of inflation, makes it hard for families to get by on one paycheck.

All but a handful of women in this study worked well along into pregnancy and then were forced either to cease or to interrupt their outside work at the time of birth. Fully one-third of them had planned either not to stop working

or to return to full-time outside employment by the time their infant was six months old, and financial necessity was the main reason for an early return. Only 6 percent of the women, however, were able to return to employment full-time within six months. Many of the families were therefore getting along on one paycheck for longer than they had anticipated. Although we did not ask about it, probably few family budgets were realistic in the sense that all the expenses associated with a birth—baby pictures, long-distance calls, husband's eating out while his wife is in the hospital—were provided for. A fair number of parents thought they were completely insured but discovered themselves liable for large hospital bills.

Another new kind of stress is that young fathers find themselves expected to measure up to fathering standards they have no role models for. They are expected to be a different kind of father from their own father. The semantic differential ratings of men in this sample revealed that they had not lived up to their own expectations for fatherhood during birth and later on. The fact that previous baby-care experience hindered lower-class fathers but helped middle-class fathers suggests how difficult it may be to alleviate such stress. Most fathers were active in their new role, however.

Because fathers of breast-fed babies participated more in infant care than fathers of bottle-fed babies, and also because fathers' emotional responses to their babies seemed to be affected by father participation in delivery and the birth event, we conclude that emotional preparation for the parent role may be more critical than practice in diapering or other caretaking.

Another stress beneath the surface is the keen disappointment that the couple, but more often the father, faced when the child's sex was not the preferred one. (Of the fathers in this study, 71 percent wanted a male child.) Rather surprisingly, no effects of this kind of stress could be uncovered in terms of either parent's feelings for, or behavior with, the infant. Nevertheless, it is hard to believe that there are no such effects. Perhaps effects appear later, or would be revealed in other kinds of measures than those used in this study. As already noted, the measures were perhaps too crude or of the wrong kind. This topic is one that requires further research.

ROLE INTEGRATION

In view of their training for childbirth, it is surprising that so many parents did not know how to respond to the infant after the birth occurred. They were eager to experience the birth together as fully as possible, but they appeared to have given little thought to what they would be thinking, feeling, or doing once the birth was over. They had little emotional preparation for anything beyond the birth event or beyond their conjugal roles in a childless family. Some did not assume the emotional role of parent for several months. A substantial number of women found the baby ugly or distasteful, and most

men had unrealistic illusions about their spouse's parental qualities. Most of the new parents were eager to be in the driver's seat until the birth occurred, but the majority were more than happy to let the hospital assume complete charge of the baby.

There are many indications that the parents required time for role integration. Although 47 percent of the men and 63 percent of the women believed parents "already love their newborn child" (Appendix B, opinion item 48), surprisingly few gave evidence that *they* had loved their unborn child or were completely ready to welcome it at its birth. Few parents were really ready to give the infant an enthusiastic welcome. As Lamb (1978:138) says: "All mothers are not the same predictable composites of breasts and caresses that our major theorists depict." Many mothers did not wish to hold their new babies right at birth. A majority of babies were kept in the hospital nursery. Couples found it easy to overlook the baby's presence in the first few weeks. Feeding schedules were more rigid than planned beforehand, and a considerable number of women let babies cry for extended periods of time. Many who did take action when the baby cried were not very disturbed by the crying. Also, even though almost all the infants were planned, about half the couples were negative about the wife's being in the pregnant state. At least with their first child, then, these parents needed time to get used to new roles. They had to become accustomed to ideas of what pregnancy entails, what it means to become a parent, and a large number required some time to learn to love the child.

Part of their difficulty may reflect a lack of guidance in how to play a new role, the modern parent role. The young woman of today cannot very well imitate her own mother. The woman's liberation movement has had a profound effect on sex-role stereotypes in the past two decades. Judging from this sample, even young women who are conservative in their views of work and marriage are liberal in their views on childbearing. Many want to experience all aspects of birth fully, including lactation. Only 25 percent of the women in this sample were sure they had been breast-fed themselves, but 68 percent planned to breast-feed their own infants. Opinions expressed by these women indicated that they were looking to their husbands to adopt a more expressive role, to share women's traditional housework or childbirth tasks, and to take an active role in early parenting. But the men had even less guidance than the women in the modern parent role.

Preparation before the birth does not appear to be very helpful in fostering role integration. One reason may be that most preparation classes give little attention to parenting. Teachers of these classes may have little choice, however, because statements of trainers who have tried adding a class on early parenthood reveal that prospective parents have little appetite for discussions of early child rearing. During pregnancy they seem unable to think past the birth event. Perhaps all couples—like the couples in this sample—are overconfident about their ability to deal with a newborn. In this sample it seemed

that couples actively avoided acquiring information about baby care in the period before the birth, even though most of the couples had little prior experience caring for infants. Role integration might be easier if some aspects of the parental role, like infant care, were rehearsed. On the other hand, the data showing negative effects of previous baby-care experience for lower-class men suggest that anticipatory socialization may backfire. Any role rehearsal should probably involve both parents simultaneously.

Acquiring the parent role took the average mother one to two months. The woman must juggle demands of the baby along with her wifely responsibilities and must learn how to stay home full-time rather than go out to a job (or else how to manage baby, house, and job). Certainly the mother's role is more demanding than the father's in the first few weeks, if only because women need time to recover physically from the birth. To do psychic work—integrate roles—requires physical well-being, and a large number of these women were physically incapacitated by the birth. All signals point to some role strain for women.

Contrary to what was expected, couples did not hold their spouses in lower regard after the birth as compared with before. Before and after childbirth, spouses assigned very high affective scores to each other. Each spouse was seen by the other in idealized terms over the entire perinatal period. On the other hand, probes in the interviews after the birth revealed incipient problems, especially about baby care. These problems probably contribute to role conflict. If baby care is partly the father's responsibility, then his opinion on whether or not to pick up the crying baby must be respected. If his opinion is disregarded, then he may have difficulty in defining the nature of his new role. Similarly, if the mother already shares her parental responsibilities, questions about how important it is for her to neglect a work role entirely in favor of a mother role become more pressing. Competition between parents with respect to child care, with one spouse monopolizing the baby, is even possible.

It was anticipated that to accomplish role integration, the mother might withdraw some affect from the father to bestow on the child. After the birth, however, wives' ratings of their husbands in most cases continued to match their "Ideal Man." Mothers accorded at least as much affect to the spouse afterward as before. They appeared, however, to withdraw affect from their idealized baby and from themselves. On the average, the women had lower opinions of themselves after delivery than before. This lessening of self-regard may be one reason why women are slow to assume the mother role. Integration of their parent role seems to carry heavier psychological costs than for the male (there was no loss in self-regard for males). The higher costs, however, might eventually lead to a stronger affective bond linking the female parent to the child.

Integration of other roles, particularly women's employment, is delayed for many women in the period of early infancy. Only a minority of the women in

this survey wanted to return to outside work during the first six months of their infants lives, even though two-thirds of them planned to resume employment by the time their children were of school age.

Some of the women who returned to full-time outside employment assumed the mother role a little sooner than women remaining home, but others were relatively late. Both outcomes seem reasonable. The burden of the new mother role may be less when the mother is employed, because women who work outside the home have a change of scene and a refreshing relief from baby care. On the other hand, outside work could threaten the new mother in her nurturing role. The evidence is that leaving their babies for part of each day to go to work is not an option that was chosen by many of these women, because far fewer returned to full-time employment than had expressed an intention to do so beforehand. Also, breast-feeders who were employed breast-fed longer on the average than breast-feeding women who stayed at home, so outside work did not affect that aspect of nurturance.

Previous experience and childbirth preparation classes seemed to help middle-class fathers adjust to their new roles, in that there were large positive direct effects of these variables on fathering behavior. The opposite was true for lower-class fathers. There is little direct information about role integration for fathers, however, except for their estimates of how long it took them to feel like a father. The average reported was less than one month. Within a couple of weeks after the birth, husbands saw things as being under control. So the present data are consistent with Russell's data (1974) and bear out Fein's conclusions (1974, 1978) based on thirty middle-class couples: men recover quickly from the birth crisis. Role integration seems less problematic for the male than for the female.[5] Both middle-class and lower-class fathers ranked work low as a source of satisfaction, and a low emotional investment in work could ease role integration for fathers. The work role may therefore not compete seriously with the new father role.

Despite the fact that it took some time for these parents to invest themselves emotionally in their new roles, role integration for parents may proceed more rapidly in this decade than in the past. Good conception control could be a key element. Although to our knowledge there are no data bearing directly on this issue, parents of a planned baby should be in a more favorable position for adopting a parental role, because it is a role they have voluntarily decided to assume.

Role integration may also be eased because most husbands and wives are better prepared than most couples a decade ago for the physical changes that accompany pregnancy and childbirth. Attendance at preparation classes is the rule rather than the exception in many urban areas. Some of the ideas and knowledge available to the well-prepared couples also may have affected

[5]Difficulty of role integration could also differ between parents for other reasons, for example, because of a difference between spouses on the strength of desire for a child—one quotation in chapter 6 notes: "You were the one who wanted the baby."

parents who did not take classes. For example, some men who did not attend preparation classes were invited to be present in delivery.

For most of the couples in this sample, actual previous experience with the parent role was slight, but whatever led some to seek out preparation classes may have also caused them to seek out information on other topics. Many of the couples had checked with friends about breast-feeding, for example. Presumably, acquiring any kind of relevant information would ease role transition.

There was a curious gap, however, between how these couples behaved prior to and during birth and how they acted as new parents. It is as though they patched roles together, a "birthing parent" role derived from the social norms of the seventies joined to a "new parent" role patterned more on customs of previous decades. This lack of role coordination probably stems from underrating the difficulty of the new-parent role. A strong indication of this is that six months after the birth (not right away) the woman wanted a longer child-spacing interval than they had wanted earlier, and there was a large increase in the number who wanted no more children. Furthermore, those who are most committed to doing well at the birth may find it the hardest to meet the unremitting demands of a new infant. Women who seek active control may be good at carrying out activities they have control over, but may be especially frustrated in caring for a helpless infant whose demands are unpredictable. Such women are likely to chafe at doing nothing else but care for the infant, which is what many young infants require.

ROLE CONFLICT

Pregnancy requires a couple to renegotiate their roles. They must alter their life-style and their relations with each other to accommodate the impending arrival of a third party. A couple's egalitarian ideals are severely tested by the birth of a child. Women who work up to the baby's arrival, and who experience all the accompanying rewards, suddenly find themselves tied to the house doing unpaid and largely menial work, isolated from other adults except their husbands. By contrast, their husbands continue much as before. Breast-feeding, in particular, calls into question the physical equality of the sexes and limits the mother's mobility. The joy of conceiving and giving birth must be tempered by such challenges to a couple's ideals, even when the child is wanted.

Couples can easily conform to all the egalitarian ideas—equal job status for women, husbands sharing equally in household tasks, enjoyment of sexuality by females, couples living together in trial arrangements, mothers of young children being employed—*until* the arrival of a child. Perhaps because they tended generally to underrate beforehand the work involved in caring for a baby, egalitarian ideals of the couples in this study "stretched"—if the baby required attention at night for a long period, the mother was the one more

likely to give it. If the mother's job and baby care could not be reconciled, she, not her husband, made the work adjustment.

Only a handful of mothers returned to full-time employment, so one might conclude that there was no conflict between work and parent roles for the remainder. This seems dubious. For one thing, not all who wanted to work were able to return to full-time employment by the time the infant was six months old. As many women tried to return to outside employment and gave up as were able to keep at it. Fewer women altogether were working than had planned to and most (twenty-one out of twenty-eight) of these were working part-time. This was true for middle-class *and* lower-class women alike. In pregnancy there was no difference in work plans by social class, either for the immediate or the more remote future.

It can be perplexing to try to follow through with egalitarian commitments after childbirth. Before the child's arrival, parents can share household tasks, and both can be employed. After the birth, women, more than men, are harnessed to tasks of baby care by their very biology, if nothing else—they bear the child and only they can breast-feed. For many women in this sample, health was below par for several weeks after the birth, and the large majority found childbirth physically more stressful than they had anticipated. Another measure of the mother's burden is that no husband stayed home longer than two weeks after the birth, and none took his infant to his workplace. Even though fathers held infants for 1½ hours daily, the lion's share of infant care was assumed by *all* mothers. The arrival of a child altered the division of labor within the home, with the mother taking on most of the new burdens. A shift to more traditional sex roles after birth of the first child was also found by Cowan et al. (1978), who followed a set of eight couples from before the birth up to the infant's six-month birthday.

Division of labor in the home seems more resistant to change than division of labor in the marketplace (Kanter 1976). Also, whether or not a woman works has surprisingly little effect on how household chores are divided, even for higher-income or professional women (see Aldous 1969).[6] Therefore, after the arrival of a child has altered the division of labor within the home, a woman's return to outside employment probably does little to restore the balance in division of labor seen beforehand. Other forces, especially a lack of institutional child-care arrangements, also conspire to keep mothers of infants at home. A mother cannot leave the house until some other caretaker arrives or she deposits the baby somewhere else. Since full-time child-care arrangements for young babies are "exceptional" and usually involve relatives or other women devoting the time that could support a full-time job, they are therefore often unreliable.

[6]Cowan et al. (1978:311) report that couples with new babies spend from 105 to 174 hours per week on combined home and baby care. To our knowledge there are no data based on a national sample concerning how much time employed mothers of children under one year of age spend on home and baby care.

The more traditional sex roles prompted by the infant's arrival are apparently not the consequence of opinion changes. The couple's ideas about delegating child care did not change. Rather, before the birth attitudes on child care had little practical consequence, whereas afterward they did. Basic conflicts in sex-role attitudes expressed by people in the country as a whole (Mason and Bumpass 1975) were echoed by people in this sample. These can be disguised or ignored before the birth but are difficult to avoid afterwards, especially if they pertain to women's employment. Several ideas about gender held by people qualify commitments couples express concerning women's working—the belief that it is better for everyone if the man is the achiever outside the family and the woman takes care of the home and family and the belief that children are harmed if they see their fathers do housework or if they have too close a relationship with their fathers, for example. There is widespread belief that a man's willingness to do housework or care for very young children is indicative of maladjustment. Some of the couples in this sample held such views.[7] The couples in this sample believed in women's sexual fulfillment and in equal pay for equal jobs, but they also leaned in the direction of "woman's place is in the home with preschool children." They believed that women are more likely to be attached, or are more easily attached, to infants emotionally. The couples, whether they consciously realized it or not, had acted in ways to decrease the pressures of egalitarian beliefs on themselves. The nature of the women's work—they held lower-level jobs than their husbands, and they had low commitment to work—made it easier for couples to sidestep conflicts between a woman's work role and her parent role after the birth. If work is not important and the job is not very prestigious, it causes little conflict to forgo outside employment.

When applied to child rearing, an egalitarian sex-role ideology probably also leads to conflict *outside* the home. Generally, the older generation seems less enthusiastic than the younger generation about mothers of young babies remaining in the labor force. For one thing, employers, who are likely to be of the older generation, are often not personally attuned to the idea of egalitarian sex roles, and many do not view a mother's absence from work for baby-connected reasons (let alone a father's absence) as legitimate. For another thing, objections of the older generation can be self-serving—a grandmother these days may wish to be employed herself rather than to serve as a baby-sitter for her daughter or daughter-in-law.

Combining an outside job with early parenting is not easily handled by a

---

[7]The issues involving role conflict for mothers vs. fathers may be much deeper than so far implied. As a consequence of women's biology, including its hormonal cyclicity, Rossi (1977:24) believes "equity of affect" between mothers and fathers in relation to the infant may be difficult to attain. There may be a "biologically based potential for heightened maternal investment" in a child, triggered by pregnancy and birth, and the potential investment women can make may exceed the investment men can make. Perhaps even if fathers stayed home and mothers went to work, the attachment of fathers to infants could not equal the mother's attachment in intensity or quality.

woman, short of making society-wide changes. The stresses generally turned out to be greater than most women and men in this sample anticipated. Other researchers (Gordon and Gordon 1967) believe that role conflict, particularly with respect to a woman's job, is the prime source of emotional difficulties in the postpartum period. In our sample it may have been a prime source mainly for the one-third of the women who stated during pregnancy that they wished to return (or to remain) in full-time employment by the baby's six-month birthday and especially for the women who tried to return to full-time employment and then had to give up outside work. Later on, however, *most* of these mothers may experience conflict, because 65 percent wished to return to outside employment by the time their children started first grade.

COMMENTARY

Exactly what successful early parenting entails is not easy to say. A warm, loving relationship between each parent and the child is certainly a principal component. Parental flexibility and / or emotional stability may be another component (Davids, Holden, and Gray 1963). In our opinion, signs of good early parenting are breast-feeding of at least a few months' duration, both parents' genuine enjoyment of the baby, a sensitivity of both parents to the infant's needs, and a deepened relationship between husband and wife.

It is probably a mistake to conceptualize "coping" too narrowly. The quality of parenting, especially its psychological flavor, most likely far outweighs factors more readily measured, such as how often the father changes a diaper. A teenage mother may be a warm and nurturant mother right from the start. In his careful study of a group of young black adolescents, Furstenberg (1976) reports that mothers who were fifteen or younger during pregnancy were not any less committed to the maternal role than older mothers were. The youngest mothers were just as enthusiastic about parenthood and were highly interested in their children. His observations run counter to "the common-sense notion that the earlier the entry into parenthood, the more difficult the adjustment to motherhood will be" (p. 180). He cautions that his observations of black mothers may not apply to whites, and the majority of mothers in his study had gained considerable experience caring for siblings and nieces and nephews, in sharp contrast to the childhood experiences of women in our sample. But since, as shown in our analysis, the effects of previous experience can be negative as well as positive, the actual causes of superior mothering in his sample are not clear. The adolescents may be good mothers partly because they have so few role conflicts and so few strong competing interests.

Preparation for parenthood is, of course, a lifelong affair, and attendance at childbirth classes or reading books on child care is only one small part of it. An immature person of any age may find it hard to place a baby's needs above his or her own convenience. And a very disorganized person may find parent-

ing difficult because a young baby has strong needs that cannot be postponed. It is ironic that an infant's needs for mothering are greatest when women have had relatively little practice in running a household and when women's abilities to be maternal are just developing.

In this sample of couples, much evidence points to lapses in parenting—especially early parenting. For example, after the birth both husbands and wives still seemed to focus most of their affection on each other. Few mentioned the baby as the nicest thing about the time in the hospital or the first few days at home. Ratings of "My Baby" dropped for scales the parents filled out after the birth in comparison with those before. Both parents found that their actual baby did not measure up to their imagined baby. Almost half of the women had negative or ambivalent feelings toward the infant when it arrived. Over half the women did not care whether they held their baby immediately or not. Quite a few fathers continued to think babies and fathers should not have much to do with each other. In reaction to the baby's crying, many mothers either indicated a disinclination to attend to the baby or responded in a perfunctory way—they met the baby's physical needs but ignored the infant's emotional needs. In fact, the responsiveness of mothers is negatively related to crying. The more the baby cried, the less responsive the mother, especially if middle-class.

Certainly for these mothers and fathers, getting used to the parent role took time. Prepared women had a more positive initial reaction to the baby and felt like mothers sooner, however, and the mothering model indicated some of the mechanisms that may mediate these effects. The *direct* effect of preparation on the lower-class women's mothering was negative, however, and there are other questions to be raised about the effectiveness of preparation. The relationship of preparation to other variables may be linear and positive only over some range. Women who pursue every possible avenue of information prior to the birth may be overanxious or so instrumental in outlook that the care of an unremittingly demanding infant is exceedingly hard for them.

Since wives felt more affect for husbands after the birth than before, husbands had little reason to be jealous of their babies. This could partly explain their more positive reactions to the babies initially and also what seems to be their easier accommodation to the parent role. But, as pointed out earlier, demands on the husband are fewer, making role assumption easier.

Many writers have commented upon the difficulties in assuming the parent role, and there may be no possible way to get parents entirely ready for their new roles. On the other hand, the psychological and physical distances that now separate couples from their own parents must make it especially hard for kin to help new parents. American society has never venerated elders, and added to this, current ideas about sexual morality frequently lead to conflict between young adults and their parents, especially in the case of daughters. Cohabitation (which had been practiced by 21 percent of the couples in this sample) is an especially touchy point. One indication of such barriers is that

men and women in this study rated their own parents very harshly with respect to ideal parents. The women's assessments of their own mothers jumped up after the birth, but were still below ideal.

Preparation for parenthood is blocked on several fronts. Large families, where older siblings routinely care for younger ones, are now less common. The severe age segregation in present-day America causes young marrieds to live in apartments or subdivisions populated mostly by others like themselves. It also causes teenagers to be locked into an adolescent society, away from very young children and away from places where they could watch young adults care for babies. Today's child-rearing patterns are biased against preparation for parenthood. Little encouragement is given to youngsters to play at parenting—doll play for girls is pretty well out of fashion, and it was always frowned on for little boys. Doll play is of little practical value for learning about the physical care of infants, but cuddling dolls, naming them, and carrying them around could prepare girls for the emotional side of motherhood.

Neither the structure of society nor people's socialization for parenthood are likely to change in the near future. The popularity of childbirth-preparation classes and their success in preparing some parents for the birth event and for breast-feeding suggest, however, that organizational innovations could bridge some of the gaps in socialization for parenthood.

Rooming-in is one way hospitals could provide instruction in parenting. It should be the rule rather than the exception. Women could then practice infant care with help at hand, freed of the burdens of caring for a house at the same time. Instead of isolating rooming-in mothers in private rooms, hospitals could encourage association between first-time mothers and other mothers.

It might be helpful for visiting nurses or child-care counselors to call upon new mothers in the first two weeks at home. This is done in several European countries. Actually, one team of obstetricians in Baltimore employs a "new baby counselor," who appears at the mother's door without being summoned, soon after she comes home from the hospital. The mothers already know her because she is the nurse who taught their childbirth-preparation classes. She is a mother herself. During her visit she provides help and reassurance with whatever problems have come up in the initial days at home. Such help is not sought voluntarily, however, because new parents are reluctant to admit a need for help, or are unaware that they need help. The timing of the help is critical—before problems are aggravated, there are usually simple solutions.

Hospitals could do a great deal to foster early contact between parents and baby. The timing of first contact between parents and child may even be critical for parent-child attachment. Klaus and Kennell (1976b) believe that physical contact between mother and child within the first twelve hours is essential for optimal parental attachment. Evidence supporting the critical nature of early contact is also found in Liefer's report (1970) that women who handled their premature infants in the hospital showed more maternal interest

later than mothers not allowed to touch their children, and even brief handling had measurable effects. Our analysis raises some questions about the efficacy of a specific period of early contact, although it may be critical for women who bottle-feed. On the other hand, it is hard to see any real drawbacks in such contact, and hospitals could rather easily alter their procedures in order to allow both the new mother and the new father unlimited contact with the infant from the moment of birth. It is astonishing that many hospitals now take it for granted that parents of sick toddlers should enter the pediatric unit and sleep alongside their sick children whenever possible, but are much less ready to foster closeness between parent and the neonate—a much younger and more vulnerable child. Parents also need education to the potential importance *for them* of these earliest associations. Parents may suffer from unfulfilled attachment needs.

EPILOGUE

This book is one small step toward a fuller understanding of pregnancy, birth, and early parenting. It begins to fill a large gap in the sociology of human development. Much remains to be done. Further work is required to test out and replicate the models proposed here. In particular, we need more adequate theories of family development.

In closing, we salute the forward-looking young couples in the sample. Their willingness to fully participate in a first birth was greater than the experience they were actually permitted. Most of them were not at all critical of their birth experience, but the rest of us should be. We agree with Mehl (1978:114), who says:

> It is interesting to speculate about what may be responsible for good outcomes of childbirth. . . . but what is clearly apparent is that we are just beginning to uncover the important factors, and, however important this process may be, it should remain secondary to the parents' right to use whatever data is available to make an intelligent, informed choice about the kind of childbirth experience they will have. . . a number of childbirth options are safe medical alternatives. The final decision must always remain the parents', for they live the rest of their lives upon that choice—not for an instant as do obstetricians, family physicians, midwives, researchers, and statisticians.

APPENDIX A: STUDY DESIGN
AND METHODOLOGY

This appendix is a technical description of the research on which this book is based. Further technical information may be obtained directly from the authors.

THE SAMPLE

Respondents were all Caucasian couples who volunteered:[1] 120 Maryland women and 60 of their husbands participated. With one exception, only couples where the *woman* was expecting her first child were studied.[2] In nine cases husbands had a previous child. No husbands who were already fathers were selected to be among the 60 husbands who were interviewed. Three of the couples were not legally married, but all couples were living in a stable relationship when the research began.

In most research on childbirth, respondents are selected from patients cared for by a single physician, or by a single hospital or clinic (Norr et al. 1977, for example). Often, a medical school directly or indirectly sponsors the research. We intentionally procured a broader kind of sample by seeking women who would be cared for by *many* different practitioners at *many* different hospitals, and even some who planned to deliver at home, in the hope that our data would more nearly represent typical birth experience.

The women were located in several different ways.

1. The local Childbirth Education Association furnished the names of all primiparous women who had recently called the organization to inquire about classes and who were currently in their sixth month of pregnancy or less. Some of these women went on to register for the series of

---

[1]The last fourteen lower-class women to be interviewed were paid a small sum (thirty dollars at the end of the third interview) to reduce attrition among the lower-class group.

[2]The exception was one woman who had had a child when she was sixteen and had immediately put it up for adoption. Eleven percent of the women had previously had abortions.

Lamaze preparation classes offered by the Childbirth Education Association for women in their eighth and ninth months of pregnancy. Others of this group decided not to take classes for various reasons. About 50 percent of the sample came from this source.

2. Another source of names of pregnant women was a local diaper service that sponsors classes for expectant mothers. The nurse who taught these classes furnished lists of all the women who signed up. About 10 percent of our sample came from this source.

3. We also located pregnant women by referral from women already in the sample. This was our main source of women who did not plan to take preparation classes. We found that women who are pregnant often know of other pregnant women, in their apartment complex or at their place of work, even though they are not close friends. About 40 percent of the sample came through this snowball technique.

These three methods of selecting respondents led to a sample of women who delivered at sixteen different hospitals in the Baltimore-Annapolis-Washington area, and it also included five planned home births. The women were attended by sixty-five different obstetricians, three different midwives, and twelve residents, and one baby was delivered by its father. Delivery was thus accomplished in many different places with eighty-one different assistants, so we would hope our findings exemplify the range of experiences of average couples during birth in a large metropolitan area.

The women were selected to fill certain demographic quotas: half middle-class, half lower-class; roughly equal numbers of Protestants, Catholics, and Jews. Also, women were selected according to whether or not they were planning to take childbirth preparation classes. The criteria for placing women into these categories will be discussed below.

After the wife of a couple had agreed to participate, we personally contacted her husband and sought his participation. As mentioned, some husbands had been married before. If the previous marriage had produced a child, the husband was not asked to participate. This requirement eliminated nine husbands. Of the remaining husbands, sixty-one[3] consented to be interviewed, including three who had previous childless marriages. Of the fifty eligible husbands who were not interviewed, thirty-three were classified as having no valid reason for declining to be interviewed. (Later, we will explore the consequences of this self-selection.) Fortunately, the participation of husbands turned out not to be contingent on social class, for twenty-eight husbands whose wives were middle-class agreed to participate and thirty-two husbands agreed whose wives were lower-class. Of the sixty husbands who consented to be interviewed, one lower-class man and two middle-class men had been previously married. These percentages are so small as to preclude any separate analysis for previously married husbands. Only two wives had been married before.

[3]One interview was lost, leaving sixty husbands for whom we have data.

RATIONALE FOR THE SAMPLE

In any kind of research, trade-offs must be made. In this research there was a trade-off between sample selection and depth of coverage. A relatively small number of persons participated in the research, but those who did participate were studied in depth. In exploratory research on topics involving deep emotions and complicated personal relationships, like the present study, there are strong reasons to favor depth over breadth of coverage. Superficial questioning is unsatisfactory. People's desire to have children and their relations with mates and children are topics of the deepest significance, not easily verbalized or necessarily even available at a conscious level. Without the opportunity to explore in depth, an investigator really has no way to interpret certain responses or to relate data to theory.

Furthermore, sampling issues for this kind of research are, at best, problematic. To procure a nationally representative sample—that is, one selected strictly so that every pregnant couple in the United States would have an equal (or known) chance to be in the final sample—would be prohibitively expensive and next to impossible. Furthermore, at this stage of knowledge, it would be wasteful. An initial sampling frame would have to be structured to guarantee a representative sample of all persons in the United States, and then within that group, a few women, those who happened to be six-months pregnant (or less), could be scheduled for interview. Rough calculations suggest that it would be fortunate—using telephone screening to eliminate women above and below childbearing age and those who were not pregnant—to find one couple in a hundred who would be eligible for study. In addition, couples so located would have to agree to participate. If any declined, as is likely when a respondent is approached by strangers and asked to submit to several hours of questioning involving intimate topics, the sample procured would be no more representative than the sample we actually procured.

The problem of volunteering has no solution. In this kind of research there is no way to question a sample of persons other than volunteers, because federal and ethical requirements mandate that all persons agree to interviews under conditions of "informed consent": they must be honestly told the purpose of the study, the topics that will be covered in the interviews, any dangers or costs to them, and the hoped-for results, and if they raise questions, the questions must be fully and honestly answered. Persons also must be told they can withdraw from the study at any time and that confidentiality will be carefully guarded. Some persons will not submit under any circumstances to questioning of the sort our study involved. (Indeed, we had a refusal rate of 22 percent.) Others, approached informally with an introduction via an acquaintance, will often agree, but they would not agree if they were approached by a complete stranger without an introduction. In addition some people agree to a first interview, but then the novelty wears off and they drop out. These are all formidable problems. A more serious problem is that, even if we persuaded a random sample of couples to respond, at the present

stage of knowledge we could not have assembled a short set of questions, suitable for use on a sizeable sample, that would tap the core issues we are interested in.

DEMOGRAPHIC CHARACTERISTICS OF THE SAMPLE

On the average, husbands in the entire sample were a little more than two years older than wives (26.9 vs. 24.7). the age of women in this sample is somewhat higher than the estimated mean age (22.4) for women bearing a first child in the United States in 1973 (U.S. Bureau of the Census 1975a). One reason could be that this sample consists almost entirely of nondisadvantaged white women. But the median age for women at first marriage is also increasing—it was 21.1 years in 1975, 20.8 years in 1970, and 20.6 years in 1965 (U.S. Bureau of the Census 1976).

On the average, wives in our sample had somewhat more than a high school education. Husbands were even better educated, with the average husband virtually a college graduate. These summary statistics, however, mask the social stratification in the sample. Twenty-nine husbands had a high school diploma or less, and twenty-six others had some post-high school training, but not a college degree. At the other extreme, fifteen husbands had either an M.D. or a Ph.D.

The distribution of women by education is narrower than the distribution of men. Ten women in this sample had a master's degree, and none held a doctor's degree. At the other end of the scale, five women had not completed high school. This kind of restriction on the range of women's education is seen in the U.S. population at large. During 1970–71, for example, women in the United States earned only 14 percent of the doctoral degrees granted (U.S. Department of Labor 1975). The difference between the sexes in educational range is also reflected in a larger standard deviation associated with husband's educational level.

The couples' occupations ranged over the entire U.S. Census occupational code. Husband's job prestige (Siegel 1971) was assigned on the basis of job information provided by the wife and is the major indicator for husband's occupation. Three husbands held jobs with a prestige rating of 17 (laborer), while eleven husbands held jobs rated 81 (medical doctor). The mean job-prestige rating was 50.4. (This would be a typical rating for such jobs as managers of hospitals, or managers of welfare and religious organizations.) As with every other demographic measure, wife's job status was lower on the average than husband's, being 46.6. (On this scale, secretary is rated 46; nurse, 62; elementary school teacher, 60.)

No census data are available on ages at which men first become fathers. Census data for 1975 give the median age at first marriage for men as 23.5 years and the age difference at first marriage between husbands and wives as 2.4 years, slightly larger than in our sample (U.S. Bureau of the Census

1976). Since some men in our sample were married before, one would expect the average age of husbands to be somewhat higher and the age differential between husbands and wives to be larger than the census figures. Nevertheless, it turns out that the average ages in our sample are not far from the census data.

Forty percent of women in this sample reported that they attended religious services fairly often or regularly. (In a recent survey, Yankelovich [1974] reports that 42 percent of noncollege youth and 23 percent of college youth see religion as a "very important personal value.") As judged from their religious practices and attitudinal information reported in chapters 2 and 3, the women in this sample are, in fact, more traditional in outlook than other women of their age. During the seventies, selecting couples who were almost all legally married and who were about to bear a first child led to selection of a traditional group, for many persons in their twenties were postponing marriage and childbearing. Since only expectant parents were sought, those with less traditional outlooks are necessarily excluded from the sample.

THE INTERVIEWS

Women were interviewed face-to-face in their homes twice before the birth and once after. In addition, we conducted a short telephone interview with the new mother when the baby was six months old and checked breast-feeding behavior up to one year. Sixty of the women's husbands were interviewed before the birth, and fifty-seven of them were interviewed again after the birth, all at home. Interviews averaged three to three and a half hours in length. All were tape-recorded and later transcribed.

Interviewers were carefully trained by conducting interviews with expectant parents who were not included in this study. White women who were mothers themselves interviewed the wives. White men—none of whom were fathers, but who were graduate students knowledgeable in the subject matter—interviewed husbands. The interviewers were approximately the same age as the respondents (middle to late twenties). Particular care was exercised to secure interviewers who could establish and maintain rapport. All interview tapes were monitored continuously by one of the authors (S.D.) to ensure that instructions were carried out exactly. In most cases, a single interviewer conducted all interviews for a given respondent, because the build-up of rapport is very important when dealing with personal and emotionally loaded questions.

The timing of the interviews is shown in figure A.1. The women were first interviewed when they were six to seven months pregnant, were interviewed for a second time when they were in their ninth month, and were then interviewed for a third time about three weeks after the birth. The men's two interviews were scheduled to match approximately the times of the second and

FIGURE A.1. Times of interviews. An interview with the wife when the baby is one year old was also planned but is not included in this report.

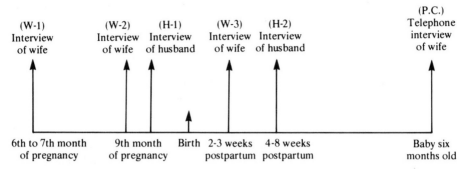

(W-1) Interview of wife	(W-2) Interview of wife	(H-1) Interview of husband	(W-3) Interview of wife	(H-2) Interview of husband	(P.C.) Telephone interview of wife
6th to 7th month of pregnancy	9th month of pregnancy	Birth	2-3 weeks postpartum	4-8 weeks postpartum	Baby six months old

third women's interviews. As mentioned above, a short telephone interview was subsequently conducted with the mothers when the babies were about six months old. The complete interview schedules are available from the authors.

Table A.1 classifies all the questions in the interviews according to broad categories. For example, questions 1 through 11 and question 13 deal with demographic information.

The interviews included a number of questions taken from well-known scales or tests. For example, in the first interview with wives twenty-one items were included from the Taylor Manifest Anxiety Scale. All scales or parts of scales were embedded in the interviews. That is, after answering several pages of questions about age, education, and so on, women replied to a number of items taken from the Taylor Manifest Anxiety Scale and some from Gough's California Psychological Inventory. Then, after a few more personal questions, the respondents were asked to complete some semantic differentials. The scales and their location in the interview are given in table A.2.

The semantic differentials were given as a group, at a point past the middle of the interview, and were preceded by careful instructions. All semantic differential scales consisted of the same twenty adjective pairs (see table A.3). Respondents were asked to characterize themselves (or other people) in various roles using these adjectives. For example, the wife was asked to rate "Myself as Mother" both before the birth and after the birth, and her husband was asked to rate "My Wife as Mother" before and after the birth, in all cases using the same twenty descriptors. These scales were aimed at picking up changes in the mother's perception of herself over the perinatal period, as well as at changes in husbands' perceptions of their wives over that same time.

Other preexisting scales or parts of scales were used to measure anxieties associated with pregnancy, general anxiety, locus of control, and masculinity-femininity. In every case the original source for such scales is listed in table A.2. In addition, a number of scales were developed specifically for

this study: a scale of menstrual symptoms; a scale for first-trimester, for second-trimester, and for third-trimester symptoms; a scale for birth experience; and others. These scales are explained in connection with the findings and are available from the authors upon request.

SCHEDULE OF INTERVIEWS

The first interview with the wife (W-1) took place in the sixth or early seventh month of pregnancy. This is late enough in the pregnancy so that the average woman, having felt fetal movements, can be expected to be dealing realistically with the fact that she is going to have a baby.

The second interview (W-2) took place in the first week of the ninth month of pregnancy, early enough so that few subjects were lost through premature deliveries, yet late enough so that those couples who took preparation classes had completed or almost completed the series. Actually, six women did miss their second interview because of early delivery. In the second interview, by repeating some of the questions and measures employed in the initial interview, we could observe changes in attitudes and emotions associated with the progression of the pregnancy and possibly with attending preparation classes.

At the time of the wife's second interview, those sixty-one husbands available to be interviewed were interviewed for the first time. (One husband interview was lost.)

A third interview with the wife was conducted in the third week following delivery. Memories were still fresh then, and the emotional openness associated with the childbirth period was still in effect, yet it was long enough after the birth so that the new mother felt well enough to have the interviewer visit. We also wished to wait long enough so that the new mother would have had the opportunity to care for her own newborn. In a few cases, it was necessary to postpone the interview until the fourth week—after a nurse had been discharged or a grandmother had gone home and the mother was finally on her own. In this third interview, we gathered information about the birth experience and about the beginning of parent-child relationships. The interviewer also observed (unobtrusively) the mother interacting with the infant. In this third interview some of the measures used in earlier interviews were repeated to ascertain changes in attitudes brought about by the impact of the birth experience. For example, a semantic differential scale by which the woman had rated her doctor or midwife before birth was given again, to see how the woman's attitude toward her birth attendant might have altered.

A second (and final) interview with participating husbands was scheduled for one month after the birth, whenever possible. The men were harder to get together with than their wives, however, and interviews were often postponed, so that, on the average interviews with husbands took place six to seven weeks after the birth.

When the infant was about six months old, a telephone interview was

TABLE A.1. Topics on questionnaires according to question numbers in each interview

Category of questions	Wife: 6 month W-1	Wife: 9 month W-2	Wife: postpartum W-3	6 month phone check (P.C.)	Wife: 1 yr* postpartum W-4	Husband: 9 month H-1	Husband: postpartum H-2
Demographic	1-11, 13				2	1-7	
Relationships with family, friends	13-15, 18-28, 41-42, 58, 63	85-86, 103-4	9-10		21-23, 30, 64, 67	8-10, 13-23, 46, 48, 61-62, 67, 94-95	8-9, 34-40, 60, 78
Psychosexual development	32-40				33-44, 69-74, 82, 103-7		
Current sexuality	99-104	27-28			92-102	111-20	
Attitudes toward femininity, masculinity	29-31				24, 68	24-26, 47	
Marriage or living together	12, 16-17, 42-58, 99-104, 110-13, 122-23	27-29, 111-12	101-4, 127-29		20-23, 25-26, 28-30, 32, 75-76, 92-102	11-12, 27-48, 95, 106	83, 87-90
Pregnancy	59-61, 64-84, 91-96, 114-16	7-8, 12, 30-33, 66-67, 92-100, 109-10			49-54, 77-79, 81	49-58, 104-10	
Fears, anxieties	85, 117-21	61-62, 68-71	42, 86, 88, 99		45-48	49, 58, 70-71, 96-97	51, 62, 76

Methods of coping with stressful situations	97–98	82–84				91–93
Work	10				6	100
Preparation for childbirth	86–90	6, 34–60, 82–84, 87–88	32–34, 125–26, 130		1	60–69, 72–84, 91–93
Preparation for parenthood	106–9, 124–27	9–11, 13–26, 72–81, 101–2, 105–8				85–90
Birth experience (expectation and reality)	85–88, 119	5–6, 34–38, 45–65, 68–69, 82–84	1–8, 11–30, 35–44		50–57	59–67, 72–84, 91–93 / 10–22, 25–30, 46–57, 103–8
Recovery period			31, 44–100, 105–24		80	23–24, 27–33
Child development and behaviors			1–4, 112, 122		3–8, 67, 83–91	92
Motherly role (expectation or reality)	79–81, 101		10, 11, 120, 121		9–19, 27, 30–31, 45–49, 58–66	68, 91–99, 109, 120–21
or Fatherly role (expectation or reality)			127, 128		19, 75–76, 81–82	101, 102
Fertility plans	16, 17	111–12	9	1, 3–5		11, 12
Infant feeding (expectation and reality)	124–27	17–26	44–55, 61, 74, 109, 112, 118–19, 135		4a, 4b, 11–16, 88–90	85–87 / 84–86, 96, 108

*To be reported at a later time.

TABLE A.2. Composition of scales included in questionnaires

Type of item	Source[1,2]	Interview	Item number
Internal-external control	Rotter[1,2] (1966)	W-1	opinion items: 1, 7, 8, 15, 20, 25, 32 (7 items)
		W-2	opinion items: 3, 8, 10, 13, 22, 25, 30 (7 items)
		W-3	opinion items: 1, 12, 33 (3 items)
		H-1	opinion items: 1, 7, 8, 15, 19, 24, 28, 38, 40, 43, 46, 49 (12 items)
		H-2	opinion items: 1, 10, 27 (3 items)
Manifest anxiety	Taylor[1] (1953)	W-1	T.G.[3]: 1, 3, 4, 6, 8, 10, 13, 14, 16, 18, 20, 21, 23, 25, 27, 28, 31, 33, 35, 37, 38 (21 items)
		W-2	T.G.: all items as in W-1 except item 33 omitted and 40 added (21 items)
		W-3	T.G.: all items as in W-1 except item 40 added (22 items)
		H-1	T.G.: same items as W-1
		H-2	T.G.: (22 items)
Femininity-masculinity and sex roles	Gough[1] (1952) Loevinger[2] (1962) and	W-1	T.G.: 2, 5, 7, 9, 11, 12, 15, 17, 19, 22, 24, 26, 29, 30, 32, 34, 36, 39, 40 (19 items)
		H-1	T.G.: same items as W-1
		W-1	opinion items: 2–6, 9–14, 16–19, 21–24, 26–31, 33–44 (37 items)
		W-2	opinion items: 1, 2, 4–7, 9, 11, 12, 14–21, 23, 24, 26–29, 31–40 (33 items)
		W-3	opinion items: 2–11, 13–32, 34–43 (40 items)

Category	Reference		Items
Menstrual symptoms	Doering (1975)	H-1	opinion items: 2–6, 9–14, 16–18, 20–23, 25–27, 29–37, 39, 41–42, 44–45, 47–48, 50–53 (41 items)
		H-2	opinion items: 2–9, 11–26, 28–37 (34 items)
	Moos[2] (1968)	W-1	questions: 39 (10 symptoms), 40 (a,c,f only)
Division of labor	Blood and Wolfe[1] (1960)	W-1	question 57
		H-1	question 47
Pregnancy symptoms	Erickson[2] (1967)	W-1	questions: 65 (1st trimester: 18 items) 67 (2nd trimester: 18 items)
		W-2	questions: 7 (3rd trimester; 18 items)
		H-1	questions: 53 (18 items)
Pregnancy and childbirth worries	Klein, Potter, and Dyk (1950) and Pleschette, Asch, and Chase[2] (1956)	W-1	questions: 96 (23 items)
		W-2	questions: 33 (24 items)
		H-1	questions: 71 (23 items)

[1] References include all the items of this type used.
[2] Some of the items were taken from the reference listed. Others of the same type were developed specifically for this research.
[3] T.G. is a list of questions drawn from the Taylor or Gough scales mixed together for presentation to respondents.

TABLE A.3. Semantic differential scales included in questionnaires

	Concept	Concept rated by wife	Concept rated by husband
BB	My Baby, If Boy	W-2	
BG	My Baby, If Girl	W-2	
HF	My Husband as Father	W-2, W-3	
HL	My Husband during Labor	W-3	
IF	Ideal Father	W-2	
IM	Ideal Man	W-1	H-1
IO	Ideal Mother	W-2	
IW	Ideal Woman	W-1	H-1
MB	My Baby	W-1, W-3	H-1, H-2
MD	My Doctor or Midwife	W-1, W-2, W-3	
ME	Myself	W-1, W-2, W-3	H-1, H-2
MF	My Father	W-1	H-1
MH	My Husband	W-1, W-2, W-3	
MM	My Mother	W-1, W-3	H-2
MW	My Wife		H-1, H-2
SF	Self as Father		H-1, H-2
SH	Self as Husband		H-1, H-2
SL	Self during Labor	W-2, W-3	H-2
SM	Self as Mother	W-2, W-3	
SW	Self as Wife	W-1, W-3	
WD	My Wife's Doctor		H-1, H-2
WL	My Wife during Labor		H-2
WM	My Wife as Mother		H-1, H-2

NOTE: All scales consisted of the same twenty bipolar adjectives. Each scale was given in the interview indicated.

Adjectives used: 1. healthy-sick; 2. happy-sad; 3. powerful-helpless; 4. active-passive; 5. large-small; 6. brave-scared; 7. calm-excitable; 8. strong-weak; 9. clean-dirty; 10. sensitive-insensitive; 11. nice-looking–ugly; 12. feminine-masculine; 13. capable-fumbling; 14. fast-slow; 15. kind-cruel; 16. peaceful-angry; 17. wise-foolish; 18. hard-soft; 19. good-bad; 20. complete-incomplete.

conducted with the mother, and follow-up data on breast-feeding were secured in later phone checks. (A fourth face-to-face interview with the mother was planned for later, when the baby was close to a year old. No data on the fourth interview are included in this book.)

STUDY DESIGN

PREPARATION LEVEL

When the research began, we planned to include an equal number of families in each of three levels of preparation. In previous work (Doering and Entwisle 1975) the extent to which women prepared for childbirth turned out to be a variable of great importance in predicting women's birth experience and their reactions to their infants. Accordingly, oversampling in the first

interview was undertaken, so that after attrition there would be a final sample with couples at many different levels of preparation.

Altogether 133 women agreed to a first interview. Because of recent trends in childbirth education, however, we had difficulty finding couples who had little or no preparation. (Other researchers in the field have recently reported the same problem; see Wente and Crockenberg 1976; Zax, Sameroff, and Farnum 1975.) We had the further problem of how to deal with couples who, at the first interview (sixth month of pregnancy), planned no preparation, but who announced when we returned for the second interview (ninth month) that they were attending training classes. We decided to keep such couples in the sample, once we had begun with them. Because of this, instead of a sample evenly divided in terms of preparation level, we ended up with thirty-five women of the sample at the lowest levels of preparation, 1 to 3 (little or none); thirty-two women at the middle levels, 4 or 5 (hospital and department store-based classes); and fifty-three women at the highest levels, 6 or 7 (intensive Lamaze training or psychoprophylaxis).[4] See table 3.2 for definitions of preparation levels.

Husbands' preparation level was so strongly correlated with wives' that each can serve as a proxy for the other.

SOCIAL CLASS

Equal numbers of women were selected from middle-class and lower-class backgrounds, according to the *occupation of the woman's father* while she was growing up. A large literature suggests that child socialization and parenting vary by social class (e.g., Kohn 1969), and that sex-role orientation also varies by class (e.g., Hess 1970). Also, degree of stress may interact with, or be affected by, social class, although little prior knowledge bears directly on this question.

For this study it seemed preferable to judge social class according to the wife's father's occupation rather than according to the husband's occupation—for several reasons, given below—although in only twelve cases is there conflict between the two classifications.

1. Because couples are in the initial years of marriage, the husband's education and / or long-term occupation is not settled. Some husbands, for example, were students with low incomes, but their eventual income will be much higher.
2. Many questions in the interviews are closely related to the wife's prior socialization and upbringing. Such matters as methods of disciplining young children, breast-feeding, or sex-role ideology, for example,

---

[4]The lowest level of preparation identified in the present study is consistent with levels I and II combined in our earlier study (Doering and Entwisle 1975). The intermediate level is consistent with level III of the earlier study, and the highest level is consistent with level IV. When data were gathered in our earlier study (1965 through 1969), it was easy to find women who had no preparation of any kind, and more difficult to find a broad range of Lamaze-trained couples.

would be expected to be more closely related to sex-role socialization in the woman's family of origin than to class-related aspects of her present family identification.

3. At this stage of family life, many decisions involving the wife would be expected to be class-related. Decisions about whether or not the wife works, for example, may depend on the wife's educational level, and decisions about what kind of preparation to seek for childbirth are likely to be strongly affected by wives' preferences.

Thus, if there is a true difference between husband and wife in social class, the wife's social class may be more important as a stratifying variable for this research. As we indicated, however, the social-class division of this sample would be little changed if husband's occupation rather than wife's father's occupation were used as the criterion of classification.

We were careful to select couples whose social-class level, when combined with the three different levels of preparation, led to an evenly proportioned 2 × 3 factorial design; there is an even division by social class within each preparation level. Such a design permits comparisons among preparation levels unconfounded by social-class differences, or comparisons between social-class groups with preparation level held constant.

RELIGION

The three major religious groups are represented about equally in the sample, with thirty-eight Protestants, forty Catholics, thirty-eight Jews, and four who professed other religions or no religion. For the same reasons as for social class, religion is assessed according to wife's religious upbringing. It was not possible to orthogonalize religion with respect to social class. There are thirty blue-collar and ten middle-class Catholic women, and nine blue-collar and twenty-nine middle-class Jewish women. The thirty-eight Protestant women and four women professing no religion are equally divided by class.

It was also impossible to orthogonalize religion exactly by level of preparation. As it turned out, there were nineteen Protestants, fourteen Catholics, and twenty Jews at the highest preparation levels (levels 6 and 7), and nineteen, twenty-six, and eighteen of each religion at lower levels of preparation (levels 1 through 5).

HUSBAND PARTICIPATION

As mentioned earlier, only half of the husbands (sixty) were interviewed. Of the remaining sixty, thirty-three refused to be interviewed, three could not be interviewed because of seemingly valid job-connected reasons, fourteen were not asked in time (their wives delivered prematurely or the interviewer

erred), nine were already fathers of other children, and one husband's interview was lost. How representative of the entire group of husbands are the
interviewed husbands? Respondents who are willing to be interviewed may
differ in important ways from those who refuse, those who are already fathers,
or those whose wives deliver early. To address this question a large number of
comparisons (236 variables) were made between interviewed husbands and
those not interviewed (see table A.4).

TABLE A.4. Differences in average values of selected variables from wives' interviews by
whether or not husband participated in the study

			Husband did not participate		
Interview	Variable	Husband participated (N = 60)	Willing, but unable or not asked (N = 27)	Unwilling (N = 33)	t-value[a]
W-1	Attitude toward cohabitation 1 = strong disapproval 4 = strong approval	2.43	2.27	2.18	
W-1	Planned feeding 1 = definitely bottle 4 = definitely breast	2.98	2.89	2.39	2.24*
W-1	Gough femininity score Low = less feminine High = more feminine	10.90	11.54	11.42	
W-1	Husband's socioeconomic status 1 = middle class 2 = working class	1.57	1.31	1.36	
W-1	Husband's interest in pregnancy 1 = uninterested 5 = enthusiastic	3.75	3.42	3.24	2.44*
W-1	How husband will feel during labor (wife's expectations) 1 = very negative 6 = very positive	4.37	4.31	3.89	
W-1	How husband will feel during delivery (wife's expectations) 1 = very negative 5 = very positive	3.57	3.50	3.46	
W-2	Opinion of home deliveries 1 = enthusiastically for 4 = emphatically against	2.64	3.00	3.09	
W-2	Plan demand or schedule feeding 1 = rigid schedule 3 = demand	2.37	2.05	2.06	
W-2	Planned feeding 1 = bottle 3 = breast	2.47	2.52	2.03	2.15*
W-2	Total worries (pregnancy and childbirth related) Low = few worries High = many worries	13.75	16.05	16.59	

(*continued*)

TABLE A.4—*Continued*

| Interview | Variable | Husband participated ($N = 60$) | Husband did not participate | | t-value[a] |
			Willing, but unable or not asked ($N = 27$)	Unwilling ($N = 33$)	
W-2	See human childbirth 1 = would *not* want to 5 = would love to	2.93	2.63	2.33	2.05*
W-2	Plan rooming-in or nursery 1 = definitely nursery 4 = definitely rooming-in	2.45	2.20	1.97	
W-2	How often see mother-in-law 1 = often 7 = never	2.20	2.72	2.69	
W-2	Frequency of sexual intercourse in last two weeks (raw numbers)	3.33	3.75	3.95	
W-2	Attitude toward sex in 9th month 1 = very negative 7 = very positive	3.23	3.43	3.78	
W-3	Final preparation level[b]	4.93	4.46	4.48	2.28*
W-3	Sum up whole birth experience 1 = very negative 7 = very positive	4.80	4.58	4.24	
W-3	Husband's feelings during labor 1 = very negative 6 = very positive	3.49	3.68	2.97	
W-3	Husband's feelings during delivery 1 = very negative 6 = very positive	4.35	3.92	3.59	2.28*
W-3	Wife's feelings about husband during labor 1 = very negative 6 = very positive	4.50	4.62	4.03	
W-3	Wife's feelings about husband during delivery 1 = very negative 6 = very positive	4.13	4.23	3.88	
W-3	Current feeding 1 = always bottle 3 = trial breast, 8–14 days 5 = still breast	3.67	3.23	2.58	2.69**
W-3	Emotions at birth 1 = very negative 6 = peak experience	3.90	3.89	3.52	
W-3	Physical feelings at recovery 1 = terrible 5 = great	2.63	3.00	3.09	
W-3	Feelings about giving birth again 1 = *never* 8 = can't wait	5.32	5.42	4.58	

(*continued*)

TABLE A.4—*Continued*

| | | Husband participated ($N = 60$) | Husband did not participate | | |
Interview	Variable		Willing, but unable or not asked ($N = 27$)	Unwilling ($N = 33$)	t-value[a]
W-3	Birth exciting experience 1 = a lot more exciting than expected 5 = a lot less exciting	2.27	2.73	2.88	
W-3	Number of feedings first 48 hrs. (raw numbers)	7.75	6.58	6.21	
W-3	Do when baby cries 1 = let cry 5 = try everything, very solicitous	3.12	3.04	2.82	
W-3	Complications 0 = none 3 = serious	1.62	1.85	1.85	
W-3	Husband changes diapers Low = never or rare High = often	17.45	13.67	11.41	
W-3	Husband feeds baby[c] Low = never or rare High = often	5.70	8.35	8.30	
	Feeding (type and length, if breast) 1 = bottle only 3 = breast up to one month 4 = breast up to three months 8 = breast over one year	4.16	3.50	2.63	2.93**

*$P < .05$, two-tailed.
**$P < .01$, two-tailed.
[a] t-tests were run between only two groups: husbands who participated (first column) and husbands who were unwilling to participate (third column).
[b] See table 3.2.
[c] Biased by high percentage of breast-feeding mothers.

Most comparisons indicated the interviewed and noninterviewed husbands were much alike, and the differences between participating and nonparticipating husbands were small. Several differences may not be negligible however. Husbands who agreed to be interviewed were over a year younger, and both they and their wives held less prestigious jobs than couples without husband interviews. Wife's present age did not differ much between groups (about three months), but wives of men who agreed to be interviewed had been younger at the time of their marriage (21.73 vs. 23.18).

According to their wives' perceptions, the participating husbands showed

more interest in the pregnancy than did the nonparticipating husbands. This finding makes sense, because in agreeing to be interviewed, men demonstrated their willingness to spend six or seven hours discussing pregnancy and childbirth. Also, the wives of husbands who agreed to interviews were themselves more interested in observing a birth (other than the birth of their own child). This suggests that they do not view childbirth as frightening, disgusting, or pathological, and their attitude may have influenced their husbands. We also note that the wives of willing husbands reported that their men had more positive emotions during the actual delivery of the baby. This observation would also fit in with their interest in being interviewed.

One consistent difference between willing and unwilling husbands seems to be in the area of infant feeding. Unwilling husbands were more likely to have wives who planned to bottle-feed when questioned in both the sixth-month and the ninth-month interviews. At the interview two to three weeks after the birth, the wives of the unwilling men were more likely to be bottle-feeding, and if they had tried breast-feeding, they were more likely to have given it up. The same finding held at the six-month phone check: wives of willing husbands breast-fed much longer (over three months compared to less than one month, on the average).

All in all, however, differences are slight, especially when one considers that the willing and unwilling groups were compared on 236 different variables (as reported by their wives). Of this set of variables, the *largest* differences are those reported in table A.4. Only eight of these differences attain statistical significance, about as many as would be expected given chance sampling fluctuations.

WHY A LONGITUDINAL STUDY?

It was, of course, expensive and time-consuming to carry out a longitudinal study. The reader might wonder why we did not locate a sample of couples with children one year old and ask them to recall their experiences prior to and following the birth of their child.

Actually, a retrospective study would be useful and might lead to insights different from those derived from a longitudinal study. For example, the importance of certain events may be more fully appreciated in retrospect. On the other hand, defects in memory are well known. Respondents edit events of the past, consciously or unconsciously, and there is a well-documented human tendency to recall pleasant happenings and to repress the unpleasant. Robbins's study (1963) provides dramatic documentation of how extensive such distortions can be. She questioned parents of three-year-olds about events such as infant feeding, thumb-sucking, and weaning. The events were relatively recent, the parents well-educated and aware that data to check their replies were

on record, yet 5 percent of the mothers were not correct in their reports of whether they had breast-fed or bottle-fed. In addition, 47 percent did not remember whether they had fed on schedule or on demand, and 65 percent were inaccurate in answers about when they had weaned from the breast. Thus, even the simplest events can be forgotten. Worse perhaps, because harder to deal with, are reconstructions of the past to fit the present. (For a study showing how the past is reconstructed to fit the present, see Davis 1961.) A young mother with a one-year-old eating three meals a day may recall that her baby started easily on solid food, whereas the baby in fact took very little food at first and then only with difficulty. Or she may recall that her husband's present affection for the baby began at birth, whereas at first the husband was jealous of the baby and resented her attention to it. For all these reasons, a longitudinal study may be better than a retrospective study for getting at the topics like those included in this research.

Another strategy might have been to conduct a series of cross-sectional studies, with different sets of couples at each time point. This design would be less advantageous for our kind of research than for other kinds of sociological studies because the subject matter is intimate. It is time-consuming to persuade respondents to submit to interviews that include detailed questions on family life and sexual habits. Thus, the usual savings in time and money expended for locating respondents for cross-sectional studies as compared to longitudinal studies would probably be minimal for our study.

But the crux of any comparison among longitudinal vs. other design strategies is in the power that a longitudinal study provides for identifying causal sequences unambiguously. If prepartum anxiety is high and is followed by complications of childbirth, there is no way that complications can be said to *lead* to prepartum anxiety. If women's anxiety and delivery complications are measured simultaneously, it is just as easy to argue that complications cause anxiety as the reverse. With several cross-sections, although the time sequencing is unambiguous, there is no correspondence from one cross-section to the next that will support the computation of covariance matrices between cross-sections. An average from one time to the next may remain unchanged when there is much significant movement on the individual level.

On the other hand, *any* design, longitudinal or otherwise, is by itself unable to guarantee correct inferences. In the example above concerning prepartum anxiety and complications, although anxiety is observed to be present *before* complications, this is still no guarantee of a causal role for anxiety. Some other factor(s) may be the actual cause of both anxiety and complications, or the relationship may be a consequence of sampling fluctuations. In other words, even if there is a statistical association between anxiety and complications and anxiety precedes complications, anxiety may be a spurious cause. The only remedy for this dilemma is, of course, a theory and a great deal of ancillary evidence pointing in the same direction.

DATA REDUCTION AND ANALYSIS

All interviews were tape-recorded, and subsequently transcribed. From the transcriptions, data were coded and then keyed into computer storage. Separate files were constructed for data from each interview (up to 500 variables per interview), and then later several master files were constructed that contained variables for tracing change over time from one interview to the next. In some cases variables were fabricated directly from questions, i.e., Cesarean delivery or its absence can be coded 0–1 and used as an attribute variable, or age can be coded in years and used as a continuously measured variable. In other cases "variables" are scores produced from several items, the Taylor anxiety score, for example.

For all data, of whatever sort, numerical codes were developed and used to construct data files. Standard routines (Nie et al. 1975) were used to produce descriptive statistics. Long discussion-type questions, such as women's attitudes toward being pregnant, how they felt immediately after the moment of birth, and when they felt like a mother, were all coded blind. Raters were not aware of any of the respondent's other answers or of what her actual experience had been when they were coding a particular question. All long-answer questions were rated by at least two coders, with a third used when there was disagreement. Inter-coder reliability was constantly being checked, and it ranged from .85 to .99.

Because interviews were face-to-face and interviewers were carefully trained and supervised, we believe the measurement error in most of the data is minimal. For example, preparation level scores were derived from information taken from several questions in more than one interview and were reviewed several times. The scale units of this variable are large compared to the volume of information available to assign scores. It is just not possible that a woman would be classified as having attended Lamaze classes when she had not, or had medical training when she had not. We knew where and when preparation classes were taught, by whom, and so on. Much of this information was cross-checked by other questions in the interview. Decisions on scores for other important variables were similarly well founded.

Alpha reliability values are given for scales constructed from more than one variable. These values estimate *scale homogeneity* and should be regarded as a lower bound on reliability of these scales rather than as good estimates of measurement error.

Because of the length of the interviews and the complexity of the questions, data from every respondent are not available on all questions. In tables N's are consistently given. For statistics cited in the text, especially correlation coefficients, the significance level appropriate for the actual sample size is reported, but N's are not. All models are estimated for listwise-present data (the subset of cases with values for all relevant variables).

In chapters 3, 4, 5, and 7 we used recursive models to guide multivariate

analyses. We assume the reader is familiar with structural equation modeling. (The basic methodology for this type of analysis is well referenced in Duncan 1975 and Heise 1976.) The strategy is each instance is to hypothesize a causal model on the basis of research evidence drawn from other studies and / or from theoretical considerations. A dependent variable(s) is seen as the outcome of several prior variables (prior in the sense of having occurred earlier in time), and then parameters in the model are estimated using ordinary least squares assuming no measurement error.

Because the work is highly exploratory, in interpreting these models we have concentrated on "significant" paths and looked for major structural links. We deliberately avoided trying to catalogue all effects exhaustively or interpreting anything but very large differences in parameter size. The case base for these analyses is marginal at best. However, because so little quantitative information is available on the issues that the models address, it seems best to try to wring out as much information from the data as possible. It seemed particularly critical to evaluate the potential impact of events around birth with some control on prior variables related to motivation. Some models are much more elaborate than we feel comfortable with in view of the sample sizes (especially the couples' feeding models and fathering models), but data of this kind are so hard to provide that we felt obliged to try the most powerful analysis possible. In evaluating effects it does not seem warranted to dwell on relatively small differences in parameter size from one group to another.

Our original plan was to use a strategy of random subsample replication in testing models (Mosteller and Tukey 1977). We divided the sample into two parts with the intention of exploring various hypotheses using one half of the data and then using the second half as a "fresh" set of data to provide a strict test of the models we developed. Unfortunately, this strategy could not be carried very far. The considerable social-class differences, and the fact that breast-feeders must be treated separately in most analyses, require that models be estimated for samples already stratified along these dimensions, so samples for analysis are always smaller than the total sample. For example, the parenting models had to be estimated separately for middle-class and for lower-class respondents. (The alternative strategy of coding class as a dummy variable and introducing interactive terms in which class was combined with every other variable is not very attractive here. The gain in stability of the error term seems more than offset by the fact that the interpretation across models is made much more cumbersome.) In short, because most analyses had to be carried out on much less than the full sample of 120, further division into random subsample replicates was ruled out. The averages of the random subreplicates were useful, however, in initial inspection of the data.

For all the major models in the book, we tried to run parallel analyses that included estimates of measurement error. To do this we used the LISREL IV program (Jöreskog and Sörbom 1978). In a few instances, models could not be estimated using this approach, either because of the limited sample size or

because of collinearity problems. In instances where parameters could be estimated, the major structural outlines of the models were the same whether or not measurement error was included, and, as would be expected, more of the variance in the endogenous variables was accounted for when measurement error was taken into account. We will be happy to furnish details of other solutions to readers upon request.

No models in this book have been "trimmed": that is, after estimating parameters, it is possible to omit those links that do not attain significance and to then reestimate the model. We have chosen not to adopt this practice for several reasons, the main one being that it seems wise to present our findings as fully as possible. A complete model informs the reader about the actual hypotheses we considered, and parameter estimates vary according to which particular set of variables is included. For all models sufficient data are given to define the covariance matrix needed for estimation of parameters.

The models tend to be cumulative. That is, in chapter 4 the woman's birth experience is explained in terms of level of preparation and husband participation. Then, in chapter 5, the woman's birth experience and level of preparation are used as predictors of breast-feeding behavior. Later, in chapter 7 birth experience and feeding both appear as possible determinants of mothering. Because the case base is so small, however, it was not possible to include the full structure at every additional step, which is tantamount to assuming that direct effects of the early omitted variables on all later endogenous variables are negligible. These assumptions seem well-founded. For example, women's and men's attitudes about breast-feeding (WOPBR and HOPBR) do not appear in the mothering model, and the only way their influence could be manifest in that model is by way of their influence upon feeding, which in the mothering model is not evaluated.

APPENDIX B: OPINION ITEMS

Agreement with opinion items according to interview

	Interview[a]				
Opinion item	W-1 (%)	W-2 (%)	W-3 (%)	H-1 (%)	H-2 (%)
I. On sex roles:					
1. In most families the father is stricter and the mother more soft-hearted.	28			57	
In most families the father and mother show equal amounts of strictness and soft-heartedness.	72			43	
2. The most important quality a good father has is that he's a good provider.		04		05	
Most important is his warmth and interest shown in his children.		96		95	
3. Deep down, most men want their first child to be a son.		73		72	
Deep down, most men don't care if their first child is a son or a daughter.		27		28	
4. Deep down, most women want their first child to be a son.	23				
Deep down, most women don't care if their first child is a son or a daughter.	77				
5. If a little girl is a tomboy, her mother should try to get her interested in dolls and playing house.	10			10	
If a little girl is a tomboy, her mother should let her play boys' games.	90			90	
6. If a little boy is interested in dolls and dressing up, his mother[b] should let him play that way.	81			63	
If he's interested in dolls and dressing up, his mother[b] should get him to play boys' games.	19			37	
7. Most new fathers would like to hold and touch their new babies right away and resent having to view them through glass in the hospital nursery.	81	87		67	68

[a] See Fig. A.1 for explanation of abbreviations.
[b] *Mother* was *parents* in the men's version.

APPENDIX B—*Continued*

	Interview[a]				
Opinion item	W-1 (%)	W-2 (%)	W-3 (%)	H-1 (%)	H-2 (%)
Most new fathers are just as happy to view their new babies in the nursery, and get to know them later.	19	13		33	32
8. Fathers usually don't get very interested in their children until they're past babyhood.	17		19	22	28
Fathers are just as interested in their children when they're still babies as when they're older.	83		81	78	72
9. In most families, husbands make the big decisions.	07			23	
In most families, the big decisions are shared by husband and wife.	93			77	
10. A married man should have at least one night per week out with the boys.	45			25	
A married man should plan his social life to include his wife.	55			75	
11. A man should make sure that his wife has time to herself when she has a small baby, even if it means he has to baby-sit.	92			100	
If a woman with a small baby wants time to herself, it's up to her to find a baby-sitter.	08			0	
12. A woman's personality suffers when she is only involved in keeping house and raising children.		65	60	68	65
A woman does not find her true self until she keeps house and raises children.		35	40	32	35
13. Raising children and keeping house is more interesting than the kind of work most men do for a living.	52		62		32
Most men have more interesting work to do than their wives have.	48		38		68
14. Most men would prefer that their wives not have a job outside the home.	52			58	
Most men would be proud if their wives had a job outside the home.	48			42	
15. Most women want the kind of husband who won't let them have a job outside the home.		09			
Most women want the kind of husband who will let them have a job outside the home.		91			
16. Married women shouldn't take jobs away from men.	01			08	
If married women can work as well as men, they should be given a chance.	99			92	

(*continued*)

APPENDIX B—*Continued*

	Interview[a]				
Opinion item	W-1 (%)	W-2 (%)	W-3 (%)	H-1 (%)	H-2 (%)
II. On menstruation, sexuality, and lactation					
17. Having to put up with menstrual periods is one of the worst things about being a woman.	14				
Menstrual periods aren't half as difficult as some women make them out to be.	86				
18. Most women[c] don't want to have sex during their menstrual periods.	70			70	
Most women[c] like to have sex during their menstrual periods as much as at any other time of the month.	30			30	
19. Men are much more interested in sex than women are.	16			07	
Women are about as much interested in sex as men are.	84			93	
20. There are more important things in a good marriage relationship than sex.	71			72	
Sex is one of the most important things in a good marriage relationship.	29			28	
21. A wife should have sex with her husband whenever he wants it.	10			07	
A wife shouldn't have to have sex with her husband when she isn't in the mood.	90			93	
22. Breast-feeding is very pleasant for the mother.		92	91		82
Breast-feeding is not very pleasant for the mother.		08	09		18
23. A woman breast-feeding her baby should always do it in private.	18		17	18	19
A woman can breast-feed her hungry baby in public as long as it's inconspicuous.	82		83	82	81
III. On pregnancy					
24. Pregnant women should stop having sexual intercourse toward the end of the pregnancy, because it might hurt the baby.		41			
Pregnant women can keep right on having intercourse up until labor starts.		59			
25. A pregnant woman is like a sick woman in many ways.	05	03			04
A pregnant woman is a perfectly healthy woman, unless she has complications.	95	97			96

[c] For men, worded: "Most men don't want to have sex with a woman during her menstrual period," etc.

(*continued*)

APPENDIX B—*Continued*

	Interview[a]				
Opinion item	W-1 (%)	W-2 (%)	W-3 (%)	H-1 (%)	H-2 (%)
26. Pregnant women should take it easy and not do as much as before pregnancy.	33				
Pregnant women can keep up the activity that they did before they were pregnant.	67				
27. No matter how much a woman wants a baby, pregnancy is a difficult experience.		28	27		
Most women find pregnancy an especially pleasant time of life.		72	73		
28. Pregnancy is a time when most women look especially lovely.	80	76	74	82	83
No matter how clever maternity clothes are made, pregnant women look clumsy and unattractive.	20	24	26	18	17
29. After a woman has a baby, her figure will never be the same again.	05		03		04
Any woman can get her figure back after she has a baby if she really tries.	95		97		96
IV. On labor and delivery					
30. Doctors should decide what drugs a woman is given during an uncomplicated labor and delivery.		14	12		12
Women should have some say about what drugs they are given in an uncomplicated labor and delivery.		86	88		88
31. Doctors know best; the patient should do what she's told without questioning too much.		01			
Doctors can't know everything; patients should feel free to ask questions and get explanations.		99			
32. Labor pains are not as bad as some women say they are.		94	74	65	58
Labor pains are the worst kind of pain there is.		06	26	35	42
33. Most women in labor would feel comforted if their husbands could stay with them.	92	94	94	95	97
Most women in labor would prefer not to have their husbands around.	08	06	06	05	03
34. Most women wouldn't want their husbands to see them during the birth of the baby.		14	15	12	11
Most women would like to have their husbands there to share the birth of the baby with them.		86	85	88	89
35. Most men would prefer not to be around when their wives are in hard labor.	36	34	31		44
Most men would prefer to be with their wives to help them during hard labor.	64	66	69		56

(*continued*)

APPENDIX B—*Continued*

Opinion item	Interview[a]				
	W-1 (%)	W-2 (%)	W-3 (%)	H-1 (%)	H-2 (%)
36. Many men would be interested in seeing the birth of their own baby, if they were allowed to.	82	77	81	72	65
Most men would not want to have to see the birth of their own baby.	18	23	19	28	35
37. Most women in labor want someone to stay with them.		95	97	92	100
Most women in labor just want to be left alone.		05	03	08	0
38. Nature didn't intend childbirth to be a painful experience.		50	42	35	28
Childbirth is painful, and only people who haven't gone through it think it isn't.		50	58	65	72
39. Nurses and doctors know that women can't help what they do or say during labor and delivery.		46	51		
Nurses and doctors know that most women can control themselves during labor and delivery if they really try.		54	49		
40. It's easiest for a woman having a baby to just be put to sleep and wakened when it's all over.		02	03		
It's worth putting up with some pain in order to be awake and see your baby born.		98	97		
41. It's worth putting up with some pain in childbirth in order to avoid drugs and actually push out your own baby.		65	59		
There's no sense in going through the pain of childbirth when there are spinals available that enable you to watch the birth while feeling nothing.		35	41		
42. Putting the mother to sleep during birth can hurt the baby.	63		56	65	60
Doctors wouldn't put mothers to sleep if it would hurt the baby.	37		44	35	40
43. There is real danger to both baby and mother when the baby is born in a taxicab by mistake.	41			53	
In most cases, both baby and mother do just as well when the baby is born in a taxicab by mistake.	59			47	
44. When labor begins, most women[d] just want to get to the hospital and let the doctors and nurses take over from there.		21	23		32
When labor begins, most women[e] want to know what's happening and how to help themselves.		79	77		68

[d] For men: "... Men just want to get their wives to the hospital...."
[e] For men: "... Men want to know what's happening and how to help their wives."

(*continued*)

APPENDIX B—*Continued*

	Interview[a]				
Opinion item	W-1 (%)	W-2 (%)	W-3 (%)	H-1 (%)	H-2 (%)
45. It's best for a new mother to get her rest and let the nurses take care of her baby while she's in the hospital.	45	37	51		42
It's best for a new mother to take care of her own baby while she's in the hospital, with occasional advice and help from the nurses.[f]	55	63	49		58
46. If hospitals weren't so crowded, it'd be better for new mothers to stay more than four days.	08		16		19
Four days in the hospital is enough time for the average mother to recover from childbirth.	92		84		81
47. It's wonderful to have your own mother with you when you come home from the hospital with a new baby.			59		
A woman is better off with outside help when she comes home from the hospital with a new baby.			41		
V. On child rearing					
48. Most mothers[g] don't really learn to love their babies till after they're born.		36	38		53
Most mothers[g] already love their babies during pregnancy.		64	62		47
49. You will spoil a tiny baby if you respond to him everytime he cries.	32		32	42	30
It's best for a tiny baby if someone responds to him everytime he cries.	68		68	58	70
50. Small babies should be fed on a regular schedule.	29		17	33	25
Small babies need to be fed whenever they're hungry.	71		83	67	75
51. It is all right for young babies to sleep in bed next to their mothers occasionally.		79	68	85	82
Young babies should never sleep next to their mothers in bed.		21	32	15	18
52. Breast-fed babies are usually healthier than bottle-fed babies.		43			
Bottle-fed babies are just as healthy as breast-fed babies.		57			
53. A six-month-old baby can be given his bottle in his crib, so that his mother will have more time for work and rest.	29		12		39

[f] Wording of this question was slightly different in the first interview. "It's best for a newborn baby to be cared for in the hospital nursery by trained nurses." vs. "It's best for a newborn baby to be cared for by his own mother in her hospital room."

[g] For men: *Parents* substituted for *mothers.*

(*continued*)

APPENDIX B—*Continued*

	Interview[a]				
Opinion item	W-1 (%)	W-2 (%)	W-3 (%)	H-1 (%)	H-2 (%)
A six-month-old baby should always be held when he has his bottle.	71		88		61
54. A one-year-old toddler is too old to still be breast-fed by his mother.		42	45		74
It's all right for a one-year-old toddler to still be breast-fed.		58	55		26
55. It's best to put breakable things where children can't reach them, when they're small.			46		63
It's best to start teaching children right away not to touch certain breakable things.			54		37
56. All parents have moments when they wish they didn't have children.			75		77
Most parents never regret having children.			25		23
57. If a mother trains her baby properly, he will not need diapers after 1½ years old.			15		
Most babies are not completely toilet-trained until after they're 1½ years old.			85		
58. It's all right for three-year-olds to run around the house without any clothes on.			59	68	
Three-year-olds should have some clothes on even in the privacy of their own home.			41	32	
59. Most mothers automatically know the best way to bring up their children.			12		09
Most mothers have doubts from time to time about the best way to bring up their children.			88		91
60. It is best for small children not to watch their parents get dressed and undressed.		16		23	
It's all right for small children to watch their parents get dressed and undressed.		84		77	
61. Mothers should prepare good meals, and then let children eat what they want.			56		
Mothers should teach their children to eat everything on their plates.			44		
62. The best kind of family life is the kind where the whole family does everything together.			13		18
Everyone, even a child, needs some privacy in his life.			87		82
63. If a child is old enough to ask a question, he's old enough to be answered.			97		96
Children ask questions about a lot of things they shouldn't know about.			03		04

(*continued*)

APPENDIX B—*Continued*

	Interview[a]				
Opinion item	W-1 (%)	W-2 (%)	W-3 (%)	H-1 (%)	H-2 (%)
64. Children should be allowed to criticize their parents occasionally.			76		60
Children should not be disrespectful to their parents.			24		40
65. If children are told too much about sex, they are likely to experiment with it.	01			05	
Children's questions about sex should be answered fully whenever they're asked.	99			95	
66. Husbands often feel slightly jealous at the sight of their wives breast-feeding the baby.		16		23	
Husbands find the sight of their wives breast-feeding the baby a very attractive one.		84		77	

APPENDIX C: DEFINITIONS OF VARIABLES USED IN MODELS

VARIABLES USED IN THE MODEL TO PREDICT PREPARATION (CHAPTER 3)

QUALITY OF COMMUNICATION IN MARRIAGE (QCOMM)

To construct a variable measuring the amount of communication between marital partners, we asked women what they and their husbands were likely to quarrel about "these days." If they said that they never quarreled, they were asked about disagreements. Both quarrels and disagreements were probed in detail, and the full response was later coded for how severe conflicts were and how the couple handled them. The placement of "never disagree" low is the scale reflects observations that a flat denial of quarreling usually reveals under probes that inevitable conflicts are not being resolved. Coding was based on long-answer responses. The scoring was: 1 = severe conflicts, little or no communication; 2 = "never" disagree or quarrel; 3 = some problems, but some communication; 4 = milder problems, better communication; 5 = very mild problems or no problems, good communication.

WIFE'S EDUCATIONAL LEVEL (WEDUC)

This variable was measured as the total number of years of schooling the woman had completed.

WOMAN'S DESIRE FOR ACTIVE ROLE (ACTRL)

This scale is the sum of scores on the three opinion items below, asked in interviews before the birth.

1. Respondents were asked if they agreed with: (a) "It's worth putting up with some pain and discomfort in childbirth in order to avoid drugs and actually push out your own baby," or (b) "There's no sense in going through the pain of childbirth when there are spinals available that enable you to watch the birth while feeling nothing" (Appendix B,

opinion item 41). Respondents agreeing with the first statement received a score of 2, while those agreeing with the second were given a score of 1.

2. Respondents were asked if they agreed with: (a) "It's best for a newborn baby to be cared for in the hospital nursery by trained nurses," or (b) "It's best for a newborn baby to be cared for by his own mother, in her hospital room" (Appendix B, opinion item 45, W-1). Respondents agreeing with the first statement were assigned a score of 1, while those agreeing with the second received a score of 2

3. Respondents were asked if they agreed with: (a) "It's best for the mother to get her rest and let the nurses take care of her baby while she's in the hospital," or (b) "It's best for a new mother to take care of her own baby while she is in the hospital with occasional advice and help from the nurses" (Appendix B, opinion item 45, W-2). Respondents agreeing with the first statement were given a score of 1, while those agreeing with the second were assigned a score of 2.

The alpha reliability for this scale is .607.

Preparation Level (WPREP)

The preparation-level variable combines all sources of women's knowledge about what to expect in labor and delivery and how to put this knowledge to use. It includes knowledge from books, classes, movies, nurse's training, and elsewhere. Scoring, derived from several questions in all three interviews with women, is shown in table 3.2.

VARIABLES USED IN THE BIRTH-EXPERIENCE MODELS (CHAPTER 4)

Preparation Level (WPREP)

This variable is defined above in connection with the chapter 3 model used to predict preparation.

Husband's Participation (HPART)

This scale is based on six items measuring the degree of husband's participation during labor and delivery, as estimated by his wife.

The first item is how the wife thought her husband felt during labor, whether he was with her for all of it, part of it, or none of it. His feelings were coded from 1 (very negative) to 6 (enthusiastic).

The second item involved the wife's perception of how her husband felt during delivery, whether he was present or not. It was coded identically to the first item.

The third item asked women how *they* felt about their husbands being or not being with them during labor. Responses were coded as for the first two items, from 1 to 6.

The fourth item asked women how they felt about their husbands being or not being with them during delivery—again, with the same scoring.

For the fifth item respondents were asked what their husbands did that helped most during labor. After that action was described, they were asked what else their husbands had done that helped and were pressed until they could not think of anything else. These discussions were coded as follows: 0 = husband wasn't there; 1 = there, but did nothing; 2 = "nothing," but turns out to be something; 3 = "just being there"; 4 = being there, plus specific help; 5 = several helpful activities; 6 = really helpful, constantly busy.

For the sixth item respondents were asked about husband's help during delivery in the same manner as for labor. The coding was similar to that for the fifth item, running from husband not there to "really helpful."

The alpha reliability for this scale is .842. The correlation between the measure of this variable based on wives' replies and a measure based on husbands' replies for couples where both responded is .832.

WORST PAIN IN FIRST STAGE OF LABOR (PAIN1)

The measure of pain was based on the woman's report of the worst pain she felt during the first stage of labor. *First stage* was initially defined for the respondent, and then the respondent was read a checklist and chose one of the following terms to describe her worst pain: 1, no pain; 2, slight pain; 3, moderate pain; 4, bad pain; 5, terrible pain.

WOMAN'S LEVEL OF AWARENESS (AWARE)

This variable is a measure of awareness at the moment of birth. A score was derived from answers to a variety of questions relating to what drugs a woman was given, the effects of these drugs, how and what the woman felt during delivery, and how clear her description of events was. The scoring may be summarized as follows: 1, unconscious; 2, gas or heavy sedation, plus conduction anesthesia; 3, gas or sedation, plus only local or pudendal block; 4, conduction anesthesia only; 5, whiffs of gas only; 6, pudendal block only; 7, local infiltration only; 8, nothing.

WOMAN'S BIRTH EXPERIENCE (BESCL)

This scale is the sum of scores on five items measuring the quality of a woman's birth experience. Respondents, after describing the birth in detail, were asked: "How did you feel?" for the moment right after the baby was born, or for the first conscious moment in the case of those who were unconscious at birth of the baby. Both physical and emotional responses were

sought. Then emotions and physical feelings (item 1 and item 2) were separately coded on a six-point and a five-point range respectively. Respondents gave similar information about their emotional and physical feelings in recovery, and these responses (item 3 and item 4) were coded like items 1 and 2. At another point in the interview respondents were asked "Many women feel, right after the birth, that they *never* want to go through all that again; did you have any feelings like that, right after?" These answers were scored from 1 (yes, never again go through birth) to 8 (no, can't wait to have another).

The alpha reliability of this scale is .734.

MAN'S BIRTH EXPERIENCE (MBESCL)

This scale is the sum of three items measuring the quality of the husband's birth experience for husbands who were interviewed after the birth of the infant.

For the first item, husbands were asked—for the moment of birth (if they were in the delivery room) or for the moment they heard about the birth (if in the waiting room)—how they felt both physically and emotionally at that instant. Only emotional responses could be coded. They were rated from 1 = very negative to 6 = peak experience, with 3 = neutral. For the second item, husbands were asked what was the "nicest thing" about labor and delivery, and probes followed. These responses were rated as follows: 0 = nothing—or "when it was over'; 1 = drugs given to wife; 2 = that it "wasn't bad"; 3 = help of medical personnel; 4 = husband being able to help his wife and / or closeness or being together with wife; 5 = witnessing the birth, passive; 6 = witnessing the birth and actively participating in it. The third item was the husband's response (with probes if required) to "Summing up the whole childbirth experience *now* [at time of interview, four to eight weeks after the birth], how would you say it was for *you*?" Responses were scored from 1 = very negative, to 6 = extremely positive, enthusiastic, with 3 = neutral.

The alpha reliability of this scale is .656.

VARIABLES USED IN THE FEEDING MODELS: DATA FROM THE 1973-76 SURVEY (CHAPTER 5)

PREPARATION LEVEL (WPREP)

This variable measured the final level of preparation women had achieved prior to the birth. It is fully described above in connection with the chapter 3 model for preparation.

LEVEL OF AWARENESS (AWARE)

This variable measured the extent to which women were mentally and physically conscious at the moment of giving birth. It is fully described above in connection with the chapter 4 birth-experience models.

Woman's Birth Experience (BESCL)

This scale measures the quality of a woman's birth experience. It is described above in connection with the chapter 4 birth-experience models.

Wife's Prepartum Feeding Intentions (WFIN)

This scale is the sum of scores on three variables: (a) whether the mother in the nine-month interview planned bottle-feeding (coded 1), was undecided about feeding mode (coded 2), or planned to breast-feed (coded 3); (b) a subjective rating by the mother of the importance to her of the feeding mode she was choosing, with "makes no difference" coded 1, "somewhat important" coded 2, and "very important" coded 3; (c) the choice of feeding mode, and if breast-fed, how long the mother planned to breast-feed, with 1 assigned to bottle-feeders, 2 assigned to breast-feeders up to three weeks, 3 = over 3 weeks to two months; 4 = over two months to four months; 5 = over four months to six months; 6 = over six months to nine months; 7 = over nine months to one year; 8 = over one year.
The alpha reliability of this scale is .426.

Wife's Attitude toward Breast-feeding (WOPBR)

This scale is the sum of five dichotomous opinion items about breast-feeding taken from the wife's interview at nine months pregnant. Each item was scored 1 for the first alternative listed below or 2 for the second alternative.

1. Breast-feeding is not very pleasant for the mother.
   or
   Breast-feeding is very pleasant for the mother. (Appendix B, opinion item 22.)
2. A one-year-old toddler is too old to still be breast-fed by his mother.
   or
   It's all right for a one-year-old toddler to still be breast-fed by his mother. (Appendix B, opinion item 54.)
3. A woman breast-feeding her baby should always do it in private.
   or
   A woman can breast-feed her hungry baby in public as long as she does it inconspicuously. (Appendix B, opinion item 23.)
4. Bottle-fed babies are just as healthy as breast-fed babies.
   or
   Breast-fed babies are usually healthier than bottle-fed babies. (Appendix B, opinion item 52.)
5. Husbands often feel slightly jealous at the sight of their wives breast-feeding the baby.
   or

Husbands find the sight of their wives breast-feeding the baby a very attractive one. (Appendix B, opinion item 66.)

The alpha reliability of this scale is .322.

WOMAN'S ATTITUDE TOWARD THE BABY ON FIRST VIEW (FSVIEW)

This variable is a rating on a scale from 1 (definitely negative) to 6 (enthusiastic) of the mother's reply to the question: "When you saw the baby for the first time, what did it look like?" An earlier analysis (1965–69 data) had indicated that this question provided a more valid measure of the mother's initial emotional response to the infant than direct questions about the mother's feelings toward the infant.

FEEDING BEHAVIOR IN THE FIRST MONTH (EFDBE)

This variable measured feeding behavior up to one month. It was scored as follows: 1 = always bottle fed; 2 = tried breast one week or less; 3 = tried breast eight days to fourteen days; 4 = tried breast fifteen days to twenty-one days; 5 = continuing breast-feeding.

FEEDING PERSISTENCE (FEED)

This variable measured long-term feeding behavior obtained by phone checks during the first year after birth. It was scored as follows: 1 = always bottle-fed; 2 = breast-fed one week or less; 3 = breast-fed eight days to one month; 4 = breast-fed over one month to three months; 5 = breast-fed over three months to six months; 6 = breast-fed over six months to nine months; 7 = breast-fed over nine months to one year; 8 = breast-fed more than one year.

HUSBAND'S INTENTIONS ABOUT BREAST-FEEDING (HSIN)

This scale is the sum of three variables: (a) whether the husband expected the baby to be bottle-fed (scored 1), or breast-fed (scored 2); (b) whether the husband was in agreement with his wife's choice of feeding mode, scored as follows: 1 = against, 2 = neutral, 3 = mildly in favor, 4 = strongly in favor; (c) how long the husband expected the baby to be breast-fed, scored as follows: 1 = up to three weeks; 2 = over three weeks to two months, 3 = over two months to four months, 4 = over four months to six months, 5 = over six months to nine months, 6 = over nine months to twelve months, 7 = over twelve months to eighteen months, 8 = more than eighteen months.

The alpha reliability of this scale is .298.

HUSBAND'S ATTITUDE TOWARD BREAST-FEEDING (HOPBR)

This scale is the sum of three dichotomous items based on husbands' replies to opinion items given in the prepartum husband interview. As was true for

their wives' answers, the first alternative was scored 1, the second alternative was scored 2. The items were:

1. Small babies should be fed on a regular schedule.

    or

    Small babies need to be fed whenever they're hungry. (Appendix B, opinion item 50.)

2. A woman breast-feeding her baby should always do it in private.

    or

    A woman can breast-feed her hungry baby in public as long as she does it inconspicuously. (Appendix B, opinion item 23.)

3. Husbands often feel slightly jealous at the sight of their wives breast-feeding the baby.

    or

    Husbands find the sight of their wives breast-feeding the baby a very attractive one. (Appendix B, opinion item 66.)

The alpha reliability of this scale is .239.

VARIABLES USED IN THE FEEDING MODELS: DATA FROM THE 1965–69 SURVEY (CHAPTER 5)

PREPARATION LEVEL (WPREP)

This variable was measured very much the same way in 1965–69 as in 1973–76. The chief difference is that in the earlier study a nine-unit scale was used, with levels 8 and 9 corresponding to levels 6 and 7 in the 1973–76 study, levels 6 and 7 corresponding to levels 4 and 5 in the 1973–76 study, and levels 1 through 5 corresponding to levels 1, 2, or 3 in the 1973–76 study.

LEVEL OF AWARENESS (AWARE)

Measurement of this variable was exactly the same in 1965–69 as in 1973–76 with one minor change. In the 1965–69 data there are no women given whiffs of gas, category 5 of the 1973–76 data. Therefore, categories 5, 6, and 7 in the 1965–69 data are equivalent to categories 6, 7, and 8 in the 1973–76 data. Categories 5, 6, and 7 (awake and feeling everything) included 62 percent of the women in 1965–69, compared to 27 percent of the women in 1973–76.

WOMAN'S BIRTH EXPERIENCE (BESCL)

Whereas in the 1973–76 analysis this measure was formed from a five-item scale, in the earlier study three questions were asked and a total score was directly assigned on the basis of all three responses together: (1) "How did

you feel," asked about the first conscious moment after the birth; (2) "Summing it all up, how would you say you feel about the childbirth experience in general?"; (3) "Do you want another baby?" and if so, "Would you do it all the same way, or is there anything you would change?" The scale ran from 1 (very negative) to 6 (peak experience).

Woman's Attitude toward the Baby on First View (FSVIEW)

The first-view index ranges from one to nine. It is based on the mother's verbal descriptions of her first two encounters with her infant. These verbal descriptions were in reply to the question: "What did he / she look like?" This neutral question appeared to be effective in eliciting negative material, i.e., mothers described the baby as "ugly," "with hair sticking up all over," "horrible . . . covered with scratches . . . head all out of shape," etc.

Feeding Persistence (FEED)

This variable was measured much the same way in 1965–69 as in 1973–76. All bottle-feeders were scored 1. Then breast-feeders were scored 2 if they breast-fed one month, 3 if they breast-fed two months, and so on up to a maximum of 9 (breast-fed eight months or longer).

VARIABLES USED IN THE MOTHERING AND FATHERING MODELS (CHAPTER 7)

Preparation Level (WPREP)

This variable is defined above in connection with the chapter 3 model to predict preparation.

Level of Awareness (AWARE)

This variable is defined above in connection with the chapter 4 birth-experience models.

Woman's Birth Experience (BESCL)

This variable is defined above in connection with the chapter 4 birth-experience models.

Woman's Attitude toward the Baby on First View (FSVIEW)

This variable is defined above in connection with chapter 5 feeding models.

Feeding Behavior in the First Month (EFDBE)

This variable is defined above in connection with the chapter 5 feeding models.

MOTHER'S PREVIOUS BABY-CARE EXPERIENCE (PREBY)

This scale is made up of the sum of two variables: (*a*) how much experience the woman had had taking care of infants under six weeks of age, coded 1 (none), 2 (some experience), 3 (full charge); and (*b*) the woman's confidence in her ability to care for a newborn baby, coded from 1 (not at all confident) to 4 (very confident).

The alpha reliability of this scale is .460.

PREPARTUM PLANS CONCERNING BABY CARE (PREPL)

This variable is made up of the sum of three standardized variables (causing them to be weighted equally). These are: (*a*) whether or not the mother plans to have rooming-in—coded 1 for "definitely nursery"; 2, "leaning toward nursery"; 3, "leaning toward rooming-in"; 4, "definitely rooming-in"; (*b*) why the mother planned rooming-in or nursery care—coded 1 for nursery because doesn't want to be bothered; 2, nursery because better for baby *and* doesn't want to be bothered; 3, rooming-in for practical reasons; 4, rooming-in for love reasons; (*c*) same as third item, choice of feeding mode and intended duration, presented under "Wife's Prepartum Feeding Intentions WFIN" in connection with chapter 5 feeding models above.

The alpha reliability of this scale is .794.

CONTACT WITH MOTHER (CONT)

This variable measures, to the nearest hour, the average number of hours per day in the first three days that mother and baby were together.

The amount of contact was actually assessed in several different ways. Contact measure A was defined as the number of minutes the mother spent with the baby in the first hour after birth. Contact measure B was defined as the number of hours (or fractions thereof) that mother and baby were together in the first twelve hours after birth. Contact measure C was the average number of hours per day spent together in the first three days after birth. The correlations between these measures were: $r_{AB} = .588$; $r_{AC} = .426$; $r_{BC} = .594$.

Several exploratory regression analyses indicated that the structural relationships involving contact were essentially the same no matter which of these measures was selected as a predictor of mothering, and the amount of explained variance in mothering was unchanged from one measure to another. In no case was the path from contact to mothering significantly different from zero. However, as would be expected, the explained variance in the contact measure itself was largest for measure C (three-day contact): 55 percent in comparison with 36 percent and 25 percent for the other two measures. Accordingly, three-day contact was the measure selected for inclusion in the model to explain mothering behavior.

MOTHERING BEHAVIOR (MOTH)

This scale is the sum of scores on seven variables measuring the extent or the quality of interaction between mother and baby. (The unweighted raw scores were summed, with the exception that the score for need feeding was multiplied by two.)

1. The first item is how the mother felt about holding the baby for the first time, coded from 1 (definitely negative) to 6 (overjoyed).
2. The type of feeding schedule in use at the time of the mother's postpartum interview was weighted by a factor of 2. This was scored as: 1, feeding on a rigid schedule; 2, semi-scheduled feeding; 3, feeding according to baby's needs.
3. Amount of crying measured the woman's report of the number of hours the baby cried in the twenty-four hours preceding the postpartum interview. This was coded from 1 (cries four or more hours per day) to 6 (cries less than one-half hour per day).
4. The women were asked how they felt about caring for a newborn. Answers were coded from 1 (strong negative) to 6 (strong positive).
5. Women were asked what they did when the baby cried. Answers were scored as follows: 1, "let cry" is woman's first response; 2, does other things, but lets baby cry regularly; 3, other things, but lets baby cry occasionally; 4, somewhat solicitous, letting cry not mentioned; 5, very solicitous, does everything can think of.
6. Women were asked how they felt when the baby cried. Answers were coded as follows: 1, no concern for baby, negative emotions; 2, neutral, crying doesn't bother her; 3, some concern for baby, some neutral or negative feelings; 4, mild concern for baby; 5, overriding concern for baby.
7. At the six-month phone check, women were asked when they first "felt like a mother." Answers were coded as follows: 0, haven't yet; 1, in fifth or sixth month; 2, during third or fourth month; 3, during second month; 4, during first month; 5, between end of first week and beginning of fourth week; 6, three to four days to one week; 7, in hospital, or within first three days; 8, at once, or during pregnancy.
   The alpha reliability of this scale is .590.

CRYING

This variable is the same as the third item in the mothering scale (MOTH), above.

MATERNAL RESPONSIVENESS

This scale is the sum of items 1, 2, 4, 5, and 6 of the mothering scale (MOTH), above.

THE CONTACT DUMMY VARIABLE

Women who were with their infants thirty or more minutes in the first hour were scored 1, other women were scored 0.

THE FEEDING DUMMY VARIABLE

Women who breast-fed their children in the first hour after birth were scored 1, other women were scored 0.

HUSBAND PARTICIPATION (HPART)

This variable is described above in connection with the chapter 4 birth-experience models.

MAN'S BIRTH EXPERIENCE (MBESCL)

This variable is described above in connection with the chapter 4 birth-experience models.

FATHER'S PREVIOUS BABY-CARE EXPERIENCE (PREEX)

This scale was formed by adding responses from two questions: (a) "Have you been around newborn babies very much?"—with answers coded: 1 = none; 2 = a little; 3 = a lot. (b) "How much do you know about how to care for a newborn?"—with answers coded: 1 = nothing; 2 = not much; 3 = some; 4 = a lot; 5 = all.

The alpha reliability of this scale is .539.

FATHER'S ATTITUDE TOWARD BABY UPON FIRST SEEING IT (FFSVI)

This variable was the husband's response to "What did the baby look like," asked about the first glimpse he had of the baby—coded: 1 = definitely negative to 6 = enthusiastic, with 3 = neutral.

FATHERING (FATH)

This scale was formed as the sum of four variables, with the last variable weighted by 3. (a) How the father felt about holding the baby for the first time—coded from 1 = definitely negative to 6 = overjoyed, with 3 = neutral; (b) How the father responded when the baby cried—with 1 = let cry or call wife to get baby; 2 = other things first, but let cry regularly; 3 = other things first, but let cry occasionally; 4 = somewhat solicitous, let cry not mentioned; 5 = very solicitous, does everything can think of; (c) How the father felt when the baby cried—with 1 = negative emotions toward baby, no concern for baby; 2 = neutral, doesn't bother father: "That's what babies do"; 3 = some concern, but some neutral or negative feelings; 4 = mild concern for

baby; 5 = overriding concern for baby; (d) Whether the father picked up the baby when it cried (answers weighted by 3): 1 = not mentioned, or tells wife to pick up baby; 2 = picks up if wife asks or wife busy; 3 = picks up on his own.

The alpha reliability of this scale is .698.

REFERENCES

Abramson, J. H.; Singh, A. R.; and Mbambo, V. 1969. Antenatal stress and the baby's development. *Archives of Diseases of Childhood* 37:42-49.

Ainsworth, M. D. S. 1969. Object relations, dependency, and attachment: A theoretical review of mother-infant relationship. *Child Development* 40:969-1025.

Ainsworth, M. D. S. 1973. The development of infant-mother attachment. In *Review of child development research,* ed. B. M. Caldwell and H. N. Ricciuti. Chicago: University of Chicago Press.

Ainsworth, M. D. S., and Bell, S. M. 1974. Some contemporary patterns of mother-infant interaction in the feeding situation. In *Stimulation in early infancy,* ed. J. A. Ambrose. London: Academic Press.

Ainsworth, M. D. S.; Bell, S. M.; and Stayton, D. J. 1971. Individual differences in strange situation behavior of one-year-olds. In *The origins of human social relations,* ed. H. R. Schaffer. London: Academic Press.

Ainsworth, M. D. S.; Bell, S. M.; and Stayton, D. J. 1974. Infant-mother attachment and social development: Socialisation as a product of reciprocal responsiveness to signals. In *The integration of a child into a social world,* ed. M. P. M. Richards. London: Cambridge University Press.

Aldous, J. 1969. Occupational characteristics and males' role performance in the family. *Journal of Marriage and the Family* 31:707-12.

Anderson, B., and Standley, K. 1976. A Methodology for Observation of the Childbirth Environment. Paper presented at meetings of the American Psychological Association, Washington, D.C.

Andrew, J. M. 1970. Recovery from surgery with and without preparatory instruction for three coping styles. *Journal of Personality and Social Psychology* 15:223-26.

Arbeit, S. A. 1975. A Study of Women During Their First Pregnancy. Ph.D. dissertation, Yale University.

Arms, S. 1975. *Immaculate deception.* Boston: Houghton Mifflin.

Arnstein, H. 1972. The crisis of becoming a father. *Sexual Behavior* 2:42-47.

Baier, P. N. d. Cited in Corea 1977.

Bain, K. 1948. The incidence of breast feeding in hospitals in the United States. *Pediatrics* 2:313.

Ban, P. L., and Lewis, M. 1974. Mothers and fathers, girls and boys: Attachment behavior in the one-year-old. *Merrill-Palmer Quarterly* 20:195-204.

Bane, M. J. 1976. *Here to stay.* New York: Basic Books.

Banta, H. D., and Thacker, S. B. 1979. *Costs and benefits of electronic fetal monitoring: A review of the literature.* NCHS Research Report, Series 79-3245. Washington, D.C. Department of HEW. April 1979.

Barnett, C. R.; Leiderman, P. H.; Grobstein, R.; and Klaus, M. H. 1970. Neonatal separation: The maternal side of interactional deprivation. *Pediatrics* 45:197-205.

Beall, E. 1977. Personal communication.

Becker, W. C. 1964. Consequences of different kinds of parental discipline. In *Review of child development research,* ed. M. L. Hoffman and L. W. Hoffman. New York: Russell Sage.

Beckwith, L. 1972. Relationships between infants' social behavior and their mothers' behavior. *Child Development* 43:397-411.

Bell, S. M. 1970. The development of the concept of object as related to infant-mother attachment. *Child Development* 41:291-311.

Bell, S. M., and Ainsworth, M. D. S. 1972. Infant crying and maternal responsiveness. *Child Development* 43:1171-90.

Belmont, N. 1976. Levana; or, how to raise up children. In *Family and society,* ed. R. Forster and O. Ranum. Baltimore: Johns Hopkins University Press.

Benedek, T. 1970a. Fatherhood and providing. In *Parenthood: Its psychology and psychopathology,* ed. A. Benedek and T. Benedek. Boston: Little, Brown.

Benedek. T. 1970b. The psychobiology of pregnancy. In *Parenthood: Its psychology and psychopathology,* ed. A. Benedek and T. Benedek. Boston: Little, Brown.

Benson, L. 1967. *Fatherhood: A sociological perspective.* New York: Random House.

Bergström-Walen, M. B. 1963. The efficacy of education for childbirth. *Journal of Psychosomatic Research* 7:131-46.

Bernal, J. F. 1972. Crying during the first ten days and maternal responses. *Developmental Medicine and Child Neurology* 14:362-72.

Bernard, J. 1975. Adolescence and socialization for motherhood. In *Adolescence in the life cycle,* ed. S. E. Dragastin and G. H. Elder. New York: Halstead.

Bernstein, R., and Cyr. F. E. 1957. A study of interviews with husbands in a prenatal and child health program. *Social Casework* 38:473-80.

Bibring, G. L.; Dwyer, T. F.; Huntington, D. C.; and Valenstein, A. F. 1961. A study of the psychological processes in pregnancy and of the earliest mother-child relationships. in *Psychoanalytic study of the child,* vol. 16. New York: International Universities Press.

Bing, E. 1967. *Six practical lessons for an easier childbirth.* New York: Grosset and Dunlap.

Bing, E. 1970. *The adventure of birth.* New York: Simon and Schuster.

Blake, J. 1972. Coercive pronatalism and American population policy. In Commission on Population Growth and the American Future, *Aspects of population growth policy.* Research reports, ed. R. Parke and C. F. Westoff, vol. 6. U.S. Government Printing Office.

Blood, R. D., and Wolfe, D. M. 1960. *Husbands and wives.* Glencoe, Ill.: Free Press.

Borgstedt, A. D., and Rosen, M. G. 1968. Medication during labor correlated with behavior and EEG of the newborn. *American Journal of Diseases of Children* 115:21-24.

Bott, E. 1957. *Family and social network.* London: Tavistock.

Bowes, W. A.; Brackbill, Y.; Conway, E.; and Steinschneider, A. 1970. *The effects of obstetrical medication on fetus and infant*. Monographs of the society for research in child development. 35, no. 4.

Bowlby, J. 1951. *Maternal care and mental health*. Geneva: World Health Organization.

Bowlby, J. 1969. *Attachment and loss*. Vol. 1 in *Attachment*. London: Hogarth.

Brackbill, Y.; Kane, J.; Maniello, R. L.; and Abramson, D. 1974. Obstetric premedication and infant outcome. *American Journal of Obstetrics and Gynecology* 118:377–84.

Bradley, R. A. 1974. *Husband-coached childbirth*. New York: Harper and Row.

Brazelton, T. B. 1961. Psychophysiologic reaction in the neonate: II. Effects of maternal medication on the neonate and his behavior. *Journal of Pediatrics* 58:513–18.

Brazelton, T. B. 1970. Effect of prenatal drugs on the behavior of the neonate. *American Journal of Psychiatry* 126:95–100.

Breen, D. 1975. *The birth of a first child*. London: Tavistock.

Brewer, T. H. 1966. *Metabolic toxemia of late pregnancy*. Springfield, Ill.: Charles C. Thomas.

Bronfenbrenner, U. 1958. Socialization and social class through time and space. In *Readings in social psychology*, ed. E. E. Maccoby; T. M. Newcomb; and E. L. Hartley. 3rd ed. New York: Holt, Rinehart, and Winston.

Broverman, I. K.; Broverman, D. M.; Clarkson, F. E.; Rosenkrantz, P. S.; and Vogel, S. R. 1970. Sex-role stereotypes and clinical judgments of mental health. *Journal of Consulting and Clinical Psychology* 34:1–7.

Brown, R. 1965. *Social psychology*. New York: Free Press.

Busfield, J. 1974. Ideologies and reproduction. In *The integration of a child into a social world*, ed. M. P. M. Richards. London: Cambridge University Press.

Campbell, A.; Converse, P. E.; and Rodgers, W. L. 1976. *The quality of American life*. New York: Russell Sage.

Caplan, G. 1960. Patterns of parental response to the crisis of premature birth. *Psychiatry* 23:365–74.

Carroll, S. J., and Morrison, P. A. 1976. *National longitudinal study of high school seniors: An agenda for policy research*. Santa Monica, Calif.: The Rand Corporation.

Chabon, I. 1966. *Awake and aware*. New York: Delacorte.

Charles, A. G.; Norr, K. L.; Block, C. R.; Meyering, S.; and Meyers, E. 1978. Obstetric and psychological effects of psychoprophylactic preparation for childbirth. *American Journal of Obstetrics and Gynecology* 131:44–52.

Cherlin, A. 1977. The effect of children on marital dissolution. *Demography* 14:265–72.

Chertok, L. 1959. *Psychosomatic methods in painless childbirth*. London: Pergamon.

Chertok, L. 1969. *Motherhood and personality*. London: Tavistock.

Chilman, C., and Elbaum, L. 1976. *The parent experience: A study of satisfactions and dissatisfactions of fathers and mothers*. School of Social Welfare, Research Report no. 1. Milwaukee: University of Wisconsin.

Christensen, H. T. 1968. Children in the family: Relationship of number and spacing to marital success. *Journal of Marriage and the Family* 30:283–89.

Clarke-Stewart, A. 1977. The Father's Impact on Mother and Child. Paper presented to the Society for Research in Child Development, New Orleans, March. Cited in Lamb, M. E., and Stevenson, M. B. 1978. Father-infant relationships: Their nature and importance. *Youth and Society* 9:277-98.

Cohen, M. B. 1966. Personal identity and sexual identity. *Psychiatry* 29:1-14.

Cohen, S. N., and Olson, W. A. 1970. Drugs that depress the newborn infant. *Pediatric Clinics of North America* 17:835-50.

Coleman, J. S.; Campbell, E. Q.; Hobson, C. J.; McPartland, J.; Mood, A. M.; Weinfall, F. D.; and York, R. L. 1966. *The equality of educational opportunity.* Washington, D.C.: U.S. Department of Health, Education, and Welfare.

Coley, S. B., and James, B. E. 1976. Delivery: A trauma for fathers? *The Family Coordinator* 25:359-64.

Colman, A. D., and Colman, L. L. 1971. *Pregnancy: The psychological experience.* New York: Herder & Herder, 1971.

Committee on Maternal Nutrition, National Research Council. 1970. *Maternal nutrition and the course of pregnancy.* Washington, D.C.: National Academy of Sciences.

Committee on Nutrition, American Academy of Pediatrics. 1976. Commentary on breast-feeding and infant care, including proposed standards for families. *Pediatrics* 57:278-85.

Condry, J., and Condry, S. 1976. Sex differences: A study of the eye of the beholder. *Child Development* 47:812-19.

Constantinople, A. 1973. Masculinity-femininity: An exception to a famous dictum? *Psychological Bulletin* 80: 389-407.

Consumer Reports. 1977. Is breast-feeding best for babies? *Consumer Reports* 42:152-57.

Corea, G. 1977. *The hidden malpractice.* New York: Morrow.

Cowan, C. P.; Cowan, P. A.; Cole, L.; and Cole, J. D. 1978. The impact of a first child's birth on the couple's relationship. In *The first child and family formation,* ed. W. B. Miller and L. F. Newman. Chapel Hill, N. C.: Carolina Population Center.

Cronewett, L. R., and Newmark, L. L. 1974. Fathers' responses to childbirth. *Nursing Research* 23:210-17.

Curtis, J. L. 1955. A psychiatric study of fifty-five expectant fathers. *U.S. Armed Forces Medical Journal* 6:937-50.

Cutright. P. 1971. Income and family events: Marital stability. *Journal of Marriage and the Family* 33:291-306.

Davids, A., and DeVault, S. 1962. Maternal anxiety during pregnancy and childbirth abnormalities. *Psychosomatic Medicine* 24:464-70.

Davids, A.; DeVault, S.; and Talmadge, M. 1961. Psychological study of emotional factors in pregnancy. *Psychosomatic Medicine* 23:93-103.

Davids, A.; Holden, R. H.; and Gray, G. B. 1963. Maternal anxiety during pregnancy and adequacy of mother and child adjustment eight months following childbirth. *Child Development* 34:993-1002.

Davids, A., and Rosengren, W. R. 1962. Social stability and psychological adjustment during pregnancy. *Psychosomatic Medicine* 24:579-83.

Davis, F. 1961. *Passage through crisis.* Indianapolis: Bobbs-Merrill.

DeChateau, P. 1976. The influence of early contact on maternal and infant behavior in primiparae. *Birth and the Family Journal* 3:149-55.

Deutscher, M. 1970. Brief family therapy in the course of first pregnancy: A clinical note. *Contemporary Psychoanalysis* 7:21-35.

Dick-Read, G. 1959. *Childbirth without fear.* New York: Harper and Row.

Doering, S. G. 1975. Femininity Scales and First Pregnancy. Ph.D. dissertation, Johns Hopkins University.

Doering, S. G., and Entwisle, D. R. 1975. Preparation during pregnancy and ability to cope with labor and delivery. *American Journal of Orthopsychiatry* 45:825-37.

Doering, S. G.; Entwisle, D. R.; and Quinlan, D. 1980. Modeling the quality of women's birth experience. *Journal of Health and Social Behavior* 21:12-21.

Douvan, E. 1978. The Marriage Role: 1957-1976. Revised from paper presented at American Psychological Association meetings, Toronto, September.

Duncan, O. D. 1975. *Introduction to structural equation models.* New York: Academic Press.

Duncan, O. D.; Schuman, H.; and Duncan, B. 1974. *Social change in a metropolitan community.* New York: Russell Sage.

Dyer, E. D. 1963. Parenthood as crisis: A re-study. *Marriage and Family Living* 25:196-201.

Eastman, N. J., and Russell, K. P. 1970. *Expectant motherhood.* 5th ed. Boston: Little, Brown.

Egbert, L. D.; Battit, G. E.; Welch, C. E.; and Bartlett, M. K. 1964. Reduction of postoperative pain by encouragement and instruction of patients. *New England Journal of Medicine* 270:825-29.

Eichler, L. S.; Winickoff, S. A.; Grossman, F. K.; Anzalone, M. K.; and Gofseyeff, M. H. 1977. Adaptation to Pregnancy, Birth, and Early Parenting: A Preliminary View. Presented at American Psychological Association meetings, San Francisco.

Eldridge, R. 1970. How to give birth to a daughter. *Redbook,* May, 135:81 ff.

Elkins, V. H. 1976. *The rights of the pregnant patient.* New York: Two Continents.

Elmer, E., and Gregg, G. S. 1967. Developmental characteristics of abused children. *Pediatrics* 40:596-602.

Enkin, M. W.; Smith, S. L.; Dermer, S. W.; and Emmett, J. O. 1972. An adequately controlled study of the effectiveness of PPM training. In *Psychosomatic medicine in obstetrics and gynecology, proceedings of the Third International Congress of Psychosomatic Medicine in Obstetrics and Gynecology,* ed. N. Morris. Basel: Karger.

Erickson, M. T. 1967. Method for frequent assessment of symptomatology during pregnancy. *Psychological Reports* 20:447-50.

Etzioni, Amitai. 1977. The family: Is it obsolete? *Journal of Current Social Issues* 14:4-9.

Fanaroff, A. A.; Kennell, J. H.; and Klaus, M. H. 1972. Follow-up of low birth-weight infants—the predictive value of maternal visiting patterns. *Pediatrics* 49:288-90.

Fawcett, J. T. 1978. The value and cost of the first child. In *The First Child and Family Formation,* ed. W. B. Miller and L. F. Newman. Chapel Hill, N.C.: Carolina Population Center.

Fein, R. A. 1974. Men's Experiences before and after the Birth of a First Child: Dependence, Marital Sharing, and Anxiety. Ph.D. dissertation, Harvard University.

Fein, R. A. 1978. Consideration of men's experiences and the birth of a first child. In *The First Child and Family Formation,* ed. W. B. Miller and L. F. Newman. Chapel Hill, N.C.: Carolina Population Center.

Feldman, H. Development of the husband-wife relationship. Cited in D. F. Hobbs, 1965.

Feldman, H., and Rogoff, M. 1977. Correlates of Changes in Marital Satisfaction with the Birth of a First Child. Mimeograph, Department of Child Development and Family Relationships, Cornell University.

Fielding, W. L. 1971. *Pregnancy: The best state of the union.* Freeport, Me.: Bond Wheelwright.

Flapan, M. 1969. A paradigm for the analysis of childbearing motivations of married women prior to birth of the first child. *American Journal of Orthopsychiatry* 39:402-17.

Foundation for Child Development, National Survey of Children. 1977. *Summary of preliminary results.* New York.

Freeman, T. 1951. Pregnancy as a precipitant of mental illness in men. *British Journal of Medical Psychology* 24:49-54.

Furstenberg, F. F., Jr. 1976. *Unplanned parenthood.* New York: Free Press.

Gerrard, J. W. 1974. Breast-feeding: Second thoughts. *Pediatrics* 54:757-64.

Gibbons, L. K. 1976. Analysis of the Rise in C-Sections in Baltimore. D.P.H. dissertation, Johns Hopkins School of Hygiene and Public Health.

Gladieux, J. D. 1978. Pregnancy—the transition to parenthood. In *The First Child and Family Formation,* ed. W. B. Miller and L. F. Newman. Chapel Hill, N.C.: Carolina Population Center.

Goetsch, C. 1966. Fathers in the delivery room—helpful and supportive. *Hospital Topics* 44:104-5.

Golluber, M. 1976. A comment on the need for father-infant postpartal interaction. *Journal of Obstetrics and Gynecology and Neonatal Nursing* 5:17-20.

Gordon, R. E., and Gordon, K. K. 1960. Social factors in prevention of postpartum emotional problems. *Obstetrics and Gynecology* 15:433-38.

Gordon, R. E., and Gordon, K. K. 1967. Factors in postpartum emotional adjustment. *American Journal of Orthopsychiatry* 37:359-60.

Gorsuch, R. L., and Key, M. K. 1974. Abnormalities of pregnancy as a function of anxiety and life stress. *Psychosomatic Medicine* 36:352-62.

Goschen-Gottstein, E. R. 1966. *Marriage and first pregnancy.* London: Tavistock.

Gough, H. G. 1952. Identifying psychological femininity. *Educational and Psychological Measurement* 12:427-39.

Greenberg, M., and Morris, N. 1974. Engrossment: The newborn's impact upon the father. *American Journal of Orthopsychiatry* 44:520-31.

Greenberg, M.; Rosenberg, I.; and Lind, J. 1973. First mothers rooming-in with their newborns: Its impact on the mother. *American Journal of Orthopsychiatry* 43:783-88.

Greenhill, J. P., and Friedman, E. A. 1974. *Biological principles and modern practice of obstetrics.* Philadelphia: Saunders.

Grey, J.; Cutter, C.; Dean, J.; and Kempe, C. H. The Denver Predictive Study from the National Center for the Prevention and Treatment of Child Abuse and Neglect. Unpublished paper, University of Colorado Medical Center. Cited in Macfarlane 1977.

Grimm, E. 1961. Psychological tension in pregnancy. *Psychosomatic Medicine* 23:520–27.

Grossman, F. K. 1978. Fathers Are Parents Too. Mimeograph, Department of Psychology, Boston University.

Guttmacher, A. F. 1950. *Having a baby.* New York: Signet.

Haas, S. 1952. Psychiatric implications in gynecology and obstetrics. In *Psychology of physical illness,* ed. L. Bellak. New York: Grune & Stratton.

Haire, D. 1972. *The cultural warping of childbirth.* Milwaukee: International Childbirth Education Association.

Haley, A. 1976. *Roots.* Garden City, N.Y.: Doubleday.

Hall, R. E. 1972. *Nine months reading.* New York: Bantam.

Halstead, J., and Frederickson, T. 1978. Evaluation of a prepared childbirth program. *Journal of Obstetrical and Gynecological and Neonatal Nursing* 7:39–42.

Harfouche, J. K. 1970. The importance of breastfeeding. *Journal of Tropical Pediatrics* 16:135–75.

Harlow, N. 1975. *Sharing the children.* New York: Harper Colophon.

Hartman, A. A., and Nicolay, R. C. 1966. Sexually deviant behavior in expectant fathers. *Journal of Abnormal and Social Psychology* 71:232–34.

Haverkamp, A. D.; Thompson, H. E.; McFee, J. G.; and Cetrulo, C, 1976. The evaluation of continuous fetal heart rate monitoring in high-risk pregnancy. *American Journal of Obstetrics and Gynecology* 125:310–20.

Heinstein, M. I. 1967. Expressed attitudes and feelings of pregnant women and their relation to physical complications of pregnancy. *Merrill-Palmer Quarterly* 13:217–36.

Heise, D. 1976. *Causal analysis.* New York: Wiley.

Helper, M. M. 1955. Learning theory and the self-concept. *Journal of Abnormal and Social Psychology* 51:184–94.

Henneborn, W. J., and Cogan, R. 1975. The effect of husband participation on reported pain and probability of medication during labor and birth. *Journal of Psychosomatic Research,* 19, 215–22.

Herzog, A. R.; Bachman, J. G.; and Johnston, L. D. 1979. Young people look at changing sex roles. *Institute for Social Research Newsletter.*

Hess, R. D. 1970. Class and ethnic influences upon socialization. In *Carmichael's manual of child psychology,* ed. P. H. Mussen. New York: Wiley.

Hill, F. L. 1967. Infant feeding: Historical and current. *Pediatric Clinics of North America* 14:255–68.

Hill, M. 1974. Models of travel to work. In *Five thousand American families,* ed. J. Morgan et al. Ann Arbor: Survey Research Center, University of Michigan.

Hill, R. 1951. *The family: A dynamic interpretation.* 2nd ed. New York: Dryden.

Hill R., and Aldous, J. 1969. Socialization for marriage and parenthood. In *Handbook of socialization theory and research,* ed. D. Goslin, Chicago: Rand McNally & Co.

Hill, R., and Rogers, R. 1964. The developmental approach. In *Handbook of Marriage and the Family,* ed. H. T. Christensen. Chicago: Rand McNally & Co.

Hirschman, C., and Hendershot, G. E. 1979. *Trends in breast-feeding among American mothers.* NCHS Vital and Health Statistics, ser. 23, no. 3; DHEW publication 79-1979. Washington, D.C.: U.S. Government Printing Office.

Hirschman, C., and Sweet, J. A. 1974. Social background and breast-feeding among American mothers. *Social Biology* 21:39-57.

Hobbs, D. F. 1965. Parenthood as crisis: A third study. *Journal of Marriage and the Family* 27:367-72.

Hobbs, D. F. 1968. Transition to parenthood: A replication and an extension. *Journal of Marriage and the Family* 30:413-16.

Hobbs, D. F., and Cole, S. P. 1976. Transition to parenthood: A decade replication. *Journal of Marriage and the Family* 38:723-31.

Hoffman, L. W. 1963. Parental power relations and the division of household tasks. In *The employed mother in America,* ed. F. I. Nye and L. W. Hoffman. Chicago: Rand McNally & Co.

Hoffman, L. W., and Hoffman, M. L. 1973. The value of children to parents. In *Psychological perspectives on population,* ed. J. T. Fawcett. New York: Basic.

Hoffman, L. W., and Manis, J. 1978*a.* Why couples choose parenthood. *Institute for Social Research Newsletter.*

Hoffman, L. W., and Manis, J. D. 1978*b.* Influences of children on marital interaction and parental satisfactions and dissatisfactions. In *Child influences on marital and family interaction,* ed. R. W. Lerner and G. B. Spanier. New York: Academic Press.

Hoffman, L. W., and Nye, F. I. 1974. *Working mothers.* San Francisco: Jossey-Bass.

Hoffman, L. W., and Wyatt, F. 1960. Social changes and motivations for having larger families. *Merrill-Palmer Quarterly* 6:235-44.

Hoge, D. R. 1976. Changes in college students' value patterns in the 1950's, 1960's, and 1970's. *Sociology of Education* 49:155-63.

Holmstrom, L. L. 1973. *The two-career family.* Cambridge, Mass.: Schenkman.

Horney, K. 1926. The flight from womanhood: The masculinity-complex in women as viewed by men and women. *International Journal of Psychoanalysis* 7:324-39.

Hubert, J. 1974. Social factors in pregnancy and childbirth. In *The integration of a child into a social world,* ed. M. P. M. Richards. London: Cambridge University Press.

Hughey, M. J.; McElin, T. W.; and Young, T. 1978. Maternal and fetal outcome of Lamaze-prepared patients. *Journal of Obstetrics and Gynecology* 51:643-47.

Hunter, R. S.; Kilstrom, N.; Kraybill, E. N.; and Loda, F. N.d. Antecedents of Child Abuse and Neglect in Premature Infants: A Prospective Study in a Newborn Intensive Care Unit. Mimeograph, Department of Pediatrics and Psychiatry, University of North Carolina School of Medicine, Chapel Hill, N.C.

Huttel, F.; Mitchell, I.; Fischer, W. M.; and Meyer, A. E. 1972. A quantitative evaluation of psychoprophylaxis in childbirth. *Journal of Psychosomatic Research* 16:81-92.

International Pediatric Association Seminar. 1975. Recommendations for action programs to encourage breast-feeding. *ACTA Paediatrica Scandinavica* 65:275-77.

Jackson, E. B.; Wilkin, L. C.; and Auerbach, M. 1956. Statistical report on incidence and duration of breast feeding in relation to personal, social, and hospital maternity factors. *Pediatrics* 17:700-715.

James, L. L. 1960. The effect of pain relief for labor and delivery on the fetus and newborn. *Anesthesiology* 21:405-30.

Janis, I. L. 1958. *Psychological stress.* New York: Wiley.

Jelliffe, D. B., and Jelliffe, E. F. P. 1978. *Human milk in the modern world.* New York: Oxford.

Jones, E. 1942. Psychology and childbirth. *Lancet* 1:695-96.

Jones, O. H. Caesarean section in present-day obstetrics. *American Journal of Obstetrics and Gynecology* 126:521-30.

Jöreskog, K. C., and Sörbom, D. 1978. *LISREL: Version IV.* Chicago: International Educational Resources.

Kanter, R. M. 1976. *Work and family in America.* New York: Russell Sage.

Kanter, R. M.; Jaffe, D.; and Weisberg, D. K. 1975. Coupling, parenting, and the presence of others. Intimate relationships in communal households. *The Family Coordinator* 24:433-52.

Kaplan, D. M., and Mason, E. A. 1960. Maternal reactions to premature birth viewed as an acute emotional disorder. *American Journal of Orthopsychiatry* 30:539-47.

Kaplan, H. S., and Anderson, D. C. 1976. Sexual revolution—the time of the woman. *New York Times Magazine,* July 4, 1976.

Kapp, F. T.; Hornstein, S.; and Graham, V. 1963. Some psychological functions in prolonged labor due to inefficient uterine action. *Comprehensive Psychiatry* 4:9-18.

Karmel, M. 1959. *Thank you, Dr. Lamaze.* New York: Lippincott.

Kartchner, F. D. 1950. A study of emotional reactions during labor. *American Journal of Obstetrics and Gynecology* 60:19-29.

Kelly, J. U. 1962. Effect of fear upon uterine mobility. *American Journal of Obstetrics and Gynecology* 83:576-81.

Kennell, J. H.; Jerauld, R.; Wolfe, H.; Chesler, D.; Kreger, N. C.; McAlpine, W.; Steffa, M.; and Klaus, M. H. 1974. Maternal behavior one year after early and extended post-partum contact. *Developmental Medicine and Child Neurology* 16:172-79.

Kennell, J. H.; Trause, M. A.; and Klaus, M. H. 1975. Evidence for a sensitive period in the human mother. In *Parent-infant interaction.* CIBA Foundation Symposium 33 (new series). Amsterdam: Elsevier.

Kinsey, A. C.; Pomeroy, W. B.; and Martin, C. E. 1948. *Sexual behavior in the human male.* Philadelphia: W. B. Saunders Co.

Kinsey, A. C.; Pomeroy, W. B.; Martin, C. E.; and Gebhard, P. H. 1953. *Sexual behavior in the human female.* Philadelphia: W. B. Saunders Co.

Kitzinger, S. 1972. *The experience of childbirth.* Baltimore: Penguin.

Klassen, D. F. 1975. Cesarean section rates: Time, trends, and comparisons among hospital sizes, census regions, and teaching and nonteaching hospitals. *PAS Reporter* vol. 13, no. 19.

Klatsky, S. N.d. *Patterns of contact with relatives.* Washington, D.C.: ASA Rose Monograph series.

Klaus, M. H., and Kennell, J. H. 1976a. Parent-to-infant attachment. In *Recent advances in pediatrics,* ed. D. Hull, no. 5. Edinburgh: Churchill Livingstone.

Klaus, M. H., and Kennell, J. H. 1976b. *Maternal-infant bonding.* St. Louis: C. V. Mosby Co.

Klein, H. R.; Potter, H. W.; and Dyk, R. B. 1950. *Anxiety in pregnancy and childbirth.* New York: Hoeber.

Klein, M., and Stern, L. 1971. Low birth weight and the battered child syndrome. *American Journal of Diseases of Children* 122:15-18.

Kloosterman, G. J. 1978. The Dutch system of home births. In *The place of birth,* ed. S. Kitzinger and J. A. Davis. New York: Oxford.

Klopfer, F. J.; Cogan, R.; and Henneborn, W. J. 1975. Second stage medical intervention and pain during childbirth. *Journal of Psychosomatic Research* 19:289-93.

Klopfer, P. 1971. Mother love: What turns it on? *American Scientist* 49:404-7.

Kohn, M. 1969. *Class and conformity.* Homewood, Ill.: Dorsey.

Korner, A. F. 1974. The effect of the infant's state, level of arousal, sex, and ontogenetic stage on the caregiver. In *The effect of the infant on its caregiver,* ed. M. Lewis and L. A. Rosenblum. New York: Wiley.

Kotelchuck, M. 1975. Cited in M. E. Lamb and M. B. Stevenson. 1978. Father-infant relationships: Their nature and importance. *Youth and Society* 9:277-98.

Kron, R. E.; Stein, M.; and Goddard, K. E. 1966. Newborn sucking behavior affected by obstetric sedation. *Pediatrics* 37:1012-16.

Laird, M. D., and Hogan, M. 1956. An elective program on preparation for childbirth at the Sloane Hospital for Women: May 1951 to June 1953. *American Journal of Obstetrics and Gynecology* 72:641-47.

Lamb, M. E. 1976. *The role of the father in child development.* New York: Wiley.

Lamb, M. E. 1977. Father-infant and mother-infant interaction in the first year of life. *Child Development* 48:167-81.

Lamb, M. E. 1978. Influence of the child on marital quality and family interaction during the prenatal, perinatal, and infancy periods. In *Child influences on marital and family interaction,* ed. R. M. Lerner and G. B. Spanier. New York: Academic Press.

Landis, J. T. 1952. Intent toward conception and the pregnancy experience. *American Sociological Review* 17:616-20.

Landis, J. T.; Poffenberger, T.; and Poffenberger, S. 1950. The effects of first pregnancy upon the sexual adjustment of 212 couples. *American Sociological Review* 15:766-72.

Lapidus, L. B. 1968. The Relationship between Cognitive Control and Reactions to Stress: A Study of Mastery in the Anticipatory Phase of Childbirth. Ph.D. dissertation, New York University.

LaRossa, R. 1976. The First Pregnancy as a Marital Crisis. Paper presented at meetings of the American Sociological Association, New York.

Larsen, V. L. 1966. Stresses of the childbearing years. *American Journal of Public Health* 56:32-36.

Lee, W. K., and Baggish, M. S. 1976. The effect of unselected intrapartum fetal monitoring. *Obstetrics and Gynecology* 47:516-20.

Leiderman, P. H., and Seashore, M. J. 1975. Mother-infant separation: Some delayed consequences. In *Parent-infant interaction.* CIBA Foundation Symposium 33 (new series). Amsterdam: Elsevier.

LeMasters, E. E. 1957. Parenthood as crisis. *Marriage and Family Living* 19:352–55.

LeVine, R. A. 1977. Child rearing as cultural adaptation. In *Culture and infancy,* ed. P. H. Leiderman, S. R. Tulkin, and A. Rosenfeld. New York: Academic Press.

Levy, J. M., and McGee, R. K. 1975. Childbirth as a crisis. *Journal of Personality and Social Psychology* 31:171–79.

Lewis, M. 1972. State as an infant-environment interaction. *Merrill-Palmer Quarterly* 18:95–121.

Liebenberg, B. 1973. Expectant fathers. In *Psychological aspects of a first pregnancy,* ed. P. M. Shereshefsky and L. J. Yarrow. New York: Raven.

Liefer, A. D. 1970. Effects of Early Temporary Mother-Infant Separation on Later Maternal Behavior in Humans. Ph.D. dissertation, Stanford University.

Lind, J. 1973. Cited in Klaus and Kennell 1976*b*.

Loevinger, J. 1962. Measuring personality patterns of women. *Genetic and Psychological Monographs* 65:53–136.

Lopata, H. Z. 1971. *Occupation housewife.* New York: Oxford University Press.

Lowenthal, M.; Thurnber, M.; and Chiriboga, D. 1974. *Four stages of life.* San Francisco: Jossey-Bass.

Lynch, M. A., and Roberts, J. 1977. Predicting child abuse: Signs of bonding failure in the maternity hospital. *British Medical Journal* 1:624–26.

Lynn, D. B. 1974. *The father: His role in child development.* Monterey, Calif.: Brooks / Cole.

Maas, H., and Kuypers, J. 1974. *From thirty to seventy.* San Francisco: Jossey-Bass.

Maccoby, E. E. 1966. *The development of sex differences.* Stanford, Calif.: Stanford University Press.

McDonald, R. L., and Christakos, A. C. 1963. Relationship of emotional adjustment during pregnancy to obstetrical complications. *American Journal of Obstetrics and Gynecology* 86:341–48.

Macfarlane, A. 1977. *The psychology of childbirth.* Cambridge, Mass: Harvard University Press.

Mann, D.; Woodward, L. F.; and Joseph, N. 1961. *Educating expectant parents.* New York: Visiting Nurse Service of New York.

Maslow, A. 1954. *Motivation and personality.* New York: Harper and Row.

Mason, K. O., and Bumpass, L. L. 1975. U.S. women's sex role ideology. *American Journal of Sociology* 80:1212–19.

Mason, K. O.; Czajka, J. L.; and Arber, S. 1976. Change in U.S. women's sex role attitudes, 1964–1974. *American Sociological Review* 41:573–93.

Masters, W. H., and Johnson, V. E. 1966. *Human sexual response.* Boston: Little, Brown.

Mehl, L. E. 1978. The outcome of home delivery research in the United States. In *The place of birth,* ed. S. Kitzinger and J. A. Davis. New York: Oxford.

Melges, F. T. 1968. Postpartum psychiatric syndromes. *Psychosomatic Medicine* 30:95–108.

Menninger, W. C. 1943. The emotional factors in pregnancy. *Bulletin of Menninger Clinic* 7:15–24.

Meyer, H. F. 1958. Breast feeding in the United States: Extent and possible trend. *Pediatrics* 22:116.

Meyer, H. F. 1968. Breast feeding in the United States. *Clinical Pediatrics* 7:708–15.

Meyerowitz, J., and Feldman, H. 1966. Transition to parenthood. *Psychiatric Research Reports* 20:78–84.

Miller, H. L.; Flannery, F. E.; and Bell, D. 1952. Education for childbirth in private practice. *American Journal of Obstetrics and Gynecology* 63:792–99.

Miller, R. S. 1973. Pregnancy: The Social Meaning of a Physiological Event. Ph.D. dissertation, New York University.

Miller, W. B. 1978. The intendedness and wantedness of the first child. In *The first child and family formation,* ed. W. B. Miller and L. F. Newman. Chapel Hill, N.C.: Carolina Population Center.

Mitchell, R. M., and Klein, T. 1969. *Nine months to go.* New York: Ace.

Moos, R. H. 1968. The development of a menstrual distress questionnaire. *Psychosomatic Medicine* 30:853–67.

Moss, H. A. 1967. Sex, age, and state as determinants of mother-infant interaction. *Merrill-Palmer Quarterly* 13:19–36.

Moss, H. A.; Robson, K. S.; and Pedersen, F. 1969. Determinants of maternal stimulation of infants and consequences of treatment for later reactions to strangers. *Developmental Psychology* 1:239–46.

Mosteller, F., and Tukey, J. W. 1977. *Data analysis and regression.* Reading, Mass.: Addison Wesley.

Nash, J. 1976. Historical and social change in the perception of the role of the father. In *The role of the father in child development,* ed. M. E. Lamb. New York: Wiley.

Newton, N. R. 1952. Attitudes of Mothers of Newborn Babies toward Their Biological Feminine Functions. Ph.D. dissertation, Columbia University.

Newton, N. R. 1955. *Maternal emotions.* New York: Hoeber.

Newton, N. R. 1963. Emotions of pregnancy. *Clinical Obstetrics and Gynecology* 6:639–68.

Newton, N. R. 1970. Effect of psychological environment on childbirth: Combined cross-cultural and experimental approach. *Journal of Cross-Cultural Psychology* 1:85–90.

Newton, N. R. 1971. Psychologic differences between breast and bottle feeding. *The American Journal of Clinical Nutrition* 24:993–1004.

Newton, N. R. 1973. Interrelationships between sexual responsiveness, birth, and breast feeding. In *Contemporary sexual behavior: Critical issues in the 1970's,* ed. J. Zubin and J. Money. Baltimore: Johns Hopkins University Press.

Newton, N. R., and Newton, M. 1962. Mothers' reactions to their newborn babies. *Journal of the American Medical Association* 181:206–11.

Newton, N. R.; Peeler, D.; and Rawlins, C. 1968. The effect of lactation on maternal behavior in mice with comparative data on humans. *Journal of Reproductive Medicine* 1:257–62.

Nie, N. H.; Hull, C. H.; Jenkins, J. G.; Steinbrenner, K.; and Bent, D. H. 1975. *SPSS, statistical package for the social sciences.* 2nd ed. New York: McGraw-Hill.

Niswander, K. R., and Gordon, M. 1972. *The women and their pregnancies.* Philadelphia: Saunders.

Norr, K. L.; Block, C. R.; Charles, A.; Meyering, S.; and Meyers, E. 1977. Explaining pain and enjoyment in childbirth. *Journal of Health and Social Behavior* 18:260–75.

Nuckolls, K. B.; Cassel, J.; and Kaplan, B. H. 1972. Psychosocial assets, life crisis, and the prognosis of pregnancy. *American Journal of Epidemiology* 95:431-41.

Nye, F. I. 1976. *Role structure and analysis of the family*. Beverly Hills, Calif.: Sage.

Onians, R. B. 1954. *The origins of European thought*. Cambridge: Cambridge University Press.

Parke, R. D. 1974. Cited in Klaus and Kennell, 1976*b*.

Parke, R. D., and O'Leary, S. 1975. Father-mother-infant interaction in the newborn period: Some findings, some observations, and some unresolved issues. In *The developing individual in a changing world*, ed. K. Riegel and J. Meachum. Vol. 2: *Social and environmental issues*. The Hague: Mouton.

Parke, R. D.; O'Leary, S. E.; and West, S. 1972. Mother-father-infant interaction: Effects of maternal medication, labor, and sex of infant. *Proceedings of the American Psychological Association*, 7:85-86.

Parke, R. D., and Sawin, D. B. 1976. The father's role in infancy. *The Family Coordinator* 25:365-71.

Parsons, T. 1955. Family structure and the socialization of the child. In *Family, socialization, and interaction process*, ed. T. Parsons and R. F. Bales. New York: Free Press.

Patterson, S. P.; Mulliniks, R. C.; and Schreier, P. C. 1967. Breech presentation in the primigravida. *American Journal of Obstetrics and Gynecology* 98:404-10.

Pearse, R. L.; Easley, E. B.; and Podger, K. A. 1955. Obstetric analgesia and anesthesia. *North Carolina Medical Journal* 16:18-24.

Pedersen, F. A., and Robson, K. S. 1969. Father participation in infancy. *American Journal of Orthopsychiatry* 39:466-72.

Peterman, D. J.; Ridley, C. A.; and Anderson, S. M. 1974. A comparison of cohabiting and non-cohabiting college students. *Journal of Marriage and the Family*, 36:344-55.

Peterson, G. H.; Mehl, L. E.; and Leiderman, P. H. 1977. The Role of Prenatal Attitude and Birth Participation in Determining Father Commitment. Paper presented at meetings of American Sociological Association, San Francisco.

Peterson, G. H.; Mehl, L. E.; and Leiderman, P. H. 1979. The role of some birth-related variables in father attachment. *American Journal of Orthopsychiatry* 49:330-38.

Pifer, A. 1976. *Women working: Toward a new society*. Annual report, Carnegie Corporation of New York.

Pleck, J. H. 1981. Husbands paid work and family roles. In *Research on the interweave of social roles: Women and Men*, ed. H. Z. Lopata, vol. 3. Greenwich, Conn.: JAI Press.

Pleschette, N.; Asch, S. S.; and Chase, J. 1956. A study of anxiety during pregnancy, labor, the early and late puerperium. *Bulletin of the New York Academy of Medicine* 32:436-55.

Poffenberger, S.; Poffenberger, T.; and Landis, J. T. 1952. Intent toward conception and the pregnancy experience. *American Sociological Review* 17:616-20.

Pohlman, E. H. 1969. *Psychology of birth planning*. Cambridge, Mass.: Schenkman.

Querec, L. J. 1978. *Characteristics of births*. Series 21, no. 30, Department of Health, Education, and Welfare no. (PHS) 78-1908.

Rainwater, L. 1965. *Family design: Marital stability, family size, and contraception*. Chicago: Aldine.

Rau, L. 1960. Parental antecedents of identification. *Merrill-Palmer Quarterly* 6:77–82.

Rebelsky, F., and Hanks, C. 1971. Fathers' verbal interaction with infants in the first three months of life. *Child Development* 42:63–68.

Richards, M. P. M. 1978. A place of safety? An examination of the risks of hospital delivery. In *The place of birth*, ed. S. Kitzinger and J. A. Davis. New York: Oxford.

Richards, M. P. M., and Bernal, J. 1972. Observational study of mother-infant interaction. In *Ethological studies of child behavior*, ed. N. Burton-Jones. New York: Cambridge University Press.

Richman, J., and Goldthorp, W. O. 1978. Fatherhood: The social construction of pregnancy and birth. In *The place of birth*, ed. S. Kitzinger and J. A. Davis. New York: Oxford.

Rindfuss, R. R., and Ladinsky, J. C. 1976. Patterns of births: Implications for the incidence of elective induction. *Medical Care* 14:685–93.

Ringler, N.; Trause, M. A.; Klaus, M.; and Kennell, J. 1978. The effects of extra postpartum contact and maternal speech patterns on children's IQ, speech, and language comprehension at five. *Child Development* 49:862–65.

Robbins, L. C. 1963. The accuracy of parental recall of aspects of child development and of child rearing practices. *Journal of Abnormal and Social Psychology* 66:261–70.

Roberts, S. 1969. We had a baby. *Good Housekeeping*, May 1969, pp. 102 ff.

Robertson, E. M. 1939. The effects of emotional stress on the contractions of the human uterus. *Journal of Obstetrics and Gynecology of the British Empire* 46:741–47.

Robertson, G. G. 1946. Nausea and vomiting in pregnancy. *Lancet* 2:336–41.

Robinson, J. P. 1977. *How Americans use time—a social-psychological analysis of everyday behavior*. New York: Praeger.

Robson, K. S., and Moss, H. A. 1970. Patterns and determinants of maternal attachment. *Journal of Pediatrics* 77:976–85.

Robson, K. S.; Pedersen, F. A.; and Moss, H. A. 1969. Developmental observations of diadic gazing in relation to the fear of strangers and social approach behavior. *Child Development* 40:619–27.

Rogerson, B., and Rogerson, C. 1931. Feeding in infancy and subsequent psychological difficulties. *Journal of Mental Science* 85:1163–82.

Rollins, B. C., and Galligan, R. 1978. The developing child and marital satisfaction of parents. In *Child influences on marital and family interaction*, ed. R. M. Lerner and G. B. Spanier. New York: Academic Press.

Rosefsky, J. B., and Petersiel, M. E. 1968. Perinatal deaths associated with Mepivacaine paracervical block anesthesia in labor. *New England Journal of Medicine* 278:530–33.

Rosen, S. 1955. Emotional factors in nausea and vomiting of pregnancy. *Psychiatric Quarterly* 29:621.

Rossi, A. S. 1968. Transition to parenthood. *Journal of Marriage and the Family* 30:26–39.

Rossi, A. S. 1973. Maternalism, sexuality, and the new feminism. In *Contemporary sexual behavior: Critical issues in the 1970's*, ed. J. Zubin and J. Money. Baltimore: Johns Hopkins University Press.

Rossi, A. S. 1977. A biosocial perspective on parenting. *Daedalus* 106:1-32.

Rothman, B. K. 1976. In which a sensible woman persuades her doctor, her family, and her friends to help her give birth at home. *Ms,* 5 (December):25 ff.

Rotter, J. B. 1966. Generalized expectancies for internal versus external control of reinforcements. *Psychological Monographs* vol. 80 Whole #609, pp. 1-28.

Russell, S. 1974. Transition to parenthood: Problems and gratifications. *Journal of Marriage and the Family* 36:294-302.

Russo, N. F. 1979. Overview: Sex roles, fertility, and the motherhood mandate. *Psychology of Women* 4:7-15.

Rutter, M. 1979. Maternal deprivation 1972-1978: New findings, new concepts, new approaches. *Child Development* 50:283-305.

Ryder, R. G. 1973. Longitudinal data relating marriage satisfaction and having a child. *Journal of Marriage and the Family* 35:604-7.

Salber, E. J.; Stitt, P. G.; and Babbott, J. G. 1958. Patterns of breast feeding. *New England Journal of Medicine* 259:707-13.

Sauls, H. S. 1979. Potential effect of demographic and other variables in studies comparing morbidity of breast-fed and bottle-fed infants. *Pediatrics* 64:523-27.

Scanlon, J. W.; Brown, W. U.; Weiss, J. B.; and Alper M. H. 1974. Neurobehavioral responses of newborn infants after maternal epidural anesthesia. *Anesthesiology* 40:121-28.

Scanzoni, J. H. 1970. *Opportunity and the family.* New York: Free Press.

Schaefer, G. 1965. The expectant father: His care and management. *Postgraduate Medicine* 38:658-63.

Scully, D., and Bart, P. 1973. A funny thing happened on the way to the orifice: Women in gynecology textbooks. *American Journal of Sociology* 78:1045-49.

Seidman, J. R., and Albert, M. H. 1956. *Becoming a mother.* New York: Fawcett.

Shainess, N. 1963. The structure of the mothering encounter. *Journal of Nervous and Mental Disease* 136:146-61.

Shereshefsky, P. M., and Yarrow, L. J. 1973. *Psychological aspects of a first pregnancy.* New York: Raven.

Shnider, S. M., and Way, E. L. 1968. Plasma levels of lidocaine in mother and newborn following obstetrical conduction anesthesia. *Anesthesiology* 29:951-58.

Siegel, P. M. 1971. Prestige in the American Occupational Structure. Ph.D. dissertation, University of Chicago.

Simmel, G. 1950. In *The sociology of George Simmel,* ed. Kurt Wolff. Glencoe, Ill.: Free Press.

Sinclair, J. C.; Fox, H. A.; Lentz, J. F.; Field, G. L.; and Murphy J. 1965. Intoxication of the fetus by a local anesthetic. *New England Journal of Medicine* 22:1173-77.

Solberg, D. A.; Butler, J.; and Wagner, N. N. 1973. Sexual behavior in pregnancy. *New England Journal of Medicine* 288:1098-1103.

Sontag, L. W. 1941. Significance of foetal environmental differences. *American Journal of Obstetrics and Gynecology* 42:996-1003.

Sosa, R.; Kennell, J. H.; Klaus, M.; and Urrutia, J. J. 1976. *Breast-feeding and the mother.* New York: Elsevier-North-Holland, Inc.

Soule, A. B. 1974. Paper presented at American Psychological Association meetings, New Orleans. Cited in M. E. Lamb, 1978.

Spotnitz, H., and Freeman, L. 1974. *How to be happy though pregnant.* New York: Berkeley Medallion.

Standley, K.; Soule, A. B.; Copans, S. A.; and Duchowny, M. S. 1974. Local-regional anesthesia during childbirth: Effect on newborn behaviors. *Science* 186:634–35.

Stender, F. 1965. *Husbands in the delivery room: Recommendations to hospital administrators and physicians on the desireability and safety of the practice.* Milwaukee, Wis.: International Childbirth Education Association.

Stewart, M., and Erickson, P. 1976. The Sociology of Birth: A Critical Assessment of Theory and Research. Paper presented at meetings of Western Social Science Association, Tempe, Arizona.

Stewart, R. H. 1963. Natural childbirth, father participation, rooming-in, or what-have-you. *Medical Times* 91:1065–68.

Stryker, S. 1964. The interactional and situational approaches. In *Handbook of Marriage and the Family,* ed. H. T. Christensen. Chicago: Rand McNally.

Syme, S. L., and Berkman, L. F. 1976. Social class, susceptibility, and sickness. *American Journal of Epidemiology* 104:1–8.

Takai, R. Forthcoming. Marital Separation in First Marriages and Remarriages of Women: An Examination of the Divergent Patterns. Ph.D. dissertation, Johns Hopkins University.

Tangri, S. 1969. Role Innovations in Occupational Choice. Ph.D. dissertation, University of Michigan.

Tanzer, D. 1967. The Psychology of Pregnancy and Childbirth: an Investigation of Natural Childbirth. Ph.D. dissertation, Brandeis University.

Tanzer, D. 1968. Natural childbirth: Pain or peak experience? *Psychology Today* 2:17 ff.

Taylor, J. A. 1953. A personality scale of manifest anxiety. *Journal of Abnormal and Social Psychology* 48:285–90.

Thoms, H., and Wyatt, R. H. 1951. One thousand consecutive deliveries under a training for childbirth program. *American Journal of Obstetrics and Gynecology* 61:205–9.

Thornton, A., and Freedman, D. 1979. *Consistency of sex role attitudes of women, 1962–1977.* Ann Arbor, Mich.: Institute for Social Research.

Towne, R. D., and Afterman, J. 1955. Psychosis in males related to childbirth. *Bulletin Menninger Clinic* 19:19–26.

Trethowan, W. H., and Conlon, M. F. 1965. The couvade symptom. *British Journal of Psychiatry* 111:57–66.

Turner, B. K. 1956. The syndrome in the infant resulting from maternal emotional tension during pregnancy. *Medical Journal of Australia* 1:222–23.

U.S. Bureau of the Census. 1975a. *Current population reports.* Series P-25, no. 613, November 1975. Washington, D.C.: U.S. Government Printing Office.

U.S. Bureau of the Census. 1975b. *Current population reports,* series P-20, no. 277. Fertility expectations of American women: June 1974. Washington, D.C.: U.S. Government Printing Office.

U.S. Bureau of the Census. 1976. *Current population reports.* series P-23, no. 58. A statistical portrait of women in the U.S.: April 1976. Washington, D.C.: U.S. Government Printing Office.

U.S. Bureau of the Census. 1978. *Current population reports.* series P-20, no. 338. Marital status and living arrangements: March 1978. Washington, D.C.: U.S. Government Printing Office.

U.S. Bureau of the Census. 1979. *Patterns of aggregate and individual changes in contraceptive practice: United States, 1965-1975.* National Center for Health Statistics, series 3, no. 17; DHEW Publication no. (PHS) 79-1401.

U.S. Department of Labor. 1975. *1975 handbook on women workers.* U.S. Department of Labor, Women's Bureau, Bulletin 297.

Vellay, P. 1960. *Childbirth without pain.* New York: E. P. Dutton.

Waller, W. W. 1938. *The family: A dynamic interpretation.* New York: Dryden.

Wapner, J. H. 1975. An Empirical Approach to the Attitudes, Feelings, and Behaviors of Expectant Fathers. Ph.D. dissertation, Northwestern University.

Warren, R. B. 1975. The Work Role and Problems in Coping: Sex Differentials in the Use of Helping Systems in Urban Communities. Paper presented at the American Sociological Association meetings, San Francisco.

Waterfall, B., and Morris, L. 1976. Trends in birth and baby care. *Mother's Manual* 12:17 ff.

Watson, J. 1977. Who attends prepared childbirth classes? A demographic study of CEA classes in Rhode Island. *Journal of Obstetrical and Gynecological and Neonatal Nursing* 6:36-39.

Wenner, N. K., and Cohen, M. B. 1968. Emotional Aspects of Pregnancy. Mimeo. Final report of Washington School of Psychiatry Project, Clinical study of the emotional challenges of pregnancy, NIMH.

Wente, A. S., and Crockenberg, S. B. 1976. Transition to fatherhood: Lamaze preparation, adjustment difficulty, and the husband-wife relationship. *The Family Coordinator* 25:351-57.

Whiten, A. 1977. Assessing the effects of perinatal events on the success of the mother-infant relationship. In *Studies in mother-infant interaction* ed. H. R. Shaffer. London: Academic Press.

Winokur, K. G., and Werboff, J. 1956. The relationship of conscious maternal attitudes to certain aspects of pregnancy. *Psychiatric Quarterly Supplement* 30:61-73.

Winters, N. 1973. The Relationship of Time of Initial Breast-feeding to Success in Breast-feeding. Master's thesis, University of Washington.

Wolff, P. H. 1969. The natural history of crying and other vocalizations in early infancy. In *Determinants of infant behavior IV,* ed. B. M. Foss. London: Methuen.

Yahia, C., and Ulin, P. R. 1965. Preliminary experience with a psychophysical program of preparation for childbirth. *American Journal of Obstetrics and Gynecology* 93:942-49.

Yalom, I. D. 1968. Postpartum blues syndrome. *Archives of General Psychiatry* 28:16-27.

Yang, R. K.; Zweig, A. R.; Douthitt, T. C.; and Federman, E. J. 1976. Successive relationships between maternal attitudes during pregnancy, analgesic medication during labor and delivery, and newborn behavior. *Developmental Psychology* 12:6-14.

Yankauer, A. 1958. *Pregnancy, childbirth, the neonatal period, and expectant parent classes.* Albany, N.Y.: Bureau of Maternal and Child Health, New York State Department of Health.

Yankelovich, D. 1974. *The new morality: A profile of American youth.* New York: McGraw-Hill.

Yankelovich, D. 1977. Raising children in a changing society. *General Mills: The American family report 1976-1977.* Minneapolis: General Mills, Inc.

Zax, M.; Sameroff, A. J.; and Farnum, J. E. 1975. Childbirth education, maternal attitudes and delivery. *American Journal of Obstetrics and Gynecology* 123:185-90.

Zemlik, M. J., and Watson, D. 1953. Maternal attitudes of acceptance and rejection during and after pregnancy. *American Journal of Orthopsychiatry* 23:570-84.

Zuckerman, M.; Nurnberger, J. I.; Gardner, S. H.; Vaudiveer, J. M.; Barrett, B. H.; and Breeijen, A. 1963. Psychological correlates of somatic complaints in pregnancy and difficulty in childbirth. *Journal of Consulting Psychology* 27:324-29.

INDEX

Three-person group, 8, 13, 165, 255
Time of birth, 89–90, 242
Toilet training, 187
Two-person group, 8, 13, 165

Volunteering, 233, 269
Vomiting, 52

Weaning, 35, 76, 135–36, 284–85
WEDUC definition, 297
Weight gain, 55–57, 84
Weight of babies, 89, 137
WFIN definition, 301
Wives: as viewed by husbands, 178–80; view
  of husbands of, 178–180, 182, 192, 237,
  241, 246, 258, 282, 284; views of self,
  177–78, 182, 232, 241, 258
Woman's role, 24, 27, 65–66, 236, 241, 247,
  297–98

Women's liberation, 77, 191; and birth experience, 146, 236
WOPBR definition, 301
Work, 2, 8, 11–12, 26, 42, 245, 253, 255,
  275; commitment to, 32, 34, 40; men's
  commitment to, 29; and men's role, 48;
  mother's return to, 165–68, 255–56, 261;
  opinions on, 190–91; and parent role, 20,
  239, 259, 262; and pregnancy symptoms,
  26, 54; and preparation, 63; as source of
  satisfaction, 26, 30, 32, 40; women's, 15,
  24, 29, 43; women's plans for, 25–26, 30,
  43
Work of worrying, 37, 41, 112
Worries: financial, 8, 12–13; of husbands',
  57–58; and stopping intercourse, 81; of
  wives', 55–57
Worry score, 53, 248, 281; and pain, 95, 171,
  277
WPREP definition, 298